# GENERAL PRINCIPLES

## OF

## ENGLISH LAW

# GENERAL PRINCIPLES OF ENGLISH LAW

BY

O. K. METCALFE, M.A., LL.M.,
OF GRAY'S INN, BARRISTER-AT-LAW

TENTH EDITION
BY
JOHN WESTWOOD, LL.B.(Lond.),
SOLICITOR (HONS.)

Published by :
Donnington Press

Distributed by :
Cassell & Collier Macmillan
Publishers Limited

DONNINGTON PRESS
Aldermaston Court
Reading RG7 4PW

Distributed by:
CASSELL & COLLIER MACMILLAN PUBLISHERS LIMITED,
35 Red Lion Square
London WC1R 4SG
Sydney, Auckland, Toronto, Johannesburg

© 1976 DONNINGTON PRESS

*All rights reserved. No part of this publication may be reproduced or transmitted in any form or by any means, electronic or mechanical, including photo-copying, recording or by any informational storage or retrieval system, without the prior written permission of Donnington Press.*

TENTH EDITION 1976
SBN 304 29883 2

Printed and bound in Great Britain by
Morrison & Gibb Ltd, London and Edinburgh

# PREFACE

THE object of this modest work is to provide a reliable text-book to meet the requirements of those professional bodies that demand at their examinations a knowledge of the general principles of English law.

It is hoped, nevertheless, that the book may be of interest to the general reader.

In preparing the present edition I have endeavoured to take into account statutory and other changes in the law which have occurred up to the end of June 1976.

*September* 1976                                                                 J. W.

# CONTENTS

| Chap. | | Page |
|---|---|---|
| | TABLE OF CASES CITED . . . . . | ix |
| | TABLE OF STATUTES CITED . . . . | xiii |
| | INTRODUCTION . . . . . . . | 1 |
| I. | SOURCES OF ENGLISH LAW AND RELATED MATTERS . | 6 |

Nature and Divisions of Law. Common Law: History; Custom; Usages; Judicial Precedent; Reports; *Ratio Decidendi* and *Obiter Dictum*; Judge-made Law. Canon Law. Law Merchant. Statute: Interpretation; Delegated Legislation. Legal Treatises. Law Reform. European Economic Community.

| II. | EQUITY . . . . . . . . | 27 |
|---|---|---|

Nature. History. Maxims. Equitable Remedies. Mortgages. Trusts. Assignment of Choses in Action. Influence of Roman Law.

| III. | ELEMENTS OF THE LAW OF CONTRACT . . . | 44 |
|---|---|---|

Nature and Classification. Essential Features of a Valid Contract. Contractual Capacity.

| IV. | ELEMENTS OF THE LAW OF CONTRACT (*continued*) . | 71 |
|---|---|---|

Legality and Possibility. Reality of Consent. Assignment. Discharge. Remedies. Quasi-contracts.

| V. | LAW OF PERSONS . . . . . . | 100 |
|---|---|---|

Natural Persons. Minors. Illegitimacy. Adoption. Marriage. Mentally Disordered Persons.

| Chap. | | Page |
|---|---|---|
| | Aliens. Nationality. The Crown. Artificial Persons. Companies. Partnership. Agency. Master and Servant. | |
| VI. | LAW OF PROPERTY | 143 |
| | Conception of Property. Ownership and Possession. Uses and Trusts. Alienation of Personal Property. Gifts. Bailment. Negotiable Instruments. Securities. Lien. Patents. Trade Marks. Copyright. Bankruptcy. Property Legislation of 1925. Estates and Interests. Alienation of Real Property by Sale, Lease, Mortgage or Settlement. Wills. Intestate Succession. | |
| VII. | ELEMENTS OF TORT | 215 |
| | Nature of a Tort. General Conditions of Liability. Parties. Substantive Torts. Remoteness of Damage. | |
| VIII. | ELEMENTS OF CRIME | 254 |
| | Nature and Classification. Constituent Elements. Liability. Degrees of Complicity. Crimes against the Person. Crimes against Property. Crimes against Public Rights. Inchoate Crimes. | |
| IX. | ENGLISH LEGAL SYSTEM | 279 |
| | House of Lords. Supreme Court of Judicature. County Court. Courts of Criminal Jurisdiction. Coroner's Court. Judicial Committee of the Privy Council. Evidence. Functions of Judge and Jury. Legal Aid. Arbitration. Administrative Tribunals. | |
| | INDEX | 307 |

# TABLE OF CASES CITED

| | PAGE |
|---|---|
| Abrath v. N.E. Railway Co. (1886) | 245 |
| Aldred's Case (1610) | 233 |
| Alexander v. Railway Executive (1951) | 57 |
| Allcard v. Skinner (1887) | 83 |
| Allsop v. Church of England Newspapers Ltd. (1972) | 239 |
| Ashbury Carriage and Iron Co. v. Riche (1875) | 69 |
| Avery v. Bowden (1855) | 89 |
| Baily v. De Crespigny (1869) | 90 |
| Baker v. T. E. Hopkins & Sons, Ltd. (1959) | 218 |
| Balfour v. Balfour (1919) | 47 |
| Bank voor Handel en Scheepvaart N. V. v. Slatford (1952) | 139 |
| Barnes v. Hampshire C.C. (1969) | 228 |
| Baroness Wenlock v. River Dee Co. (1888) | 68 |
| Bativala v. West (1970) | 234 |
| Beach & Anor. v. Freeson (1971) | 242 |
| Beatty v. Gillbanks (1882) | 121 |
| Bell v. Lever Bros. (1932) | 77 |
| Beloff v. Pressdram Ltd. & Anor. (1973) | 139 |
| Beswick v. Beswick (1966 and 1967) | 55 |
| Board of Trade v. Owen (1957) | 255 |
| Bolton v. Mahaveda (1972) | 96 |
| Bonnewell v. Jenkins (1878) | 60 |
| Bonsor v. Musicians' Union (1955) | 127 |
| Boston v. W. S. Bagshaw & Sons (1966) | 242 |
| Boulton v. Jones (1857) | 75 |
| Bowater v. Rowley Regis Corporation (1944) | 217 |
| Brace v. Calder (1895) | 141 |
| Bradford v. Robinson Rentals (1967) | 248 |
| Bradford Corporation v. Pickles (1895) | 216, 226 |
| Bradley v. Carritt (1901) | 37 |
| Branca v. Cobarro (1947) | 60 |
| Bridlington Relay v. Yorkshire Electricity Board (1965) | 298 |
| British Railways Board v. Herrington (1972) | 231, 298 |
| Brooke v. Bool (1928) | 220 |
| Broome v. Cassell & Co. sub. nom. | |
| Cassell & Co. v. Broome (1972) | 253 |
| Buckle v. Holmes (1926) | 13 |
| Buckley v. N.U.G.M.W. (1967) | 127 |
| Burnard v. Haggis (1863) | 219 |
| Burnett v. British Waterways Board (1972) | 217 |
| Buron v. Denman (1848) | 216 |
| Butler v. Fife Coal Co., Ltd. (1912) | 227 |
| Byrne v. Van Tienhoven (1880) | 59, 62 |
| Byrne v. Boadle (1863) | 229 |
| Cadell v. Palmer (1833) | 202 |
| Candler v. Crane, Christmas & Co. (1951) | 228 |
| Carlill v. Carbolic Smoke Ball Co. (1893) | 59 |
| Case of Ship Money (1637) | 116 |
| Cassidy v. Daily Mirror Newspapers (1929) | 239 |
| Central London Property Trust, Ltd. v. High Trees House, Ltd. (1947) | 53, 87 |
| Chapelton v. Barry U.D.C. (1940) | 57 |
| Chic Fashions (West Wales) Ltd. v. Jones (1968) | 223 |
| Church of Scientology v. Johnson-Smith (1972) | 241 |
| Clarke v. Army & Navy Co-operative Society (1903) | 232 |
| Clayton's Case (1816) | 88 |
| Coggs v. Bernard (1703) | 161 |
| Collen v. Wright (1857) | 126 |
| Combe v. Combe (1951) | 53 |
| Conway v. George Wimpey & Co. (1950) | 220 |
| Cooper v. Phibbs (1867) | 76 |
| Coral v. Kleyman (1951) | 73 |
| Coulson v. Coulson (1887) | 243 |
| Couturier v. Hastie (1856) | 76 |
| Cowern v. Nield (1913) | 65 |
| Cox v. Philips Industries (1976) | 141 |
| Crook v. Derbyshire Stone, Ltd. (1956) | 220 |
| Cundy v. Lindsay (1878) | 51, 75 |
| Currie v. Misa (1875) | 53 |
| Curtis v. Chemical Cleaning and Dyeing Company Ltd. (1951) | 57 |
| Curtis v. Maloney (1950) | 155 |
| Cutter v. Powell (1795) | 96 |

# TABLE OF CASES CITED

| | PAGE |
|---|---|
| D. & C. Builders Ltd. v. Rees (1965) | 87 |
| Davis Contractors Ltd. v. Fareham U.D.C. (1956) | 96 |
| Decro-Wall International S.A. v. Practitioners in Marketing Ltd. (1971) | 89 |
| Derry v. Peek (1889) | 80 |
| Dickinson v. Dodds (1876) | 62 |
| D.P.P. v. Beard (1930) | 260 |
| D.P.P. v. Bhagwan (1970) | 276 |
| D.P.P. v. Kent and Sussex Contractors (1944) | 261 |
| D.P.P. v. Majewski (1976) | 260 |
| D.P.P. v. Withers (1974) | 276, 277 |
| Donoghue v. Stevenson (1932) | 13, 14, 227, 232 |
| Doyle v. White City Stadium, Ltd. & B.B.B.C. (1935) | 66 |
| Draper & Anor. v. Hodder (1972) | 234 |
| Duncan v. Jones (1936) | 120 |
| Entores Ltd. v. Miles Far East Corporation (1955) | 62 |
| Fardon v. Harcourt-Rivington (1923) | 234 |
| Felthouse v. Bindley (1862) | 58 |
| Fletcher v. Rylands (1868) | 235 |
| Foster v. Mackinnon (1869) | 74 |
| Friend v. Young (1897) | 88 |
| Froom v. Butcher (1975) | 229 |
| Gallie v. Lee (1970) | 74 |
| Gayler & Pope Ltd. v. Davies & Son Ltd. (1924) | 234 |
| General Billposting Co. v. Atkinson (1909) | 141 |
| Gomberg v. Smith (1962) | 234 |
| Goodwin v. Robarts (1876) | 15 |
| Gough v. Thorne (1966) | 219 |
| Grant v. Australian Knitting Mills, Ltd. (1936) | 233 |
| Grist v. Bailey (1966) | 78 |
| Grover v. Matthews (1910) | 135 |
| Hadley v. Baxendale (1854) | 94 |
| Hallet's Estate, Re (1880) | 88 |
| Hambrook v. Stokes Bros. (1925) | 249 |
| Hampson v. Powell (1970) | 296 |
| Harris v. Lubbock (1971) | 241 |
| Harrison & Jones v. Bunten & Lancaster (1953) | 77 |
| Harrison, W. F. & Co. Ltd., v. Burke (1956) | 84 |
| Harvey v. Facey (1893) | 63 |
| Haughton v. Smith (1973) | 278 |
| Haynes v. Harwood (1935) | 217, 218 |
| Heaven v. Pender (1883) | 232 |

| | PAGE |
|---|---|
| Hedley Byrne & Co. v. Heller & Partners (1963) | 228 |
| Herschtal v. Stewart & Ardern, Ltd. (1940) | 233 |
| Heydon's Case (1584) | 21 |
| Hill v. William Hill (Park Lane), Ltd. (1949) | 73 |
| Hochster v. De La Tour (1853) | 89 |
| Hoenig v. Isaacs (1952) | 96 |
| Hollins v. Fowler (1875) | 224 |
| Hollywood Silver Fox Farm Ltd., v. Emmett (1936) | 226 |
| Holmes v. Director of Public Prosecutions (1946) | 265 |
| Home Counties Dairies Ltd. v. Skelton (1970) | 72 |
| Home Office v. Dorset Yacht Co. Ltd. (1970) | 228 |
| Horne v. Midland Railway Co. (1873) | 94 |
| Horrocks v. Lowe (1972) | 242 |
| Houghland v. R. R. Low (Luxury Coaches) Ltd. (1962) | 161 |
| Hughes v. Lord Advocate (1963) | 248 |
| Hulton v. Jones (1910) | 238, 243 |
| Hyde v. Wrench (1840) | 59 |
| Ingram & Little (1960) | 75 |
| Jackson v. Horizon Holidays (1975) | 94 |
| Jarvis v. Swans Tours Ltd. (1973) | 94 |
| Jones v. Livox Quarries Ltd. (1952) | 229 |
| Joyce v. Director of Public Prosecutions (1946) | 272 |
| Kaufman v. Gerson (1904) | 82 |
| Kemp v. Baerselman (1906) | 84 |
| Knight v. Knight (1840) | 39 |
| Knightsbridge Estates Trust Ltd. v. Byrne (1940) | 38 |
| Knuller (Publishing etc.) Ltd. v. D.P.P. (1972) | 276 |
| Kreglinger v. N.P. Meat & Cold Storage Co. (1914) | 38 |
| Langridge v. Levy (1837) | 244 |
| Law v. Jones (1973) | 60 |
| Leeson v. Leeson (1936) | 88 |
| Leigh v. Taylor (1902) | 180 |
| Le Lievre v. Gould (1893) | 227 |
| Lemmon v. Webb (1894) | 226 |
| Leslie (R.) Ltd. v. Sheill (1914) | 64 |
| L'Estrange v. Graucob (1934) | 57 |
| Lewis v. Averay (1971) | 75 |
| Lloyds Bank Ltd. v. Bundy (1974) | 82 |
| London Tramways Co. v. London County Council (1898) | 10 |
| Lumley v. Wagner (1852) | 97 |
| Lumley v. Gye (1853) | 246 |

## TABLE OF CASES CITED

| | PAGE |
|---|---|
| Macdonald v. Green (1950) | 73 |
| Macdonnel v. Evans (1852) | 295 |
| McGreevy v. D.P.P. (1973) | 296 |
| Maddison v. Alderson (1883) | 50 |
| Magee v. Pennine Insurance Co. Ltd. (1969) | 78 |
| Mancini v. Director of Public Prosecutions (1942) | 265 |
| M'Naghten's Case (1843) | 259 |
| Manton v. Brocklebank (1923) | 234 |
| Marion White Ltd. v. Francis (1972) | 72 |
| Mercantile Union Guarantee Corporation, Ltd. v. Ball (1937) | 65 |
| Merritt v. Merritt (1973) | 48 |
| Mills v. Brooker (1919) | 226 |
| Moore v. Bresler (1944) | 261 |
| Moore v. Fox (1956) | 229 |
| Morgan v. Odhams Press Ltd. (1971) | 238 |
| Morris Ltd. v. Saxelby (1916) | 72 |
| Mount v. Oldham Corporation (1973) | 298 |
| Munday v. Metropolitan Police District Receiver (1949) | 121 |
| Munton v. Greater London Council (1976) | 61 |
| Nash v. Inman (1908) | 65 |
| National Union of General and Municipal Workers v. Gillian (1945) | 126 |
| Newstead v. London Express Newspaper, Ltd. (1940) | 238, 243 |
| Newton v. Edgerley (1959) | 219 |
| Nissan v. Attorney-General (1967) | 216 |
| Noakes v. Rice (1902) | 37 |
| Noble v. Harrison (1926) | 14 |
| O'Connell v. Jackson (1971) | 229 |
| O'Kelly v. Harvey (1883) | 121 |
| Olley v. Marlborough Court, Ltd. (1949) | 57 |
| Oldfield, Re, Oldfield v. Oldfield (1904) | 40 |
| O'Neil v. Armstrong (1895) | 96 |
| Parker v. Clark (1960) | 48 |
| Parnall v. Parnall (1878) | 40 |
| Pearce v. Gardner (1897) | 49 |
| Peek v. Gurney (1873) | 244 |
| Peters v. Anderson (1814) | 88 |
| Pharmaceutical Society of Great Britain v. Boots Cash Chemists (Southern) Ltd. (1952) | 63 |
| Phillips v. Brooks (1919) | 75 |
| Pitcher v. Martin (1937) | 233, 234 |
| Polemis & Furness Withy & Co., Re, (1921) | 248 |

| | PAGE |
|---|---|
| R. v. Bourne (1939) | 267 |
| R. v. Brindley; R. v. Long (1971) | 263 |
| R. v. Casement (1917) | 272 |
| R. v. Charlson (1955) | 261 |
| R. v. Clarke (1972) | 259 |
| R. v. Collins (1969) | 284 |
| R. v. Cunningham (1958) | 265 |
| R. v. Dolman (1950) | 275 |
| R. v. Dudley and Stephens (1884) | 261 |
| R. v. Dunbar (1957) | 260 |
| R. v. Dunn (1973) | 269 |
| R. v. Electricity Commissioners (1924) | 118 |
| R. v. Gould (1968) | 274 |
| R. v. Hancock (1931) | 284 |
| R. v. I.C.R. Haulage, Ltd. (1944) | 261 |
| R. v. Jones (R. W.) (1969) | 298 |
| R. v. Lloyd (1887) | 273 |
| R. v. Manley (1933) | 276 |
| R. v. Newland (1953) | 276 |
| R. v. Onufrejczyk (1955) | 264 |
| R. v. Osborn (1919) | 278 |
| R. v. Potter (1958) | 270 |
| R. v. Ring (1892) | 278 |
| R. v. Robinson (1915) | 278 |
| R. v. Robson; R. v. Harris (1972) | 295 |
| R. v. Singh (1973) | 258 |
| R. v. Taylor (1950) | 274 |
| R. v. Tolson (1889) | 274 |
| R. v. Watkins (1976) | 269 |
| R. v. Windle (1952) | 259 |
| Raffles v. Wichelhaus (1864) | 76 |
| Ramsgate Victoria Hotel Co. v. Montefiore (1866) | 59 |
| Ratten v. Reginam (1971) | 297 |
| Rawlinson v. Ames (1925) | 50 |
| Read v. J. Lyons & Co., Ltd. (1946) | 236 |
| Reid v. Metropolitan Police Commissioner (1973) | 154 |
| Roberts v. Gray (1913) | 65 |
| Rondel v. Worsley (1967) | 290 |
| Rookes v. Barnard (1964) | 252 |
| Roscorla v. Thomas (1842) | 55 |
| Rose & Frank Co. v. J. R. Crompton & Bros. Ltd. (1925) | 48 |
| Rowland v. Dival (1923) | 98 |
| Rylands v. Fletcher (1868) | 235, 236 |
| Salomon v. Salomon & Co. Ltd. (1897) | 122 |
| Samuel v. Jarrah Timber & Wood-Paving Corporation Ltd. (1904) | 197 |
| S and K Holdings Ltd. v. Throgmorton Publications Ltd. (1972) | 239 |
| Saunders (Exec. of Gallie decd.) v. Anglia Building Society (1970) | 74 |
| Scott v. Shepherd (1773) | 249 |
| Searle v. Wallbank (1947) | 253 |

| | PAGE |
|---|---|
| Sedleigh-Denfield v. O'Callaghan (1940) | 226 |
| Seymour v. Pickett (1905) | 88 |
| Shadwell v. Shadwell (1860) | 54 |
| Shaw v. Director of Public Prosecutions (1961) | 276, 277 |
| Shears v. Mendeloff (1914) | 65 |
| Simpkins v. Pays (1955) | 48 |
| Six Carpenters' Case (1610) | 222, 223 |
| Société Anonyme des Grands Etablissements, etc. v. Baumgart | 73 |
| Solle v. Butcher (1949) | 78 |
| Soltykoff, Re (1891) | 64 |
| Southern Portland Cement Co. v. Cooper (1974) | 231 |
| Steinberg v. Scala (Leeds) Ltd. (1923) | 66 |
| Stevenson v. MacLean (1880) | 60 |
| Stevenson Jordon & Harrison Ltd. v. MacDonald & Evans (1952) | 139 |
| Sturges v. Bridgman (1879) | 226 |
| Suisse Atlantique Case (1966) | 57 |
| Sumpter v. Hedges (1898) | 96 |
| Swain v. West (Butchers) Ltd. (1936) | 54 |
| Taff Vale Railway Co. v. Amalgamated Society of Railway Servants (1901) | 126 |
| Taylor v. Caldwell (1865) | 91 |
| The Queen v. Brown (1841) | 115 |
| Thomas v. Sawkins (1935) | 121 |
| Thompson v. Price (1973) | 251 |
| Thornton v. Shoe Lane Parking Ltd. (1971) | 57 |
| Tillet v. Ward (1882) | 234 |
| Tiverton Estates v. Wearwell Ltd. (1973) | 60 |

| | PAGE |
|---|---|
| Tolley v. Fry (1931) | 239 |
| Trego v. Hunt (1896) | 134 |
| Turner v. Goldsmith (1891) | 136 |
| Turner v. National Coal Board (1949) | 229 |
| Tweddle v. Atkinson (1861) | 54 |
| Van Lynn Developments Ltd. v. Pelias Construction Co. Ltd. (1968) | 84 |
| Vinogradoff, Re (1935) | 149 |
| Von Hartzfeldt-Wildenburg v. Alexander (1912) | 60 |
| Wagon Mound (1961) | 248 |
| Wakenham v. Mackenzie (1968) | 50 |
| Walsh v. Lonsdale (1882) | 32, 34, 194 |
| Walton Harvey Ltd. v. Walker & Homfrays, Ltd. (1931) | 90 |
| Ward v. Herts C.C. (1970) | 228 |
| Warder v. Cooper (1970) | 253 |
| Warren v. Keen (1953) | 194 |
| Webster v. Cecil (1861) | 78 |
| Weld-Blundell v. Stephens (1920) | 249 |
| White v. Bluett (1853) | 54 |
| White v. Garden (1851) | 52 |
| White & Carter (Councils) Ltd. v. McGregor (1961) | 89 |
| Whitehead's Will Trusts, Re (1971) | 149 |
| Whittaker v. Minister of Pensions and N.I. (1966) | 139 |
| Winn v. Bull (1877) | 60 |
| Wise v. Dunning (1902) | 121 |
| With v. O'Flanagan (1936) | 81 |
| Woolmer v. Delmer Price, Ltd. (1955) | 57 |
| Woolmington v. Director of Public Prosecutions (1935) | 264, 293 |
| Wormald v. Cole (1954) | 235 |

# TABLE OF STATUTES CITED

|  | PAGE |
|---|---|
| Abortion Act, 1967 | 267 |
| Act for the Submission of the Clergy, 1534 | 14 |
| Act of Settlement, 1701 | 279 |
| Acts of Parliament Numbering and Citation Act, 1962 | 18 |
| Administration of Estates Act, 1925 | 175, 179, 207, 209 |
| Administration of Justice Act, 1960 | 283, 295 |
| Administration of Justice Act, 1964 | 286 |
| Administration of Justice Act, 1969 | 204, 280 |
| Administration of Justice Act, 1970 | 3, 43, 280, 282, 291, 301 |
| Administration of Justice Act, 1973 | 301 |
| Administration of Justice (Miscellaneous Provisions) Act, 1938 | 117 |
| Adoption Act, 1958 and 1968 | 103 |
| Adoption Act, 1976 | 103 |
| Affiliation Proceedings Act, 1957 | 101 |
| Agriculture Act, 1947 | 213 |
| Agricultural Holdings Act, 1948 | 213 |
| Animals Act, 1971 | 26, 218, 223, 233 et seq. |
| Arbitration Act, 1950 | 301 |
| Atomic Energy Act, 1954 | 237 |
| Attachment of Earnings Act, 1971 | 5 |
| Bankruptcy Act, 1914 | 177, 283 |
| Betting Act, 1853 | 21 |
| Betting and Loans (Infants) Act, 1892 | 64 |
| Betting and Gaming Act, 1960 | 73 |
| Betting, Gaming and Lotteries Act, 1963 | 18, 73 |
| Bills of Exchange Act, 1882 | 3, 18, 55, 166 |
| Bills of Sale Acts, 1878 and 1882 | 168 et seq. |
| British Nationality Act, 1948 | 109 |
| Building Societies Act, 1962 | 100 |
| Charities Act, 1960 | 122, 148 |
| Children Act, 1975 | 101, 103 |
| Children and Young Persons Act, 1963 | 259 |
| Children and Young Persons Act, 1969 | 255, 259 |
| Civil Aviation Act, 1949 | 222 |
| Civil Evidence Acts, 1968–1972 | 297, 299 |
| Coinage Act, 1971 | 87 |
| Common Law Procedure Act, 1852 | 195 |
| Community Land Act, 1975 | 214 |
| Companies Acts, 1948–1967 | 69, 79, 122 et seq. |
| Consolidation of Enactments (Procedure) Act, 1949 | 2 |
| Consumer Credit Act, 1974 | 48, 162, 163, 164, 170, 305 |
| Contracts of Employment Acts, 1963 and 1972 | 48, 139 |
| Copyright Act, 1956 | 175 |
| Corporate Bodies Contracts Act, 1960 | 69 |
| County Courts Act, 1959 | 282, 283, 301 |
| Court of Probate Act, 1857 | 15 |
| Courts Act, 1971 | 3, 280 et seq. |
| Criminal Appeal Act, 1964 | 284 |
| Criminal Appeal Act, 1966 | 283 |
| Criminal Appeal Act, 1968 | 283, 284 |
| Criminal Damage Act, 1971 | 270 |
| Criminal Evidence Act, 1898 | 299 |
| Criminal Evidence Act, 1965 | 297 |
| Criminal Justice Act, 1925 | 258, 261 |
| Criminal Justice Act, 1948 | 277 |
| Criminal Justice Act, 1961 | 259 |
| Criminal Justice Act, 1967 | 259, 288, 294, 298 |
| Criminal Justice Act, 1972 | 255, 259, 293 |
| Criminal Justice Administration Act, 1956 | 285 |
| Criminal Law Act, 1967 | 25, 121, 256, 257, 262, 276, 277 |

## TABLE OF STATUTES CITED

| | PAGE |
|---|---|
| Criminal Procedure (Attendance of Witnesses) Act, 1965 | 299 |
| Criminal Procedure (Insanity) Act, 1964 | 259, 260 |
| Crown Proceedings Act, 1947 | 113, 114, 219 |
| Dangerous Drugs Act, 1965 | 255 |
| Deeds of Arrangement Act, 1914 | 178 |
| Defamation Act, 1952 | 237 et seq. |
| Defective Premises Act, 1972 | 231 |
| Disposal of Uncollected Goods Act, 1952 | 162, 173 |
| Divorce Reform Act, 1969 | 106, 293 |
| Dogs Acts, 1906 and 1928 | 235 |
| Domicile and Matrimonial Proceedings Act, 1973 | 111 |
| Dramatic and Musical Performers Act, 1958 | 176 |
| Employment Agencies Act, 1973 | 140, 262 |
| Employment Protection Act, 1975 | 139, 262 |
| Equal Pay Act, 1970 | 140 |
| European Communities Act, 1972 | 26, 69, 122, 137, 273, 298 |
| Fair Trading Act, 1973 | 300, 305 |
| Family Law Reform Act, 1969 | 43, 51, 63, 100, 102, 105, 153, 205, 209, 211 |
| Family Provision Act, 1966 | 204, 209 |
| Fatal Accidents Acts, 1846–1976 | 102, 250, 251, 252 |
| Finance Act, 1950 | 17 |
| Finance Act, 1963 | 183 |
| Finance Act, 1972 | 305 |
| Foreign Jurisdiction Act, 1890 | 289 |
| Forfeiture Act, 1870 | 256 |
| Forgery Act, 1913 | 270 |
| Friendly Societies Act, 1974 | 127 |
| Gaming Acts, 1835–1968 | 72, 73 |
| Guardianship Act, 1973 | 101 |
| Guardianship of Minors Act, 1971 | 101 |
| Health and Safety at Work Act, 1974 | 142 |
| Hire-Purchase Act, 1964 | 155, 164 |
| Homicide Act, 1957 | 259 et seq. |
| Hotel Proprietors Act, 1956 | 161 |
| House of Commons Disqualification Act, 1975 | 289 |
| House of Commons (Indemnification of Certain Members) Act, 1949 | 18 |
| Housing Act, 1961 | 195, 213 |
| Industrial Relations Act, 1971 | 127, 142, 293 |
| Infant Life Preservation Act, 1929 | 267 |
| Infanticide Act, 1938 | 267 |
| Infants Relief Act, 1874 | 51, 64 |
| Infant Settlements Act, 1855 | 43 |
| Inheritance (Family Provision) Act, 1938 | 102, 204 |
| Inheritance (Provision for Family and Dependents) Act, 1975 | 102, 206, 283 |
| Innkeepers Act, 1863 | 161 |
| Insolvency Act, 1976 | 177 |
| Interpretation Act, 1889 | 19 |
| Intestates' Estates Act, 1952 | 204, 205, 207, 209 |
| Judicial Committee Act, 1833 | 289 |
| Judicature Act, 1873 | 2, 3, 27, 31, 42, 83, 145, 280 |
| Judicature Act, 1925 | 42 |
| Juries Act, 1974 | 294 |
| Justices of the Peace Act, 1949 | 287 |
| Justices of the Peace Act, 1968 | 286 |
| Land Charges Acts, 1925 and 1972 | 179 et seq. |
| Land Registration Acts, 1925–1971 | 179 et seq. |
| Land Registration and Land Charges Act, 1971 | 191 |
| Landlord and Tenant Acts 1927 and 1954 | 195, 213, 283 |
| Larceny Act, 1916 | 258, 268 |
| Law Commissions Act, 1965 | 26 |
| Law of Libel Amendment Act, 1888 | 242 |
| Law of Property Act, 1922 | 180 |

# TABLE OF STATUTES CITED

|  | PAGE |
|---|---|
| Law of Property Act, 1925 | 36, 37, 41, 44, 49, 50, 55, 83, 139, 144 *et seq.* |
| Law of Property Act, 1969 | 188 |
| Law Reform (Contributory Negligence) Act, 1945 | 25, 229 |
| Law Reform (Enforcement of Contracts) Act, 1954 | 49 |
| Law Reform (Frustrated Contracts) Act, 1943 | 91, 96 |
| Law Reform (Husband and Wife) Act, 1962 | 25, 218 |
| Law Reform (Limitation of Actions, Etc.) Act, 1954 | 92, 113, 252 |
| Law Reform (Married Women and Tortfeasors) Act 1935 | 67, 177 |
| Law Reform (Miscellaneous Provisions) Act, 1934 | 250, 251 |
| Law Reform (Miscellaneous Provisions) Act, 1970 | 54, 66, 92 |
| Law Reform (Miscellaneous Provisions) Act, 1971 | 251, 252 |
| Leasehold Reform Act, 1967 | 213 |
| Legal Aid Act, 1974 | 3, 300, 301 |
| Legal Aid and Advice Acts, 1949–1964 | 300 |
| Legitimacy Acts, 1926, 1959 and 1976 | 102, 103 |
| Limitation Act, 1623 | 18, 19 |
| Limitation Act, 1939 | 25, 46, 55, 92, 173, 195, 197, 198 |
| Limitation Act, 1963 | 92, 252 |
| Limitation Act, 1975 | 251, 252 |
| Limited Partnerships Act, 1907 | 129 |
| Local Land Charges Act, 1975 | 194 |
| London Government Act, 1963 | 286 |
| Lord Campbell's Act (Fatal Accidents Act, 1846) | 250 |
| Lord Tenterden's Act (Statute of Frauds (Amendment) Act, 1828) | 245 |
| Magistrates Courts Act, 1952 | 288 |
| Magna Carta (reissue), 1225 | 17 |
| Maintenance Orders Acts, 1960 and 1968 | 108 |
| Malicious Damage Act, 1861 | 270 |
| Marriage Acts, 1949–1970 | 100, 105, 106 |
| Married Women's Property Act, 1882 | 108, 218 |
| Married Women's Property Act, 1964 | 108 |
| Matrimonial Causes Act, 1857 | 15 |
| Matrimonial Causes (Property and Maintenance) Act, 1958 | 205 |
| Matrimonial Causes Act, 1965 | 2 |
| Matrimonial Causes Act, 1967 | 106, 283 |
| Matrimonial Causes Act, 1973 | 3, 106, 107 |
| Matrimonial Homes Act, 1967 | 191, 193 |
| Matrimonial Proceedings and Property Act, 1970 | 68, 108 |
| Matrimonial Proceedings (Magistrates' Courts) Act, 1960 | 108 |
| Mental Health Act, 1959 | 67, 109, 260 |
| Misuse of Drugs Act, 1971 | 255 |
| Misrepresentation Act, 1967 | 25, 58, 79, 80 |
| Murder (Abolition of Death Penalty) Act, 1965 | 264 |
| National Health Service Acts, 1946–1973 | 116 |
| National Insurance Act, 1965 | 139 |
| National Insurance (Industrial Injuries) Acts, 1965–1973 | 116, 139 |
| Nullity of Marriage Act, 1971 | 106 |
| Obscene Publications Acts, 1959–1964 | 119 |
| Occupiers Liability Act, 1957 | 25, 230, 231 |
| Offences Against the Person Act, 1861 | 274 |
| Parliament Acts 1911 and 1949 | 17 |
| Partnership Act, 1890 | 2, 129 *et seq.* |
| Patents Acts, 1949–1957 | 174 |
| Pawnbrokers Acts, 1872–1960 | 171 |
| Payment of Wages Act, 1960 | 72 |
| Perjury Act, 1911 | 272, 273 |
| Performers Protection Act, 1963 | 176 |
| Perpetuities and Accumulations Act, 1964 | 25, 202 |
| Policies of Assurance Act, 1867 | 172 |
| Poor Law Act, 1601 | 21 |
| Post Office Acts, 1947 and 1969 | 113 |
| Powers of Attorney Act, 1971 | 134, 138, 139 |

# TABLE OF STATUTES CITED

| | PAGE |
|---|---|
| Powers of Criminal Courts Act, 1973 | 255, 259 |
| Prescription Act, 1832 | 187 |
| Private Street Works Act, 1892 | 194 |
| Provisions of Oxford, 1258 | 29 |
| Public Order Acts, 1936–1963 | 119, 120 |
| Public Trustee Act, 1906 | 151 |
| Race Relations Acts, 1965–1968 | 283 |
| Radioactive Substances Act, 1960 | 237 |
| Redundancy Payments Act, 1965 | 141 |
| Registered Designs Act, 1949 | 175, 304 |
| Registration of Business Names Act, 1916 | 129 |
| Rehabilitation of Offenders Act, 1974 | 241 |
| Rent Act, 1957 | 181 |
| Rent Act, 1965 | 253 |
| Rent Act, 1968 | 213, 214 |
| Rent Act, 1974 | 213 |
| Resale Prices Act, 1964 | 3, 283 |
| Restrictive Practices Court Act, 1976 | 3, 283 |
| Restrictive Trade Practices Acts, 1956 and 1976 | 3, 283 |
| Rights of Light Act, 1959 | 187, 194 |
| Riot Act, 1714 | 121 |
| Riot (Damages) Act, 1886 | 121 |
| Road Safety Act, 1967 | 298 |
| Road Traffic Act, 1930 | 21 |
| Road Traffic Act, 1960 | 2, 21, 58, 266 |
| Road Traffic Act, 1972 | 3, 58, 266 |
| Sale of Goods Act, 1893 | 2, 58, 65, 80, 143, 154, 155, 163, 233 |
| Settled Land Act, 1925 | 178, 201, 202 |
| Short Titles Act, 1896 | 18 |
| Slander of Women Act, 1891 | 239 |
| Slaughterhouses Act, 1974 | 3 |
| Social Security Act, 1973 | 115, 116 |
| Statute of Frauds, 1677 | 49, 52 |
| Statute of Frauds (Amendment) Act, 1828. *See* Lord Tenterden's Act. | |
| Statute of Uses, 1535 | 39 |
| Statute of Westminster II, 1285 | 29 |
| Statute of Westminster, 1931 | 289 |
| Statutory Instruments Act, 1946 | 22 |
| Suicide Act, 1961 | 266 |
| Summary Jurisdiction (Separation and Maintenance) Acts, 1895–1949 | 108 |
| Supply of Goods (Implied Terms) Act, 1973 | 26, 58, 155, 156, 164 |
| Theatres Act, 1968 | 119 |
| Theft Act, 1968 | 25, 256, 262, 268 *et seq.*, 288 |
| Town and Country Planning Acts, 1962–1971 | 3, 212, 304 |
| Trade Descriptions Acts, 1968–1972 | 255, 256, 262 |
| Trade Disputes Act, 1906 | 127 |
| Trade Marks Act, 1938 | 175 |
| Trade Union and Labour Relations Act, 1974 | 127, 141, 247 |
| Trade Union and Labour Relations (Amendment) Act, 1976 | 127, 247 |
| Transport Act, 1962 | 57 |
| Treason Act, 1351 | 272 |
| Tribunals and Inquiries Acts, 1958–1971 | 304, 305 |
| Truck Acts, 1831–1940 | 72 |
| Trustee Act, 1925 | 148 *et seq.*, 179, 208 |
| Trustee Investments Act, 1961 | 151 |
| Unsolicited Goods and Services Act, 1971 | 162 |
| Unsolicited Goods and Services (Amendment) Act, 1975 | 162 |
| Variation of Trusts Act, 1958 | 152 |
| War Damage Act, 1965 | 18 |
| Wills Act, 1837 | 158, 203, 204 |
| Wills Act, 1968 | 204 |

# GENERAL PRINCIPLES OF ENGLISH LAW

## INTRODUCTION

The history of the law is an interesting subject worthy of detailed study, but it lies outside the scope of this work, which is intended to set forth the principles of English Law in simple language. Much of what is mentioned in this Introduction will be dealt with in greater detail in subsequent Chapters, but it will perhaps be advantageous for the reader to have before him at the outset an outline of the growth of the English Legal System, a brief mention of the various Courts in which cases are tried, and a summary of the mode of commencing proceedings and enforcing judgments.

### Common Law and Equity.

Before the 12th century, law consisted solely of local customs and practices handed down orally from generation to generation, some of them dating from the times of the early Britons. These customs were recognized and enforced, and gradually extended by the "law-givers" of each succeeding period. Usages of other races, of the Romans, for instance, were incorporated, and, after the Norman Conquest, the body of law common to the whole country, as distinct from local customs, was administered in the King's Courts and was designated the *Common Law*. This uniformity was accomplished by the "Circuit Judges," as a result of their interchange of opinions, when they discussed their individual experiences in London.

By degrees the Common Law became a somewhat rigid system from which substantive rules of law emerged only from the interstices of formalistic procedural law governing the writ necessary for the pursuit of a claim. This inflexibility proved most inconvenient to the trading community, and in many cases caused great hardship. Consequently various customs and usages adapted to mercantile transactions grew up amongst traders, and these tended to simplify commercial intercourse. Frequently foreign practices were introduced and retained, and large numbers of principles from international codes of rules, which were created and observed by the merchant communities of all countries, were adopted by British merchants, in particular those rules which had reference to maritime matters. The English

Courts did not originally recognize this *lex mercatoria*, or law merchant, which merchants applied in their own courts ; but gradually it obtained recognition by the Courts and, towards the middle of the 18th century, it became firmly established as part of the Common Law largely owing to the vigour of Lord Chief Justice Mansfield.

A direct outcome of the harshness and inflexibility of the Common Law was the creation of what is known as *Equity*. The Common Law Courts did not provide a remedy for every civil wrong, and the relief that they were able to give was often insufficient. It therefore became customary for those seeking redress to petition the King, as the " Fountain of Justice ", who directed the Chancellor to review the petitions and bring before him such matters as he thought proper. Edward III ordered the Chancellor to deal with these petitions himself, and by the end of the 15th century he regularly dealt with petitions on his own initiative, and the Court of Chancery came into being. The principles upon which the Chancellor decided disputes came to be known as Equity. Equity was based upon the idea of natural justice, as opposed to the strict letter of the law. Equity did not claim to override the Common Law but to supplement it. The two systems have worked well together since the 17th century and finally the administration of the principles of law and Equity was fused by the Judicature Act, 1873, and it was laid down that all the Courts should administer both sets of principles ; and that where the rules of law and Equity differed, those of Equity should prevail. These matters are given more detailed treatment in Chapter II.

In addition to this gradual growth of a system of law, much new law has been added and much of the existing law has been altered by Acts of the Legislature, comprising the Queen, the House of Lords and the House of Commons in Parliament assembled. These acts are known as *statutes*, and the law thus created is referred to as *Statute Law*. Statute Law is superior to, and overrides, all rules of Common Law and Equity inconsistent therewith and is the major source of new law today. Since the middle of the 19th century attempts have been made to *codify* into one statute or series of statutes all the rules relating to one particular branch of the law ; e.g., the Partnership Act, 1890, and the Sale of Goods Act, 1893. The Consolidation of Enactments (Procedure) Act, 1949, lays down the procedure for *consolidating* statutes on a particular branch of law, with such minor corrections as the consolidation may entail. The Road Traffic Act, 1960 and the Matrimonial Causes Act, 1965, are examples of the use hitherto made of this procedure. It so happens, that both enactments have figured in subsequent consolidating statutes ; the

INTRODUCTION 3

former in the Road Traffic Act, 1972 and the latter in the Matrimonial Causes Act, 1973.

Whereas a *codifying* statute, such as the Bills of Exchange Act, 1882, assembles the known law at a given time and in a given field both statutory and case-law, a *consolidating* statute, such as the Town and Country Planning Act, 1971, does no more than collect into one statute all the relevant statute law on a given topic, leaving relevant case-law still operative. A recent example of a consolidating statute is the Slaughterhouses Act, 1974 consolidating enactments relating to slaughterhouses and knackers' yards and the slaughter of animals. Another is the Legal Aid Act, 1974 consolidating enactments relating to legal aid and legal advice and assistance.

## The Courts.

Before the Judicature Act of 1873 came into operation, there were in existence several distinct Courts: (1) The Courts of Common Law, comprising the Queen's Bench, the Court of Common Pleas, and the Court of Exchequer, and (2) the Court of Chancery. The Judicature Act created the SUPREME COURT OF JUDICATURE, which consists of the HIGH COURT OF JUSTICE and the COURT OF APPEAL. The High Court became divided into three Divisions—viz., the Chancery Division, the Queen's Bench Division, and the Probate, Divorce and Admiralty Division, but as a result of the re-organisation effected by the Administration of Justice Act, 1970 the last-named Division was supplanted by the new Family Division. In theory all the Divisions are of equal competence, dispensing both Law and Equity, but, for convenience, certain business is assigned to each. The Crown Court was, pursuant to the Courts Act, 1971, made a part of the Supreme Court.

The Supreme Court of Judicature, together with the House of Lords and the Judicial Committee of the Privy Council are classified as *Superior Courts of Record*. Inferior Courts of Record, so called because their proceedings are subject to supervision of some superior Court, include the County Courts.

Courts of Record are so called because a record is kept of the proceedings before them, such records being conclusive evidence of what is contained therein.

The Restrictive Practices Court established under the Restrictive Trade Practices Act, 1956 (and given further functions by the Resale Prices Act, 1964) is a Superior Court of Record. Its jurisdiction is now covered by the Restrictive Practices Court Act, 1976 (a consolidating Act).

## Actions.

Actions are founded on the infringement of a person's legal rights; thus if a contract has been broken by one party, or an act which the law regards as wrongful is committed, the other party to the contract or the person who has been injured by the wrongful act has a right of action.

An action in the Queen's Bench Division is normally commenced by a *Writ of Summons* which commands the defendant to enter an appearance, usually within eight days of service. On the writ are endorsed particulars of the plaintiff's claim; and, if the defendant wishes to contest the claim, he must "enter an appearance" within the stated time. If he does not do so, judgment may be entered against him, which will be "final" if the claim is for a liquidated amount—that is, for an ascertained sum—but, if it is for an unliquidated amount, what is termed an "interlocutory" judgment is signed and a *writ of inquiry* is issued to assess the amount of damages.

If the defendant enters an appearance, then after various intermediate steps, known as interlocutory proceedings, have been taken, the action will be tried by a Judge and jury, or by a Judge alone, and a decision, known as a judgment, will be given in favour of either the plaintiff or the defendant.

Appeals against this decision may be carried to the Court of Appeal and thence, with the consent of the Court of Appeal or of the House of Lords, to the House of Lords.

A judgment may take the form of an award of damages to be paid in cash; or of a decree for specific performance, that is, the actual carrying out of a contract in accordance with the agreed terms; or of an injunction issued by the Court prohibiting a party from doing certain things or compelling him to do certain things.

## Enforcement of Judgments.

Judgments sounding in money may be enforced in several ways, the most common being the issue of:—

(1) *A writ of fieri facias*, for the purpose of seizing the debtor's money and selling his goods (including leasehold property)—usually termed *fi. fa.*
(2) *A garnishee order*, which is an order commanding a third party, who owes money to the judgment debtor, to pay it to the judgment creditor instead.
(3) *A charging order*, for the purpose of seizing stocks and shares, or a partner's interest in the firm's property or whereby the land of the judgment debtor may be subjected to a registrable charge.

(4) *Equitable execution*, available in cases where the debtor has a legal or an equitable interest in land or other property which cannot be taken in execution by any of the above modes. If money be due to the debtor from any source, a receiver may be appointed by way of equitable execution to receive the money and to satisfy the creditor therewith.

(5) *An Attachment of Earnings Order* under the Attachment of Earnings Act, 1971. By virtue of this Act the High Court has power to make an attachment of earnings order to secure payment under a High Court maintenance order (as defined in s.2(b)). The Court must be satisfied that the debtor's failure to make payments is due to his wilful refusal or culpable neglect (s.3(5)). The attachment of earnings order is to be directed to the person appearing to the court to have the debtor in his employment (s. 6).

Under the Act a County Court and a Magistrates' Court are likewise empowered to make such an Order in certain cases.

If the debtor does not pay a High Court maintenance order or a County Court maintenance order or a judgment for taxes and certain other public charges, a judgment summons can be taken out ; and if it can be shown that he had had the means of paying since the date of the judgment, he may be imprisoned for a period of up to six weeks. With this exception, however, there is no imprisonment for civil debt.

The most important of the inferior Courts of Record are County Courts, the jurisdiction of which is limited geographically and to cases involving only comparatively small amounts of money or money's worth. The jurisdiction of these Courts is referred to in greater detail in Chapter IX.

The jurisdiction of the High Court extends only to England and Wales and to the town of Berwick-on-Tweed. It may, however, take cognizance of matters arising abroad if the parties are within the jurisdiction, except in cases of actions for trespass to land situate abroad : and it may, in certain circumstances, give leave for a defendant to be sued in this country although he is abroad ; but the Court has no jurisdiction against independent Foreign Rulers, Sovereign States, or Foreign Ambassadors and their staffs even if they are in this country, unless, of course, they choose to submit themselves to its jurisdiction, that is to say, they expressly, or by conduct, evince an undertaking to be bound by the decision of the English Court.

# CHAPTER I

## SOURCES OF ENGLISH LAW AND RELATED MATTERS

**Nature of Law.**

A law is a rule—this connotes the idea of order—regularity—straightness. The term law, in this sense, however, is used in many connections—the laws of golf, the laws of health. A legal rule also is a rule of conduct—the uniformity of behaviour of the various members of the State. A rule, however, is of little use unless it can be enforced. This element of compulsion is known in law as a *sanction*—the threat of coercion to ensure that the command is obeyed. If a man persists in disobeying the rules of football, he will come under the ban of the authorities controlling the game. By whom is the offender against a rule of law dealt with? How is obedience secured? The enforcement is by the State, acting through the medium of the Courts. But it is not all rules of conduct that are so enforced. Social misbehaviours—private drunkenness, debauchery and the like are not the direct concern of law. Thus, a law has been defined as " A rule of civil conduct enforced by the State ".

The preceding represents an analytical approach. It is possible to adopt a functional approach and regard law as a medium by means of which, man being a gregarious animal capable of living a satisfactory life only in intercourse with others, order is preserved and communal life within a complicated society is organized. The compulsive or " police " nature of law should not be overstressed, however, for it is a misconception to think in terms of law being there " to take care of raskills " (Mr. Tulliver in George Eliot's *Mill on the Floss*). In developed society the ordinary citizen acts much more frequently in consonance with the law than he does in breach of it and indeed uses it, whether consciously or not, as an instrument in his everyday affairs.

**Divisions of Law.**

Owing to the interaction and overlapping of the various spheres of law it is difficult to essay a satisfactory classification.

Leaving aside the distinction between International Law and the law of the State, a convenient division of the latter is that between public and private law.

*Public law* is normally subdivided **into** constitutional, administrative and criminal law. The first, is the " body of rules which prescribe (a) the structure and (b) the functions of the organs of central and local government " (Wade and Phillips). The second is concerned with the reconciliation of efficient administration with individual freedom and rights or interests. The third is that set of rules which characterize certain kinds of wrong-doing as offences and matters of public concern and provide for redress by sanction to be imposed by courts of criminal jurisdiction.

*Private law* (which the Romans facilely put into the tripartite division of the law relating to persons, to things and to actions) is concerned with the rights and obligations of individuals *inter se*. These rights may be created directly by the law or be created by consent, a consideration which suggests the following subdivisions :

*The law of tort* has as its general purpose the securing to a man of " indemnity against certain forms of harm to person, reputation or estate, at the hands of his neighbours, not because they are wrong but because they are harms " (Holmes : *The Common Law*). These harms are what the Law regards as harms : the result of conduct which is wrongful by reference to legal rather than moral standards. Hence the law will grant a remedy for the invasion of a right to inviolability of, say, property, person or reputation that right being conceded by the law itself.

*The law of contract* " attempts the realization of reasonable expectations that have been induced by the making of a promise " (Prof. Corbin). Hence the law will grant a remedy for a breach of contract, as a wilful denial of the right to performance conceded consensually.

*The law of property* governs the relation between a person and some item of material or human resources. It is through property that a man can in some ways express his individuality and independence. This department of the law is concerned with the concepts of ownership and possession and the methods by which these may be acquired or alienated. The Law of Succession on death may fairly be said to be a facet of this branch ; so may the topic of Trusts.

*Family law* may be broadly regarded as the law which defines the rights, duties, and status of husband and wife, parent and child and other members of a household.

*The law of procedure* is " adjective " law supporting, so to speak, the " substantive " law under the foregoing heads, by " providing machinery for the settlement of disputes on lines that do justice to both parties " (Paton).

Interaction between and overlapping of the various spheres of law can be seen most vividly as between criminal law and the law of tort. In developed English law, a crime has come to be regarded as an offence against the community or State as such, a power to absolve which lies exclusively with the Crown ; whereas a mere civil wrong (tort) is a matter between private individuals, the injured party being at liberty to sue or not or to enforce or not enforce a judgment obtained by him. The matter is explored in greater detail at the beginning of Chapter VIII.

Overlapping in contract and tort could occur, for instance, in the case of employment. Here an employer could be liable to an employee for breach of contract to pay agreed remuneration and in tort, for breach of duty to provide a safe system of work. See end of Chapter V.

### Sources of Law.

In general, systems of law have followed similar lines of development. A community *finds* the advantages of some form of uniformity of behaviour : thus, " custom " emerges, and " Law is the child of custom and habit is the parent of the latter ". Usages become standards of conduct, suited to what are considered to be the needs of the community. But, of necessity, there is no " looking ahead ". Different circumstances arise beyond the scope of the original scheme. Accordingly, the second stage emerges : some means of expansion, of extension, perhaps of improvisation, are devised to deal with the altered circumstances —not to supersede the existing order, but to supplement it. At this stage the idea of a person or a body of persons with power to lay down the law is conceived—a body of " law-makers ". The sources of English law conform to this pattern—they are the Common Law, Statute Law and Equity.

### Common Law.

Before the Norman Conquest there was no common speech, no common dress—*no Common Law*. Civilization, such as it was, was primitive—and a primitive civilization is a local civilization. One main cause was the lack of adequate communications. Then came the Normans who were neither swashbuckling invaders nor mere colonizers, but supreme administrators. No drastic changes were made in the English customs, the " law "—but it was made uniform. The chief means by which this was achieved was the introduction of the " circuit system ", whereby the King's Judges went regularly round the shires and gradually moulded the numerous customs into one uniform law common to the whole Kingdom. The process was complete by 1250, and before the end of the 13th century appeared the first exposition of the Common Law, the treatise of Bracton, a Justice Itinerant of Henry III. (Itinerant Justices were Judges who went round from place to place in the Kingdom administering the King's justice.) He established the true origin of the Common Law—a Judge-made law, originating in ancient native customs. But the Common Law was not all derived from local custom. That part which deals with the ownership of land was derived from the system of feudal tenures, adopted throughout Western Europe after the break-up of the Roman Empire. It was introduced into this country by the Normans and developed by the royal Judges during the 12th and 13th centuries.

**Custom.**

Although the Common Law, as described above, was, in origin, the " universal custom of the realm ", many local customs still survive, and in so far as they have received judicial recognition they constitute qualifications upon the Common Law, and, in the matters to which they relate and in their own locality, replace the Common Law. Judicial recognition will be afforded if the following conditions are satisfied :—

(a) Immemorial existence : the custom must have existed at the commencement of legal memory (arbitrarily fixed at the first year of the reign of Richard I, 1189), which will be readily presumed, unless it can be shown that the custom could not have existed at that date.
(b) Continuity, i.e., unbroken observance.
(c) Locality : the custom must be confined to some district known to law.
(d) Reasonableness.
(e) Certainty, i.e., as to subject-matter, locality and the persons benefited by it.
(f) Peaceable user, i.e., it must not have been the subject of dispute.
(g) Compulsory : once established, the custom must be the local Common Law.
(h) Consistency : obviously, contradictory customs cannot be recognized.

Customs must be distinguished from usages—a term applied to a particular course of dealing customary in a particular occupation or department of business life, e.g., trade customs or customs of the port. Every usage must be certain and reasonable and must be shown to have acquired notoriety in the trade or business to which it relates, but it need not have existed from time immemorial. Where a usage is proved, the effect thereof is to incorporate in a contract a certain term which is not specifically included. For instance, if a usage is established to entitle workers in a particular occupation to three months' notice of termination of their engagements, then this usage becomes a term of each contract relating to the employment of such workers, unless negatived or varied by express provision.

**Doctrine of Judicial Precedent.**

From the earliest days the Judges were wont, in cases of difficulty, to give not merely their decisions, but also the reason for their decisions : thus, eventually, principles were established.

Obviously, if a case, involving similar facts, came before the Courts subsequently, reference would be made to the reasons given in the earlier case. If the principle involved was the same, then it would be applied in this case also : thus, emerged the doctrine of "judicial precedent". In effect, a judgment is a lecture on the particular point of law involved. The doctrine was of slow growth for various reasons, particularly the difficulties of communication. As soon as the value of these decisions was realized, however, the practitioners, quite naturally, began to make collections of them, both for their own use and for the use of their brethren. The growth of printing enabled these collections to be made in a permanent form, and, as a consequence, they could be more widely distributed. Thus, the number and value of the reported judicial decisions increased.

As, in general terms, the whole of the Common Law has been built up by the decisions of the Judges in this way, the importance of judicial precedent is apparent, and has not diminished. In all cases where no statute governs the position, the case will be argued and decided by reference to previous decisions on similar facts, in so far as the same principle is applicable.

Until a decision by an English Court has been overruled by Parliament, or a superior tribunal, it is binding on all inferior Courts and will be disregarded only with caution by Courts of equal standing. Thus, a judgment of the House of Lords is binding as a precedent upon the Court of Appeal, the High Court, and inferior Courts. It was not, however, until the 19th century that it was definitely established that a principle enunciated in a previous decision of a superior Court was binding on an inferior Court. Towards the end of that century the House of Lords ruled (in *London Tramways Co. v. London County Council* (1898)) that it was bound to follow its own previous decisions given in a judicial capacity. However, in mid-1966 the Lord Chancellor announced a relaxation of the rule and stated that in future while the House will normally follow its earlier precedents it will now depart from a previous decision "when it appears right to do so". Some commentators consider this relaxation will assist law reform but the relaxation has so far been sparingly used.

Despite its undoubted merit in tending to eliminate uncertainty in the law, at any rate in the case of a decision of the House of Lords, the doctrine of the binding force of precedent (or *stare decisis*, as it is sometimes called) has been criticized on the ground that it fetters the Judges with obsolete principles from which relief can be obtained only by legislative action.

Precedents may be either declaratory or original. A declaratory precedent is one which is merely the application of an already existing rule of law. An original precedent, on the other hand, is one which creates and applies a new rule. Original precedents alone develop the law. Declaratory precedents are merely evidence of it. According to one theory, as we shall presently see, all precedents are merely declaratory and our Judges do not make law.

It is not unknown for an English Court to quote as a precedent a case decided in a foreign country. This is particularly true of decisions of American or Commonwealth Courts, but such precedents (like those of the Judicial Committee of the Privy Council see p. 287 *post*) are of *persuasive* authority only and are therefore to be distinguished from the *binding* precedents arising from the hierarchical principle outlined above.

Among the advantages of Case Law may be mentioned, according to Professor Geldart :—

(i) Certainty.
(ii) The possibility of growth.
(iii) The great wealth of detailed rules.
(iv) The practical character of these rules.

The same writer claims that its main disadvantages, on the other hand, are :—

(i) *Rigidity*. " The binding force of precedent is a fetter on the discretion of the Judge." This defect, however, can be overcome by the judicious use of *statutes*. Where a rule which has become rigid causes hardship, it can be altered by statute.
(ii) *The danger of illogical distinctions*, resulting from the fact that a precedent sometimes leads the law into a " blind alley ", escape from which is possible only by making minute and somewhat unreal distinctions between one case and another. Here again, a statute may be enacted to provide the logical way out.
(iii) *Bulk and complexity* : the law can be ascertained only by a search through a large number of reports, a process which, however, may in the comparatively near future be facilitated by the computer system.

**Reports.**

It is obvious that the doctrine of judicial precedent could not have been established unless judicial decisions had been recorded in some form.

From very early times records of cases were kept on the " rolls " of the Courts, but these merely set forth the pleadings and the decisions given, and contained no record of the reasons for such decisions. The earliest form of Law Report is the *Year Books*, gossipy and fragmentary notes of cases, written in Anglo-Norman, covering a period of two and a half centuries, from the reign of Edward I to that of Henry VIII. Originally, they were in manuscript form, being printed about the end of the 15th century. They were not of official origin, but were compilations by practitioners and students of cases which they heard in the Courts and which they considered to be of professional interest. Collections of such notes were compiled by enterprising publishers and sold. During the 16th and 17th centuries summaries of such notes were published under the title of *Abridgments*. The Year Books are little used by the modern practitioner by reason of their many inaccuracies and of the language in which they were written. They are, nevertheless, of great interest to research students.

The invention of printing contributed to the production of many Reports appearing under the names of individual reporters such as Coke, Plowden and the famous " teams " of Barnewall and Cresswell, and Meeson and Welsby. The value of such reports will necessarily vary with the reputation of the reporter and that of the Judge whose decisions he records.

Modern reports date from the early part of the 19th century, when there was a revival of mass-reporting. In 1833 the Law Journal Reports were started. In 1864, *The Law Reports* came into being. These did not represent a commercial venture, but were compiled under the supervision of a body comprising representatives of the Inns of Court and of the Law Society. Many of the judgments are revised by the Judges who pronounce them. Nevertheless, the Reports are not " official ", because their accuracy may be challenged. If a Judge before whom a case is quoted thinks that the report is erroneous, he may send for the official record of the particular case from the Record Office. The Law Journal Reports and another series, the Law Times Reports, are now incorporated in the All England Reports, a useful series which started in 1936.

Since January, 1953, the Incorporated Council of Law Reporting for England and Wales has published Weekly Law Reports (without arguments) and Monthly Law Reports (with arguments). The various series of Law Reports are identified in text-books and elsewhere by appropriate abbreviations. Thus, a common law case decided in the Queen's Bench Division in 1965 and reported in *The Law Reports* would be referred to as to source as, say, " 1965, 1 Q.B. 511 ".

Decisions in County Courts and Magistrates' Courts are seldom initially reported, but outstanding cases sometimes figure in professional journals. The County Courts not infrequently have to deal with interesting and difficult points of law which sometimes are the subject of appeals to the Court of Appeal or House of Lords : it is then that the matter figures in a Law Report.

### Ratio Decidendi and Obiter Dictum.

The mere reading of the report of a case will not reveal what was decided in that case : the reader must extract the *ratio decidendi*, i.e., the principle of law on which the decision was based. For instance, in *Donoghue* v. *Stevenson* (1932), referred to below and in Chapter VII, the actual facts of the case are of small importance compared with the principle on which the decision proceeded. This principle is the only factor which a Court can take into account in a subsequent case where the same principle apparently applies. The chance of two cases occurring with identical facts is obviously very remote.

The Judge in his approach to the solution of the problem in issue may well have given illustrations of a general principle not professing to be applicable to the particular question. Such words are *obiter dicta*—things said by the way. They are of persuasive value, but are not binding in effect, though they will be considered with respect, according to the reputation of the Judge. Professor Goodhart has suggested that, to determine the principle of a case, one must take into account :—

(a) The facts treated by the Judge as material ;
(b) His decision as based on them. It may also be of value to consider why certain facts were excluded on the ground of immateriality.

### Judge-Made Law.

Although the Common Law is the product of judicial decisions, the Judges have always maintained that they do not make law, judicial decisions being merely evidence of custom and of the law derived therefrom. Salmond declares : " Doubtless Judges have many times altered the law whilst endeavouring in good faith to declare it. But we must recognise a distinct law-creating power vested in them and openly and lawfully exercised." C. K. Allen is of similar opinion, but considers the different meanings which may be attributed to the word " make ". He says : " We must use this word ' make ' with caution, and I think we shall find that in one sense of it at least, Judges are not merely resorting to what Bentham called a ' childish fiction ' when they disclaim the capacity to create new law ". Nevertheless, modern conditions have created new situations, unanticipated combinations of circumstances, which have rendered new rules of law inevitable. Thus, it was not until 1926 that a definite ruling was given as to the liability of a man whose cat raids his neighbour's hen-roost (*Buckle* v. *Holmes*). In the same year there was determined, for the first time, the liability of the occupier of premises adjoining a highway, whose tree, without his negligence, falls into the highway and injures a passer-by (*Noble* v. *Harrison*). The notable case of *Donoghue* v. *Stevenson* (1932)—the snail in the ginger-beer bottle case discussed in Chapter VII—aligned the law of negligence and the concept of duty to take care to the modern manufacturing age. Such cases are known as " leading cases ", since they formulate important principles.

Allen suggests that the solution may be found in the two possible meanings to be attributed to " making " law. Parliament " makes " law in the primary sense—it *manufactures* law. Not so the Judge : he does not manufacture the law ; his province is to *find* the law. But there may be no precedent to guide him ; then, he must apply " natural justice " or " common sense ", but this he applies in accordance with his study of the law and in accordance with what he considers to be the principles of English jurisprudence. It is in this sense of the term that the Judge " makes " law. And Allen concludes : " The creative power of the Courts is limited by existing legal material at their command. They *find* the material and *shape* it. The Legislature may manufacture entirely new material."

That English law is, however, a live and constantly developing system is demonstrated by a statement recently made by a Judge as follows :—" the law of England is a living law. It develops and must develop according to changes in social life and social outlook. It has long since been pointed out under our system that the novelty of a claim is no answer to it."

## Canon Law.

As has been said already, not all English law is derived from native custom. There is the Canon Law, the Law of the Church, administered in the " Courts Christian ", which arose as the result of the decree of William I ; this provided that ecclesiastical matters should no longer be discussed in the local secular Courts of the Shire and Hundred, but in separate Ecclesiastical Courts. Certain matters fell naturally within the jurisdiction of such Courts, for example, the punishment of offences against doctrine and morality, and the control of marriage, and of divorce, in so far as the latter was recognized by the Church. But these Courts also claimed jurisdiction in certain secular matters, in particular, the administration of the estates of deceased persons, so far as personal property (as opposed to real property, i.e., land) was concerned.

With regard to purely ecclesiastical matters, the Church applied the Canon Law and, in consequence of the Act for the Submission of the Clergy, 1534, in the few matters still within the purview of the Church Courts, and in such matters as have not been transferred to the secular Courts, e.g., divorce, the canons existing in 1532 are still binding on clergy and laity alike, except in so far as modified by Parliament or by Measure of the General Synod of the Church of England. In 1857, the Matrimonial Causes Act transferred the jurisdiction in matrimonial affairs to a new civil Court known as the Divorce Court.

As regards jurisdiction in purely secular matters, probates of wills, and the administration of the estates of deceased persons, the Church Courts drew largely upon the great body of Roman Law, the Corpus Juris Civilis of Justinian, and thus a body of Judge-made or case law arose. This jurisdiction passed to the Probate Court, under the Court of Probate Act, 1857.

Finally, in 1875 the Probate and Divorce Courts were incorporated in the newly created Supreme Court of Judicature (see *ante* p. 3), the legal principles evolved in the Ecclesiastical Courts being expressly incorporated into the Laws of England.

### Law Merchant.

This body of customary law was described in *Goodwin* v. *Robarts* (1876) as, " neither more nor less than the usages of merchants and traders . . . ratified by the decisions of Courts of law which, upon such usages being proved before them, have adopted them as settled law ".

The landowner's disputes concerning land, and his remedies for personal violence, were provided for in the Common Law Courts. But naturally enough such Courts contained no machinery for dealing with disputes of merchants arising out of the development of trade, both internal and external. Hence arose the Courts Merchant and Maritime—Courts of Piepowder, Courts of the Staple, and local maritime Courts. The first-named were possibly so called from the dusty feet (*pieds poudrés*) of the merchants—travelling from market to market—whose disputes were settled there. The Courts of the Staple were Courts established in the Staple towns, i.e., towns which had a monopoly in dealings with the more important articles of commerce. The principles administered in such Courts were not those of the Common Law, but the accepted customs of merchants prevailing over a large part of Western Europe. Maritime law had a distinctly " international " flavour.

The work of the local Courts was gradually absorbed by the Common Law and Admiralty Courts. During the 17th and 18th centuries the Law Merchant, apart from maritime law and prize law, was absorbed into the Common Law of England. The main agent in this work of incorporation was Lord Mansfield (Chief Justice, 1756). Yet he continued to treat the Law Merchant as a special branch of the Common Law with its own special rules. He established the principle that, once a considered judgment on a custom has been given, the custom is judicially recognized and no further proof of it is necessary in the future. He heard cases with specially selected juries of merchants, thus ensuring continuity and experience in development. His work was carried on by his successors, in particular, Lord Ellenborough. By 1827 the Law Merchant was settled in principle, but still retains its peculiarities. Its principles are capable of extension by proof of a new custom of merchants. The test is not "immemorial antiquity", but universality of observance.

### Law Merchant and Equity.

There are distinct resemblances between the Law Merchant and Equity (the nature of which will be described in the next Chapter).

The principles of the Law Merchant were not founded on the ancient customs of the realm, but upon the practice of the merchant community, a kind of *ius gentium* (Law of Nations); similarly, Equity claimed to derive its principles from natural justice. The procedure in the Courts administering the two systems was of a summary nature. Moreover, the Law Merchant was not complete in itself: it was an appendix and complementary to the Common Law. Equity, similarly, was a " gloss " upon the Common Law. Further examples of similarity were :—

(*a*) Equity and the Law Merchant viewed alike the assignability of contractual rights and obligations. The Common Law refused to recognize the assignability of choses in action (i.e., rights of ownership incapable of physical possession and enforceable only by process of law, e.g., debts) on the ground that such recognition would lead to multiplicity of actions, but Equity had no such qualms, compelling an assignor to allow the assignee to sue the debtor in his, the assignor's, name. Similarly, the Law Merchant recognized the assignability of bills of exchange.

(*b*) Both systems recognized what was later termed the doctrine of notice. Thus, by the Law Merchant the holder for value of a bill of exchange took the bill free from any defects in the title of his transferor, provided that he had no knowledge of such at the time of transfer. Similarly, in Equity, the transferee for value of the legal estate held the property free from any equities affecting the transferor, if he had acquired such estate without notice of such encumbrances.

(*c*) The Common Law demanded performance of a contract on the day fixed, not so Equity and the Law Merchant: the former did not recognize time as the essence of the contract, the latter allowed " days of grace ".

(*d*) According to the Common Law, until the middle of the 19th century, the parties to an action, being interested parties, were not allowed to give evidence, whereas they were always competent witnesses in the Courts of Chancery and of the Law Merchant.

(e) Equity had no particular regard to the sanctity of seal or consideration. Neither had the Law Merchant until it was incorporated into the Common Law.

## Statute.

Although the term "statute" has a wider meaning, to be explained later, normally it means an Act of Parliament, the necessary parties to which are the Queen, the House of Lords and the House of Commons—although the assent of the Lords may be dispensed with, in certain circumstances, under the Parliament Acts, 1911 and 1949. Acts are recorded in the Statute Book, beginning with the reissue of Magna Carta in 1225, although, of course, at that time, the respective parts to be played by the King, Lords and commons in legislation had yet to be determined.

The essential differences between Statute Law and Common Law are apparent from the definition of a statute: *An express and formal laying down of a rule or rules of conduct to be observed in the future by persons to whom the statute is expressly, or by implication, made applicable.* Thus a statute differs from a judgment in the following ways:—

(a) A statute openly creates new law, whereas a judgment disclaims any attempt to do so.

(b) Whilst a statute lays down general rules for the guidance of future conduct, a judgment merely applies an existing law to a particular set of circumstances.

(c) A judgment gives reasons and is argumentative. A statute, on the other hand, gives no reasons and is imperative.

Despite the increasing spate of statutes, the basis of our law still remains the Common Law. Even if all the statutes were repealed, there would still be a legal system, albeit inadequate. But if there were only statutes there would be no system— merely a set of disjointed rules, making no provision for many of the problems of daily life. Yet the statute is supreme: its validity cannot be brought into question by any Court, and if in conflict with the Common Law, the Statute must prevail. Indeed, one of the functions of Statute Law is to abolish those Common Law rules which have outlived their usefulness. Statutes may also amend or adapt Common Law rules to meet the requirements of changing circumstances.

The omnipotence of Statute Law is nowhere more clearly illustrated than by section 26 of the Finance Act, 1950, which imposed liability to income tax on certain payments made to individuals which, under the law existing when the payments were made, were not liable to tax. Similarly the War Damage Act, 1965, removed vested rights to compensation from the Crown found to be payable under a decision of the House of Lords in its judicial capacity made shortly before. This is known as "retrospective" or "retroactive" legislation. A statute can also grant relief from the consequences of an illegal act, e.g., the House of Commons (Indemnification of Certain Members) Act, 1949, relieving certain members from the penal consequences of having sat and voted in the House of Commons whilst they were legally disqualified from so doing. These are illustrations emphasising the importance of the doctrine of the " Sovereignty of Parliament ", but it should be stressed that retrospective legislation is comparatively rare and that the majority of statutes operate only from the date when the preliminary measure has received the Royal Assent or some later date specified in the legislation.

Statute law is *written*, i.e., contained in documents, and enacted by the Legislature. The Common Law, on the other hand, is *unwritten* in the sense that it is nowhere to be found officially written down. It is found mainly by reference to a large number of reports of decided cases. This is different from the system prevailing in certain countries having a "code" of laws, e.g., France, Germany and Italy. The functions of Judges in these countries is merely to interpret and apply the relevant provision of the particular code.

Any legal text-book to which one may refer contains numerous abbreviations which refer chiefly to relevant statutes and reported cases.

There are three methods of referring to an Act of Parliament :—

(a) Short Title ; the reference by which it is generally known ; e.g., Bills of Exchange Act, 1882. The Short Titles Act, 1896, names many Acts of Parliament that were formerly known only by their official reference, e.g., the Limitation Act, 1623, referred to below.

(b) Official Reference : which quotes the Session of Parliament and the number (or chapter) of the particular statute ; e.g., " 45 and 46 Vict. C. 61 " is the official reference to the Bills of Exchange Act, 1882. Fully expanded, it means the 61st enactment passed in the Session of Parliament held in the 45th and 46th year of the reign of Queen Victoria. The Acts of Parliament Numbering and Citation Act, 1962, simplifies matters in respect of statutes passed in and after 1963 in that the numbering and citation of these statutes are to be by reference to the *calendar* year (and not the Session) in which they are passed. Thus the Betting, Gaming and Lotteries Act, 1963 (a consolidating Act) bears the reference " (1963, c. 2) ".

## SOURCES OF ENGLISH LAW

(c) Full Title : which is the official title, in its full form, together with a short description of the object of the statute ; e.g., to the words quoted in (b) are added " being an Act to codify the law relating to Bills of Exchange, Cheques and Promissory Notes ".

In order to determine the title of an Act passed before 1963 of which one knows the Official Reference only, it is, therefore, necessary to know the Table of Regnal Years in order to determine the year in which the statute was passed ; thereafter reference may be made to the complete list of statutes passed in that year. For example, the statute 21 Jac. 1 C. 16, we can readily compute, was passed in 1623 ; in fact, it is the official reference to the Limitation Act, 1623 (now superseded).

Subordinate legislation is referred to by the year in which it was made and the number of the Order in question, e.g., S.I., 1968 (No. 404) refers to Order No. 404 of the Statutory Instruments made in the year 1968.

Obsolete statutes are periodically " weeded out " by what are known as Statute Law Revision Acts. As to codification and consolidation see *ante* p. 2.

**Interpretation.**

When the Court is concerned with the rules of Common Law, it must find what was the *ratio decidendi*, the principle of law on which a particular decision was based, and then apply it to the facts before the Court. Where, however, a statute covers a case, the express words (*litera legis*) of the statute must be applied (in the light of the statutory aids to interpretation afforded by the Interpretation Act, 1889).

The Courts themselves have developed principles of construction. One of them is that if the words of a statute are ambiguous, the Court must endeavour to ascertain their meaning and in so doing will interpret them in such a manner as to avoid an absurdity. Where, however, the words are clear, they must be followed literally, even though an absurdity results.

The Court presumes that Parliament does not make mistakes and applies this principle strictly, on the ground that Parliament alone can correct mistakes in legislation. Faults of language, however, will be corrected by the Court when the intention is clear. An erroneous statement of facts does not bind the Court, such statement in a statute not being conclusive evidence of that fact. Nevertheless, for the purpose of construing a statute, the Court may :—

    (i) Correct obvious misprints ;
    (ii) Supply omitted words ;

(iii) Substitute one word for another ;
(iv) Transpose words ;
(v) Treat an affirmative word as negative, and *vice versa* ;
(vi) Treat a disjunctive word as a conjunctive, and *vice versa* ;
(vii) Extend the literal meaning of words.

**Rules of Interpretation of Statutes.**

1. The " Golden Rule " is to construe the statutes according to the *grammatical and ordinary* sense of the words *unless* that would lead to some absurdity or some repugnancy or inconsistency with the rest of the statute, in which case the grammatical and ordinary sense of the words may (subject as above) be modified so as to avoid that absurdity or inconsistency, but *no further*.

Thus, the meaning of the words may be extended :—

(i) If the language falls short of the whole object of the legislature and the words are capable of such extension. Thus " to sell beer to a drunken man " has been held to include the supply of beer to a drunken man and his sober companion when the latter paid for it.

(ii) To avoid evasion. Thus, evasion of an Act by putting forward documents which give a false description of a matter will not be allowed.

Similarly, the meaning of words may be restricted in the following ways :—

(i) There is a presumption against the general alteration of the law. Thus, where a statute provided that every conveyance of land in a particular form would be valid, it was held that compliance with the formalities did not remedy an inherent defect of title in a given case.

(ii) Where an act is done under an honest and reasonable belief in the existence of a state of things, which if true, would have afforded a complete justification for such act, such act will not *as a general rule* fall within a statute which prohibits that act. Thus, if a man demands goods with threats, *bona fide* believing them to be his, he will not be guilty of robbery.

(iii) Statutes imposing taxes or infringing rights will be construed strictly.

It has been recently stated, however, that if there are two reasonable interpretations, grammatically speaking, of the words in a statute, the Court adopts that which is just, reasonable and sensible. On the other hand, where there is any doubt concerning the wording of a statute, the words are to be understood in a way which harmonises with the policy of the statute. In this connection guidance was given so long ago as 1584, when in *Heydon's Case*, the judges ruled that the following matters should be considered :—

(i) What the law was before the Act was passed ;
(ii) What was the mischief or the defect for which the law had not provided ;
(iii) What remedy Parliament had provided ;
(iv) The reason for the remedy ;

the office of the judge then being to make such construction " as shall suppress the mischief and advance the remedy ".

2. In ascertaining the object and scope of the statute, all the parts of the statute, e.g., the title, preamble and headings to sections may be considered as well as the sections themselves. No account must, however, be taken of the substance of debates in Parliament while the statute was still in the Bill stage, i.e., before it was passed by Parliament and received the Royal Assent. However, the Courts are now tending (in effect in connection with applying the Rule in *Heydon's Case* referred to in the preceding paragraph) to examine and consider the Reports of Law Reform Committees or of the Law Commission (see *post* p. 26) leading to the enactment of specific legislation.

3. The "*Ejusdem Generis*" rule, whereby general words following specific words will be construed as applying only to persons or things of the same class as already mentioned. Thus, in the Betting Act, 1853, the words prohibiting the keeping of a " house, office, room or other place " for betting were held not to include an uncovered enclosure adjacent to the racecourse, where the public went to bet with bookmakers. Also, the definition of a traffic sign in the Road Traffic Act, 1930, to include " all signals, warning sign-posts, direction posts, signs or devices " was held not to include a white painted line on a road.

4. *Expressio unius est exclusio alterius* (" The express mention of one thing implies the exclusion of another ") is a rule dealing with the exclusion of implied terms. If specific words in a statute are not followed by general words, the statute will be applied only to those things which are mentioned. Thus, in the Poor Law Act, 1601, " lands, houses, coal mines, or saleable underwoods " was held not to extend to any mines other than coal mines.

## Delegated Legislation.

Parliament, being omnipotent, can depute to a non-Parliamentary body or authority, e.g., a Government Department, Minister or a Rule-making body, the power to make Orders, Regulations and Rules having statutory force. This is termed delegated legislation. The tendency of modern Acts of Parliament is to lay down general principles or policy, and to leave the working out of the administrative details to the authority responsible for the carrying out of the Act. For instance, under the Road Traffic Act, 1960, the Minister of Transport was given power to make Regulations governing (*inter alia*) the issue of licences under the Act.

The following reasons are usually advanced for the increase of delegated legislative powers :—

(a) *Lack of Parliamentary Time.* Parliament has too much to do, and too little time in which to do it.
(b) *Urgency.* Parliament is not always in session and its procedure is slow.
(c) *Necessity for Future Provisions.* Parliament cannot foresee all the conditions that may arise out of a measure under consideration. It is, therefore, necessary to give an administrative authority power to deal with future situations, as they arise, by means of Rules and Regulations.
(d) *Elasticity.* Subordinate legislation is more elastic than an Act of Parliament. If a regulation proves impracticable it may be readily withdrawn—not so an Act.

The usual types of delegated legislation are :—

(a) Orders made by the Queen in Council under statutory authority, and usually issued without further reference to Parliament.
(b) Rules and Orders made by Ministers which normally require submission to Parliament either before or after coming into force.
(c) Bye-laws of Local Authorities, usually requiring confirmation by a Central Department.

The Statutory Instruments Act, 1946, created a new term, " statutory instrument ", applicable to any document by which Her Majesty in Council or a Minister of the Crown, or a rule-making authority exercises the statutory power to make, confirm or approve orders, rules, regulations and other subordinate legislation. The Act lays down the procedure to be followed in enacting delegated legislation.

Delegated legislation has been the subject of much criticism in the past, but is inevitable in modern times and the following may be said to be checks upon the abuse of delegated legislative powers :—

(a) Parliament retains its authority to revoke or vary the delegated power.

(b) There is the judicial safeguard. Although the Courts may not declare invalid an Act of Parliament, they may, and do declare the exercise of a delegated power, e.g., by Rules and Orders, to be invalid on the ground that it is *ultra vires*, " beyond the powers ", conferred by the Act under the authority of which such Rules and Orders are made. The modern Parliamentary draftsman has, however, to some extent diminished the value of this safeguard by introducing special clauses tending to exclude the intervention of the Courts.

Another judicial safeguard resides in the fact that as concerns Bye-Laws (which are a form of delegated legislation entrusted to local government and other authorities) the Courts may declare void any such Bye-Laws as are found, in all the circumstances, to be unreasonable.

(c) Sometimes it is provided that a public inquiry shall be held before an Order can be made. Also, the law-making authority may be required to give public notice of intention to exercise its powers, and to give to public bodies interested an opportunity to make revisions or suggestions regarding proposed Rules.

(d) *The Select Committee.* In 1944 there was set up, as a permanent organ, a Select Committee of eleven members, chosen from the House of Commons, to scrutinize the statutory Rules and Orders made by the Executive in the exercise of delegated powers of legislation, the Rules and Orders being such as require Parliamentary sanction or admit of Parliamentary challenge.

The Committee reports to the House on any Order or Regulation deserving special attention on the ground :—

(i) That it imposes a charge on the public revenues or contains provisions requiring payments to be made to the Exchequer or any Government Department or to any Local or Public Authority in consideration of any licence or consent or of any service to be rendered, or prescribes the amount of any such charge or payments ;

(ii) That it is made in pursuance of an enactment containing specific provisions excluding it from challenge in the Courts, either at all times or after the expiration of a specified period ;

(iii) That it appears to make some unusual or unexpected use of the powers conferred by the statute under which it is made ;

(iv) That there appears to have been unjustifiable delay in its publication ;

(v) That for any special reason its form or purport calls for elucidation.

The Committee may require a Government Department to submit a Memorandum explaining any Rule, Order or Draft under consideration, or to depute a representative to appear and explain any such document. Before the Committee reports that the special attention of the House should be drawn to any such document, it affords the Department concerned an opportunity of furnishing an explanation.

**Legal Treatises.**

Finally, one must not lose sight of the fact that legal treatises, regarded as authoritative, such as the works of the great lawyers, Glanvil, Bracton, Coke and Blackstone, also helped to shape our law.

The famous treatise of Bracton, produced towards the end of the thirteenth century, and establishing the true origin of the Common Law to be a Judge-made law originating in ancient native custom, is one of the earliest sources of the Common Law.

Later treatises were Littleton's Tenures, Coke's Institutes and Hales' Pleas of the Crown. Only these treatises already referred to and their like are treated as "books of authority" in the sense of being minor sources of actual law. As such they are accorded authority for the propositions of law they contain, certainly as to the state of the law when they were written and occasionally to be relied upon where modern sources are conflicting or silent upon a given point.

When more than three-quarters of the great eighteenth century had already passed, Blackstone, the first Vinerian Professor of Law at Oxford, member of Parliament and Judge of the Court of Common Pleas, published his *Commentaries of the Laws of England* in four volumes, giving a systematic exposition of the then current law. It was widely read equally by lawyer, country squire and cultured student of affairs, but, in particular, it had immense influence in the then "New World" and was a contributory cause of the law of the Colonies and Dominions and of the United States being Common Law systems.

Since Blackstone's day and nearer our own time there have been many influential writers on legal topics: Maitland and Sir William Holdsworth in the realm of History; Sir Frederick Pollock in departments of history and the Common Law and Prof. Dicey in the matter of Constitutional Law.

Statements of the law in encyclopaedic works like Halsbury's *Laws of England* (now in its fourth edition and kept up to date by supplements) are of immense value to the busy practitioner but are not regarded as authoritative, but like considered views of highly reputable writers in text-book or learned periodical are sometimes "adopted" by a judge as being a correct statement of the law during the course of the hearing of a case.

To sum up, then, the ultimate sources of English law may be enumerated as Custom, Usages, Judicial Decisions, Statutes, Legal Treatises, the Canon Law and the Law Merchant.

## Law Reform.

It is evident that in any system of law there is much room for reform in cutting out relics of the past and amending rules which cause injustice.

The device of appointing a Royal Commission has been often used in England. A Commission is appointed to investigate the problem thoroughly and to make recommendations for legislation based on consideration of all the evidence available, including the experience of other countries, e.g., recent Royal Commissions on divorce and on capital punishment.

Such a Royal Commission, however, is only temporary, and cannot serve as a permanent stimulus to law reform. Such stimulus was to a certain extent provided by the Lord Chancellor's Law Revision Committee, appointed in 1934. It was reconstituted in 1952 and is now known as the Law Reform Committee. This Committee consists of Judges and both practising and academic lawyers. The Committee is limited to reporting upon such topics as are referred to it by the Lord Chancellor but can of their own initiative indicate topics on which a reference would appear to be desirable. Indeed, any member of the public wishing to suggest subjects for consideration by the Committee may communicate with the Secretary. Much useful work has been done and many statutes passed as a result of its work, e.g., the Limitation Act, 1939, the Law Reform (Contributory Negligence) Act, 1945, the Occupiers' Liability Act, 1957, the Law Reform (Husband and Wife) Act, 1962, the Perpetuities and Accumulations Act, 1964 and the Misrepresentation Act, 1967. However, not all the reports of the Committee have been implemented by statute either promptly or at all. Much work has also been done by the Committee in preparing lists of statutes which have outlived their usefulness and are fit for removal from the statute book.

Another Committee is that appointed in 1959 to consider such aspects of the criminal law as the Home Secretary may refer to it, to consider whether the law requires revision and to make recommendations. It is known as the Criminal Law Revision Committee. The Seventh Report of the Committee recommended the abolition of the archaic and artificial distinctions between felonies and misdemeanours (see *post* Chapter VIII) a result achieved by the Criminal Law Act, 1967. The Eighth Report led to the recasting of the law as to larceny and kindred offences in the Theft Act, 1968 (see also *post* Chapter VIII).

In September, 1964 the Criminal Law Revision Committee and the Lord Chancellor's Law Reform Committee were jointly entrusted with a comprehensive review of the law of evidence.

In January, 1965 a White Paper was issued (Cmnd 2573) in commendable brevity, drawing attention to the lack of a just, up-to-date, accessible and intelligible system of law and calling for the appointment of Law Commissioners to keep the law as a whole, under constant review and make recommendations for comprehensive reform. A Bill was subsequently introduced into the House of Lords to establish a Law Commission. A Minister without Portfolio would answer in the Commons for this and allied matters.

The Bill became law with effect from 15th June, 1965, under the title of the Law Commissions Act, 1965. So far as England and Wales are concerned, it established a Law Commission to promote the reform of the law. The Commission has the duty to keep the law under review with a view to its systematic development and reform, including the codification of such law, the elimination of anomalies, the repeal of obsolete enactments and generally the simplification and modernisation of the law.

The Commission has already been very active. Statutes " sponsored " by the Commission have included the important Animals Act, 1971 and the Supply of Goods (Implied Terms) Act, 1973. The Commission circulates Working Papers and invites comments from interested bodies thereon, so that in due course a " Law Com " can be issued (perhaps containing the draft of a suggested statute) ; it also issues an annual report.

**Law of the European Economic Community (E.E.C.).**

By reason of the entry of the United Kingdom into the Common Market as from 1st January, 1973, and the concurrent coming into force of the European Communities Act, 1972, under which, within its own field, Community Law becomes directly applicable law within the United Kingdom (see section 2 (1) of the 1972 Act) the Courts must apply that law to the exclusion of any internal law (including statute-law) inconsistent therewith.

The primary legislation of the Community consists of the relevant Treaties (including the Treaty of Rome establishing the Community).

Secondary legislation consists (*inter alia*) of Regulations and Directives. Regulations are directly binding on and applicable to the member states. Directives are binding, as to the results to be achieved, upon member states, but it is left to the national authorities to choose the form and method of implementing them.

## CHAPTER II

## EQUITY

**Nature of Equity.**

The term Equity, as popularly used, appears to be equivalent to natural justice, i.e., a decision based upon current conceptions of right and wrong, but that is not the meaning of Equity as administered in the English Courts. No Court could administer natural justice in the full sense of that term, as no Court could enforce the " duties " relevant to charity, gratitude and kindness. Such must be left to the dictates of the individual conscience. Moreover, as regards those principles of natural justice which *are* judicially enforceable, the Equity Court had no monopoly—to a large extent the law administered in the Common Law Courts was equally based on natural justice and good conscience. But there were " gaps " in the Common Law system, and the early function of Equity was to " fill in the gaps ". Thus, it has been said that, " Equity came to fulfil the Law, not to destroy it ". Equity, as part of the English legal system, is not to be regarded as connoting favour or clemency or justice. It is, and has been for a long time, a system of law, as definite and binding as the Common Law itself. It includes that portion of natural justice which is judicially enforceable but which for various reasons was not enforced by the Courts of Common Law.

Equity, unlike the Common Law, is not an independent system : it cannot stand alone. It presupposes the existence of the Common Law, the rules of which it supplements and modifies. The rules of Equity, which are based on conscience, are not fundamentally opposed to the rules of the Common Law, although they frequently produce an effect directly opposite to that contemplated by the Common Law. The two systems are complementary. Where a rule of Equity comes into irreconcilable conflict with a rule of the Common Law, the Judicature Act of 1873 provides that the former shall prevail. Equity proceeds by decrees, which it enforces by means of its own remedies, principally specific performance and injunction. The Common Law, on the other hand, is concerned with rights rather than decrees based on conscience, and its remedy for the violation of a right is an award of damages.

## CHAPTER II

**History.**

The history of Equity is intimately connected with the Writ System and the Chancellor.

Most early medieval Kings had their Chancellors, and the Chancellor may be described conveniently as the Royal Secretary. The authenticity of documents emanating from the Crown was testified by the Seal of which the Chancellor was the natural custodian. Edward the Confessor was the first English King to have a seal and the first to have a Chancellor. The early Chancellor was not primarily, or, indeed, largely, a legal officer; he was invariably an ecclesiastic, and usually a bishop or an archbishop.

His connection with the law is due to the writ system, which is of great antiquity and is the means of commencing an action to redress a legal wrong or to claim some form of relief. A writ is issued in the King's name and orders the person to whom it is addressed, known as the defendant, to appear before the Court to answer the claim of the person, known as the plaintiff, at whose instance it is issued. Since writs issued from the Crown they were sealed with the Great Seal, and, therefore, issued from the Chancery, which is, thus, described as the "Writ-shop". By the close of the 12th century the Chancery had become an independent Department. "In the 13th and 14th centuries, as the Courts of Common Law gradually grew to an independent existence separate from the central government, the Chancellor and the Chancery came to occupy a key position midway between them and the Council." (Radcliffe and Cross: "The English Legal System," 5th Edition, p. 115.) (The "Council" was the Privy Council, the State governing authority comprising the King and his chief Ministers.) There were two reasons for this: on the one hand, the Chancellor was an important member of the Council; on the other hand, as the issuer of writs he was kept in close touch with the Common Law Courts.

The Chancellor's equity appeared in consequence of the inflexibility of the Common Law. In order to be able to bring an action in one of the King's Courts, the aggrieved person had to obtain from the Chancery a writ for which he had to pay. Writs could, however, only be issued in a limited number of cases, and if a writ could not be issued no action could be brought. It was, therefore, necessary to fit the facts of a particular case within the four corners of one of the existing writs. For a time the Register of Writs (which set out the cases in which a writ was available) expanded rapidly but was considered "complete" at a comparatively early date.

Changing conditions gave rise to novel disputes. For well-known complaints the Chancellor issued writs from the Register, writs in common form—*de cursu*. If the complaint was not covered by an existing writ, then the clerks in Chancery framed a new writ. But this amounted to legislation, and, consequently, the Provisions of Oxford, 1258, forbade the practice. The consequent inconvenience was soon felt, and an attempt to alleviate the situation was made by the Statute of Westminster II, 1285, whereby the clerks in Chancery were empowered to issue new writs by analogy, *in consimili casu* (in like case), adapting an existing writ to fit new circumstances. But, for some unexplained reason, full use was not made of this provision. Then, when for one reason or another a person thought he could not obtain justice in the ordinary Courts, he was apt to petition the King for relief, the King being the Fountain of Justice. Such petitions were in practice referred by the King to the Council, which usually referred them to the Chancellor. This latter practice was put on a permanent basis by a royal decree of 1349. Before the end of the 14th century petitions were addressed often to the Chancellor himself, and, although the earlier decrees were issued on the authority of the Chancellor and Council, by the end of the 15th century the Chancellor sat alone to hear petitions and the decrees were issued in his name. Thus emerged the Court of Chancery.

The early petitions were of three types :—

(*a*) Those alleging that because of the power of the defendant in the county (i.e., because the defendant was a person who, by reason of his wealth and power would intimidate the jurors and defy the Court), the Common Law Courts were powerless against him.
(*b*) Those alleging a want of jurisdiction, e.g., where foreign merchants were parties to disputes.
(*c*) Those alleging actual defects in the existing law.

In the course of time the Court of Star Chamber acquired jurisdiction over the first type and the Admiralty Court took over the second type, leaving the Chancellor to deal with the third type of petition.

At first the Common Law Courts and the Court of Chancery worked in harmony, but relations became strained and, eventually, matters came to a head in the dispute between Sir Edward Coke, Chief Justice of the Court of King's Bench, and Lord Ellesmere, the Chancellor. The cause of the dispute was the frequent interference of the Chancellor, by means of injunctions, with judgments and proceedings in the Common Law Courts. He endeavoured to prevent successful parties from enjoying the benefit of their judgments if he thought that they had obtained them unfairly. So frequent was such interference that the term

*Common Injunction* was applied to the machinery by which it was effected. 1616, a plaintiff obtained a verdict, in a case heard by Coke himself, by a gross fraud. The Chancellor was petitioned and granted an injunction preventing the plaintiff from executing his judgment. At the instance of Coke, proceedings were thereupon taken to punish those persons at whose instance the Chancellor had been petitioned. The matter was referred to James I, who upheld the Chancellor. In consequence, the right of the Chancellor to grant injunctions against parties to a Common Law action was not afterwards seriously disputed.

But despite this victory there were grave defects in Equity. Thus, critics in the early 17th century could say : " *Equity varies with the length of the Chancellor's foot* " ; and again : " *Equity is a roguish thing. For Law we have a measure, know what to trust to. Equity is according to conscience of him that is Chancellor, and as that is larger or narrower, so is Equity* ". These criticisms were not without justification. Any person invoking the aid of the Common Law had some guide as to his chance of success in the existing statutes and decided cases, for precedent was followed. But if he invoked the aid of Equity he had no such measure. Relief that one Chancellor would grant, his successor might refuse, as such relief was granted *ex gratia*, not of right but as a matter of conscience. The only measure was that of the conscience of the Chancellor, and this varied with the individual Chancellor. " So many Chancellors so many consciences." Thus, Equity at this stage was both flexible and uncertain. This flexibility was an advantage in so far as it was able to give relief which the law, on account of its rigidity, could not give ; but the uncertainty of Equity was often a hardship, as persons could not ascertain their rights. However, Equity gradually came to be administered on fixed principles, and precedents began to be more and more rigidly followed. Ultimately, these became the measure, and the conscience of the individual Chancellor was no longer of account. The chief agents in bringing about this result were Nottingham, Hardwicke and Eldon.

Lord Nottingham (holding office 1673–1682) is called the " Father of Equity ". He considered that his discretion and that of succeeding Chancellors should not be an arbitrary discretion, but should be exercised, where possible, in accordance with known principles. If there was conflict, or if there was no precedent, then, and only then, was the Chancellor's own conscience to determine the matter.

Lord Hardwicke (1736–1756) established firmly the rule that a Judge in Equity should follow existing principles. Many of his judgments are still of vital importance to the student of Equity, as are also a few judgments of Nottingham. Before his time there were few principles; after Hardwicke the principles were settled and Equity had become an intelligible and predictable system. Equity had lost the last traces of the " Chancellor's foot " ambiguity.

Lord Eldon (1801–1806, 1807–1827) completed, in one sense, the development of Equity. If Hardwicke may be said to have turned Equity into a system of principles, Eldon turned it into a system of case-law almost as rigid as the Common Law itself.

But there was another side of Eldon's Chancellorship—which readers of *Bleak House* will appreciate—the appalling state of confusion and delay on the administrative side of the Court of Chancery, for which Eldon's dilatory manner was partly responsible, but the nature of the machinery much more so. Various attempts at reform were made, culminating in the Judicature Act, 1873. Before the Act there were, as we have seen, two distinct systems of justice administered in the Courts—Common Law and Equity. Such Courts administered different systems of law, used different procedure, recognized different principles.

The object of the Act was to fuse the *administration* of the two systems, but to leave the principles distinct. This is sometimes loosely described as the " fusion of Law and Equity ", a description which is apt to mislead the reader into thinking that the two sets of principles were fused. What the expression is in fact intended to mean is the fusion of the *Courts*, some of which had administered the Common Law, while others had administered Equity. The result of the fusion is that Common Law and Equity are administered in the same Courts by the same Judges. A simplification of procedure has thus been attained. The mode adopted was to amalgamate all the superior Courts into one Supreme Court of Judicature, divided into the High Court and the Court of Appeal. The High Court was itself divided into three Divisions, viz., the Queen's Bench Division, the Probate, Divorce and Admiralty Division and the Chancery Division. For convenience of administration, certain matters were assigned to particular Divisions, e.g., the administration of trusts to the Chancery Division. Apart from other provisions, the Act provided :—

(a) That Law and Equity were to be administered in every Court by every Judge. Henceforward, a Judge in the Queen's Bench Division can grant equitable relief, and a Judge of the Chancery Division can give legal remedies.

(b) That claims, defences and rights were to be recognized in the same manner as the old Courts of Equity would have recognized them. Thus, no longer was it necessary for a party in a Common Law action to resort to a Court of

Equity to protect equitable rights. Complete redress may be obtained from the same Court and in the same action.

(c) That in case of conflict between the rules of Equity and those of Common Law, the rules of Equity were to prevail.

### Walsh v. Lonsdale (1882).

L agreed, in writing, to grant a seven years' lease of a mill to W at a rent payable a year in advance. W entered into possession without any lease having been granted, and he paid his rent quarterly, *and not in advance*. Subsequently, L demanded a year's rent in advance, and as W refused to pay, he distrained. At Common Law, as no formal lease had been granted, W was a tenant from year to year at a rent not payable in advance. W argued that the legal remedy of distress was not open to L.

*It was held* by the Court of Appeal that, as the agreement was one of which the Court would order specific performance, and as Equity regarded as done that which ought to have been done, W held on the same terms as if a lease had been granted. The equitable rule prevailed, and a distress could be made.

## Maxims of Equity.

The following " maxims ", or general principles, illustrate some of the functions of Equity :—

(i) " *Equity will not suffer a wrong to be without a remedy* ", provided that such wrong is capable on judicial redress. This is the basic idea of Equity. It was on this maxim that the Court of Chancery based its interference to enforce trusts.

(ii) " *Equity follows the law.*" Equity did not purport to overrule the Common Law : it was a " gloss " upon it : it supplemented the Common Law. Even when creating rules peculiar to itself (equitable rules), Equity, where possible, formulated principles similar to corresponding Common Law principles. Thus, an equitable interest has generally been treated as having the same incidents as the corresponding legal estate.

(iii) " *He who seeks Equity must do Equity.*" Thus, if a husband had resort to Equity to put him in possession of property to which he was entitled (under the Common Law rule concerning the effect of marriage on the wife's property) merely because he was " the husband of his wife ", Equity would not assist him, unless he acted fairly by his wife, as by drawing up a document enabling his wife to benefit from certain of his property.

(iv) " *He who comes to Equity must come with clean hands.*"

Thus, a minor who misrepresented herself to be of full age, and, thereby, obtained money from her trustees to which she was entitled only on attaining full age, was refused aid when she tried subsequently to make the trustees pay over the money to her again.

(v) "*Equity looks to the intent rather than to the form.*" On the strength of this maxim Equity sought to relieve the harshness of the rigid Common Law rules. In particular, this dictated the attitude of Equity with regard to mortgages. Thus, a mortgage was regarded simply as a security, and provided the money was repaid, the estate had to be reconveyed to the borrower, even though repayment was not made on the covenanted date.

(vi) "*Equity acts in personam.*" In this maxim is embodied the fundamental difference between the Common Law and Equity. An order of a Court may be *in rem*, against the thing or property, or *in personam*, against the person. The former represents the Common Law attitude, the latter the outlook of Equity. Thus, if certain property is intended to pass from A to B, the Common Law Court may put the sheriff in possession of the property, instructing him to hand it over to B. This is an instance of procedure *in rem*. If, however, pressure is brought to bear upon A—it may be by threat of a fine—to compel him by his own act to convey the property to B, this is procedure *in personam*. In other words, Courts of Equity did not take away property from the defendant, they compelled him to hold it for the benefit of, or even to transfer it to, the rightful owner. The methods of compulsion used were imprisonment or sequestration of property—until the order was obeyed.

This maxim also operated to extend the jurisdiction of the Chancery Court beyond that exercised by the Courts of Common Law. If a dispute concerned land situate outside England, the latter Courts would not hear it, because obviously a judgment against such land could not be executed by its officers (land as immovable property being subject to the law of the place where it is situated). But, as Equity acts *in personam*, there would be no such obstacle to the jurisdiction of the Court of Equity, wherever the land might be situate, if the defendant was in England. The judgment could be executed against him. The Court, however, will not exercise this jurisdiction unless the situation is such that one of the remedies devised by Equity, e.g., specific performance or injunction (referred to below), is sought, and a matter of conscience involved. Moreover, equitable remedies being discretionary, the Court will refuse its assistance if of opinion that there is a competent Court to settle the dispute where the land is situate, and that it would be more convenient to settle the dispute in such Court.

(vii) "*Equity imputes an intention to fulfil an obligation.*" Thus, where A owes B £100 and by his will leaves £100 to B, the general principle is that B cannot claim both the debt and the legacy. It will be presumed in most cases that A's act in leaving the legacy to B was intended to be in satisfaction of his debt to B.

(viii) "*Equity looks on that as done which ought to have been done.*" It was on this principle that the decision in *Walsh* v. *Lonsdale* (referred to above) was decided.

(ix) "*Delay defeats equities.*" Where there is a case for equitable relief, the rule is that the person entitled to relief must not "sleep on his rights" but must go before the Court as soon as possible to ask for the necessary relief.

(x) "*Where the equities are equal the law prevails.*" In Chapter VI it will be made clear that any person dealing with an equitable interest can do so only subject to the rights of the legal owner whether or not he is aware of such rights. But if the legal owner has been guilty of conduct which the Court considers unreasonable or fraudulent, his rights will be postponed to those of the person dealing with the equitable interest. Where, however, neither party is at fault, then the legal owner has priority. As an example, if A, the owner of land, forges a duplicate set of the title deeds with intent to defraud, deposits the genuine deeds with B to secure a loan, and then conveys the property to C for value, handing over the forged duplicate deeds, it is clear that if C has no notice of B's equitable mortage his rights are superior to those of B. Neither B nor C is at fault, that is to say, "the equities are equal". Consequently, "the law prevails", and C, the legal owner, has priority.

(xi) "*Equality is equity.*" If A and B are entitled to Blackacre as joint tenants beneficially (see Chapter VI), then on the death either of A or B, the whole of Blackacre passes to the survivor. But Equity decrees that the above principle has no application where A and B are partners. It is presumed that partners are to be treated on a basis of equality, and on the death of one of the partners his share in Blackacre forms part of his estate.

## Contributions of Equity.

(*a*) Remedies of *Specific Performance* and *Injunction*.

Equity did something more than merely " fill in the gaps " of the Common Law : it supplied superior reliefs or remedies to a successful plaintiff. The characteristic remedy of the Common Law was, and still is, *damages*—monetary compensation. If A proves that B has made a contract with him and has broken such contract, A is entitled to a judgment for damages. But that may well be poor satisfaction to A, who would much rather have the contract performed than be solaced with damages. A may have set his heart on a particular plot of land, and may have persuaded B, the owner, to sell it to him. If B goes back on his word, if he breaks his contract, the Common Law will award A damages, but that is cold comfort to A who wants the land, not money. Or again, your neighbour's conduct or his use of his premises may seriously inconvenience your use and enjoyment of your premises. In the appropriate circumstances, the Common Law will award you damages. But what you desire is to put a stop to an intolerable nuisance. Your neighbour threatens to interfere with your right of light. At Common Law, if and when the threat has been executed, you may obtain damages, but your desire is to prevent the threat being carried into execution. It was to deal with the inadequacies of the Common Law in these matters that Equity invented the great remedies of *specific performance*, compelling a man to carry out his promise, and *injunction* forbidding him to do what he has promised not to do, or what he has no right to do.

Nevertheless, although the Common Law remedy of damages is claimable as of right, the equitable remedies of specific performance and injunction are granted only at the discretion of the Court, guided by the dictates of conscience. Yet there are well-defined rules as to the granting or withholding of these equitable decrees. Thus, specific performance will be decreed of an agreement for breach of which damages would be an inadequate remedy. But even if damages do constitute an inadequate remedy, specific performance will not be decreed if the remedy is not mutual, i.e., not available against the party seeking it. A contract of sale by a minor, for example, will not be enforced at his request, because, owing to the minor's right to repudiate such a contract, such a contract cannot be enforced against him. Furthermore, it must be proved (*a*) that specific performance would be an effective remedy ; (*b*) that the Court could efficiently supervise the specific performance of the agreement—thus, the decree would not be granted to enforce a contract for personal services ; (*c*) that specific performance would not inflict undue hardship upon the defendant.

Where A specifically contracts that he will not do a certain thing, e.g., that he will not build on his land so as to obstruct the flow of light to his neighbour's windows, then on breach of such an agreement, an injunction will follow as a matter of course. Many contracts for personal services contain a negative term. For example an actor may covenant that he will not for so many years work for any other but a certain film company. Here again the Court will automatically restrain the breach of such a covenant. In the case, however, of other wrongs in respect of which an injunction is sought, e.g., trespass or nuisance, the Court will not grant the same as a matter of course, but will reserve the remedy for cases where damages would not be an adequate remedy.

Injunctions may be (*a*) interlocutory, i.e., granted before the hearing of the action, the plaintiff giving an undertaking to be responsible for any damage caused to the defendant if it is found at the hearing that he was not entitled to the relief, or (*b*) perpetual, after the Court has determined finally the point at issue between the parties. Another broad division of injunctions is into (*a*) prohibitory and (*b*) mandatory. In the first case the Court orders that a certain act shall not be done. In the latter, the Court orders the carrying out of a positive act, e.g., the pulling down of a building erected in breach of covenant.

An injunction may be obtained in a *quia timet* action in order to secure the plaintiff against an apprehended future loss. The action is so described because the plaintiff is in *fear* of loss.

Other remedies provided by Equity are :—

(i) *Appointment of a Receiver.* A Court may appoint a receiver of property in order to preserve it pending the result of proceedings affecting that property.

(ii) *Rectification and Cancellation of Documents.* Where a document has been procured by fraud, or where, through some mistake, it does not represent the true intention of the parties thereto, the Court will sometimes order that the document in question be surrendered (that is rescinded), or will rectify it so that it may show the proper rights of its signatories.

(iii) *Administration of Estates, including Trusts.* In many cases, in order to procure the proper administration of trust property, Equity will itself take charge, and carry out all the necessary work in connection with the trust.

(iv) *Declaratory Order.* Where it is anticipated that a dispute may arise in respect of circumstances already in existence, the Court may make an order declaring the rights of the parties.

(v) *Relief against Penalties and Forfeiture of Leases.*

(*b*) *Equity of Redemption.*

Prior to the Law of Property Act, 1925, the ordinary mode of creating a mortgage of freehold lands was for the borrower (the mortgagor) to convey the fee simple (i.e., the greatest estate in land known to law) to the lender (the mortgagee), with the condition that if the mortgagor repaid the loan on a specified day the mortgagee would reconvey the land to him. At Common Law this condition was construed strictly and if the loan was not repaid on the specified day the borrower was deprived permanently of his land. This caused great hardship until the Chancellor invented the Equity of Redemption. He regarded the conveyance simply as a security, and so long as the money was repaid the estate had to be reconveyed to the borrower, even though repayment was not made on the specified date. As Lord Nottingham said, in 1675, " the principal right of the mortgagee is to the money, and his right to the land is only as a security for the money ". In other words, even after the day for redemption had passed, the mortgagor was entitled in Equity to an interest in the land. But this right of redemption was not perpetual : it could be cut short, in the appropriate circumstances, by an order of the Court known as a foreclosure decree. Since the coming into force of the Act of 1925, it is no longer possible to create a mortgage of land by transferring the whole of the borrower's interest therein to the lender. The modern method is to grant to the lender as security a lesser interest than that possessed by the borrower (see *post* p. 196.) But the idea of the equity of redemption still exists, that is to say, the essence of the transaction is still considered to be a loan, and the mere fact that the legal date for redemption (i.e., the date stipulated in the mortgage deed) has passed, will not prevent the borrower from redeeming thereafter by virtue of his equitable right to redeem. (See also *post* p. 197.)

Equity was jealous to preserve this right of redemption and regarded any provision in the mortgage deed tending, even indirectly, to make the mortgage irredeemable, or leaving the mortgagor still encumbered in his enjoyment of his property after payment of principal and costs, as a " clog " upon the equity of redemption and, therefore, unenforceable. Thus, in *Noakes* v. *Rice* (1902), the lessee of a public house, whose lease had twenty-six years to run, mortgaged his lease to a firm of brewers and in the mortgage promised that *for the whole of the remainder of the lease* he would buy all his beer from the brewers. This was considered to be a clog on the equity of redemption as the mortgagor would be left with a " tied " house (i.e., a public house obliged to acquire its beer from a particular source only) when he had mortgaged a " free " house (i.e., one free to acquire its beer from any source). Again, in *Bradley* v. *Carritt* (1901), a shareholder in a tea company mortgaged his shares to a tea broker and promised thereafter he would *always* pay the mortgagee a commission if the sale of the company's wares was entrusted to another broker. It was held that he might redeem his shares freed from the condition.

Nevertheless, not every collateral advantage to the mortgagee is void. Thus, in *Kreglinger* v. *N. P. Meat and Cold Storage Co.* (1914), a firm of woolbrokers lent £10,000 to a meat company on mortgage, and it was agreed that for a period of five years the company should not sell sheepskins to anyone other than the lenders, provided the latter were willing to pay the best prevailing price. The loan was repaid after two years, but it was held that the option continued for five years, as it was not in the nature of a penalty. The general principle was enunciated that a collateral advantage is valid provided that it is not in the nature of a penalty clogging the equity of redemption, and is not unconscionable or repugnant to the right to redeem. Even postponement of redemption for a lengthy period, e.g., forty years, is no clog on the equity of redemption if there is nothing oppressive or unconscionable in such postponement: *Knightsbridge Estates Trust, Ltd.* v. *Byrne* (1940).

(c) *The Trust.*

The conception of the trust is one of the outstanding characteristics of English law, and although it is beyond the scope of this book to deal with the subject in detail, some mention must be made of the origin and growth of trusts. The holding of land in feudal times, when several tenants held land of the Lord of the particular Manor, was attended by many burdensome incidents. For example, if the tenant died, the person succeeding to the land usually had to pay a sum of money to the Lord before he was allowed into possession. Where the person entitled on death was under age, the Lord of the Manor had the right to manage the holding for his own benefit until such person became of age. Another great difficulty of the legal system of those times was that a feudal tenant was unable to transfer his land by will. To circumvent these and other difficulties, the equitable idea of the " use " was invented. The idea was that the tenant should transfer his holding to two or more friends, instructing them that they were to hold the same to the *use*, or, in other words, for the benefit of the person actually intended to be benefited. To take a concrete example, A would transfer his land to B and C to hold to the use of D. Although D was obviously intended to benefit, the Common Law ignored his rights and was concerned only with B and C, the legal owners. If, however, B and C attempted to deal with the land in a manner inconsistent with their obligations (moral, if not legal) towards D, the Court of Chancery would step in to protect D's interests, and B and C would be compelled, under threat of imprisonment, to carry out their obligations to D. This is the foundation of the modern theory of "duality of ownership" whereby certain persons, known as trustees (in our example B and C) are entitled to the legal estate, but where the beneficiary (D in our example) has the beneficial interest.

An attempt was made by the Statute of Uses, 1535, to abolish uses, the operation of which was contrary to the financial interests of the numerous Lords of the Manor, and of the King himself, but for various technical reasons the operation of the Statute was for all practical purposes nullified within one hundred years thereafter. The conception of duality of ownership, therefore, continued to flourish and is of outstanding importance even at the present day, since it lies at the root of the trust conception.

It is most difficult to formulate a satisfactory definition of a trust, but perhaps the clearest definition is : " A trust is an equitable obligation imposing upon a person (who is called a trustee) the duty of dealing with property over which he has control (which is called the trust property) for the benefit of persons (who are called beneficiaries or *cestuis que trustent*) of whom he may himself be one, and any one of whom may enforce the obligation " (Underhill).

Thus, A, the owner of a freehold farm, may convey it to B in trust for C for his life, and at C's death to D absolutely. A who creates the trust is called the settlor, and B, the trustee. B becomes the legal owner under the trust, but he is bound to let C, the beneficial owner, run the farm and enjoy all its benefits. At C's death, B must convey the farm to D, the remainderman, who then becomes the legal owner, for the trust then comes to an end. Similarly, A may leave shares to the value of £50,000 to B in trust for C for his life, and at C's death to D absolutely. In this case, C, the beneficiary, will enjoy the dividends as long as he lives, and at his death D will become the legal owner of the shares. C's interest under the trust is called the beneficial interest, as opposed to B's legal interest.

The importance of trusts has been greatly increased by the Property Acts (see *post* Chapter VI) for trusts constitute the only method by which future and concurrent beneficial interests in land can now be created.

Apart from trusts of land, which must be evidenced by writing, a trust may be created in any informal way which adequately expresses an intention to create it.

The essential elements of an express private trust are well settled. Lord Langdale, in *Knight* v. *Knight* (1840), declared that three " *certainties* " are essential for the creation of a trust :—

(i) Certainty of intention : the settlor must have intended to create a trust binding by law—the words used must be imperative. In *Re Oldfield, Oldfield* v. *Oldfield* (1904), a testatrix, after leaving property to her two daughters absolutely, added : " My desire is that each of my said two daughters shall during the lifetime of my son pay him one-third " of the income accruing from the property given. It was held that no trust in favour of the son was created. The reason for this decision is that the Court construed the wording of the will as an expression of the testatrix's hope that her daughters would carry out her wishes, but the Court decided there was no binding obligation on the daughters to benefit the son.

(ii) Certainty of subject-matter. In *Parnall* v. *Parnall* (1878), a testator gave property to A and directed that so much as might not be required by A or might be possessed by A at his death, should go over to B. It was held that B took nothing. The attempted provision for B was of too undefined a nature to be capable of legal enforcement.

(iii) Certainty of objects. For instance, it is a principle of the law of trusts that where a person leaves property by his will to someone, such property to be held for the benefit of persons whose names are to be disclosed subsequently, a disclosure after the donor's death is ineffective, and the intended trust will fail. At the date of the testator's death there is no certainty as to the identity of the persons supposed to benefit, and there is, therefore, no enforceable trust.

Trusts (including charitable ones) are referred to again in Chapter VI.


(d) *Assignment of Choses in Action.*

With certain exceptions, as in the case of bills of exchange and assignments to or by the Crown, choses in action (i.e., personal property of an intangible nature capable of enforcement only by action, e.g., a debt) could not be assigned at Common Law. Thus, if A assigned to B a debt owed to him by C, B could not bring an action in his own name against C.

Equity, however, gave effect to assignments. If the assignment was of an equitable thing in action, that is to say, a right enforceable only in the Court of Chancery, such as a legacy or an interest in a trust fund, the assignee could sue in his own name. In the case of a legal chose in action, that is to say, a right enforceable in a Court of Law, such as a debt, this could not be done, and so Equity would force the assignor to lend his name for the purpose of the action.

The requirements for an assignment at law of a chose in action will be discussed in Chapter IV. Where these requirements are not complied with, an assignment is said to be an " equitable " assignment. The interest of a beneficiary under a trust, being necessarily equitable in nature (as explained above) can form the subject only of an equitable assignment. Thus, although there can be either a legal or an equitable assignment of a *legal* chose in action, there cannot be a legal assignment of an equitable interest. The assignment of equitable interests under trusts can give rise to questions of priorities. Suppose that X, the beneficiary under a trust, makes an assignment of his interest first to Y and then to Z. If the value of such interest is insufficient to satisfy the claims of both Y and Z, it is important to decide which of them has priority. It is laid down by section 137 of the Law of Property Act, 1925, that priorities in such cases are to be decided by the dates on which notices of the assignments are respectively given to the trustee. Thus, if in the above example Z gave notice first, he would have priority unless, at the time of giving notice, he was aware of the prior assignment to Y.

(e) *Generally.*

By applying considerations of conscience and good faith, Equity was able to afford relief against fraud, accident and mistake as well as to victims of undue influence or oppressive conduct. It developed the remedies of rescission and rectification of documents.

## Influence of Roman Law.

As has been seen, Canon Law had its roots in Roman Law. In early days, all ecclesiastical officers owed fealty to the Pope in Rome. Those who acquired learning did so under the protection of Rome and any legal knowledge acquired would be that of the Roman Church.

Prior to the Conquest, there were no Ecclesiastical Courts in this country, and Canon Law was in a very undeveloped state. Consequently, any influence exerted by Roman Law before the Conquest could be due only to survivals from the Roman civilization found here by the Angles and Saxons. There is much, however, to be said for the view that there was a rapid decay of Roman civilization and that this decay was accompanied to a certain extent by a revival of British civilization. Roman influence was, therefore, very superficial, and all trace of it seems to have vanished by the time of the Norman invasion. The Common Law, therefore, originated in ancient native customs.

After the Conquest, as has been observed, the effect of Canon Law was considerable. Moreover, as the early Chancellors were ecclesiastics, their early development of Equity was influenced by Roman Law conceptions. Again, the early Judges, being ecclesiastics trained in Roman Law, filled in gaps in the Common Law by borrowing from Roman Law. Further, teachers like Vacarius, and text-book writers like Bracton, similarly supplied deficiencies. The Law Merchant, maritime law in particular, had its origin in Roman Law, and was developed in the Admiralty Courts by Judges and advocates trained in Roman Law. Eventually, the Common Law was developed on its own footing, the influence of the Church and its Canon Law gradually waning for the following reasons :—

- (i) The barons resented interference by the Church, and refused to allow the introduction of certain of its principles ;
- (ii) The practice grew of appointing lawyers instead of clerics to be Judges, with the result that clerical influence was no longer present in the development of the Common Law ;
- (iii) Statute, in the reign of Henry VIII, provided that Canon Law must not operate contrary to the Common Law or to any Act of Parliament ;
- (iv) Lawyers trained at the Inns of Court knew little or nothing of any system but their own.

The principles of Roman Law are, however, of use even at the present day in the development of English Law. For instance, there may be no precedent available, and no statute on a particular point. In such cases it is not unknown for Judges to refer to the relevant principles of Roman Law to resolve the point at issue. They are also applied in appeals to the House of Lords from Scotland, where a system of law strongly influenced by Roman Law prevails.

**Main Fields of Equity.**

It has been previously pointed out that notwithstanding the fusing of the administration of Common Law and Equity by the Judicature Act, 1873, certain matters are, for convenience, assigned to a particular Division of the High Court.

By the Judicature Act, 1925, the following matters (amongst others) were assigned to the Chancery Division :—

- (a) All causes and matters in respect of which the old Court of Chancery was given exclusive statutory jurisdiction, e.g., under

the Infant Settlements Act, 1855 (since repealed by the Family Law Reform Act, 1969), under which the Court might sanction the making of a binding settlement by a minor.
(b) The administration of estates.
(c) Dissolution of partnerships.
(d) Redemption or foreclosure of mortgages.
(e) The raising of portions and other charges on land.
(f) The sale of property subject to a lien or charge.
(g) The execution of charitable and private trusts.
(h) The rectification or setting aside or cancellation of deeds or other written instruments.
(i) Specific performance of contracts for sale and leases.
(j) The partition or sale of real estate.
(k) Any matters specially assigned to the Division, e.g., the winding-up of limited companies.

Following the re-organisation effected by the Administration of Justice Act, 1970 the Chancery Division acquired jurisdiction in contentious probate matters. (See *post* Chapter IX) (perhaps as compensation for the loss to the new Family Division of jurisdiction over the wardship of minors.)

Perhaps no clearer illustration is possible of the many and diverse fields in which equitable principles are operative today.

## CHAPTER III

## ELEMENTS OF THE LAW OF CONTRACT

**Classification.**

It is customary to classify contracts as follows :—

(a) *Contracts of Record.* This type of contract is formed by the entry of a debt upon the record of a Court of Record. Such contracts are obligations imposed upon a person by the Crown in its judicial capacity, e.g., a judgment or a recognizance. They are not true contracts : the person obliged has no option : there is no voluntary agreement.

(b) *Contracts under Seal.* These are also termed contracts by deed, or specialty contracts. Obviously, a specialty contract must be in writing. In addition there are three requisites : the contract must be sealed, it must be delivered, and, since the 1st January, 1926, it must be signed by the promisor, i.e., the person making the promise. Sealing is now a mere formality—the touching of a wafer or seal, already attached, by the finger of the executing party, whereby he acknowledges the seal as his. " Delivery " does not involve parting with physical possession of the document : it suffices that the executing party clearly shows that he intends the instrument to be binding upon him, the usual formula being, " I deliver this as my act and deed ". A deed has no operation until delivery. A person having sealed a deed may deliver it in such terms as to qualify or suspend its binding effect. A deed so conditionally delivered is termed an *escrow*, and, until the condition is fulfilled, there is no true deed. The principal contracts required to be under seal are transfers of British ships ; conveyances of land, and all leases for more than three years. [These differ from mere agreements for the sale or lease of land, which must be evidenced by writing, not necessarily under seal, under s. 40 of the Law of Property Act, 1925. See *post*, pp. 49 and 188.]

(c) *Simple Contracts.* These are alternatively termed *parol* contracts. A simple contract, disregarding contracts of record, is any contract not made under seal. It may be made orally, it may be made in writing, or it may be implied by conduct. Thus a contract is completed when a person puts the requisite coin in an automatic machine which is visibly " charged " and is otherwise in working order.

In the main, the remainder of this Chapter will be concerned with the simple contract, but it is proposed first to deal with the chief differences between specialty and simple contracts, certain of which will be better appreciated at a later stage in this Chapter.

| Specialty Contract | Simple Contract |
|---|---|
| \(1\) *Form.* | |
| The deed actually *creates* the contract : it is not merely evidence of it. | In most cases, even if a simple contract is reduced to writing, such is merely evidence of the contract. But a few simple contracts, e.g., bills of exchange, *do* depend upon writing for their existence ; i.e., without writing there is no contract. |
| \(2\) *Consideration.* | |
| Consideration is not essential. | Consideration is essential in all cases. |
| \(3\) *Limitation of action.* | |
| Action must be brought within *twelve* years from the date when the cause of action arises. | Action must be brought within *six* years. |
| \(4\) *Estoppel.* | |
| Statements in a deed are conclusive against the parties to it, unless fraud, duress or mistake is proved, or unless a latent ambiguity, i.e., an ambiguity not apparent on the face of the contract, exists. | Statements in a simple contract are only *prima facie* evidence of their truth. |

MERGER.

A simple contract subsequently embodied in a deed is swallowed up, or " merged " in a specialty contract embodying the same promise. For instance, if A agrees to pay B £250 for services to be rendered, and subsequently A covenants under seal to pay B this same £250, action can be taken only on the covenant, the obligation created by the former simple contract being merged in the covenant.

ESTOPPEL.

Estoppel is a rule of evidence whereby a man who, by his words or conduct, has led another to believe in the existence of a certain state of facts, with the result that the latter acts on that belief to his detriment, is thereafter " estopped ", or prevented from denying the existence of such a state of facts.

Estoppel is of three kinds :—

(1) Estoppel by record, i.e., by judgment of a Court of Law.
(2) Estoppel by deed, as explained above.
(3) Estoppel *in pais*, or estoppel by conduct, where a person by his conduct has led another to take a certain course.

Thus, a man who has held himself out as a partner, and has thereby induced another to contract with a firm, is not allowed to disclaim liability by pleading that he is not, in fact, a member of the firm.

It will have been gathered that a specialty contract has certain peculiar advantages :—

(1) *Formality*. The law attaches great importance to the solemnities of a deed, and will not lightly allow interference with its terms. Thus, the doctrine of estoppel applies. Moreover, whereas writing in the case of a simple contract is only evidence of the contract's existence and nature, the writing of a contract under seal, i.e., the deed, *is* the contract.
(2) *Permanence*. The Limitation Act, 1939, provides that action to enforce a contract under seal or to obtain damages for its breach must be taken within twelve years from the accrual of the right of action, whereas in the case of a simple contract the right of action is extinguished after six years.
(3) *Definiteness*. A deed contains all the terms of the contract and cannot be varied or added to by oral evidence. The terms of a simple contract are not always easy to discover, as they may be partly written, and partly unwritten, or they may need elucidation from the conduct of the parties.

But the simple contract also has its advantages :—

(1) *Convenience*. It can be more easily entered into than a deed.
(2) *Cheapness*. A simple contract does not attract the heavy stamp duties often payable in the case of a deed.

Apart from the basic classification of contracts as those of record, specialties and simple contracts, there is a further division into (*a*) *Express* contracts, where the terms of the contract are definitely agreed upon, either in writing or orally, and (*b*) *Implied* contracts, where the contract is capable of being inferred from the conduct of the parties. Thus, the act of a bus company in placing a bus on the road, and the act of a passenger on entering the bus bring into existence a contract which is to be implied from the conduct of the two parties.

A contract may also be *executed* or *executory*, the former denoting a contract that is wholly performed on one side, the latter applying to a contract which is wholly unperformed, or in which there still remain obligations to be performed, by both parties. Thus, if A agrees to pay B the sum of £5 for a book which the latter hands over immediately, this is said to be an executed contract, as B has completely performed his obligations under the contract. But if A agrees to pay B the sum of £20,000 for a house which B is to erect, the contract is executory. The obligations of both parties under the contract are yet to be carried out, A to pay the £20,000, and B to build the house.

## Nature of an Agreement.

A contract has been defined as " *a legally binding agreement made between two or more persons, by which rights are acquired by one or more to acts or forbearances on the part of the other or others* ".

It will be seen later that there are certain valid contracts which are not enforceable by *action at law*. A contract results from the combination of the two ideas of agreement and obligation. Agreement exists when two minds come together with a common intention. The parties are then " of the same mind " and there is what is known as *consensus ad idem*. The essence of the idea of obligation is that certain definite persons are able to enforce against other definite persons an agreement by the latter either to carry out or not to carry out, as the case may be, certain definite acts, the whole of the agreement being capable of estimation in terms of money.

Although every contract includes an agreement, every agreement is not a contract. There must be an intention that as a result of the agreement the legal relations of the parties should be altered. There must be something more than an agreement affecting social or moral relations. A may agree to go to the theatre with B, or to dine with him : such may give rise to social or moral obligations, but there is no contract.

### Balfour v. Balfour (1919).

A husband, about to return to his employment in Ceylon, promised to make his wife an allowance for housekeeping and clothing. He failed to keep up his payments, and his wife sued him for breach of contract.

*Held* that the agreement was a mere domestic arrangement without any legal obligation attaching thereto, and that, therefore, the wife could not maintain an action against her husband for breach of it.

A contract may, however, arise out of ordinary domestic or social relations, if the parties indicate clearly that they intend to affect their legal relations. For instance in *Simpkins* v. *Pays* (1955) an arrangement, informal but possessing essential elements of mutuality, whereby three persons were to " go shares " in a weekly newspaper competition, was held to amount to a contract, notwithstanding that the defendant, on being sued for a share in the prize received by her on behalf of the " syndicate ", pleaded that there had been no intention to create legal relations. Likewise in *Parker* v. *Clark* (1960) an aged couple were held bound in contract on an arrangement made by correspondence with their niece and her husband whereby the latter sold up their own home in order to go to live with the old people and share the household and other expenses. Similarly the principle of *Balfour* v. *Balfour* (*supra*) did not fall to be applied in *Merritt* v. *Merritt* (1973) since the firm undertakings by a husband no longer in amity with and about to separate from his wife were held to be enforceable. On the other hand, in ordinary commercial dealings an intention to create legal relations may well be presumed, unless the terms of the agreement clearly show that there was no such intention.

**Rose & Frank Co. v. J. R. Crompton & Bros., Ltd. (1925).**

Three firms entered into a mutual arrangement concerning their business dealings. A written document was drafted in which appeared the following clause : " This arrangement is not entered into, nor is this memorandum written, as a formal or legal agreement, and shall not be subject to legal jurisdiction in the Law Courts."

*Held* that the agreement was not a contract, because the parties showed no intention to create legal obligations.

The reader will be familiar with similar declarations on the part of persons promoting competitions of various descriptions such as the football pools.

## Form.

In general, apart from specialty contracts, no form is prescribed for a contract. However, certain simple contracts must be *in* writing, e.g., a contract of marine insurance or an assignment of copyright. In such a case without writing there is no contract.

Under the Contracts of Employment Act, 1972 (replacing earlier legislation from the Contracts of Employment Act, 1963 onwards) an employer is required within a specified time to give his employee written particulars of the terms of employment (although the contract of service itself may be informal).

Regulated agreements within the Consumer Credit Act, 1974 (being non-exempt consumer credit agreements or consumer hire agreements) must be properly executed in a document complying with the Act, otherwise they are enforceable against the debtor or hirer on an order of the Court only.

Certain other contracts need not be in writing, but they must be *evidenced* by writing. In the absence of that evidence there is still a contract, but it cannot be enforced by action (see *post*).

Examples of such contracts are :—

(1) *Under section* 4, *Statute of Frauds*, 1677, *as amended by the Law Reform* (*Enforcement of Contracts*) *Act*, 1954 :—

Any special promise to answer for the debt, default or miscarriage of another person. Although this wording is wide enough to include liability for the wrongful or tortious act of another person, in general the section is confined to contracts of guarantee. A guarantee must be distinguished from an indemnity (to which the statute has no application). A guarantee is the undertaking of a secondary liability : " If he does not pay you, I will ". An indemnity is the undertaking of a primary liability : "Let him have the goods, I will see that you are paid ". Moreover, in a contract of guarantee there are three parties, the creditor, the debtor and the guarantor or surety, whereas in an indemnity there are only two parties.

(2) *Under section* 40, *Law of Property Act*, 1925.

This refers to contracts for the sale or leasing of land, or for the transfer of any interest in land. (See further *post*, p. 188.)

**Nature of the Memorandum.**

There is no need for any particular formality. The memorandum need not be made at the time of the contract, but it must be in existence before action may be brought. The memorandum may consist of a number of documents, and, provided there is some internal evidence of connection, external oral evidence is permissible to prove that the various documents constitute one memorandum. Thus, in *Pearce* v. *Gardner* (1897), all the terms of the contract, except the name of the person to whom it was addressed, appeared in a letter ; evidence was admitted to connect the envelope with the letter, and so complete the memorandum.

CONTENTS OF THE MEMORANDUM.

The memorandum must contain :—

(a) The names, or identifiable descriptions, of the parties.
(b) The subject-matter of the contract.
(c) The consideration. In the case of *guarantees*, the consideration need not be mentioned in the memorandum, but must exist in fact.

(d) The signature of the person to be charged (i.e., the person proposed to be made the defendant in an action) or that of his duly authorized agent.

Thus, only one signature is necessary, and, therefore, it may be that the contract is only enforceable against one of the parties. An auctioneer is the agent of both parties for the purpose of signing a memorandum, provided he signs at the time of the sale or at the earliest possible moment after it. A signature may be printed or stamped, and may appear anywhere in the document, provided that it is intended as a signature which is to govern the whole contract.

Effect of Non-compliance.

In the absence of a memorandum the contract is not void but merely unenforceable by action. Ownership will pass under such a contract, but the contract cannot be enforced by action in a Court of law.

Doctrine of Part Performance.

Where there is no memorandum as required by section 40, Law of Property Act, 1925, Equity may still grant a decree of specific performance if the following conditions are satisfied :—

(a) The plaintiff has performed some act of part performance unequivocally referable to the existence of a contract.

**Rawlinson v. Ames (1925).**

Mrs. A orally agreed to take a lease of Mrs. R's flat. At Mrs. A's request Mrs. R carried out certain alterations to the flat. Mrs. A refused to complete, and, when sued, pleaded the Statute of Frauds, there being no memorandum.

*Held* that the statute did not apply. The conduct of Mrs. R clearly constituted acts of part performance " unequivocally referable to the contract ". They could bear only this interpretation.

This decision must be contrasted with that in *Maddison* v. *Alderson* (1883), where a woman entered the service of a farmer as housekeeper without any wages on the faith, as she alleged, that he would leave her a life estate in the farm. She served the farmer for many years, but he died without having made provision for her. Here, the Court held that there had not been a sufficient part performance. The fact of her service without wages was capable of various explanations : she might have been willing to give her services in return for board and lodging. The plaintiff in *Wakeham* v. *Mackenzie* (1968) had greater success as she was able to pin liability on a widower for his breach of

ELEMENTS OF THE LAW OF CONTRACT 51

undertaking to benefit her if she would give up her council flat and come to act as his housekeeper.
(b) The circumstances are such that it would amount to fraud on the defendant's part to take advantage of the lack of written evidence.
(c) There is adequate and admissible oral evidence of the terms of the contract.

It should be noted that part performance is a *doctrine*, while specific performance is a *remedy*.

## Essentials of a Valid Simple Contract.

The essential requisites of a valid simple contract are :—

(1) The making of an offer by one of the parties and its *acceptance* by the other.
(2) The presence of *consideration*.
(3) The contractual *capacity* of the parties : they must be recognized by law as having power to bind themselves by contract.
(4) *Legality*; i.e., the subject-matter of the contract must not be contrary to law.
(5) *Possibility*; i.e., performance of the contract must not be obviously impossible, e.g., " to swim the Atlantic ".
(6) *Reality* or *Genuineness* of the *Consent* of the *Parties*.

There must have been *consensus ad idem*, i.e., agreement about the same thing, and each party must have entered into the contract of his own free will and accord. Thus, the agreement of the parties may be vitiated by proof of fraud, misrepresentation, mistake, undue influence or duress.

A failure to observe one or more of these essentials may render the contract *void* or *voidable*. A void contract is no contract : it is destitute of legal effect. A contract may be void on the ground of illegality, e.g., a contract to commit a crime, or a contract which is opposed to public policy. It may be void for mistake, e.g., a contract to sell a thing which, unknown to either party, is non-existent. Furthermore, certain contracts entered into by minors (i.e., person under 18 years of age) are declared void by the Infants Relief Act, 1874 (as read with the Family Law Reform Act, 1969). The absence of consideration may also render a contract void.

A *voidable* contract is one which, although *prima facie* valid and enforceable, may be affirmed or repudiated by one of the parties on proof of fraud, duress, misrepresentation or undue influence by the other party. But, unless and until avoided, there is a valid subsisting contract. A voidable contract must not be confused with a *determinable* contract which is one where the contract itself provides for cessation of obligation on the happening of a specified event.

The vital importance of the distinction between a void and a voidable contract arises in connection with third parties. Thus, a third party, however innocent he may be, whatever value he may give, cannot acquire rights under a void contract. But such a person, acting in good faith and giving value, will acquire rights under a voidable contract if he has acted before the contract has been avoided.

Two cases illustrate this distinction.

### Cundy v. Lindsay (1878).

A fraudulent person named Blenkarn, imitating the signature of a respectable firm named Blenkiron, an old customer of Lindsay, sent an order to the latter which was executed. Blenkarn then sold the goods to Cundy, who gave value and acted in good faith. Blenkarn then decamped. Lindsay claimed the goods from Cundy, who refused to return them, pleading that the contract between Blenkarn and Lindsay was merely voidable for fraud, and that he had obtained a good title before the contract had been avoided.

*Held* that Cundy must return the goods. The contract was *void* for the vital mistake of identity. Lindsay had only one person in mind, his old customer. There was no contract, no title had passed to Blenkarn, and he could pass no title.

### White v. Garden (1851).

P bought from G 70 tons of iron, never intending to pay for them but giving in purported payment a fictitious bill of exchange. P sold the iron to W, who gave value in good faith with no notice of the fraud. G then discovered the fraud and sought to recover the goods from W.

*Held* that he could not now avoid the contract, W having obtained title whilst a valid contract was in existence.

A contract which is void or voidable must be distinguished from an *unenforceable* contract. An unenforceable contract is a valid contract in all respects and ownership will pass under it, but it cannot be enforced by action until some evidential requirement imposed by statute has been observed ; e.g., an oral guarantee not evidenced by writing as required by section 4, Statute of Frauds, 1677, cannot be enforced by action.

## Consideration.

Every simple contract must be supported by consideration. If it is not supported it is treated as gratuitous. A gratuitous contract may, of course, be enforced if it is entered into under seal.

The existence of a blood or marriage relationship is often described as " *good* " consideration. But this kind of consideration is not recognised by the law of contract, which demands " *valuable* " consideration.

*Valuable* consideration was defined in *Currie* v. *Misa* (1875) as " some right, interest, profit or benefit accruing to one party, or some forebearance, detriment, loss or responsibility given, suffered or undertaken by the other ".

Consideration may be *executed* or *executory*.

*Executed Consideration* is that which is wholly performed on one side immediately the contract is entered into, e.g., a purchase of goods in a shop on credit ; the shopkeeper has done all that is due from him in handing over the goods.

*Executory Consideration* is a promise to confer a benefit or to suffer some detriment at some future time. In the example given above the consideration due from the customer is executory in that having received the goods he promises to pay at some future date.

In English law, consideration is an essential part of the contract, not, as in other systems of law, merely one form of *evidence* of the *existence* of a contract.

In *Central London Property Trust, Ltd.* v. *High Trees House, Ltd.* (1947), the principle was enunciated, that when a promise is made which is intended to create legal relations, which to the knowledge of the promisor will be acted on by the promisee and which is so acted on, the law, *though it does not give a cause of action in damages if the promise is broken, will require it to be honoured* to the extent of refusing to allow the promisor to act inconsistently with it, notwithstanding that the promise is not supported by consideration in the strict sense of the term. In *Combe* v. *Combe* (1951), however, the Court of Appeal held that consideration still remains a cardinal necessity of the formation of a contract and that the principle in the *High Trees* case operated only as a shield or defence to a person sued and not as a weapon of attack enabling him to sue on a gratuitous promise. The *High Trees* case is now regarded as an illustration of promisory estoppel, which has become progenitive in many and hitherto unsuspected fields. Cf. the case under the Redundancy Payments Act, 1965, of *Evenden* v. *Guildford City Football Club* (1975)—assurance given by employer succeeding to the employee's previous employer that the employment is to be regarded as unbroken, precludes the succeeding employer from seeking to rebut the presumption of continuity of employment arising under s. 9 (2) of the Act.

It is natural to associate the idea of benefit with consideration, but this is not essential : the promisor need not have received any direct benefit ; it suffices that the promisee has suffered a detriment. Consider the ordinary contract of guarantee : in consideration of A's lending £1,000 to B, C promises to repay the loan if B defaults. C derives no tangible benefit, but A suffers detriment by lending his money.

There are the following rules relating to consideration :—

(a) Consideration need not be adequate. A person cannot seek the assistance of the Court merely because he has made a " bad " bargain. Inadequacy may, however, be relevant if fraud is alleged.

(b) Consideration must have *some* ascertainable value, however slight.

(c) Consideration must be definite : an undertaking to " do the right thing " or " not to bore " is too vague : *White* v. *Bluett* (1853).

(d) The consideration must be something which the promisee is not already legally bound to do in favour of the other party : *Swain* v. *West (Butchers) Ltd.* (1936). But if A, at B's request, agrees to do something which he is already bound to do under a contract with C, this may be consideration as between A and B, because A owes a duty now, to perform the specified act, not merely to C, but also to B, who may have some special reason for wishing A to carry out his contract with C.

### Shadwell v. Shadwell (1860).

An uncle promised his nephew an annuity of £50 in consideration of the nephew marrying a lady whom he had already promised to marry [a binding and enforceable agreement as the law stood then and until the Law Reform (Miscellaneous Provisions) Act, 1970, abolished the action for breach of promise of marriage]. The nephew married her and this was held to be sufficient consideration for the uncle's promise. By marrying, the nephew incurred responsibilities, and had changed his position. Moreover, the uncle might well derive benefit from the satisfaction of seeing his nephew " settled ".

(e) Consideration must move from the promisee. When a contract is made between two parties, no obligation under it can normally be enforced by a third party, since there is no " privity of contract " between the third party and the contracting parties.

### Tweddle v. Atkinson (1861).

T was married to the daughter of X. To provide for the couple, X promised to pay T £200 in consideration of T's father paying T £100. X died without having paid the £200, and T sued Atkinson, X's executor.

*Held* that T could not succeed as no consideration for X's promise had moved from him, T.

The principle has, however, become eroded by (i) procedural possibilities of the third party being able to require the promisee to sue on the promise for the benefit of the third party ; (ii) an obligation being in appropriate cases (rare) capable of being regarded as imposing a trust (see pages 38 and 144) ; (iii) statutory provision (such as that relied on in *Beswick* v. *Beswick* (1966) namely s. 56 of the *Law of Property Act*, 1925, which enables a person to take the benefit of any agreement respecting land or other property (including a chose in action [see page 141], although not named as a party). It was on the strength of this provision that a majority in the Court of Appeal held that widow Beswick was able to compel her defaulting nephew to honour his engagement (in a contract transferring his uncle's business to him to which she was not a party) to pay her an annuity from the death of his uncle.

However, on the case coming before the House of Lords in 1967, that House gave s. 56 of the 1925 Act a more restricted meaning, but nevertheless recognised the availability to the widow (in her capacity of personal representative of her deceased husband) of a decree of specific performance which she could enforce for her own benefit.

(*f*) Consideration must be lawful. Thus, a promise given in consideration of an agreement to commit a civil injury would be void because the consideration on which it is based is illegal.

(*g*) Consideration must not be past. Past consideration is an act or a forbearance to act, sufficient to support a contract, but not done or exercised in pursuance of a contract, although it subsequently gives rise to a promise. Motives of gratitude for a benefit received in the past will not support a promise not embodied in a deed.

**Roscorla v. Thomas (1842).**

*After* T had sold a horse to R with no conditions attached, T warranted the horse to be free from vice. The horse did not prove so.

*Held* that R had no right of action, T's warranty not being supported by consideration. Had it been made before or at the time of the sale, the sale would have been the consideration for the warranty.

There are said to be three exceptions to the rule that consideration must not be past :—

(*a*) Where it can be shown that services have been rendered at the express or implied request of the promisor, it has been held that this is sufficient consideration to support a subsequent promise to pay. This is no true exception, because the request for services implies a promise to pay a reasonable reward, and the later promise to pay is merely an assessment of the actual amount to be paid.

(*b*) A debt barred by the Limitation Act (see *post* p. 92) may be revived by a written acknowledgment, so that it will be enforceable, although the consideration is past. This, again, is only *apparently* an exception to the general rule, for the acknowledgment, which revives the right of action, is *not* the promise on which the action is brought : it is only *evidence* of the original obligation, and the action is brought on the promise originally given.

(*c*) The third exception, which is statutory, is created by section 27 of the Bills of Exchange Act, 1882, which provides that consideration for a bill may be constituted by any consideration sufficient to support a simple contract, *or by an antecedent debt or liability*. This is the only genuine exception to the rule.

## Forbearance to Sue.

A promise not to sue, i.e., the surrender, not of a legal right the existence of which has not yet been tested, but of the claim to such a right, will constitute valuable consideration provided that :—

(i) The claim is reasonable in itself ;
(ii) The plaintiff had an honest belief in the soundness of his claim ;
(iii) He had not concealed any fact which to his knowledge might affect the validity of his claim. The forbearance to prosecute a claim which the person forbearing knows must fail is no consideration.

It does not appear to be relevant that the claim abandoned was ill-founded, provided the plaintiff believed that he had a right of action. The test is, not whether the claim given up is good in law, but whether it is a *bona fide* claim.

## Offer and Acceptance.

A contract does not come into being until a definite offer has been unconditionally accepted.

" Any words or conduct from which an offer by one party and an acceptance of that offer by the other party may be reasonably inferred, are sufficient to constitute an agreement by offer and acceptance."

The nature of an offer may be illustrated by the following rules :—

(1) *An offer may be made to a definite person, or to individuals generally ; but until the offer has been accepted by a definite person there is no contract.* An offer may be made to the " whole world ", but it can be accepted only by those persons who are willing to, and do, perform the terms of the offer. Advertisements of rewards for services are common examples of this type of offer. The reward must be brought to the notice of the person to whom it is made and if, therefore, a person finds stolen goods and returns them to their owner in ignorance of the fact that a reward has been offered, he cannot claim the reward. In other words, a person who is ignorant of the existence of the offer cannot be said to have accepted it. " How can there be consent or assent to that of which the party has never heard ? "

(2) *The person who makes the offer may attach to it any conditions he pleases and prescribe any terms of acceptance he chooses.* But to bind an acceptor such conditions must be brought to his notice at the time of the contract. This requisite will be satisfied if

the offeror does all that is *reasonably* necessary to bring the existence of the conditions to the mind of the offeree. This is evident in the so-called " ticket cases ", where conditions limiting liability frequently appear on the back of a ticket evidencing the terms of a contract. In general, there must be some sufficient reference on the face of the ticket to the conditions on the back before those conditions can be regarded as incorporated in the contract, e.g., the words " for conditions see back ".

*L'Estrange* v. *Graucob* (1934) shows that a person entering into a written contract for the purchase of goods will be bound by the terms contained in the document if he signs it without reading it, unless the scope of the terms are misrepresented as in *Curtis* v. *Chemical Cleaning and Dyeing Company, Ltd.* (1951).

The foregoing principles have no application to documents which are not contractual in the sense of being the documents on which the contract was actually based. Illustration of this is afforded by *Chapelton* v. *Barry U.D.C.* (1940) where the plaintiff took a deck-chair from a stack near which was a notice which gave the price of hire at so much per session of so many hours and requested the public to obtain tickets from the chair attendant and retain them for inspection. The plaintiff obtained a ticket and put it into his pocket without reading it. The chair collapsed and he sued the Council, who relied on a provision printed on the ticket excluding liability. The Court of Appeal held that the contract was formed by way of offer from the notice and acceptance by taking the chair and that the ticket was a mere *receipt* for the hire charge. Likewise in *Olley* v. *Marlborough Court, Ltd.* (1949) a notice in a hotel bedroom was held to be too belated to be effectual since the parties had already concluded their contract without reference to the notice. Cp. *Thornton* v. *Shoe Lane Parking Ltd.* (1971).

Moreover, the Courts are tending to decline to give effect to exemption clauses where the party seeking to rely upon such a clause is himself in fundamental breach of contract : see *Alexander* v. *Railway Executive* (1951) ; *Woolmer* v. *Delmer Price, Ltd.* (1955). The doctrine so developing (but seemingly confined by the decision of the House of Lords in the *Suisse Atlantique Case* (1966) holding that the ambit and effect of an exemption clause is a question of construction) has, in some quarters and perhaps not happily, been labelled as the doctrine of the " fundamental term ". See further *post* p. 78.

> Exemption clauses are not only controlled by the action of the Courts, but may be subjected to legislative interference. For instance, under s. 43 (7) of the Transport Act, 1962, the Boards succeeding the Transport Commission " shall not carry passengers by rail on terms or conditions which :—

(a) purport, whether directly or indirectly, to exclude or limit liability in respect of the death of, or bodily injury to, any passenger other than a passenger travelling on a free pass, or

(b) purport, whether directly or indirectly, to prescribe the time within which or the manner in which any such liability may be enforced,

and any such terms or conditions shall be void and of no effect ". This provision follows the pattern for public service vehicles set by s. 151 of the Road Traffic Act, 1960 [not affected by the consolidating Act of 1972 referred to *ante* p. 3] and, indeed, numerous statutes (particularly in the field of Housing) prohibiting a " contracting-out ".

More recently s. 3 of the Misrepresentation Act, 1967, provides that if any agreement contains a provision which would exclude or restrict :—

(a) any liability to which a party to a contract may be subject by reason of any misrepresentation made by him before the contract was made ; or

(b) any remedy available to another party to the contract by reason of such a misrepresentation ;

that provision shall be of no effect except to the extent (if any) that, in any proceedings arising out of the contract, the court or arbitrator may allow reliance on it as being fair and reasonable in the circumstances of the case.

Provisions in the Supply of Goods (Implied Terms) Act, 1973, amending the law previously obtaining under the Sale of Goods Act, 1893, disclose a growing tendency to afford " consumer protection " by rendering void certain exemption clauses. See also provisions in the Consumer Credit Act, 1974.

(3) *The offeror cannot dispense with the necessity of communicating acceptance of the offer.* A mere mental acceptance will not suffice.

### Felthouse v. Bindley (1862).

F offered to buy his nephew's horse for £30 15s., adding, " If I hear no more about him I shall consider the horse is mine at £30 15s." The nephew did not reply to the letter, but he told Bindley, an auctioneer, to keep the horse out of a sale of farm stock, as it was sold to his uncle. Bindley, by mistake, sold the horse, and Felthouse sued him for conversion.

*Held* that, as the nephew had never signified his acceptance to his uncle, there was, in fact, no acceptance, the horse did not belong to the uncle, and, therefore, there had been no conversion.

The offeror may, however, indicate that the performance of the act may be sufficient communication, as in cases where rewards are offered by advertisement for the performance of specified acts. It is thought that an automatic machine charged with commodities constitutes a general offer capable of acceptance by insertion of the appropriate coin.

### Carlill v. Carbolic Smoke Ball Co. (1893).

A patent medicine company advertised that they would give £100 to any person who contracted influenza after using their " smoke ball " for a certain period in accordance with given directions. A, who had read the advertisement, bought and used the article in accordance with the directions but afterwards contracted influenza. She brought an action to recover £100 from the Company.

*Held* that there was a sufficient offer, and that the plaintiff, by performing the conditions, had accepted the offer, although she had not communicated her acceptance directly to the Company.

(4) *An offer, unlike acceptance, may lapse or be revoked.*
It may lapse :—

(a) On the death of either offeror or offeree *before* acceptance ;
(b) When it is rejected by the offeree ;
(c) When the time stipulated for acceptance has expired or, if no such time is specified, after the expiration of a reasonable time. In *Ramsgate Victoria Hotel Co.* v. *Montefiore* (1866), Montefiore by letter on the 28th of June applied for shares. No answer was made until the 23rd of November. He refused to accept shares allotted to him on that date, and it was held that his offer had lapsed through the unreasonable delay in accepting.

(5) *Revocation, to be effective, must be communicated to the offeree before he has accepted.* This point is exemplified by the case of *Byrne* v. *Van Tienhoven*, discussed later.

Acceptance ". . . is what a lighted match is to a train of gunpowder " (Anson). It is the intimation by the offeree of his willingness to be bound by the proposed obligation ; it binds not only him but the offeror. There are the following rules relating to acceptance :—

(1) *The acceptance must be absolute and unconditional.*

Any discrepancy between the terms of the offer and a purported acceptance is a rejection of the offer, which thereby lapses and is incapable of acceptance on a change of mind.

### Hyde v. Wrench (1840).

A offered to sell a farm for £1,000. X said that he would give £950. A refused, and X then said that he would give £1,000, and, when A declined to adhere to his original offer, sought specific performance.

*Held* that there was no contract, as X's offer to pay £950 was a refusal of the offer and a counter offer ; when he said later that he would pay £1,000, he was making a new offer, which would have to be accepted by A before a binding contract could come into existence.

But an enquiry as to whether the offeror would be willing to modify the terms of his offer is not to be regarded as a rejection of the offer, which may still be accepted by the offeree, if the offeror is unwilling to alter its terms; *Stevenson* v. *MacLean* (1880).

When the parties to a proposed contract agree to the general terms of the contract, but qualify it by reference to a formal contract, the position is as was explained by Parker, J., in *Von Hartzfeldt-Wildenburg* v. *Alexander* (1912): "It appears to be well settled by the authorities that if the documents or letters relied on as constituting a contract contemplate the execution of a formal contract between the parties, it is a question of constructtion whether the execution of the further contract is a condition or term of the bargain or whether it is a mere expression of the desires of the parties as to the manner in which the transaction already agreed on will in fact go through. In the former case there is no enforceable contract either because a condition is unfulfilled or because the law does not recognize a contract to enter into a contract. In the latter case there is a binding contract and the reference to the more formal document may be ignored."

In general, the words "subject to" indicate that there is, as yet, no contract concluded.

### Winn v. Bull (1877).

By a written agreement, Bull agreed with Winn to take a lease of a house for a certain term at a certain rent, "subject to the preparation and approval of a formal contract".

*Held* that there was no contract until the formal contract had been prepared and approved; indeed, such formal contract might have contained terms not yet agreed upon by the parties.

On the other hand, the fact that the parties contemplate the preparation of another document evidencing the terms of the contract, does not prevent the contract from being unconditional. Thus, if A writes to B offering certain property for sale at a stated figure and B writes back "I accept your offer and have asked my solicitors to draw up a contract," there is a binding contract, even if no such formal contract is ever drawn up: *Bonnewell* v. *Jenkins* (1878).

In *Branca* v. *Cobarro* (1947) a vendor agreed to sell the lease and goodwill of a farm on the terms of a document which was declared to be "a provisional agreement until a fully legalized agreement, drawn up by a solicitor and embodying all the conditions herewith stated is signed". The Court of Appeal held that the use of the word "provisional" indicated that the parties intended the document to be binding, although to be replaced subsequently by a more formal contract.

[N.B. The two inconsistent decisions of the Court of Appeal (with different Lords Justices) in *Law* v. *Jones* (1973) and *Tiverton Estates* v. *Wearwell Ltd.* (1973) have rendered the "subject to contract" formula in relation to transactions concerning land less cast-iron than as at one time thought. However, *Munton* v. *Greater London Council* (1976) appears to have restored the suspensive or conditional character of the formula.]

(2) *The acceptance must be made in the manner and form, if any, prescribed in the terms of the offer.*

If the offeror *stipulates* for acceptance in a certain way, then that method must be used. If A, a Sheffield business man, sends an offer by his lorry driver to B in London, writing, "If you agree, send your acceptance by my driver, *and by him only*," then, if B purports to accept by post, there is no contract. But if A merely wrote, "Send your acceptance by my driver," then, if B sent his reply by post, and his letter reached A at least as soon as it would have done if sent by the driver, there may well be a contract.

(3) *The acceptance must be made either within the time stipulated, or if no period is stipulated, within a reasonable time.* It has been held that where an offer is made by *telegram* an acceptance by *letter* is too late.

(4) *The acceptance must be communicated, either by words or by conduct, to the person making the offer, or to his authorized agent.*

(5) *If the offer is made to a specified person, it can be accepted only by that person.*

(6) *An acceptance, once communicated, cannot be revoked, for a contract has been concluded. In this respect it is unlike an offer, which, as we have seen, may be revoked.*

A promise to keep an offer open for a certain time is of no effect unless something is given in return for the promise and so an "option" is created. In the absence of such a binding element, an offer may be revoked or withdrawn, by communication to the offeree, before acceptance. Such communication need not come from the offeror, nor from his agent: it will suffice if it comes from a *reliable* source.

### Dickinson v. Dodds (1876).

A offered to sell a house to B. The offer provided, "This offer to be left over until Friday, 9 a.m.". Before Friday B heard from X that A had sold the house to C. Nevertheless, B handed his "acceptance" to A a few minutes before 9 a.m. on the Friday.

*Held* that there was no contract between A and B, the latter being aware, at the time of his purported acceptance, that the offer had been revoked.

## Use of the Post.

When the post is the means of communication between the parties, the question arises: When does the contract come into being ? What is the position if the letter of acceptance is lost in the post ? Generally speaking, an offer can be of no effect until communicated to the offeree. Similarly, as a general rule, there is no acceptance until the acceptance reaches the offeror. But if the post is the proper mode of communication between the parties, the acceptance is communicated and the contract is concluded *immediately the letter is posted*, notwithstanding that it is delayed in the post and even though it is destroyed and never reaches the offeror.

The post is the proper mode of communication when expressly or impliedly indicated by the offeror, as "where the circumstances are such that according to the ordinary usages of mankind, the post might be used as a means of communicating the acceptance of an offer . . ."

For the rule to apply, however, the letter must be properly *posted*, not merely handed to a third party, even a postman, to be posted.

Revocation of an offer, on the other hand, is never effective until it is actually brought to the notice of the offeree.

### Byrne v. Van Tienhoven (1880).

The defendant made an offer in writing to the plaintiff on the 1st October asking for a reply by cable. The plaintiff received the offer on the 11th, and at once accepted in the manner indicated. On the 8th October, the defendant had posted a revocation of the offer. This letter reached the plaintiff on the 20th. Two questions arose :—(1) Had revocation any effect until communicated ? (2) Did the posting of a letter of revocation amount to a communication to the person to whom the letter was sent ?

*Held* that the acceptance made by cable was not affected by the fact that a letter of revocation was on its way, as revocation must be brought to the actual notice of the offeree before he intimates his acceptance.

## Use of the Telephone.

Where a contract is made by "instantaneous communication", e.g., by telephone, the contract is not complete when the acceptance is spoken into the telephone at the offeree's end of the line, but only when received by the offeror at *his* end of the line. Thus, if the line " goes dead " during the communication of the acceptance, there is no contract. If the words are not distinctly heard by the offeror, then there is no contract until the words of acceptance have been repeated and heard by the offeror. But if the offeror, not having heard the words distinctly, does not ask for a repetition, he may be estopped from denying that there has been communication of acceptance : *Entores, Ltd.* v. *Miles Far East Corporation* (1955). The same principle applies to use of the telex system.

That an acceptance *inter praesentes* must be unequivocal and that its repetition is advisable in circumstances giving rise to doubt may be illustrated by the following attractive examination question :—

> " D is an art collector and E an art dealer. E has a picture by a minor Dutch painter which D admires. As they are lunching in a restaurant, E says to D, ' that Dutch painting that you like so much—you can have it for £250 '. D momentarily taken aback then says ' Done ' at the same time shaking his head to get rid of a fly. The orchestra started to play at the same time ; in consequence E did not hear D's ' Done ' and seeing him shake his head, thought that D was rejecting the offer. Thereafter E sent the picture for cleaning before putting it up for auction. The cleaner discovered beneath the present picture an old Flemish master, and on E's direction, completely restored it. The Flemish painting so revealed was at once assessed as worth £30,000. D then claimed the picture as his and E refused to give it up. Discuss."

In conclusion, an offer must be distinguished from :—

(a) An intention to make an offer. A mere declaration of intention, unlike an offer, is not capable of being converted into an agreement by acceptance. So long as advance booking of seats is not permitted, a mere advertisement of a concert is not an offer to hold such concert ; it is a mere declaration of intention. In *Harvey* v. *Facey* (1893) A telegraphed to B : " Will you sell us Bumper Hall Pen ? Telegraph lowest cash price ". B replied : " Lowest price for Bumper Hall Pen £900 ". A telegraphed : " We agree to buy Bumper Hall Pen for £900 asked by you ". It was held that there was no contract, as the mere statement of the price did not contain an implied offer to sell.

(b) An invitation to make an offer. Such is sometimes termed an invitation to treat. This is the mere initiation of negotiations from which an agreement may or may not result. Normally, a circular or catalogue advertising goods for sale is not an offer, but a mere inducement to others to make offers. Similarly, where goods are exhibited for sale in a shop window, marked with a price, that is not an offer to sell at the price named, but is an invitation to persons generally to come into the shop and make offers, and the price-ticket indicates the price at which the shop-keeper will consider (but not necessarily accept) an offer to buy. This principle has been applied to the modern Self-Service of grocery, provision and other shops : *Pharmaceutical Society of Great Britain* v. *Boots Cash Chemists (Southern) Ltd.* (1952).

**Contractual Capacity.**

While, in general, any person in the eye of the law may freely enter into and be bound by a contract, there are qualifications of the general rule the most important of which are the following :—

A. MINORS.

The " Latey Report " on the Age of Majority (1967 Cmnd. 3342) recommended (but not unanimously) that for most purposes of the Civil Law (including the realm of Contract) the age of majority should be fixed at eighteen (the age being calculated from the commencement of the relevant anniversary of the date of birth of the person concerned). The Committee preferred the use of the term " minor " to that of " infant ".

The Family Law Reform Act, 1969 implemented the main recommendations of the Committee. Section 12 of the Act reads " A person who is not of full age may be described as a minor instead of as an infant and accordingly . . . ' minor ' means such a person as aforesaid." Section 1 (2) also provides (amongst other things) that references in earlier statutory provisions to " infant " or " infancy " shall normally be taken to be references to " minor " and " minority " respectively.

Accordingly, in the ensuing discussion, the more satisfactory expression " minor " will normally be used to describe a person who has not yet attained full age under the law for the time being in force.

A minor's contracts may be classified as follows :—

(*a*) *Void.* Under the Infants Relief Act, 1874, three types of contract are void :—

    (i) **Any agreement for the repayment of money lent or to be lent.**
    (ii) **Any contract for the supply of goods other than necessaries.**
    (iii) **All accounts stated, i.e., admissions of money due.**

If a minor, by a fraudulent misrepresentation as to his age, induces a contract which is not binding upon him, the other party cannot recoup himself by suing for damages in tort for fraud, because that would be an indirect way of enforcing a void contract : *R. Leslie Ltd.* v. *Sheill* (1914). (It will be pointed out in Chapter VII that, generally speaking, a minor is liable for his torts, i.e., wrongs independent of contract.) If goods have been obtained by such a fraud the Court may order the restoration of them if still in the minor's possession and identifiable, but he cannot be made to refund *money* obtained on loan by a fraudulent representation, for " restitution ends where repayment begins " (per Lord Sumner in *Sheill's* case (*supra*).

An agreement after full age to repay a loan of money obtained during minority is void under the Betting and Loans (Infants) Act, 1892, which also provides that any instrument, negotiable or otherwise, given under such an agreement, is void as against all parties.

*Re Soltykoff* (1891) shows that a minor cannot be made liable on a bill of exchange even though given in payment of a debt incurred for necessaries (this term will be explained later). In the case of necessaries, however, he can be sued on the consideration for which the bill was given, i.e., for a reasonable price for the necessaries supplied.

(*b*) *Valid.* There are two types of contract which are binding upon a minor :—

(i) Contracts for necessaries, i.e., " goods suitable to the condition in life of such infant [minor] *and* to his actual requirements at the time of the sale and delivery ". Thus, there are two factors : the social status of the minor and his actual stock of the article at the time of the sale *and* delivery. Goods may be " necessary " according to the first test, but if he is already sufficiently supplied they are luxuries, as was the case with the undergraduate's fancy waistcoats involved in *Nash* v. *Inman* (1908). If the goods are necessaries, the minor may be compelled to pay a " reasonable " price for them, and this is not necessarily the contract price. Although the above definition (given in the Sale of Goods Act, 1893) refers to goods, a similar principle applies to necessary lodgings, medical attendance and necessaries for his wife and children, even the necessary hire of a conveyance.

(ii) Contracts for the minor's benefit. This does not apply to trading contracts, however beneficial such may be to the minor : *Shears* v. *Mendeloff* (1914). In *Cowern* v. *Nield* (1913), it was held that a hay and straw dealer who was under age was not liable to repay the price of a consignment of hay that he had failed to deliver and in *Mercantile Union Guarantee Corporation, Ltd.* v. *Ball* (1937) the Court refused to uphold a hire-purchase agreement entered into by a minor in respect of a lorry. To be " beneficial ", the contract must be an apprenticeship contract, a contract concerning education, a service contract or one closely analogous to such contracts. The terms of the contract must be reasonable and substantially in the interests of the minor. Certain contracts of a professional billiards player under age [*Roberts* v. *Gray* (1913)] and of a boxer under age [*Doyle* v. *White City Stadium Ltd., and B.B.B.C.* (1935)] were declared valid on this ground.

(*c*) *Voidable.* This class includes contracts of a continuing nature, or contracts under which the minor obtains an interest in property of a permanent kind to which obligations attach, e.g., a lease, a contract to become a partner or to take shares in a company. Such contracts are binding upon a minor unless he repudiates them expressly either before he comes of age or within a reasonable time thereafter. If benefits under such a contract are accepted by a minor *after* he comes of age, or if he fails to repudiate within a reasonable time thereafter, the former minor will be liable on the contract.

(*d*) Contracts not coming within any of the classes described above cannot be enforced against a minor, but he can himself enforce them if he chooses. The chief example of this type used to be a promise to marry. If A, a minor, promised to marry B, an adult, in return for B's promise to marry him, A, then he could enforce the contract against B, but the latter could not enforce it against him; however, the Law Reform (Miscellaneous Provisions) Act, 1970 abolished the action for breach of promise to marry. It has been pointed out in Chapter II that since, generally speaking, a contract for the acquisition of property by a minor is not enforceable *against* him, a decree of specific performance will not be granted at his instance. He may, however, sue for damages for breach of contract, as damages are a Common Law remedy in which want of mutuality is not relevant.

> It may be mentioned that under s. 50 of the Consumer Credit Act, 1974, it is made an offence for a person who, with a view to financial gain, sends to a minor any document (e.g. by way of circular) inviting him to :—
> (*a*) borrow money, or
> (*b*) obtain goods on credit or hire, or services on credit, or
> (*c*) apply for information or advice on borrowing money or otherwise obtaining credit or hiring goods.
>
> It is a defence for the person charged to prove that he did not know and had no reasonable cause to suspect that the addressee was a minor; however, where a document is received by a minor at any school or other educational establishment for minors, a person sending it to him at that establishment knowing or suspecting it to be such an establishment is to be taken to have reasonable cause to suspect that he is a minor.

RECOVERY OF MONEY PAID BY A MINOR. When a minor has paid money under a voidable contract, then, although he may repudiate the contract, disclaiming future liability, he cannot recover money paid unless he can prove a *total* failure of consideration, i.e., that he has received no benefit under the contract.

### Steinberg v. Scala (Leeds), Ltd. (1923).

> The plaintiff, a minor, applied for shares and paid the amount due on allotment and on the first call. She neither received any dividends nor attended any meetings, but the shares had been " quoted " during the period of her holding. Whilst still a minor, she repudiated the contract and sought recovery of moneys paid.

*Held* that she was entitled to have her name removed from the register of shareholders, thus avoiding liability for future calls, but she could not recover the moneys paid, because there had not been a total failure of consideration, the shares having a " potential " market value.

Similarly, unless there has been a total failure of consideration, a minor cannot recover any specific chattel or money which has passed under a *void* contract.

It has been held that a minor can be made bankrupt in respect of enforceable debts.

B. MENTALLY DISORDERED PERSONS.

Contracts entered into by a person at a time when, by reason of mental disorder, he is incapable of appreciating the effect of his act are voidable *by him* on regaining sanity, if the other party was aware of his incapacity at the time of execution of the contract. The mentally disordered person must, however, pay a reasonable price for necessaries supplied to him. There is no liability if goods have been supplied voluntarily by a relative or from motives of charity, there being no intention, at the time of the supply, of requiring payment.

> With regard to contracts that are binding it may be pointed out that under section 103 (1) (*g*) of the Mental Health Act, 1959, the Court is given power to make orders and give directions for ". . . the carrying out of any contract entered into by the patient " (i.e., a " person suffering or appearing to be suffering from mental disorder "—section 147).

C. INTOXICATED PERSONS.

Similar rules apply here as in the case of mentally disordered persons (except that the Act of 1959 referred to in the preceding paragraph does not apply), but it may be more difficult for the party contracting with an intoxicated person to prove that he was unaware of the condition of the latter at the time of the contract.

D. MARRIED WOMEN.

A married woman now has full legal capacity by virtue of the Law Reform (Married Women and Tortfeasors) Act, 1935.

The position of a husband with regard to his wife's contracts may be considered here. In general, he incurs no liability thereon in his capacity as husband, but he will incur liability in the following circumstances :—

(i) When he had expressly authorized his wife to act as his agent. (On the topic of agency, see *post*, p. 134).
(ii) When he has impliedly authorized her to pledge his credit. This is an example of the doctrine of " holding out ", i.e., so acting that third parties are led to believe that one

person has authority to make certain contracts on behalf of another person. If his wife has purported to contract on his behalf but without his authority, and he settles her bills without demur, she has implied authority to pledge his credit in similar transactions with the tradesman, unless and until the husband has given express notice to the tradesman of the withdrawal of his authority.

(iii) When his cohabiting wife, or his mistress, or other person managing his household, purchases household and personal necessaries. Here, there is a presumption of authority to pledge his credit, but this may be rebutted by proof that :—

    (*a*) She is already sufficiently supplied with household necessaries ;
    (*b*) He has provided her with adequate funds for the purpose ;
    (*c*) The goods were not necessaries, being excessive in quantity, or beyond the standard prescribed by him ;

The fact that the tradesman is ignorant of the position in the above three cases will not render the husband liable.

    (*d*) He has forbidden her to pledge his credit. Provided he has not held her out as his agent, notice to her is sufficient, the tradesman dealing with her " at his peril ".

Of course, where a husband and wife engage in business as partners, a situation of agency subsists between them. See *post* p. 129.

[Note. Formerly and at Common Law a deserted wife was treated as agent of necessity of her husband to purchase necessaries according to her station in life. The agency was terminated by her adultery. This form of agency of necessity was, however, abolished by a provision in the Matrimonial Proceedings and Property Act, 1970.]

E. CORPORATIONS.

The contracts of corporations fall to be considered in their legal aspect from two angles : (*a*) capacity, (*b*) form.

As to *capacity* :—

(i) A Common Law Corporation, i.e., incorporated by Royal Charter, may contract like an ordinary person. If any limitations imposed by the Charter are exceeded, the effect is not to avoid the contract but to make the Charter liable to forfeiture : *Baroness Wenlock* v. *River Dee Co.* (1888).

(ii) Other Corporations. The capacity for all other corporations is defined by the statute or memorandum of association by which the corporation is constituted and which states the purposes and objects of its formation, and in some cases powers are implied from the nature of the company's business. Any exercise of powers in excess of those laid down in the constitutive instrument or necessarily implied as being incidental thereto, is termed *ultra vires*, and any contracts thus entered into are (in theory) void on the ground of incapacity, cannot be ratified by the members and are ineffectual to impose any obligation on the corporation : *Ashbury Carriage and Iron Co. v. Riche* (1875). In the case of a company registered under the Companies Acts the " constitutive instrument is a combination of Memorandum of Association, Articles of Association and Certificate of Incorporation. It is to the Memorandum of Association (and particularly its " objects clause ") that one must look to ascertain what is *intra* and what is *ultra vires*. (See further *post*, p. 121.)

So far as concerns persons dealing in good faith with a company, the *ultra vires* doctrine lost most of its force on the United Kingdom joining the " Common Market " on 1st January, 1973, for the European Communities Act, 1972 (making provision in connection with such entry) provides in s. 9 (1) that :

" In favour of a person dealing with a company in good faith, any transaction decided on by the directors shall be deemed to be one which it is within the capacity of the company to enter into, and the power of the directors to bind the company shall be deemed to be free of any limitation under the memorandum or articles of association ; and a party to a transaction so decided on shall not be bound to enquire as to the capacity of the company to enter into it or as to any such limitation on the powers of the directors, and shall be presumed to have acted in good faith unless the contrary is proved."

The doctrine remains, however, in relation to a person not dealing with the company in good faith as also does it in relation to the accountability of the directors for their acts to the company.

As to *form* :—

At Common Law all corporations' contracts had to be under seal. The rule became modified, however, by decisions of the Courts and the Companies Act, 1948, permitted companies registered under that Act to contract in the same way as private individuals. The Corporate Bodies' Contracts Act, 1960, completed the process by permitting other corporations (which include Local Authorities) to contract, in matter of form, in the ways open to or required of private individuals.

Other aspects of the law relating to corporations (including limited liability companies) are discussed in Chapters V, VI and VIII.

## F. ALIENS.

In time of peace aliens have the same contractual capacity as British subjects, but they cannot acquire a share in a British ship, save as members of an English registered company.

A contract made with an alien enemy—which includes not merely a subject of a State at war with Her Majesty but also a British subject resident in hostile or enemy-occupied country —is void. The contracts of an alien enemy present in England by licence of the Crown are valid and enforceable even during hostilities. Contracts made with alien enemies before the outbreak of hostilities are suspended for the duration of the war, unless they are such as to involve intercourse between the parties, as in the case of a partnership, or are such as to operate to the prejudice of this country, when they are wholly dissolved.

It has already been pointed out in the Introduction that foreign sovereigns and ambassadorial representatives of foreign States cannot be sued in this country unless they submit to the jurisdiction. This disability applies, of course, to actions for breach of contract.

## CHAPTER IV

## ELEMENTS OF THE LAW OF CONTRACT
### (continued)

**Illegality.**

An illegal contract, however made, is void. The illegality may exist in respect of the promise, the consideration or the subject-matter. If the contract is illegal only in part, the valid portion may be enforced unless the contract is such that severance of the good from the bad is impossible.

Contracts may be illegal at Common Law or by statute. Of the former description are contracts to commit a crime or a civil wrong or which are contrary to public policy. Contracts contrary to public policy include those for an immoral purpose, of a champertous nature, those entered into to defeat the Revenue or those in undue restraint of trade since they restrict the trade or professional activities of one of the parties.

CONTRACTS IN RESTRAINT OF TRADE.

The general rules as to restraint are :—

(1) Every agreement in restraint of trade is *prima facie* illegal and void.
(2) An agreement in restraint of trade will be upheld if :—
   (a) It is reasonable between the parties ;
   (b) It is reasonable having regard to the interests of the public.

Thus, the key-word is " reasonableness ". A distinction is drawn by the Courts between a covenant exacted by the purchaser of a business from the vendor of the goodwill and a covenant exacted by an employer from an employee. The tests of reasonableness are applied more strictly to the latter class of covenant. A covenant directed solely to preventing competition by an employee after he has left his employer's service will not be upheld. The employer is entitled to protect himself only against the misuse of knowledge gained by employees while in his service. This knowledge may take the form of information as to private processes, or of acquaintance with his employer's customers. But the employee's skill, although gained in the employer's service, is his own to take away and use permanently for his own benefit, and a covenant which merely has the effect of interfering with the use of it is unreasonable, and, therefore, void.

The leading case in the employment field is :—

**Morris Ltd. v. Saxelby (1916)**
In this case, the defendant, a draughtsman employed by the plaintiffs, covenanted that he would not for seven years after leaving their employment carry on business in any capacity in the United Kingdom in regard to the sale or manufacture of various kinds of machinery. Within a year, however, after leaving their service, he accepted employment with a competing firm. Held by the House of Lords that the restraint was bad, and the contract unenforceable against the defendant. [Cp. and contrast the milk roundsman case of *Home Counties Dairies Ltd. v. Skelton* (1970) and that of the hairdresser in *Marion White Ltd. v. Francis* (1972).]

Certain contracts are rendered illegal by statute. Examples are gaming and wagering contracts and contracts infringing the Truck Acts, 1831–1940, i.e., contracts whereby workmen are required to receive their wages, or part of them, in kind and so not in cash. The Payment of Wages Act, 1960, mitigated the rigours of these Acts by permitting payment of wages to a workman by credit to a banking account. The arrangement between the parties must be voluntary and is revocable.

The law as to gaming and wagering contracts is somewhat complex, but may be summarized as follows :—

(i) A wager is a promise to give something upon the ascertainment of an uncertain event, the consideration for such promise being the promise by the other party to give value should the uncertain event be determined in a particular way.
(ii) The Gaming Act, 1845, makes all such contracts void and unenforceable, but it does not make them illegal.
(iii) The Act of 1892 renders irrecoverable all moneys earned by way of commission in respect of such transactions.
(iv) By virtue of the same Act, an agent employed to make bets cannot recover from his principal money paid in respect of a loss, but the principal may recover the amount of bets won and received by his agent.
(v) The validity of negotiable instruments given for money lost at wagering depends upon whether or not the bets were made on the result of " games or pastimes ". If so made, the *consideration* is *deemed illegal* (Gaming Act, 1835), and subsequent holders must prove that they are *bona fide* holders for value having no knowledge of the illegality. If, however, the bet was on some event other than " games or pastimes ", e.g., the result of an election, there is a mere *absence* of *consideration*, and a subsequent holder need only prove that value has been given at some time in the history

of the instrument to enable him to enforce it, his knowledge of its origin being immaterial. Thus, if A loses a bet on a horse race to B, and gives a cheque for the amount lost, B cannot sue A on the cheque. If B cashes the cheque with C, who does not know that it was given in payment of a lost bet, C can enforce the cheque against A. If, however, the bet had been, e.g., on the result of a general election, then the fact that C knew that the cheque had been given in payment of a lost bet will not prejudice him. He himself has given value by cashing the cheque.

(vi) Money lent to pay bets *already* lost is recoverable, but not so if the lender himself pays the money to the winner. In *Macdonald* v. *Green* (1950), where the plaintiff, the managing director of a company of bookmakers, in a private capacity lent money to the defendant with the obvious intention that the money should be applied solely in payment of the defendant's betting debt to the company, it was held, however, that it was not recoverable.

(vii) Money due in respect of a gaming transaction is not recoverable even if a new consideration is given for the promise to pay : *Hill* v. *William Hill (Park Lane), Ltd.* (1949). In this case, H owed a company of bookmakers a large sum as a result of betting transactions. He eventually agreed to pay so as to avoid being posted as a defaulter. When he failed to pay, the company brought an action to recover what was owing to them. The House of Lords held that, although the agreement contained a new promise by H for good consideration, it was a promise to pay money won upon a wager, and the company's action was brought to recover money alleged to be so won. The money was irrecoverable under the Gaming Act, 1845. Cp. *Coral* v. *Kleyman* (1951).

(viii) Money knowingly lent in England for gaming purposes is irrecoverable ; but money lent for gaming purposes in a country where gaming is not unlawful is recoverable in England : *Société Anonyme des Grands Etablissements, etc.* v. *Baumgart* (1927).

The legislation starting with the Betting and Gaming Act, 1960 (consolidated in the Betting, Gaming and Lotteries Act, 1963, Part II of which has been replaced by the Gaming Act, 1968) which, amongst other things, established a system of licensed betting offices and legalized certain forms of hitherto illegal gaming provided certain conditions are satisfied, does not appear to have affected the propositions set forth above in so far as they concern the law of contract. Note, however, s. 16 of 1968 Act which gives a right of action on certain cheques accepted in exchange for cash or tokens in a licensed club. The conditions are stringent.

## Impossibility of Performance.

Antecedent impossibility must be distinguished from subsequent impossibility. Contracts which at the time of making are, to the knowledge of the parties, or according to the state of knowledge of the day, impossible of performance are void because of the failure of consideration, e.g., an undertaking to swim the Atlantic, or to transmute lead into gold. In this case a contract never arises. *Subsequent* impossibility (to be considered later) will sometimes discharge a contract which has already come to existence.

## Reality of Consent.

A contract otherwise regular as regards form and consideration, etc., may be vitiated on the ground that there is no real consent to it by one or both of the parties. A consent which appears on the surface to be genuine may in fact be unreal owing to the presence of mistake, innocent misrepresentation, fraud, duress or undue influence.

MISTAKE.

It is the exception, not the rule, that mistake will vitiate consent. A mistake which has this effect is termed " operative ". Operative mistake must be mistake of fact ; mistake of law, save in certain exceptional cases, does not render a contract void. But mistake as to private rights is construed as mistake of fact. Thus, when A and B contract that A shall grant to B a lease of property which both of them think belongs to A but which actually belongs to B, this is treated as a mistake of fact. There is no true consent between A and B, and the contract, therefore, is void. Operative mistake may be classified as follows :—

(1) *Mistake as to the nature, scope and effect of the instrument.*

Where a person signs a contract, or executes a deed, in the mistaken belief that it is of a totally different kind from that which it is in fact, there is no contract, and he can plead " *non est factum* ", certainly so where he was fraudulently induced to sign the contract.

The case of *Saunders (Exec. of Gallie decd.)* v. *Anglia Building Society* (1970) in the House of Lords shows that the old doctrine of *non est factum* has little scope in the modern literate age and carelessness will not be an excusing factor. The case is also cited under its title at first instance of *Gallie* v. *Lee.*

### Foster v. Mackinnon (1869).

M, an old man of feeble sight, was induced to indorse a bill of exchange for £3,000 on the assurance that it was a mere guarantee.

Later the bill was indorsed for value to F, who sued M on the bill.
*Held* that there was no negligence on the part of M, and, although F was innocent of the fraud, he could not recover as M's mind did not go with his signature, which was a nullity.

(2) *Mistake by one party as to the identity of the other party.*
This type of mistake will vitiate a contract only if it is proved that identity was a material factor. In the case of an ordinary purchase contract, accordingly, a mistake of identity will not affect the contract, but even here there are exceptions. Thus, in *Boulton* v. *Jones* (1857), B had purchased the business of Brocklehurst, with whom J had been in the habit of dealing, *and against whom he had a set-off* (i.e., a contra account). J ordered further goods, and B executed the order without notifying J of the change of ownership of the business. It was held that J was not liable to pay B for the goods as there was no contract with him.

The test in mistake as to identity is : Did the mistaken party intend to contract with one person *and with him only* ? That was the test applied in *Cundy* v. *Lindsay* (the facts of which were given in Chapter III) and again in *Ingram* v. *Little* (1960). It makes no difference that the contracting parties met face to face. Here, the test is : Did the seller intend to contract with the person physically before him, irrespective of his identity or did he intend to contract with the person whom he mistakenly thought this person to be and with him only ?

### Phillips v. Brooks (1919).

X went into P's shop and purchased some jewellery. *Then* X, saying " I am Sir G.B.," drew a cheque in that name and was allowed to take away one of the jewels, which he pledged with B, who acted in good faith.

*Held* that B obtained a good title. The contract was not void for mistake, but voidable for fraud. At the time of the contract, the jeweller intended to deal with the person physically before him, irrespective of his identity.

[Cases of mistaken identity clearly have to be decided on their own special facts. *Ingram* v. *Little* (*supra*) is a case in point. There a rogue offered to buy a car from a lady on visiting her house and to pay by cheque. The lady refused the offer and cheque since she did not know the gentleman before her. However, he convinced her that he was a responsible person living at a given address and the corresponding telephone number given by him was checked, whereupon she accepted his cheque and let him take the car away. The rogue then sold the vehicle to the defendant and the cheque was dishonoured. Held that the contract between the lady and the rogue was *void* for mistake and that the defendant must restore the car to the lady as neither the rogue nor he had acquired any title to it. Contrast *Lewis* v. *Averay* (1971) (C.A.)]

(3) *Mistake as to the subject-matter.*

There may be mistake as to the identity or existence of the subject-matter of a contract. Where there is a contract for something which does not bear a distinctive name and the contract does not clearly specify a particular thing, then evidence may be given that one party intended to contract with regard to one thing, and the other with regard to something else.

**Raffles v. Wichelhaus (1864).**

The defendant agreed to buy a cargo of cotton " *ex Peerless* sailing from Bombay ". There were two cotton ships thus called, and both sailed from Bombay. Wichelhaus meant the one which arrived in England in October, Raffles meant the one due in December.

*Held* that there was no contract.

Where the subject-matter of the contract does not exist at the time of the contract, although neither party is aware of this fact, the contract is void on the ground of mistake.

**Couturier v. Hastie (1856).**

A contract was made between two parties for the sale of a cargo of corn which was presumed to be on the high seas in course of transit. Unknown to the parties, the cargo in question was not then in existence, as it had become overheated and had been landed at the nearest port and sold.

*Held* that the contract was void.

This principle, however, does not apply when goods are sold under their class name. If X agrees to sell a case of " W. H. Whisky " to Y, thinking to fulfil the contract out of a stock which he believed to be in his cellar, but which has in fact been destroyed, he is not excused from his contract and must buy whisky elsewhere to fulfil his contract.

(4) *Mistake as to the existence of a state of affairs forming the basis of the contract.*

This renders the contract void if the mistake is common to both parties, as where A contracts to lease to B property which, unknown to both of them, actually belongs to B, as in *Cooper* v. *Phibbs* (1867).

(5) *Mistake as to the quality of the subject-matter.*

This renders the contract void only if it is the mistake of both parties and is a mistake as to the existence of some quality which makes the thing without the quality essentially different from the thing as it was believed to be by both parties. This does not mean a mere mutual mistake as to the value of a thing. Thus, if both buyer and seller believe a picture to be the work of an old master, in consequence of which the buyer pays a high price, he cannot avoid the contract on discovering that it is merely a modern copy, provided the seller made no representation or warranty. The following case will illustrate the kind of mistake meant.

**Bell v. Lever Bros. (1932).**

B was engaged under a contract of service with the X Co., Ltd. During the period of his service and in breach of his contract of employment he engaged in secret trading. The consequence of this breach was that the X Co., Ltd. could have, had it so desired, terminated the engagement immediately. The X Co., Ltd. was fused with another company, and B was paid the sum of £30,000 as compensation for terminating the contract before the due date. Later the company discovered that B had been guilty of a breach of his contract of employment and sought to recover the sum of £30,000 from him.

*It was held* that the company could not recover. The mutual mistake of the parties did not destroy the identity of the subject-matter, but related only to a quality which was not material. The company had got precisely what it asked for, namely the termination of the service agreement on compensatory terms and it was irrelevant that, in the commercial sense, the company had made a bad bargain.

*Bell* v. *Lever* is a difficult case but it has been suggested by more than one commentator that its effect is to confine the doctrine of operative mistake to cases where there is mistake as to the actual existence or identity of the subject-matter of the contract.

*Harrison & Jones* v. *Bunten & Lancaster* (1953) seems to support this view ; at any rate it shows that in ordinary commercial transactions mistake as to quality will rarely be treated as " operative ". There the buyers agreed to buy " 100 bales of Calcutta kapok, Sree brand " equal to standard sample. The seller delivered in accordance with the description and sample. It emerged that both parties had made the contract in the belief that " Calcutta kapok, Sree brand " was pure kapok consisting exclusively of tree cotton, whereas in fact it contained a mixture of bush cotton and was commercially a very different and inferior category of goods. The buyer's contention that this common mistake rendered the contract void was rejected by the Court.

It will have been appreciated that, where mistake does affect a contract, it renders it void. This is in direct contrast to the other possible vitiating factors, which render the contract merely voidable.

The following additional comment may be made particularly as it concerns mistake, fraud and the granting of equitable relief.

Very often (but not always) it will be found in dealing with cases of mistake that an element of fraud is involved. The usual effect of fraud in itself is to make a contract voidable and although fraud may in fact be present, that is entirely irrelevant when the question to be considered is whether a *mistake* has arisen, for mistake of the operative kind outlined above makes a contract *void*, and not merely voidable, however it arises.

Even where a contract is not void at Common Law because the parties " had agreed in the same terms and on the same subject-matter," a mistake common to them, if sufficiently fundamental, may allow Equity to intervene at the instance of the party seeking to set up the mistake (but not himself at fault) and set the contract aside (if necessary on terms) : *Solle* v. *Butcher* (1949) ; *Grist* v. *Bailey* (1966) ; *Magee* v. *Pennine Insurance Co. Ltd.* (1969). Likewise the equitable remedy of specific performance will be denied to a plaintiff who has taken advantage of a serious error made by the defendant on making an offer to sell property, as in the " snap acceptance " case of *Webster* v. *Cecil* (1861).

RECTIFICATION.

When the parties are in fact agreed, but the written instrument which purports to be their contract does not truly represent their agreement, the Court may rectify the instrument and then enforce it as rectified. Before rectification can be obtained, the following conditions must be satisfied :—

(a) The mistake must be one of expression only.
(b) There must be a concluded contract antecedent to the instrument.
(c) There must be clear evidence of the real intention.
(d) The mistake must be common to both parties.
(e) The mistake must have existed at the time of the execution of the instrument.
(f) The mistake must be proved exactly ; i.e., the party seeking rectification must show the precise form in which the instrument should have been drawn up.

INNOCENT MISREPRESENTATION.

A misrepresentation may be *innocent* or *fraudulent*. A representation must be distinguished from an actual term of a contract, which is either a *condition* or a *warranty*. A *condition* is an undertaking that a certain state of affairs exists, or will exist, or a promise that a certain thing shall or shall not be done, the fulfilment of which undertaking is one of the fundamental bases on which the contract is founded. A condition is an essential term which goes to the root of the whole contract, and breach of a condition entitles the aggrieved party to treat the contract as at an end. The doctrine of the " fundamental term " referred to in Chapter III should not be confused with a *condition*, since the latter is an actual term, whereas the application by a Court of the doctrine involves, in essence, the implication of a fundamental assumption concerning what may, perhaps, be described as the " core of the contract ". A *warranty* is an agreement with reference to goods which are the subject of a contract of sale, but collateral to the main purpose of such contract, the breach of which (as a contractual term) gives rise to a claim for damages, but not to a right to reject the goods and treat the contract as repudiated. A representation, in the strict sense, is a statement that precedes and induces a contract but is not itself a term of the contract; nevertheless it may, by incorporation or coalescence, become a term as either a condition or a warranty.

Both innocent and fraudulent misrepresentation have certain common factors which will be treated under fraudulent misrepresentation.

The effect of an innocent misrepresentation (in the strict sense) is to render a contract voidable, although the injured party may, if he chooses, affirm the contract. If he decides to repudiate the contract, he may (*a*) bring an action for rescission of the contract, or (*b*) set up the misrepresentation as a defence to an action for breach of contract brought by the other party. The right to rescind only exists where the plaintiff acts promptly.

> Before the Misrepresentation Act, 1967, the right to rescind was lost where the representation had become a term of the contract (thus giving rise to the remedies for breach referred to above); it was also lost once the contract had been executed. Thus in the latter connection, if the transaction had been completed by the conveyance of land, the grant of a lease, the actual transfer of shares or the acceptance of goods the subject of a contract of sale, the right to rescind was lost. The right to repudiate was lost if an innocent third party had acquired rights for value in the subject-matter of the contract, or if it was not possible to restore the parties to their original positions. In general, damages (as opposed to an indemnity) might not be recovered for innocent misrepresentation, but there were two exceptions :—
> 
> (*a*) In an action under section 43, Companies Act, 1948, damages, termed " compensation ", might be recovered from a director or a promoter of a company in respect of false statements in a prospectus.
> 
> (*b*) In an action for breach of warranty of authority, damages might be claimed from an agent who had unwittingly exceeded his authority or represented himself to have authority to act as agent for another when he had no such authority, and it was immaterial that the " agent " acted innocently. The so-styled agent alone was liable.

The Misrepresentation Act, 1967 (following the main recommendations of the Law Reform Committee in their Tenth Report) substantially amended the previous complicated and unsatisfactory law concerning the remedies for non-fraudulent misrepresentation. In the first place, it makes rescission available (subject to satisfaction of the basic requirements) notwithstanding that such misrepresentation had become a term of the contract or the contract had been performed. Secondly, it confers a right to damages in respect of loss suffered by a person who has entered into a contract after a misrepresentation made to him by another party thereto and that other party is unable to prove (the onus being upon him) that he had reasonable ground to believe and did believe up to the time the contract was made that the facts represented were true ; this appears to introduce liability for what may be termed " negligent misrepresentation ". Thirdly, it confers on the Court power to award damages or confirm or order rescission in the alternative, according to the merits or justice of the case ; but if damages are awarded under this power they are to be taken into account in assessing liability to damages for any " negligent misrepresentation ". Fourthly, it controls exclusion clauses (See *ante* p. 57).

The Act also made certain amendments to the Sale of Goods Act, 1893, not material to the present discussion.

FRAUD OR FRAUDULENT MISREPRESENTATION.

A fraudulent misrepresentation is an untrue statement of fact made with knowledge of its falsity, or without belief in its truth, or, recklessly, not caring whether it be true or false : *Derry* v. *Peek* (1889). The features common to innocent and fraudulent misrepresentation are :—

(a) The misstatement must be one of fact, not of law.
(b) The misstatement must be made by a party to the contract.
(c) The party seeking relief must have relied and acted upon the misrepresentation in entering into the contract.
(d) He must have suffered damage thereby.

A fraudulent misrepresentation may be analysed thus :—

1. There must be a *false* representation ; i.e., there must be an actual intent to deceive, and not merely a non-disclosure of facts which might be morally censurable, but an actual fraudulent statement, or a fraudulent fragmentary statement, or an intentional half-truth.
2. It must be a misrepresentation of *fact*. Mere expressions of opinion or intention do not involve fraud. But, of course, a man may tell a lie about his opinion or his intention, and that will be a misstatement of a matter of fact.
3. To constitute fraud a statement must be made with a knowledge of its falsity or without belief in its truth. A man who makes a statement recklessly, careless whether it be true or false, can have no actual belief in its truth.
4. The statement must be made with the intention that it should be acted upon by the injured party.
5. The representation must deceive. Deceit which does not deceive is not fraud. If the complainant was not influenced in his conduct by the misrepresentation, or if he relied upon his own judgment, there is no fraud. In other words, deceit which does not affect conduct cannot create liabilities. But

the fact that the plaintiff had and neglected the opportunity of ascertaining the falsity of the representation will not prejudice him.

In addition to rescission, the injured party may seek damages for fraud. This is not an action on the contract; it is an action in tort known as Fraud or Deceit, but for convenience it may be pursued in the action for rescission of the contract. This latter remedy of rescission is claimable, in the case of fraudulent misrepresentation, even though the contract is no longer executory. For example, where A, by B's fraud, is induced to buy the latter's land, A can rescind the contract even though the land has been already formally conveyed to him.

CONTRACTS UBERRIMAE FIDEI.

These are contracts of the utmost good faith. In the case of certain contracts it is not sufficient to refrain from saying what is untrue : there must be full disclosure of all material facts, i.e., all facts knowledge of which might influence the judgment of the other party as to whether or not to enter upon the contract, or as to the terms of the contract. The consequence of non-disclosure is to enable the other party to avoid the contract.

The contracts to which this doctrine applies are those of insurance, where the knowledge of facts and circumstances affecting the risk, lies substantially with the person seeking the insurance cover, his answers to the enquiries made by the insurance company being most material to the question whether the company will accept the risk either at the normal or a higher premium or indeed at all. Thus the proposer must make a full and truthful disclosure if he is not to run the risk of the insurance contract being repudiated.

The term is sometimes applied to contracts of suretyship and to certain contracts involving a fiduciary relation, such as contracts between partners, and between solicitor and client, but here the duty to disclosure does not arise during the preliminary negotiations but exists during the continuance of the relationship, and, therefore, they are not true examples of the application of the doctrine.

Even in the case of negotiations for a contract which is not strictly *uberrimae fidei*, although, in general, failure to disclose material facts (as opposed to making active misrepresentations) is not a ground for upsetting the contract subsequently made, yet as *With* v. *O'Flanagan* (1936) shows, if a statement has been made which was true when made but by the time the contract falls to be finalised has become false owing to a change of circumstances, it is the duty of the person who made the statement not to remain silent but to reveal the truth to the other party. If he remains silent the contract may, as in that case (which concerned the sale of a medical practice), be rescinded at the instance of that other party.

DURESS.

Duress is the pressure brought to bear upon one of the contracting parties by the other to induce him to enter into the contract. It consists in actual or threatened personal violence, imprisonment or restraint of personal liberty. The violence or threats may be offered to himself, his wife, child or parent. A contract entered into under duress is voidable.

Kaufman v. Gerson (1904).

G misappropriated the money of his employer, K, who threatened G's wife that, if she did not promise to make good the amount out of her own property, he would prosecute her husband. In consequence, G's wife agreed so to do on the express terms that there should be no prosecution.

*Held* that the contract could not be enforced against her, there having been " moral " coercion.

UNDUE INFLUENCE.

This (as developed by Equity) means any influence by which the exercise of free and deliberate judgment is excluded. It may arise in various ways, but in all cases the root of the matter is that the parties to a contract were not on a footing of equality with regard to forming a true conception of the implications of the contract.

It may arise from an obvious unfairness or inequality existing between the parties to a contract, as where one party is an educated and experienced man and the other is an uneducated and inexperienced individual, so that the relation becomes that of " the wolf and the lamb ". The onus is on the party benefiting from a contract of this nature to show that the other party did in fact exercise a free and independent judgment.

Thus in *Lloyds Bank Ltd.* v. *Bundy* (1974) (C.A.) the Court declined to assist the Bank to recover possession of premises owned and occupied as his sole asset by an old man who had mortgaged the property to the Bank to support the guarantee given by him in respect of his son's overdraft at the Bank. The Court stressed the fiduciary nature of the relationship between banker and customer (the old man was one such), the inequality of bargaining power between the parties and the need for independent advice.

The actual relations of the parties may set up the *presumption* that one of them has exerted an overbearing influence upon the other. Such recognised relations are those of parent and child, solicitor and client, medical man and patient, spiritual adviser and devotee. With the exception of solicitor and client, it is doubtful whether the presumption arising from these relations is as strong as it was a hundred years ago.

Where there is no manifest unfairness between the parties and there is no such recognised relation existing between them, then the presence or otherwise of undue influence is a question of fact.

It is most important to note that where there is a presumption of undue influence, it is necessary for the party presumed to have exercised the same to prove negatively that he did not do so. In other cases, the party in the weaker position must prove affirmatively that undue influence was in fact exercised.

The effect of undue influence is to confer a right of rescission upon the party of whom advantage has been taken. But he must act promptly, within a reasonable time of the withdrawal of the overbearing influence, or his lethargy may be construed as consent.

**Allcard v. Skinner (1887).**
The plaintiff, as a young woman, entered a religious order, and at various times made gifts of her property to the Superior. Eventually, she left the order, but not until five years afterwards did she seek to set aside the gifts on the ground of undue influence.

*Held* that the length of time elapsing, during which she had ample opportunity of independent advice, was evidence that she had acquiesced after the over-bearing influence had been withdrawn.

## Assignment of Contractual Rights.

Rights under a contract are termed *choses in action*, i.e., rights which can be enforced only by legal action, e.g., a debt, as opposed to *choses in possession*, which are things capable of physical possession, such as a tin of salmon. Assignment means transfer, and in this connection involves a change in the parties to the contract.

As explained in Chapter II, choses in action were not assignable at Common Law. Equity allowed assignment, the assignee bringing his action in the name of the assignor, who could be compelled to allow his name to be used for this purpose. Since 1873, however, legal assignments of debts and other legal choses in action have been possible.

Under the Judicature Act, 1873 (the relevant provision of which was repealed and re-enacted in section 136, Law of Property Act, 1925), a legal assignment may be made of debts and other *legal* choses in action, provided that :—

  (i) The assignment is in writing, signed by the assignor ;
  (ii) The assignment is absolute, and not by way of charge ; i.e., the assignment must be of the whole debt, not of a portion of it, but the assignment of the whole of a debt, with the proviso that the assignee is to have the benefit of part only, is an absolute assignment ;

(iii) Written notice is given to the person liable. This amount must be accurate as to the amount of the debt : *W. F. Harrison & Co., Ltd.* v. *Burke* (1956) ; *Van Lynn Developments Ltd.* v. *Pelias Construction Co. Ltd.* (1968).

An assignment complying with the section will enable the assignee to maintain an action in his own name without making the original creditor a party to the action.

All assignments are *subject to equities* ; i.e., an assignee takes subject to any right of set-off which the person bound may possess against the assignor, and subject, also, to the rights of third parties.

Assignments of rights arising out of certain choses in action, e.g., insurance policies and shares, are governed by statute or articles of association, and the prescribed form must be adopted.

Rights under contracts of a personal nature cannot be assigned. Thus, if A contracts with B to sing at B's theatre, B cannot assign his right under the contract to C, another theatre owner.

This rule is not limited to contracts of personal service.

**Kemp v. Baerselman (1906).**

B undertook to supply K, a confectioner, with all the eggs which he should require for his business for one year. K. on his part agreed not to purchase eggs elsewhere within the year, so long as B was ready to supply them. Within the year K sold his business to a company and purported to assign his contract with B to the company.

*Held* that, as the number of eggs to be supplied depended on K's personal requirements the contract was not assignable.

We have been considering assignments of *rights* under a contract. A liability under a contract cannot be assigned : the party to benefit cannot be compelled to accept performance from any other than the party bound. A creditor may assign his debt, but a debtor cannot relieve himself of liability by assigning it to another.

But liability under a contract may be transferred from one person to another by *novation*, i.e., a new contract, entered into by the parties to the old contract and the third party, which rescinds the old contract and substitutes a new one. This differs from assignment, where despite transfer the contract continues to exist. In return for the promise of the party entitled under the original contract to waive his rights under it, consideration must be given : the provision of a substitute to take over the obligation of the party originally liable constitutes the necessary consideration. Thus, suppose that A and B are in partnership and B wishes to retire, C to be a partner in his place. With the consent of the creditors of the firm of " A and B " B may be released in consideration of C taking his place and assuming his liabilities.

Assignments dealt with so far are known as assignments *by act of parties*. But there may also be assignments *by operation of law*, i.e., the involuntary assignment of rights *and liabilities*. These arise by :—

(i) *Death.* The personal representative of the deceased (i.e., his executor or administrator) stands in his shoes and acquires his rights and his liabilities to the extent of the deceased's estate. Rights and obligations arising out of contracts for personal services, however, are extinguished by the death of either party.

(ii) *Bankruptcy.* The Trustee in bankruptcy has vested in him all the rights of the bankrupt, except those of a purely personal nature, which in no way affect his property. Thus, rights of action for slander or assault, to mention but two examples, do not pass to the Trustee. Contracts for personal services to be performed by the bankrupt are not affected unless the bankrupt is willing to perform such services. The Trustee is also liable to the extent of the estate for any liabilities formerly due from the debtor. The Trustee may, however, disclaim onerous, i.e., burdensome, contracts, any person injured by the disclaimer proving in the bankruptcy for any damage he suffers thereby.

## Discharge of Contract.

A contract is discharged when the obligation created by it ceases to be binding on the promisor, who is no longer under a duty to perform his side of it.

Discharge may take place in various ways.

## A. Agreement.

An agreement to terminate a contract may take one of three forms :—

(1) *Waiver.*

Here the parties to a contract agree that it shall no longer be binding upon them. Just as consideration is necessary for the formation of a contract, so is it necessary for the discharge of it by agreement. When both parties still have obligations to perform the consideration will consist of mutual forbearances to demand fulfilment of those obligations. But if one party has performed all that he has to do under the contract, then there must be a new consideration moving from the other party for the former's promise to abandon the contract, or the agreement to abandon the contract must be under seal.

(2) *Substituted Contract.*

When the parties to a contract introduce fresh parties or fresh terms, so that, in effect, a new contract arises, the former contract is discharged.

(3) *Provisions for Discharge.*

The contract itself may provide for its own discharge. It may, for instance, make the completion subject to the fulfilment of a condition precedent ; i.e., there may be a provision that the contract is not to come into existence until a certain condition is fulfilled, e.g., " I will buy your car if you fit two new tyres to it." Unless and until two new tyres are fitted there is no obligation to take the car.

Again, the parties to a contract may agree that it shall be discharged by a condition subsequent ; i.e., there may be a condition that upon the occurrence of a certain event the contract shall become void, e.g., the ordinary " Excepted Perils " clause in a charterparty, whereby the occurrence of one of the stated " perils " discharges the shipowner from his duties under the contract.

Again, the terms of the contract may provide for the withdrawal of either party from the contract on terms. Contracts of employment usually contain a clause of this nature.

## B. Performance.

If performance is to be an absolute discharge of a contract, nothing must remain to be done thereunder by either party. When one party has performed all that he has to do under the contract, and there yet remain obligations to be performed by the other party, the contract is, of course, not discharged ; it is merely the obligations of the former party which are terminated.

Two forms of performance are worthy of detailed analysis.

(1) *Payment.*

This may operate as a discharge in that :—

(a) It may be the fulfilment of the contract itself.
(b) It may discharge a contract substituted for the original contract.
(c) It may be the fulfilment of a contract to waive the rights of action arising from the breach of the original contract.

Where a cheque or bill of exchange is accepted in discharge of a monetary obligation, its acceptance may operate as an absolute discharge or as a discharge conditional upon its being subsequently honoured. If taken in absolute discharge, the creditor has only one right of action, that on the cheque or bill itself. If, however, it is taken in conditional discharge, there are two rights of action, those on the cheque or bill and on the original contract. In the absence of evidence to the contrary, the presumption is in favour of a conditional discharge.

(2) *Tender.*
Strictly speaking, tender is not a performance of a contract, but an attempted performance which may, or may not, be a discharge of a contract according as it is applied to the performance of a promise to *do* something or to a promise to *pay* something. In the former case, tender, if refused, discharges the obligation. In the latter case, tender is not a discharge but may be a protection to the person making the tender, in that if, after refusal, the amount of the tender is paid into Court in the subsequent action and no greater amount is awarded by the Court, the debtor will be awarded his costs incurred in the action. To constitute a valid tender :—

(a) There must be an actual production of the money.
(b) The tender must be unconditional, but tender " under protest " is not conditional.
(c) It must not be less than the amount of the debt ; it may be more, but if so, " change " cannot be demanded.
(d) The tender must be a continuing one.
(e) The tender must be made to the creditor himself, or to his agent.
(f) It must be in legal tender ; that is, within the limits of particular forms of currency or coinage for the time being laid down by law. Those limits resulting from the introduction of decimal currency are at present laid down in s. 2 of the Coinage Act, 1971.

PAYMENT OF A LESSER AMOUNT IN DISCHARGE OF A GREATER.
This will not discharge the debt even where the creditor accepts the payment as in full settlement, unless there is some consideration for the creditor's promise to forego the balance : *D. & C. Builders Ltd.* v. *Rees* (1965). In the following cases, consideration is deemed to have been given :—

(a) Payment of a *liquidated* (i.e., definite) smaller sum in discharge of a *greater, unliquidated* amount (i.e., an uncertain sum). Thus, suppose that A has broken a contract with B and the latter maintains that he has suffered damage to the extent of £100. If B agrees to accept £50 in full settlement, this agreement is binding. The £50 is a liquidated sum, whereas damages for breach of a contract are unliquidated.
(b) Payment made *before it is legally due, or made by a third party* with the consent of the creditor.
(c) Composition made by a debtor with his creditors.

In other words, in order that the payment of a smaller amount may operate as a discharge, the thing done or given must be in some way *different from that which the recipient is entitled to demand*. Something other than money will operate as a full discharge if it is accepted as such.

The case of *Central London Property Trust, Ltd.* v. *High Trees House, Ltd.* (1947), discussed in Chapter III, shows that the absence of consideration is not material where the creditor has promised to reduce rent or other periodical payments, the promise was intended to create legal relations and has been acted upon by the promisee-debtor. Any such suspension of contractual rights may, of course, operate only temporarily, since the party making concessions may properly give notice that he intends to resume his full strict rights as from a future date.

APPROPRIATION OF PAYMENTS.

Where a debtor owes a creditor more than one amount, and makes a payment insufficient to satisfy the whole, the money is appropriated in accordance with the following rules :—

(a) To whichever debt the debtor desires, provided he exercises his option, either by word or by conduct, at the time of payment or such other time as the opportunity to appropriate *first* presents itself to him : *Peters* v. *Anderson* (1814).

There must be something more than a mere intention on the part of the debtor, uncommunicated to the creditor, to amount to an appropriation by him : *Leeson* v. *Leeson* (1936).

(b) If the debtor does not elect, the creditor may do so : *Peters* v. *Anderson* (*supra*). The appropriation by the creditor may be at any time prior to the communication of appropriation by the debtor, or prior to, or during, an action : *Seymour* v. *Pickett* (1905), and it may be to any legal or equitable claim, even though statute-barred (i.e., even though action has not been taken within the period of time stipulated by law), but not to a debt arising upon an illegal contract. An appropriation by a creditor may be revoked at any time prior to its communication to the debtor, but not after : *Friend* v. *Young* (1897).

(c) If there is a *current account*, i.e., a continuing account of successive credits and debits, e.g., a current account with a bank, and neither party appropriates, the appropriation is made by presumption of law to the debit items in the order in which they were incurred, beginning with the first *enforceable* debt : Rule in *Clayton's Case* (1816). This means that the first payments in are appropriated to the first items on the debit side of the account. This presumption may be rebutted either by direct evidence or by an opposite legal presumption of greater force : *Re Hallet's Estate* (1880) (trust moneys).

## C. Breach.

Whilst every breach of contract gives a right of action to the injured party, it does not necessarily follow that he is absolved from his obligations under the contract. The breach may be of the whole contract or of only a part of it, and of such a minor part that the foundation of the contract may remain. Even if the partial breach is so important that the contract may be regarded as discharged, the injured party may content himself with an action for damages. A breach of contract in the strict sense destroys the contract, it relieves the injured party from further obligations under the contract and gives a right of action in its place. Where the complaint is that an obligation under a contract remains unfulfilled, there is no true breach ; the contract is still in existence, but it is executory.

A breach in the strict sense may take place in varying circumstances. One party to the contract, for instance, may repudiate his liabilities thereunder. This means the definite assertion by a party that he has no intention to fulfil his obligations, and enables the other party to regard the contract as discharged, even though the time for performance has not yet arrived ; the party in default then being said to have committed an "anticipatory breach" : *Hochster* v. *De la Tour* (1853). A similar principle applies when repudiation takes place *during* the performance of a contract. On the other hand, the party not at fault may elect to treat the contract as still binding and hold the other party responsible for the consequences of non-performance. Where he so elects, however, the party at fault may take advantage of any circumstances which may subsequently release him from the contract, e.g., the outbreak of war, as in *Avery* v. *Bowden* (1855).

[*White & Carter (Councils), Ltd.* v. *McGregor* (1961)—a decision of the House of Lords—underlined the availability of the "election" referred to above, Lord Hodson saying : " I have never been able to understand what effect repudiation by one party has unless the other party accepts [it] . . . ; if . . . there was no acceptance, the contract remains alive for the benefit of both parties . . ." On that footing, the plaintiffs recovered the contract price, as such, and were not relegated to securing merely damages for an anticipatory breach by the defendants which the plaintiffs had not accepted as a repudiation. The need for acceptance of repudiation (if at all) was stressed in *Decro-Wall International S.A.* v. *Practitioners in Marketing Ltd.* (1971).]

Again, one party to the contract may render its performance impossible. If a party has rendered himself incapable of carrying out his obligations under a contract, the other party has an immediate right to regard the contract as having been broken.

Again, there may be a failure of performance on the part of one of the parties. Where one party to a contract refuses or renders himself unable to perform his obligations, the other party has not only a right of action, he has the right to consider himself absolved from carrying out *his* obligations. Where, however, the breach is the result of a *failure* of one party to carry out his obligations in whole or in part, the question arises : Is the other party absolved from the contract in addition to having his right of action, or is he still bound to perform his obligations and then sue for damages? There are three possibilities :—

(i) If the promises of the parties are simultaneous or interdependent, the failure of one party absolves the other.
(ii) A term of a contract may be either a prime element upon the fulfilment of which the whole contract is based, or it may be a mere subsidiary element the failure to implement which will give a right to an action for damages but will not act as a discharge to the injured party. This is the difference between a condition and a warranty (see p. 77).
(iii) A contract may consist of a number of terms so that it may be partially performed. That is to say, there may be divisible promises. Here, the question is : What degree of failure of performance will discharge the contract ? This situation often arises in instalment contracts—contracts to receive and pay for goods by instalments. There is no absolute rule, but if the failure to perform is such as to amount to an implied repudiation of the contract, or if what is left undone renders what is done of little or no value to the injured party, he may well claim that the contract is discharged and that he is freed from his obligations thereunder.

## D. Subsequent Impossibility (Frustration).

As a general rule, the fact that a contract has become incapable of performance does not discharge the contract, and the defaulting party is liable in damages despite the fact that his inability to perform is occasioned by circumstances outside his control. The apparent harshness of this rule is justified when one considers that, if a person voluntarily makes an absolute promise, without any reservation or qualification that he has full opportunity of imposing, then he must stand to his promise. This rule, however, will not apply if the contract depends for its operation on the existence or occurrence of a particular object or state of things as its very foundation, so that both parties must have intended that the contract should be at an end if such foundation ceased to exist. If the Court so construes a contract, it will *imply* a term in the contract to that effect. Thus, there are the following circumstances in which a contract will be discharged by subsequent impossibility :—

(i) *Where the impossibility is caused by a change in the law.* Thus, in *Baily* v. *De Crespigny* (1869), D had leased land to B and had covenanted not to build on adjoining land retained by him. Acting under a subsequent Act of Parliament, a railway company compulsorily acquired D's land and built on it. The Court held that D's liability under the covenant was extinguished. There must, however, be a *change* in the law. If *at the time of the contract* statutory powers exist for the *exercise* of certain rights which will prevent the performance of the contract, a *subsequent exercise* of such powers will not discharge the contract. Thus, in *Walton Harvey, Ltd.* v. *Walker & Homfrays, Ltd.* (1931), X had the right for a certain period to exhibit advertisements on Y's premises. During this period the premises were compulsorily bought by the Local Authority in pursuance of its existing powers. It was held that the contract was not thereby discharged, as Y was aware of the risk of compulsory requisition and must be taken to have accepted the risk. He was, therefore, held liable for damages for breach of contract.

(ii) *Where the accidental destruction of a specific thing upon the existence of which the contract depends renders performance impossible.* C agreed to let a music-hall to T for a series of concerts. Before the appointed day the music-hall was accidentally destroyed by fire. The contract was held to be discharged : *Taylor* v. *Caldwell* (1865).

(iii) *Where the contract depends upon the happening of a specific event which does not occur.* Thus, contracts to hire seats or windows along the line of route of a procession for the particular day on which it is to take place are discharged when it is postponed. Many examples of this nature arose out of the postponement of the coronation of King Edward VII. If, however, the occurrence of the event is not the sole basis on which both parties contracted, the non-occurrence of the event does not discharge the contract. Thus, where a ship was chartered for the purpose of seeing a coronation review *and* to cruise round the fleet, the cancellation of the review did not discharge the contract.

(iv) *Where a person bound by a contract to perform personal services is unable to carry out his obligations by reason of death or serious illness.* Contracts for musical, artistic or histrionic activities come within this exception.

(v) *Where through a vital change of circumstances the contract as a commercial venture is frustrated.* Thus, a contract whereby a ship is chartered for a *short* span of time will be frustrated as a commercial venture and rendered void by reason of subsequent impossibility if the vessel is requisitioned by the Government for the duration of a war.

Formerly, it was considered that when subsequent impossibility discharged a contract, it did not discharge it *ab initio* (from the beginning) but only from the time of the occurrence of the impossibility. Thus, the loss lay where it fell, so that (*a*) money not due at the time of the dissolution of the contract could not be claimed, (*b*) money due but not paid could be recovered, and (*c*) money rightly paid under the contract before its dissolution could not be recovered by the payer. However, the legal consequences of frustration were regulated afresh by the Law Reform (Frustrated Contracts) Act, 1943. Under this Act, with certain exceptions such as insurance contracts, all sums paid to a party under a frustrated contract shall be recoverable from him as money received by him to the use of the paying party, and all sums payable under the contract shall cease to be payable. The Court may, however, in its discretion, allow the party to whom the money was paid or payable to retain or recover, as the case may be, a sum equivalent to any expenses incurred in, or for the purpose of, the performance of the contract. Further, where any party to such a contract has before its discharge obtained a valuable benefit from the other party other than a payment of money, the party so benefited must pay to the other party such sum, not exceeding the value of the benefit to him, as the Court thinks just.

### E. Lapse of Time.

In general, apart from some provision in the contract, lapse of time does not discharge a contract, but the *remedy by action* is extinguished under the Limitation Act, 1939 (as amended). Under this Act :—

(*a*) All actions on simple contracts or to enforce a recognizance (i.e., an obligation or bond acknowledged before a Court of record or authorized officer and enrolled in some Court of record, the object being to secure performance of some act, e.g., to keep the peace) are barred after six years.

(*b*) Actions on specialty contracts or judgments are barred after twelve years.

(*c*) Actions to recover money secured by a mortgage or charge on property, or to recover the proceeds of sale of land, are barred after twelve years.

(*d*) Actions to recover arrears of interest on a judgment debt or on money secured by a mortgage or charge are barred after six years from the date when the interest became due.

(*e*) Actions to recover land are barred after twelve years. *Here the title to the land, not merely the right of action, is extinguished.*

Formerly, special periods of limitation were provided by statute in certain cases, e.g., in actions against Public Authorities, but these provisions have been repealed by the Law Reform (Limitation of Actions, Etc.) Act, 1954. This Act also provides that an action for personal injuries arising out of breach of contractual duty is barred after three years (but there may be an extension by leave of the Court pursuant to the Limitation Act, 1975).

The time runs not from the date of the contract, but from the date on which the plaintiff can first bring his action. Where, however, he is under a disability, such as minority or insanity when the cause of action accrues, the period is, in ordinary cases, six years from the cessation of the disability or from the death of the plaintiff, whichever first occurs. Once the time has begun to run, however, subsequent disabilities do not affect the operation of the Act.

Ignorance of a right of action does not as a rule prevent time from running under the Act; but where the action is based on the defendant's fraud, or where the plaintiff is unaware of his right of action by reason of the defendant's fraud, or where the action is for relief from the consequences of a mistake, the period will begin to run from the time when the fraud or mistake could, by the exercise of reasonable diligence, have been discovered.

The remedy by action is revived by a written acknowledgment, part payment or payment of interest, the date of which is then deemed to be the date of accrual of the right of action.

### F. Merger and Estoppel.

These matters have already been dealt with in Chapter III.

### G. Material Alteration.

An alteration of a material part of a deed or written contract, made by one party intentionally and without the consent of the other, will discharge the contract.

A material alteration is one *which alters the legal effect of the contract*, not, for example, the correction of a misdescription of a party, or the insertion in a deed of the true date of execution after execution thereof.

### H. Death and Bankruptcy.

As has been said already, the death of either party to a contract for personal services discharges the contract. It has also been seen that a Trustee in bankruptcy cannot enforce a contract involving personal services.

### Remedies for Breach of Contract.

The remedies available to a person injured by a breach of contract are :—

1. A right of action for damages in respect of the breach of the contract or some term of it.
2. A right of action on a *quantum meruit*, i.e., a right to sue in respect of what he had already done before the breach occurred.
3. A decree of specific performance compelling the other party to carry out his obligations, or an injunction restraining him from violating them.

1. **Damages.** In an action for breach of contract, a real attempt is made to award damages in money which will compensate the injured party, in so far as money can be a compensation, for the breach of the contract. The injured party will not necessarily be recouped to the full extent of his loss. Only such loss will be considered as would have been contemplated by an ordinary prudent man in the position of the parties as likely to follow from a breach of the contract. If *special* damages are claimed for a peculiar loss, the claimant must prove that the possibility of unusual loss was brought to the notice of the other party at the time of the contract, and that he contracted on the basis of this possibility. These propositions emerge from the leading case of *Hadley* v. *Baxendale* (1854). Express notice is not required if the special circumstances are, or should be, in fact known to the other party at the time of the contract.

Thus, in *Horne* v. *Midland Railway Co.* (1873), H delivered a consignment of shoes to the company for carriage to London. The shoes were supplied for use by the French Army at a price greatly above the market price, a condition being that they should be delivered by a certain date. Horne told the company that the contract would be " off " if the shoes were not delivered by the specified date, but he did not advise them of the exceptional price. Owing to unreasonable delay in transit, the shoes were not delivered to time, and the purchasers refused acceptance. It was held that H could recover damages for delay, but such must be limited to the difference between the price at which H ultimately sold the shoes and the ordinary market price, not the contract price.

Furthermore, damages for breach of contract must be awarded on the purely impersonal basis of compensation : no account must be taken of injured feelings ; although in *Jarvis* v. *Swans Tours Ltd.* (1973) (C.A.) damages were awarded for mental distress and for inconvenience suffered by reason of a holiday not living up to the brochure advertising it. Cp. *Jackson* v. *Horizon Holidays* (1975). In other words, damages must be compensatory, not punitive. But in one case exemplary damages, damages in excess of the actual loss, may be awarded, namely for a banker's wrongful dishonour of his customer's cheque.

On the other hand, *nominal* damages, e.g. ten new pence, are awarded when the defendant has committed a breach of contract but the plaintiff has in fact suffered no damage.

Moreover the injured party must take reasonable steps to minimize the damage resulting from breach. In the case of non-delivery of goods, for instance, he should at once buy others to replace them, not wait until the market price has risen.

The above remarks apply to *unliquidated* damages, damages " made clear " or awarded by the Court on the trial of an action and not provided for in the contract. Where the contract does provide for the payment of a certain sum on breach, such sum may be either liquidated damages—an agreed and reasonable compensation for loss—or a penalty—an imposition fixed irrespective of the extent of the loss, with a view to ensuring performance of the contract. Where the parties have made a genuine attempt to pre-assess the consequences of breach, the Court will regard the amount stated as liquidated damages and will enter judgment therefor, without proof of the actual loss. If, however, there has been no such attempt, if the sum specified has been inserted *in terrorem*, as a " frightener ", to ensure performance of the contract, the Court will disregard it and will assess damages in the ordinary way.

The term used by the parties themselves to describe the sum is not conclusive. The following propositions have been established by the Courts :—

(i) The sum must be treated as a penalty if it is extravagant and unreasonable in amount by comparison with the greatest loss that could ensue from breach of the contract.

(ii) Where the payment of a smaller sum is secured by a larger sum, the latter is a penalty.

(iii) There is a *presumption* that the sum inserted is a penalty when " a single lump sum is made payable by way of compensation on the occurrence of one or more or all of several events, some of which may occasion serious damage, and others but trifling damage."

If the agreed sum is in the nature of liquidated damages, no higher sum may be awarded, even though, in the event, the consequences of breach have been much more serious than the parties anticipated.

2. *Quantum meruit* (" As much as he has earned "). In the event of a breach of contract, the injured party may have a claim other than that for damages. He may have performed services under the contract, and for such he is entitled to claim on a *quantum meruit*. This action is quite distinct from the action for breach of contract. The basis of the pleading is that certain work has been done and that such has been accepted without demur by the other party. The work may have been part of the

original contract, or it may be work done under it, or it may be quite independent of the contract. In any case the defendant must have had a reasonable opportunity of rejecting the offer. Even the party in fault may have a right to a claim on a *quantum meruit* if the other party has accepted and had the benefit of so much of the work as he had performed. This, however, does not apply if the contract is indivisible, i.e., if it is a contract to do one piece of work in consideration of a lump-sum payment.

### Cutter v. Powell (1795).

A sailor was hired for a voyage from Jamaica to Liverpool, on the terms of being paid 30 guineas after arrival of the ship at Liverpool, provided he continued to do his duty until that time. He died on the voyage.

*Held* that his executors were not entitled to receive anything. They could not receive 30 guineas because the contract imposed one indivisible obligation which had not been performed. They could not recover a reasonable sum for the work done, because that would imply an obligation to pay such a sum and that obligation would contradict the terms of the express contract.

It would appear that the decision in this case has been modified by the Law Reform (Frustrated Contracts) Act, 1943, which allows a party who has done something in performance of the contract prior to the frustrating event to claim compensation for any benefit thereby conferred upon the other.

If the performance of the contract is prevented by the act of the other party, then, even though the contract is indivisible, a claim on a *quantum meruit* may be made by the aggrieved party.

### O'Neil v. Armstrong (1895).

The plaintiff, an Englishman, was engaged by the captain of a Japanese warship to act as fireman on a voyage from England to Japan. During the voyage Japan declared war on China, and the plaintiff's continued performance of his engagement would have been illegal under the Foreign Enlistment Act, 1870.

*Held* that the plaintiff was entitled to refuse to continue performance of the contract and to sue for the wages he had earned up till the time when performance of the contract became illegal.

But if the contract is not divisible, the party in default cannot claim the value of what he has done. In *Sumpter* v. *Hedges* (1898) a builder contracted to erect a house for a specified sum. He abandoned the work before it was completed. It was held that he could not claim the value of the materials he had used and the labour he had expended. Where, however, the work is substantially completed, even if there be small defects in the work and differences from what was originally agreed on, the full amount due under the contract may be claimed, with an allowance for the defects and differences: *Hoenig* v. *Issacs* (1952). This is the doctrine of " substantial performance ". It could not be applied in *Bolton* v. *Mahaveda* (1972) because of the extent of the deficiencies in the heating system installed under the contract.

The doctrine of frustration has never been applied to a case where completion of the contract is possible but has been delayed (e.g. by scarcity of labour), and a *quantum meruit* claim will not, therefore, be entertained in that respect : *Davis Contractors, Ltd.* v. *Fareham Urban District Council* (1956).

3. Specific Performance and Injunction. These remedies have two characteristics in common : they are supplementary and they are discretionary.

The following principles are followed by the Court in deciding whether to grant the remedy of specific performance :—

> (a) Where damages alone are an adequate remedy, specific performance will not be given, for Equity " follows the law " ; it does not supplant it. A contract for the sale of land will usually be a fit subject for a decree for specific performance, for an award of damages would not necessarily put the injured party in the position he would have occupied if the contract had been duly performed by his obtaining the particular land. On the other hand a contract to lend money or to sell goods otherwise readily obtainable in the open market would not be specifically enforced;
> (b) If supervision by the Court of the performance of the contract is impossible, specific performance will not be given. Examples : A contract of a continuing nature like an instalment contract (this does not mean a hire-purchase transaction but a contract envisaging " performance " in stages) or a contract involving personal services ;
> (c) The contract must be certain, fair and just, and the conduct of the party asking for specific performance must be irreproachable, e.g., he must not have induced the contract by unethical conduct as, for example, by snap acceptance of an offer which he knows was made in error as to a material term such as price ; £500 when £5,000 was intended ;
> (d) There must be mutuality, i.e., the contract must be specifically enforceable against both parties, e.g., specific performance of a specialty contract lacking consideration would not be given, nor would it be granted against, or at the suit of, a minor.

The Court may grant an injunction to restrain the breach of a negative contract, provided that it is enforceable, for in such cases the injunction " does nothing more than give the sanction of the process of the Court to that which already is the contract between the parties ". As a general rule, the Court does not *offer* either of its discretionary remedies in contracts of a personal nature, because their enforcement would (as previously mentioned) entail continuous supervision by the Court. But it has been pointed out in Chapter II that where a contract for personal service contains a *negative* term, e.g., that the party bound will not work for any person other than the other party to the contract, this negative stipulation may be enforced by injunction as it was in *Lumley* v. *Wagner* (1852). Even here, however, the Court will not intervene if the granting of an injunction would compel the defendant either to work for the plaintiff alone, or remain idle, as this would amount to the indirect enforcement of a contract for personal services.

### Quasi-Contracts.

It is not possible in a book of this scope to give a detailed analysis of this subject, which is a territory not fully explored even yet and a matter of judicial and academic controversy. Professor Winfield has defined " genuine quasi-contract " as " liability, not exclusively referable to any other head of law, imposed on a particular person to pay money to another particular person on the ground of unjust benefit ".

The rights and liabilities involved do not arise from agreement but are implied by law by virtue of the particular relations of the parties. The matters dealt with under this head have little or no affinity to contract : there is no " consent ". The following are examples :—

(a) *Money paid by A to the use of B.* If B requests or allows A to take up a position in which he is compelled by law to discharge B's legal liabilities, the law imports a request and a promise made by B to A : a request to make the payment, and a promise to repay. Thus, a surety who has paid the whole of a debt may recover contribution from his co-sureties in an action for money paid to the use of the others.

(b) *Money received by A to the use of B.* For example, the plaintiff pays money to the defendent in pursuance of a transaction which he believes to be a contract but which proves to be no contract. Thus, there may be a *total* failure of consideration. In *Rowland* v. *Divall* (1923), the plaintiff bought a motor car from the defendant and used it for several months. He then discovered that the defendant had no title to the car, and he was compelled to restore the car to the true owner. The plaintiff was allowed to recover the price paid from the defendant, the latter's plea that there was only a partial failure of consideration failing because the plaintiff had contracted to buy the car, not to hire it. Similarly, a person may recover money he has paid under a void contract. But, if the contract is not merely void but illegal, then, in general, money paid thereunder is irrecoverable.

(c) *Money paid under a mistake of fact.* Money so paid is recoverable. Money paid under a mistake of law cannot, save in exceptional circumstances, be recovered. We have seen, however, that a mistake as to private rights is treated as a mistake of fact.

(d) *Alternative rights of action.* It may sometimes happen that A has a right of action against B, not founded on contract. A does not wish to exercise that right, but, at the same time, desires recompense. He may sue B on a quasi-contract, waiving his former rights.

For example, if A buys an excursion ticket on a railway and one of the conditions is that A shall not take more than 28 lbs. of luggage with him, but nevertheless A takes 56 lbs. of luggage, the law will imply a promise by A to pay freight on the extra 28 lbs. and an action will lie for it.

## Interpretation of Contracts.

In construing a contract, the Court will give to the words used their ordinary and literal sense, but seek to give effect to the intentions of the parties so far as lawful. Proved commercial customs or trade usages may be read into the contract unless inconsistent with the express terms and oral evidence be admitted to explain a latent as opposed to a patent ambiguity ; to prove collateral terms or warranties ; or to prove rescission of a written contract. Moreover, the Court will, when to do so would not override an express term, imply a term in order to give efficacy to the contract in accordance with the intention of the parties.

## CHAPTER V

## LAW OF PERSONS

Persons in law (bearers of rights and duties) may be natural or artificial. Natural persons are ordinary individuals, whereas artificial persons are a creation of law, e.g., a limited liability company which, although artificial, is nevertheless regarded as a " person " for many legal purposes.

### A. NATURAL PERSONS

**Minors.**

At birth a child becomes for most purposes of civil law a minor, and remains such until majority is reached on the attainment of the eighteenth anniversary of such birth. The effect of minority upon contractual liability has been described already in Chapter III. The position of a minor with regard to the ownership of land and his liability for tort will be considered in later Chapters as will the effect of age in relation to crime.

As regards marriage, the Marriage Act, 1949, renders void the marriage of persons either of whom is under the age of sixteen. Even above that age, until the minor attains eighteen, the parents or guardians may veto the marriage by withholding their consent, but the Court has power to override such refusal of consent.

As regards testamentary capacity, a minor cannot make a valid will unless he is a soldier or airman on active service or a mariner at sea. A person who has attained majority but is still under the age of twenty-one is unable to sit as a member of either House of Parliament.

It may be noted that a person under the age of eighteen may, if the rules do not otherwise provide, be admitted as a member of a Building Society and give all necessary receipts ; he cannot, however, while remaining under full age vote or hold any office in the society : sections 9 and 47, Building Societies Act, 1962 (as read with the Family Law Reform Act, 1969). Since a minor cannot hold a legal estate in land (see p. 153) he is in the position of being competent to be an investing member of a Building Society but incompetent to be a borrowing member.

## How a Minor Sues or is Sued.

Where it is necessary to take action in the Courts to protect or enforce the rights of a minor, a responsible person (generally the father) is appointed to act as his " next friend ". Where the minor is properly made a defendant to proceedings, similarly a responsible person is appointed as his guardian *ad litem* [the second italicized word comes from the Latin ' lis ' meaning a law suit : hence our word " litigation "].

## Parents and Guardians.

It is the duty of the father to maintain his children while under age, a duty which, in the appropriate circumstances, is cast upon the widow. Similarly, he must ensure that his children take advantage of the educational facilities provided by the State, in so far as he himself does not make adequate provision for this purpose. By the consolidating Guardianship of Minors Act, 1971 (as read with the Guardianship Act, 1973, and the Children Act, 1975), father and mother are equally entitled to the care, custody and upbringing of their children who are minors. Any dispute in respect of such matters is decided by the Court, the welfare of the child being the paramount consideration. On the death of either parent, guardianship devolves upon the survivor, who must, however, act in conjunction with any guardian appointed by the deceased parent by deed or will. In the event of misconduct or unfitness, or, in an emergency, the Court may appoint a guardian. A parent or guardian has the right to administer *reasonable* punishment, and this power may be delegated, expressly or impliedly, to such persons as schoolmasters.

## Illegitimacy.

There is a strong presumption that a child born in lawful wedlock, or within due time after the termination thereof, is legitimate. Illegitimate children, as such had at Common Law no right of succession to the property of their fathers, but an illegitimate child succeeded to the property of its mother in the absence of legitimate issue. Of course, a father might provide expressly for his illegitimate children by his will, but in general, the term, " children ", was (at Common Law) construed as meaning legitimate children.

The custody of an illegitimate child is vested in the mother and she is primarily liable for its maintenance, but, by taking the appropriate proceedings before justices, under the Affiliation Proceedings Act, 1957 (as amended) and on due proof of paternity, she may obtain a limited contribution from the father until the child attains the age of sixteen.

In recent years, however, statute has moved considerably in the direction of placing, for the most part, legitimate and illegitimate offspring on the same footing. For example, illegitimate relations are included among the dependants on whose behalf an action may be brought under the Fatal Accidents Acts, 1846 to 1959 (see now consolidating Fatal Accidents Act, 1976), in respect of the death of a person through the wrongful act, neglect or default of another.

More importantly, under the Family Law Reform Act, 1969 at least two beneficial results occur. In the first place it is provided in Section 15 that in any disposition (this includes a will or codicil) made after the coming into force of the section (1st January, 1970) " any reference to the child or children of any person shall, unless the contrary intention appears, be construed as, or as including, a reference to any illegitimate child of that person . . .". Nevertheless, the technical meaning of " heir " is preserved and the Act does not affect the devolution of property limited so as to devolve with a dignity or title of honour. Moreover, an illegitimate child is entitled to the benefit of the provisions of the Inheritance (Family Provision) Act, 1938 (as amended) (now replaced by the Inheritance (Provision for Family and Dependants) Act, 1975) see *post* p. 204. Secondly, as far as the law of intestacy is concerned (see *post* p. 211) an illegitimate child may now succeed on the intestacy of either parent and vice versa.

By the Legitimacy Act, 1926, Parliament recognized at last the principle of *legitimation* of an illegitimate child by the subsequent marriage of its parents. Legitimation could take place only where :—

(a) The father was domiciled (i.e., permanently resident) in England or Wales at the date of the marriage ;
(b) Neither parent was married to a third person at the date of the birth ;
(c) The legitimated person was living on or after the 1st January, 1927.

The legitimation took effect (1) from the 1st January, 1927, where the parents married before that date, or (2) from the date of the marriage in any other case.

The Legitimacy Act, 1959, removed obstacle (b), so that suppose a child is born to A during the subsistence of her marriage to B, the child being offspring of an adulterous association between A and C ; B then obtains a divorce from A on the score of that adultery, whereupon, after decree absolute, A and C marry, the effect of the latter marriage is to legitimate the child. Where the father was not domiciled in England or Wales at the date of the marriage, but was, at the time of the marriage, domiciled in some other place the law of which recognizes legitimation by subsequent marriage, English law recognizes such legitimation.

The Children Act, 1975, made some amendments and clarifications to the legislation and the Legitimacy Act, 1976, has now consolidated the relevant statutory provisions.

Upon the death of a relative intestate, i.e., without making a will disposing of his entire property, a legitimated person is entitled to succeed as if he had been born legitimate, provided that the intestate dies after the date of legitimation.

In the case of an entailed interest, i.e., property given to a person, and, after his death, to a specified class of his heirs, legitimated persons may take the property only where the interest is created after the date on which the legitimation takes effect (see page 180).

The legislation excludes legitimated persons from succeeding to titles of honour, or to property limited to devolve along with a title of honour. Where the title to property depends upon the relative seniority of a number of persons, e.g., where entailed property descends to the heir, legitimated persons rank as if they had been born on the date on which their legitimation became effective.

Upon the death intestate of a legitimated person, those persons succeed who would be entitled, had the deceased been born legitimate.

## Adoption.

Prior to 1927, English law accorded no recognition to the practice of adoption, which created no legal relationship between the parties. However, under the Adoption Act, 1926, the institution of adoption was recognized and it is possible to obtain an " adoption order " from the Court having prescribed legal consequences and constituting a definite legal relationship between the adopting and the adopted parties. The Act regulating this matter (subject to certain amendments made in 1960 and 1964 as well as provisions in the Adoption Act, 1968, giving effect to the Hague Convention on the Adoption of Children and facilitating the making and recognition of adoption orders accordingly) came to be the Adoption Act, 1958. However, provisions in the Children Act, 1975, made some substantial amendments (including the tightening up of controls over adoption agencies and imposing additional duties on local government authorities) and the Adoption Act, 1976, consolidated the statutory provisions on the topic. Under the legislation, the rights and duties of the natural parents or the guardians of the adopted person are extinguished and the parental rights and duties become vested in the adopter(s). The powers and duties relating to the custody, maintenance and education of the child are vested in the adoptive parent or parents, who have, in the event of death, the same power of appointing guardians as natural parents. An adopted person who has attained the age of 18 years is entitled to obtain from the Registrar General a certified copy of the record of his birth.

For the purpose of succession to property under intestacies occurring after the adoption order, the adopted person is deemed to be the legitimate child of the adopter, and is not deemed to be the child of his natural parents. Similarly, a reference to a child or children made in any disposition or will coming into force after the adoption order shall, unless the contrary intention appears, be construed as referring to the adopted person. The general effect of these provisions is to extinguish, for the purposes of succession to property, the relationship between the adopted person and his natural parents, and to substitute the relationship between the adopted person and his adopted parents.

Basically, the conditions which must exist before a child can be legally adopted in England under the legislation are as follows :—

(a) There must be an application to the High Court or the appropriate County Court or Magistrates' Court and the applicant(s) must be domiciled in a part of the United Kingdom or the Channel Islands or the Isle of Man or the application must be for a Convention adoption order (that is, one made under the 1968 Act above referred to).

(b) The child must be under the age of 18 and unmarried but have attained a minimum age (varying from 14 weeks to twelve months according to the circumstances) and have had its home with the applicant(s) for a given period before the making of the adoption order.

(c) The applicant must be :—
  (i) the mother or father of the child (special provisions apply where one of the natural parents is dead or cannot be traced) ; or
  (ii) A relative of the child who has attained 21 ; or
  (iii) A stranger-in-blood who has attained 21.

(d) An adoption order is not to be made in respect of a child who is a female in favour of a sole applicant who is a male, unless the court is satisfied that there are special circumstances which justify as an exceptional measure the making of an adoption order.

(e) Requisite consents must (unless dispensed with) be obtained, e.g., of the parent or guardian ; or of the other of two spouses one of whom makes the application.

(f) Unless the child has been placed with the applicant(s) by an adoption agency, the local authority has been notified of the application and made an investigation and report to the Court, the Court must be satisfied that the making of an adoption order will be for the welfare of the child; in this regard first consideration must be given to the need to safeguard and promote such welfare throughout his childhood. The Court " shall so far as practicable ascertain the wishes and feelings of the child regarding the decision and give due consideration to them, having regard to his age and understanding."

As an alternative to adoption the Court may make a custodianship order introduced by the Children Act, 1975.

## Marriage.

According to the English conception, marriage is the permanent union of one man with one woman to the exclusion of all others.

A marriage may be celebrated according to the predilection of the parties in the form they desire, always presupposing that the statutory requirements are complied with (these being those laid down in the Marriage Acts, 1949–1970). Thus it may be celebrated either in the presence of a clergyman of the Church of England or of a Registrar of Marriages. Where the parties are not " Anglicans ", the marriage may take place according to the religious or other tenets of the parties but either as a preliminary the authority of a Superintendent Registrar's certificate is required or his attendance arranged for a separate civil ceremony. Thus armed, Jews, Quakers, Roman Catholics and others may go through the customary ceremonies in their own places of worship.

Every marriage must be preceded by a step or steps intended to secure publicity before the celebration, like banns, Bishop's licence, Archbishop of Canterbury's special licence or Registrar's licence.

A concomitant of every marriage ceremony is the recording thereof in the appropriate register under the ultimate control of the Superintendent-General of Births, Marriages and Deaths.

Under the Acts a marriage solemnized between persons either of whom is under the age of sixteen is void. Above that age but below the age of majority (18 by virtue of the Family Law Reform Act, 1969) consent is required by the parents or in the last resort by the Court.

The legislation states the prohibited degrees of relationship precluding marriage.

**Nullity.**

The Nullity of Marriage Act, 1971 (as since slightly amended) re-stated the law on the topic inherent in its title. The only ground on which a marriage taking place after the commencement of the Act is *void* is that it is not a valid marriage under the provisions of the Marriage Acts, 1949–1970, e.g., because either of the parties was under the age of sixteen or within the prohibited degrees of relationship. Although a decree of nullity is not required, it is advisable to seek one for the sake of certainty. Grounds on which a decree of nullity can be obtained of a marriage that is alleged to be *voidable* include lack of consent to the marriage by one party or his or her lack of capacity to consummate the marriage.

The Act of 1971 was repealed by the Matrimonial Causes Act, 1973 and its provisions replaced therein.

Notwithstanding the annulment, a child born of a *voidable* marriage is deemed legitimate.

**Divorce.**

Under the Matrimonial Causes Act, 1973 (a consolidating Act incorporating the radical changes effected by the Divorce Reform Act, 1969—with its abandonment of the old concept of the matrimonial offence as committed against an " innocent party ") a decree of dissolution of marriage may be granted on one ground and one ground only, namely, irretrievable breakdown of marriage, of which breakdown one or other of the five factual situations listed in the Act are symptomatic or a manifestation.

The factual situations covers such matters as adultery by the respondent in a context in which the petitioner finds it intolerable to live with the respondent ; conduct by the respondent which it would be unreasonable to expect the petitioner to overlook in deciding whether to continue to live with the respondent ; desertion by the respondent for at least two years ; separation for an extended period (in the case of two years' separation the consent of the respondent is requisite to a decree ; in the case of separation for five years or more the decree can be granted *in invitum* subject to the protection of the financial interests of the respondent).

Desertion is the wilful cessation of cohabitation without the other party's consent. It may be either (a) *actual*, where the offending party withdraws from cohabitation, or (b) *constructive*, where the conduct of the offending party is sufficiently gross to justify the other party's withdrawal from cohabitation. One of the aims of the legislation being to promote reconciliation, it is provided that resumption of cohabitation for a period not exceeding three months for the purpose of reconciliation is not to interrupt desertion.

No petition for divorce may be presented to the Court until after the expiration of three years from the marriage, unless the Court is satisfied that the case is one of exceptional hardship suffered by the petitioner, or of exceptional depravity on the part of the respondent.

All petitions must now be presented in the first place to the relevant County Court (first given jurisdiction in this field by the Matrimonial Causes Act, 1967) but defended cases or those giving rise to special difficulties have to be transferred to the Family Division of the High Court.

The Court has powers under the legislation to grant ancillary relief in the way of maintenance and orders as to property or payment of a lump sum (matters referred to in the 1973 Act as Financial Provision) and as to the custody of or access to the children of the marriage.

Under the 1973 Act, a married person who can show good grounds for supposing the other spouse to be dead, may apply to the Family Division for an order to presume death and to dissolve the marriage. In any such proceedings, continuous absence of the other spouse for seven years, provided the petitioner has no reason to believe such other spouse to have been alive within that time, shall be *prima facie* evidence that the other spouse is dead.

In addition to the above decrees the Court may grant a decree of judicial separation. Here the five factual situations referred to above in connection with divorce are in effect made " grounds " as such, since irretrievable breakdown does not have to be proved. This does not affect the continuance of the married state, but during the continuance of the decree, the wife is in the position of a *feme sole* (a single woman) and the parties are no longer bound to cohabit. It is provided in the 1973 Act that while a decree of judicial separation is in force and the separation is continuing either of the parties to the marriage dies intestate, the property as respects which he or she died intestate shall devolve as if the other party to the marriage had then been dead.

In addition, a Magistrates' Court has wide jurisdiction in connection with " domestic proceedings ". The Court for this purpose is constituted of not more than three Justices, including both a man and a woman. As far as is possible, the matters before such Court must be separated from other business. The magistrates have power to make an order providing for the separation of the spouses, their maintenance and that of the children of the family and as to the custody of such children. The Matrimonial Proceedings (Magistrates' Courts) Act, 1960, consolidated with important amendments the Summary Jurisdiction (Separation and Maintenance) Acts, 1895–1949. In particular it :—

    (i) made the grounds of relief available to a husband substantially the same as those available to a wife ;
    (ii) widened the Court's powers and duties in relation to the children of the family ;
    (iii) increased the amounts of maintenance which the Courts can order in respect of a spouse or child. The Maintenance Orders Act, 1968, removed the upper limits imposed by the 1960 Act so that at present the amount which can be awarded will depend on the financial position of the parties.

It should be noted that as an example of (i), the Court may now make an order on the application of the husband on a complaint that the wife has " wilfully neglected to provide, or to make a proper contribution towards, reasonable maintenance for the husband or for any child of the family who is, or would but for that neglect have been, a dependant, in a case where by reason of the impairment of the husband's earning capacity through age, illness, or disability of mind or body, and having regard to any resources of the husband and the wife respectively which are, or should properly be made, available for the purpose, it is reasonable in all the circumstances to expect the wife so to provide or contribute ".

Property disputes between spouses can be settled under the special procedure provided by section 17 of the Married Women's Property Act, 1882. It may be noted that the Married Women's Property Act, 1964 usefully provides that, in the absence of agreement to the contrary, any surplus of money derived from a housekeeping allowance made by a husband to a wife (or property acquired out of such money) is to be treated as belonging to the spouses in equal shares. Similarly, a Section in the Matrimonial Proceedings and Property Act, 1970 attempts to deal with a situation where a husband or wife contributes to the improvement of property in which either or both of them has or have a beneficial interest. Subject to any agreement to the contrary, the contribution so made is to give to him or her a share or enlarged share in the beneficial interest and the share may ultimately fall to be fixed by the Court.

**Mentally Disordered Persons.**

The position of such persons with regard to contracts, torts and crimes is dealt with in other Chapters, but mention may be made here of the fact that certification, treatment and administration of the property of these unfortunate people has for long been provided for by statute. The Mental Health Act, 1959—a most comprehensive enactment—is the statute at present in force.

## Aliens.

The status of an *alien friend* is in most respects similar to that of a subject. Apart from a few exceptions, he may acquire and dispose of any kind of property, a title to such property being derived through him as through a British subject. He can sue and be sued in the Courts of this country, and enforce his rights even against the Crown; thus he can sue out a writ of *Habeas Corpus*. He is, however, subject to certain disqualifications :—

(a) He cannot directly own a share in a British ship, although he may have shares in a company owning one ;
(b) He cannot act as master, chief officer or chief engineer of a British ship registered in the United Kingdom unless it is habitually engaged in voyages between ports outside the United Kingdom ;
(c) He cannot be a Privy Councillor or Member of Parliament, hold any office of trust or vote at any Parliamentary or municipal election.

An *alien enemy* has no rights and privileges. Contracts made by him after the outbreak of war are void, while those made before are annulled, or at least suspended during continuance of hostilities. The Crown may, under the Prerogative, claim any property of his in this country. Whether or not a person is an alien enemy depends upon where he is *resident*, not necessarily on his nationality. Even a British subject may be considered as an alien enemy if he is resident in enemy, or enemy-occupied, territory.

An alien has no enforceable right to enter British territory and powers exist to exclude or indeed to expel him from the United Kingdom.

## Nationality.

The British Nationality Act, 1948, in giving effect to a developed conception of common citizenship between the various parts of what has come to be called the Commonwealth provided for the achievement of British nationality through citizenship of the United Kingdom and Colonies or of some other Commonwealth country.

After making provision for persons of various categories in being before the commencement of the Act it provides that every person born within the United Kingdom and Colonies after the commencement of the Act shall be a citizen of the United Kingdom and Colonies by birth, unless his father is not a citizen and enjoys diplomatic immunity or unless his father is an enemy alien and the birth occurs in a place in enemy occupation.

Every person born after the commencement of the Act whose father is a citizen of the United Kingdom and Colonies at the time of the birth shall be a citizen of the United Kingdom and Colonies by descent. Where, however, the father of such a person is a citizen of the United Kingdom and Colonies by descent only, that person shall not be a citizen of the United Kingdom and Colonies unless :—

> (a) That person is born, or his father was born, in a Protectorate, Mandated Territory or Trust Territory, or any place in a foreign country where Her Majesty has or had jurisdiction over British subjects ; or
> (b) That person is born in a foreign country other than such as is mentioned in (a) and the birth is registered at a United Kingdom consulate within one year or, with the Secretary of State's permission, later ; or
> (c) That person's father is, at the time of the birth in the service of the Crown in the United Kingdom ; or
> (d) That person is born in a specified territory.

The Act has been applied or restricted from time to time as changes in the membership of the Commonwealth have occurred.

A British woman who marries an alien retains United Kingdom citizenship unless she renounces it. An alien woman who marries a British subject acquires British nationality only by registration.

British nationality may be lost :—

> (a) By a declaration of renunciation of citizenship of the United Kingdom and Colonies ; or
> (b) By deprivation by the Home Secretary of such citizenship in certain cases, e.g., disloyalty, twelve months' imprisonment within five years of naturalization, or fraud in obtaining citizenship or naturalization (see below).

## Naturalization.

At his absolute discretion, the Home Secretary may grant a certificate of naturalization to an alien, provided that :—

> (a) He has either resided in the United Kingdom or been in Crown service in the United Kingdom, or partly the one and partly the other, throughout the twelve months immediately preceding his application for naturalization ;
> (b) He has, during the seven years immediately preceding those twelve months, either resided in the United Kingdom or any Colony, Protectorate, United Kingdom Mandated Territory or United Kingdom Trust Territory, or been in Crown service as aforesaid, or partly the one and partly the other, for periods amounting in the aggregate to four years ;
> (c) He is of good character ;
> (d) He has sufficient knowledge of the English language ; and

(e) He intends :—
  (i) To reside in the United Kingdom or in any Colony, Protectorate or United Kingdom Trust Territory ; or
  (ii) To enter into, or continue in, Crown service in the United Kingdom, or service in the employment of a society, company or body of persons established in the United Kingdom or in any Colony, Protectorate or United Kingdom Trust Territory.

The Home Secretary may revoke a certificate where he is satisfied that it was obtained by fraudulent means or where the grantee has shown himself to be disaffected or disloyal or of bad character.

## Domicile.

Of outstanding importance in the law of persons is the question of *domicile*. A person's domicile is the country in which he has his permanent home, or where his " roots " are ; it is thus more than mere residence, which may be casual.

The concept is of particular importance in that department of law known as the " Conflict of Laws "—where an English Court may be concerned with a case having a foreign element.

Domicile must be distinguished from nationality, which is the political relation that exists between an individual and the State to which he owes allegiance. Domicile determines *civil* rights and obligations, e.g., rights of marriage and succession, whereas nationality determines *public* rights and obligations, e.g., the right to vote or to hold political office. Thus, it has been previously pointed out that anyone born in the United Kingdom is *ipso facto* a citizen of the United Kingdom. But a foreigner, coming to England and having the intention to remain here indefinitely acquires English domicile, whatever his nationality ; he could ultimately, if he wished, on complying with the statutory requirements, become naturalized.

There are two inflexible rules regarding domicile :—

(a) Every person must possess a domicile ; and
(b) No person can have more than one domicile.

There are three different classes of domicile :—

(a) *Domicile of origin.* This attaches automatically at birth, and the domicile of a newly born child is that of its father if living, or, if the father is dead, or the child is illegitimate, that of its mother. However, by virtue of the Domicile and Matrimonial Proceedings Act, 1973 (hereafter referred to as the 1973 statute) the child will take his mother's domicile instead of the father's where the spouses are separated and the child makes his home with the mother. Furthermore under the 1973 statute a person who has attained the age of sixteen (or marries under that age, if such is permitted by that person's domiciliary law) is now capable of acquiring an independent domicile. A foundling is domiciled in the place where it is found. A domicile of origin can never be entirely extinguished, and if a person with a domicile of choice (see below) abandons such domicile without simultaneously acquiring a new domicile of choice, the domicile of origin will revive.

(b) *Domicile of choice*. Where a person of full age and capacity (or falling within the provisions of the 1973 statute) takes up residence in a country other than his last domicile, with the intention of remaining there indefinitely, he is said to acquire a domicile of choice there. Acquisition and abandonment of a domicile of choice depends on intention, the burden of proof of which lies on the person asserting the change.

(c) *Domicile of dependent persons*. The rules for the acquisition of domicile by children at birth and subsequently have already been mentioned. Furthermore, until the 1973 statute a woman, on marriage, acquired her husband's domicile and was not free to acquire a separate domicile of choice during the marriage. However under the 1973 statute a married woman is now capable of acquiring a domicile independent of her husband.

The importance of domicile can be illustrated by referring to some of the many matters in which the question of domicile is all important, e.g.,

(a) Jurisdiction of the Courts in divorce.
(b) **The validity of wills and the distribution of movable property on an intestacy.**
(c) Legitimation.
(d) The essential validity of marriages.

## The Crown.

" The Queen can do no wrong." This maxim is still true of the Queen as regards acts or omissions committed or made in her private capacity, but it has been shorn of most of its strength in regard to those committed or made in her public capacity. Formerly, her personal immunity extended to such acts or omissions, and a subject could not bring an ordinary action to recover damages from a Government Department in the absence of statutory authority. For such, as an act of grace, the Queen might allow proceedings by a procedure known as a " petition of right ", but even this was not available in the case of a breach of contract of service, or in the case of a tort.

LAW OF PERSONS                                113

The Crown Proceedings Act, 1947, provides that the Crown shall be subject to all those liabilities in tort to which, if it were a private person of full age and capacity, it would be subject :—

(a) In respect of torts committed by its servants or agents provided that, apart from this Act, such torts would have given rise to an action against them ;
(b) In respect of any breach of those duties which a person owes to his servants or agents at Common Law by reason of being their employer ; and
(c) In respect of any breach of the duties attaching at Common Law to the ownership, occupation, possession or control of property.

[Formerly under the Act the Crown and any officer of the Crown enjoyed an immunity from civil action in respect of an *unregistered* postal packet, telegram or telephone message. No proceedings lay in respect of loss of, or damage to, a *registered inland* packet under section 9(2) of the Act, unless the proceedings were commenced within the twelve months beginning with the date on which the packet was posted : Law Reform (Limitation of Actions, etc.) Act, 1954.

However, by virtue of the Post Office Act, 1969, the Post Office ceased to be a department of the Crown and became a public corporation. Accordingly, section 9 of the Crown Proceedings Act, 1947, was repealed, but section 30 of the 1969 Act (repeating the scheme of section 9 of the 1947 Act) subjects the Post Office to limited liability in respect of registered inland packets and proceedings must likewise be begun within twelve months of the posting of the packet.]

Nothing done or omitted by a member of the Armed Forces of the Crown, while on duty as such, shall subject him or the Crown to liability for inflicting death or personal injury on another member of the Armed Forces whilst the latter is on duty as a member or is on any land, premises, ship, aircraft or vehicle used for the purposes of the Armed Forces, if the appropriate Minister certifies that the victim will receive an award.

Under the Act, claims against the Crown for breach of contract may now be enforced as of right.

Civil proceedings by, or against, the Crown may be instituted in the High Court or in a County Court. Proceedings by the Crown may be instituted either by an authorized Government Department in its own name, or by the Attorney-General. Proceedings against the Crown must be instituted against the appropriate Government Department, or, if none is appropriate, against the Attorney-General. No injunction is available against the Crown and a judgment cannot be enforced by execution in the manner customary as between private litigants. Moreover, the Crown enjoys certain other procedural advantages, including the right to decline to produce documents the production of which would be contrary to the public interest.

The Act contains a general overriding provision that nothing in the Act shall authorize proceedings in tort to be brought against the Queen in her private capacity.

**Servants of the Crown.**

The position with regard to the Crown is clear : all Crown servants, whether civil or military, hold office at the pleasure of the Crown, and have no right of action on summary dismissal unless their tenure of office is protected by statute. Even though a special contract of service is proved, the Crown is not bound thereby.

The Crown's position with regard to third parties may be stated thus :—

(a) For the enforcement of a public duty the appropriate instrument is the Order of *Mandamus*, which requires the duty to be performed, but the subject may not avail himself of this procedure if the duty is one owed to the Crown alone.

(b) As regards liability in contract, where a public servant, *acting on behalf of the Crown*, makes a contract, he incurs no personal liability thereon. Moreover, it appears that, where a servant of the Crown makes a contract in his public capacity, there is a presumption that he contracts as agent for the Crown, and not personally. If he contracts personally, he will, of course, be liable personally.

(c) As regards liability in tort, where a Crown servant commits a tort in the performance of his official functions, the Crown, generally speaking, is liable (Crown Proceedings Act, 1947). The servant also is liable.

Nevertheless, the normal liability of a master for the wrongful acts of his servants, committed during the course of employment, has no application as regards Crown servants, for all are equally servants of the Crown. Thus, a superior Crown official cannot be held liable for the tortious act of a subordinate official, unless the former personally directed or authorized the tortious act.

**Allegiance.**

" Allegiance " is " the tie which binds the subject to the ruler, in return for the protection which the ruler affords to the subject ": *Stephen's Commentaries on the Laws of England.*

An oath or affirmation of allegiance is exacted from Members of Parliament, aliens seeking naturalization and certain persons on acceptance of office, but apart from any express oath or affirmation, there is an implied allegiance owing from every subject to his sovereign from the moment of the latter's accession to the throne. This tie between subject and ruler is also called "natural allegiance".

The duty of allegiance is not, however, confined to subjects. Even an alien friend resident in this country owes such a duty to the Queen whose protection he enjoys. This duty owing from a resident alien friend is called " local allegiance " to distinguish it from the duty owed by a subject, but its effect on his relations to the Crown is similar.

## Duties of a Subject.

The chief duties of a British subject in the United Kingdom are :—

(1) To serve the Crown when required. This is a Common Law duty. Thus, a person chosen as sheriff cannot generally refuse to accept office. In many continental countries, the citizen is liable to military service, but, in England, this liability is now imposed by special Acts of Parliament.

(2) To assist the police in quelling disturbances and maintaining the Queen's peace. A member of the general public may be punished for unjustifiably refusing to accede to a police officer's request for assistance in an emergency : *The Queen* v. *Brown* (1841). These duties of service and assistance have, in practice, been wholly or partially superseded by the establishment of paid forces or officials, and are, therefore, enforced only in an emergency.

(3) To give evidence as an ordinary witness in a trial, and, with certain qualifications, to serve on a jury. Peers, clergymen, Judges, practising members of the legal, medical and dental professions and members of the Armed Forces are exempt from this liability.

(4) To pay rates and taxes. This is a duty imposed by statute.

(5) To make returns, not merely the return necessary for the determination of the amount of taxation payable, but also returns under the Factory Acts, the Road Traffic Acts, the Insurance Acts, and the Census Act.

(6) To register the births and deaths of members of his family.

(7) Under the Education Acts, to see that his children attend school.

## National Insurance and National Health Service.

The Social Security Act, 1975 (consolidating and extending statutory provisions introducing in the forties the " Welfare State ") provides for a comprehensive scheme of National Insurance which embraces employed persons (those gainfully occupied in employment under a contract of service in Great Britain), self-employed persons, and non-employed persons. With certain minor exceptions, therefore, the whole population consisting of persons over school-leaving age and under pensionable age, are insurable under the Act. The benefits provided are :—

Sickness Benefit.  
Unemployment Benefit.  
Guardian's Allowance.  
Retirement Pension.

## CHAPTER V

Maternity Benefits :
  (a) Maternity Grant.
  (b) Maternity Allowance.
  (c) Home Confinement Grant.
Death Grant.

Widows' Benefits :
  (a) Widow's Allowance.
  (b) Widowed Mother's Allowance.
  (c) Widow's Pension.

The legislation is administered by the Department of Health and Social Security.

The National Health Service Acts, 1946 to 1973, make provision for health services to be available for everyone, and there is no insurance qualification, although part of the cost is met by contributions under the Acts and certain charges are made for spectacles, dentures and other appliances. The services are :—

  (i) Hospital and specialist services, comprising all forms of general and special hospital treatment, together with sanatoria, maternity accommodation, treatment during convalescence, medical rehabilitation and other institutional treatment.
  (ii) General practitioner services, either at home, at doctors' surgeries or Health Centres to be set up by Local Authorities.
  (iii) Various supplementary services, including midwifery, maternity, child welfare and family planning.
  (iv) The provision of spectacles, dentures and other appliances, drugs and medicines, at Hospitals, Clinics and elsewhere, as may be appropriate.

The Acts are administered by the Department of Health and Social Security in conjunction with certain bodies, such as the Regional Health Authorities.

### National Insurance (Industrial Injuries) Acts, 1965 to 1973

This legislation consolidates and extends earlier legislation in this field which had repealed the Workmen's Compensation Acts from the 5th July, 1948 and superseded the procedure whereby a workman claimed compensation from his employer under those Acts and substituted a procedure whereby a workman may claim benefit from a State-administered Fund, supported by contributions from employers, employees and the State. Subject to a few exceptions, all persons employed under a contract of service or apprenticeship are insurable. There is no income limit and no age limit. No provision is made for " contracting out ", i.e., making arrangements for insurance outside the State scheme. The legislation has now in very large part been worked into the consolidating Social Security Act, 1975.

### The Rule of Law.

Whatever duties are imposed on the subject by the State, they must be enforced only in a legal manner and on legal authority. The antithesis of the Rule of Law is arbitrary government. In the *Case of Ship Money*, 1637, it was decided that no tax can be levied except under an Act of Parliament.

The essence of the Rule of Law is that the government has no arbitrary power over the subject, the latter having by Common Law or statute certain unassailable rights not subject to executive interference. The Rule further presupposes the principle of equality before the law, all persons being subject to the same law and amenable to the jurisdiction of the same tribunals.

### Prerogative Writs and Orders.

To safeguard the private rights of individuals, the decisions of administrative organs and other public authorities may be brought under review by the Courts. The machinery by which this is done is provided mainly by what were known as the Prerogative Writs of *Habeas Corpus, Mandamus, Prohibition* and *Certiorari*. They were so called because they were originally issued only at the suit of the Crown and never issued as a matter of course on the mere application of an aggrieved party. The last three, however, have been replaced respectively by Orders of *Mandamus, Prohibition* and *Certiorari* : Administration of Justice (Miscellaneous Provisions) Act, 1938.

The writ of *Habeas Corpus* enables a person unlawfully imprisoned to obtain his release. The writ may be applied for by the person detained or by some person on his behalf. Application is made to a Divisional Court of the Queen's Bench Division, or, in vacation time, to any Judge of the High Court. The Court or Judge orders the " detainer " to appear and the case is argued on its merits. If the Court or Judge decides against him, he is ordered to produce the prisoner, who is then released. Even if there is sufficient cause for his detention, he can secure a speedy trial.

The *Order of Mandamus*, which lies in the absolute discretion of the Court, provides the means by which an administrative organ or other public authority may be peremptorily commanded to do its duty. It has, for instance, been employed to compel the Housing Tribunal to hear and determine an appeal, to compel a lawful election of aldermen to be held, following an irregular election, and to compel a Local Authority to produce its accounts for the inspection of a ratepayer. It may in fact be employed to enforce performance of any acts which a Local Authority is under an obligation to do, such as, for example, the construction of a road in place of one that has been stopped up. The procedure cannot, however, be employed to enforce a purely private or domestic duty, e.g., the duty of the Chairman of the Convocation of London University to summon a meeting in accordance with the University Statutes. Nor can it be used against the Crown as such.

The *Order of Prohibition* issues against public or semi-public bodies for the purpose of controlling the exercise of judicial or *quasi*-judicial, but not legislative, functions. Thus, in *R.* v. *Electricity Commissioners* (1924), *Prohibition* was invoked to quash a scheme formulated by the Commissioners for the incorporation of a joint electricity authority. It may also be used to control usurpation of jurisdiction by *quasi*-judicial tribunals such as the Income Tax Commissioners.

The *Order of Certiorari* may be employed to review the acts and orders of any competent authority having power to impose a liability or to give a decision determining the rights of the affected parties. For example, it can be invoked to challenge the action of the Secretary of the Environment in altering or confirming a housing scheme. It is frequently sought along with Prohibition, so that not merely may an *ultra vires* act be reviewed but its operation restrained. *Certiorari* does not lie to an Ecclesiastical Court.

A remedy of greater elasticity now being increasingly used is the action for a Declaratory Judgment. It is not a Prerogative Writ and is less subject to technicalities than, say, *Certiorari*.

The remedies described above are becoming increasingly used to test the validity of Ministerial decisions. Thus, in 1976 one or other of them was used to question the power of the Home Office to revoke television licences not granted in accordance with a scheme involving the timing of payment of increased licence fees ; to test the withdrawal of aviation facilities from an operator ; to pronounce upon the validity of the exercise by the Secretary for Education and Science of alleged power to pronounce on the reversal by a local authority of the decision of its predecessor to introduce a plan to impose a scheme of comprehensive education in its area, which would deny the rights of parents to opt for a continuance of the " selective system " previously obtaining.

### Right of Personal Freedom.

Personal freedom is secured under the British Constitution by the existence of ready remedies available to a citizen whose personal freedom is in any way interfered with. For any interference with personal freedom (unless it is justified by law, e.g., arrest on a criminal charge, or imprisonment for contempt of Court), the citizen has one or more of the following remedies :—

(a) Extra-judicial, namely, self-defence.
The amount of force which can justifiably be used in self-defence must be :—

(i) Necessary for the protection of oneself or one's property ; and
(ii) Proportionate to the harm which it is intended to avert.

(b) Judicial :
    (i) A civil action for damages for assault and/or false imprisonment.
    (ii) A civil action for damages for malicious prosecution.
        These actions may be brought against anyone, including public officials, members of the police, hospital officials, etc.
    (iii) Criminal proceedings for assault or false imprisonment.
    (iv) The Prerogative Writ of *Habeas Corpus*. This is used to procure the release of a person imprisoned without legal justification. It is not a means of punishing the offender, who can be proceeded against by one or more of the methods mentioned above (i-iii).

## Liberty of Discussion.

All that the " right " means is the right to speak or write freely on any matter, subject to the following limitations :—

(a) An action for libel or slander.
(b) A prosecution for libel.
(c) A prosecution for blasphemy.
(d) A prosecution for sedition.
(e) A prosecution for abusing the law in any other manner, e.g., by using obscene language or by blackmail.

Recent statutes have imposed further restrictions. Thus, the evidence in divorce and separation cases must not be published, or the identity of defendants in the Juvenile Courts revealed, while words spoken at public meetings may be dealt with under the Public Order Act, 1936. The Obscene Publications Acts, 1959–1964 proscribe the publication of obscene articles and the Theatres Act, 1968 (which incidentally abolished the censorship functions of the Lord Chamberlain and transferred the licensing of theatre premises to the appropriate local authority) contains provisions (creating offences) in relation to the performance of plays analogous to those contained in the Obscene Publications Acts in relation to the publication of books. In effect the Act makes it a criminal offence to present or direct an obscene performance in public or (with certain exceptions) in private.

## Right of Public Meeting.

" The right of assembling ", says Dicey, " is nothing more than a result of the view taken by the Courts as to individual liberty of a person and individual liberty of speech ".

The right is limited in the following ways :—

(a) By the law of trespass.
(b) By the criminal law with reference to riots and unlawful assemblies.
(c) By local bye-laws.
(d) By the law of nuisance.

Under the doctrine enunciated in *Duncan* v. *Jones* (1936), it appears that the police can forbid any meeting on the ground that it is likely to cause a breach of the peace, and if it is persisted in, can proceed against those holding it for obstructing the police in the execution of their duty.

The Public Order Act, 1936, makes it unlawful for any person in a public place or at a public meeting to wear a uniform signifying his association with any political organization or with the promotion of any political object. It is also unlawful for any person to take part in the organization, training, control or management of any association the members or adherents of which are organized, trained or equipped for the purpose of enabling them to usurp the functions of the police or the Armed Forces, or for the purpose of enabling them to be employed for the use or display of physical force in promoting any political object. The chief officer of police, if he has reasonable ground for apprehending that a public procession may occasion serious public disorder, may impose conditions prescribing the route to be taken by the procession or prohibiting the procession from entering any specified public place, or he may apply to the Council of the borough or district for an order prohibiting for a period not exceeding three months the holding of all public processions or any class of public processions. The Act also covers the special needs of the Metropolis. Further, any person who, in any public place or at any public meeting, uses threatening, abusive or insulting words or behaviour with intent to provoke a breach of the peace, or whereby a breach of the peace is likely to be occasioned, is guilty of an offence under the Act.

Penalties were increased by the Public Order Act, 1963.

### Unlawful Assemblies.

An unlawful assembly is an assembly of three or more persons with intent to execute some common design in circumstances calculated to inspire in persons of reasonable firmness and courage a fear of a breach of the peace.

A rout is a disturbance of the peace by three or more persons unlawfully assembled who take some preliminary steps towards achieving their common design but do not complete it, e.g., a procession of strikers on their way to attack premises.

A Common Law riot is a tumultuous disturbance of the peace by three or more persons who assemble together with intent mutually to assist one another by force against any who oppose them in the execution of their common design and who actually execute, or attempt to execute, the same in a violent and turbulent manner calculated to alarm at least one person of reasonable firmness and courage. A further degree of accomplishment is

## LAW OF PERSONS

necessary than is found in a rout. An illustration of a Common Law riot occurs in *Munday* v. *Metropolitan Police District Receiver* (1949), where a large crowd, unable to secure admission to an important football match, invaded the garden of the plaintiff's premises close to the ground, to see the match.

The importance of establishing a Common Law riot is that a person suffering damage to his property by reason of such a riot can demand to be compensated out of the Police Fund of the district in question under the Riot (Damages) Act, 1886.

> Formerly a Common Law riot had to be distinguished from a statutory riot. Under the Riot Act, 1714, an offence was committed where a riotous assembly of twelve or more persons failed to disperse within one hour after the reading by a magistrate of the proclamation set out in the Act. The rioters might then be dispersed or apprehended, the persons assisting in dispersing or apprehending them being free from all liability for any injury or loss of life ensuing. The Act of 1714 was, however, repealed by the Criminal Law Act, 1967 (which abolished the former distinctions between felony and misdemeanour—see *post*, p. 254). Thus " reading the Riot Act " is no longer a pre-requisite. The 1967 Act provides (s. 3) that a person " may use such force as is reasonable in the circumstances in the prevention of crime or in effecting . . . the lawful arrest of offenders. . . ."

A lawful assembly is not rendered unlawful merely because people announce their intention of preventing it by force : *Beatty* v. *Gillbanks* (1882).

If a meeting is engaged in no unlawful act, but yet a magistrate believes on reasonable and probable grounds that it is being held with unlawful intent and that there would be a breach of the peace if the meeting continued, he is justified in taking steps to stop and disperse the meeting if there is no other way of avoiding a breach of the peace : *O'Kelly* v. *Harvey* (1883).

If a person seeks to enforce his " right of public meeting so as to give a good reason for a belief that he will cause a breach of the peace, he may be bound over to keep the peace " : *Wise* v. *Dunning* (1902).

Where a public, or perhaps even a private, meeting is held on private premises and the police have reasonable grounds for anticipating a breach of the peace, they are entitled, in the execution of their duty, to enter and remain on the premises during the meeting : *Thomas* v. *Sawkins* (1935).

### B. ARTIFICIAL PERSONS

**Corporations.**

One of the most important conceptions of jurisprudence is the corporation, a legally recognized person, consisting of a group of persons acting in combination. But the group, as such, has a definite legal personality quite distinct from the individual personalities of the constituent members. This was emphatically stated by the House of Lords in the following leading case.

*Salomon v. Salomon & Co. Ltd.* (1897)

S sold his private business to a company which he formed. There were seven members, his wife and four sons and one daughter taking one £1 share each, and S, himself, taking 20,000 fully paid shares, representing part of the purchase price of S's business ; S accepted the balance of the price by taking £10,000 in debentures ; i.e., in effect, he lent the company £10,000 on mortgage. The company failed, with assets of £6,000. There was the debt of £10,000 due to S, secured by the debentures, and, in addition, £7,000 due to unsecured creditors. S claimed priority on the strength of his security. The unsecured creditors claimed that as S & Co. was in effect the same person as S, he could not owe money to himself, and that they were entitled to prior payment.

*Held* that, once a company is incorporated, it must be treated as an independent person. Thus S kept the £6,000 in part payment of his loan to the company.

A corporation may be defined as a legal entity, or artificial person, with a distinctive name, perpetual succession, and a common seal. Certain writers argue that a corporation has a real not a merely artificial personality, that an association of persons has a real group personality quite distinct from the individual personalities of the group members. However that may be, a corporation is a being recognized by law as capable of legal rights and legal liabilities. But there are obvious limits to the activities of a corporation : it cannot commit bigamy, it cannot suffer corporal punishment. Yet, unlike the natural person, a corporation has perpetual succession ; the death of members, the withdrawal of members, or the introduction of new members, does not affect the continuity or identity of the corporate body. It has already been explained in Chapter II that valuable rights accrued to the great feudal landowners on the death of the tenant. Since, however, a corporation never dies, the Common Law forbade the acquisition of land by a corporation. This was the Mortmain Rule, " mortmain " meaning " dead hand ". Any land transferred in breach of this Rule was forfeited to the Crown. The Rule did not operate if the corporation had power to hold lands under licence from the Crown or under the provisions of some statute, e.g., the Companies Act, 1948 and the Rule itself was swept away by a provision in the Charities Act, 1960. The contractual position of corporations and the doctrine of *ultra vires* (including the impact of the European Communities Act, 1972) have been discussed in the Chapters on Contracts.

Corporations may be classified as :—

(1) Corporations Sole. Here, the corporation has only one member at any given time, and it consists of the successive holders of certain offices, e.g., the Bishop of London, the incumbent of a parish.
(2) Corporations Aggregate. Here, the corporation consists of many members. There are three types of such corporation :—
  (a) Common Law Corporations, i.e., corporations created by express or presumed charter of the Queen.
  (b) Statutory Corporations, formed under special Acts of Parliament, e.g., Water Companies.
  (c) Registered Companies formed under the various Companies Acts.

## Companies.

The early trading companies, when incorporated, were incorporated by Royal Charter ; and some of these companies still exist, e.g., Hudson's Bay Company. A chartered company is not affected by the doctrine of *ultra vires* ; its contractual capacity is not limited to acts necessary for or incidental to the pursuit of the objects for which it was formed, though the Crown may annul the charter if the conditions on which it was granted are disregarded. Later, when companies were formed to conduct public utility undertakings, such as railways, canals, gasworks and waterworks, it was found convenient to incorporate each such company by a special Act of Parliament, which gave the company any special powers required, e.g., to acquire land compulsorily. These statutory companies are subject to the doctrine of *ultra vires*.

Incorporation by either of the means mentioned above is impracticable for all but the largest undertakings. Until 1844 most industrial and trading undertakings were formed as partnerships, or as unincorporated companies. In the latter, the capital was subscribed by numerous members, who took no part in the management, which was delegated to directors. But in law, both forms were treated as partnerships ; they had no legal existence separate from their members, and could hold no property, whilst each member had unlimited liability for the debts of the undertaking. Now, such undertakings are usually incorporated as registered companies, with limited liability, under the provisions of the Companies Act, 1948 (as amended), or one of the earlier Companies Acts. Incorporation is secured by registering with the Registrar of Companies (a) a memorandum of association which states the name, objects and capital of the company and the limitation (if any) on the liability of its members, and (b) articles of association which define the rights of members *inter se* and as against the company, and the extent to which the powers of the company are delegated to the directors. The memorandum and articles together constitute a contract between the company and its members. The two documents must be signed by at least seven subscribers (at least two, in the case of a private company), and these subscribers become the first members. When the memorandum and articles have been registered with the Registrar and the necessary fees and capital duty have been paid, the Registrar issues a certificate of incorporation. This brings the company into legal existence, and is conclusive evidence that all requirements relating to registration have been satisfied.

Registered companies may be companies with or without a share capital. They may be (a) limited by shares, (b) limited by guarantee, or (c) unlimited. In a company limited by shares (the usual form of company) each member takes a number of shares, of a certain nominal value, e.g., £1, and is liable, in the event of the company being wound up, to contribute such amount (not exceeding that which remains unpaid on his shares) as may be required to pay the company's debts and the costs of winding-up, and to adjust the rights of members amongst themselves. Once he has fully paid up the nominal amount of his shares—and shares are usually so paid up when allotted, or within a short time thereafter—he is under no further liability. In a company limited by guarantee, each member undertakes to contribute, in the event of winding-up, a certain sum for the purposes mentioned above. Such companies are formed for purposes not requiring a large capital, e.g., professional associations.

A registered company cannot undertake anything outside the pursuit of the objects stated in its memorandum of association, though it may do anything reasonably necessary or incidental to the attainment of its main object (see *ante*, pp. 68 and 69).

For the protection of investors and creditors the Companies Acts, 1948–1967, regulate the proceedings of registered companies in a large number of matters. A company may not invite subscriptions from the public for its shares or debentures without issuing a prospectus which gives comprehensive particulars of the company. The company must (*inter alia*) hold (a) an annual general meeting of members, and submit to the members a directors' report on the state of affairs of the company, together with an audited balance sheet and profit and loss account and (if the company has subsidiaries) group accounts; and (b) an extraordinary general meeting, when so required by a certain proportion of the members, to consider any matter they desire to raise. The company must keep a register of members; a register of directors and secretaries; a register of charges on the company's property; and a register of directors' shareholdings, to disclose directors' holdings and dealings in the company's shares and debentures; and these registers are open to inspection. The company must file with the Registrar an annual return, giving particulars of the members and their holdings, and of transfers since the last return and, if it is a limited company, copies of its audited accounts and its directors' reports. The company's file containing these and other returns is open to public inspection. A limited company can, if all its members agree, convert itself into an unlimited company and so avoid having its accounts and directors' reports open to the public.

For certain acts the sanction of a resolution of members in general meeting is necessary. A special resolution (one passed by three-fourths of the votes cast, at a meeting of which at least twenty-one days notice has been given) is required to alter the objects, within certain limits allowed by the Act; to alter the name, with the consent of the Board of Trade [now for practical purposes the Companies Division of the Department for Trade and Industry]; to reduce capital, with the consent of the Court; or to alter the articles.

The capital of a company may be divided into classes, usually (a) Preference Shares, entitled to a dividend at a fixed rate out of the profits in priority to any other class, and frequently to priority in the return of capital in the event of winding-up, and (b) Ordinary Shares. The rights of the classes are prescribed in the articles. Funds may also be raised by the issue of debentures, i.e., loans, usually secured by a charge on the company's assets. Such a charge may be a fixed charge, i.e., a mortgage; or a floating charge. The latter is peculiar to companies. By it a company is enabled to offer as security its undertaking as a whole, including assets which change from day to day and on which a fixed charge would be impracticable, e.g., stock-in-trade. The company is free to deal with such assets until it defaults in respect of the loan; the charge then crystallizes, i.e., becomes fixed on the assets in the state in which they then are.

The first directors are usually appointed by being named in the articles. Subsequent directors are appointed by the members in general meeting. In a public company the articles usually require a proportion, usually one-third, of the directors to retire by rotation each year, the retiring directors being eligible for re-appointment. The articles also usually require directors to hold a share qualification; if a director fails to obtain or retain sufficient shares for his qualification, he loses his seat. Directors are in some respects agents, in some respects trustees, for the company; they reach their decisions at board meetings, and so long as they act as a board, within their powers, in good faith and without gross negligence, they incur no liability to the company or its members.

A private company is one which, by its articles: (a) limits the number of its members to fifty, exclusive of employees, and of past employees who have remained members; (b) restricts the right to transfer its shares; and (c) prohibits any invitation to the public to subscribe for its shares and debentures. Unlike a public company, which must have at least seven members, a private company need have only two ; and it is relieved from certain other obligations of public companies.

The existence of a company is usually terminated either by (i) the Registrar striking its name off the register, after taking steps to satisfy himself that it is defunct ; or (ii) winding-up. The winding-up may be voluntary, being initiated by a resolution of the members ; or compulsory, when it is ordered by the Court, following a petition presented by a member or creditor or the Board of Trade, which must specify one of a number of grounds. These include inability to pay its debts ; failure to commence business for a year, or to maintain the minimum number of members ; or any other ground which makes it just and equitable that the company should be wound up.

## C. OTHER GROUPS AND RELATIONSHIPS

### Unincorporated Associations.

There are, of course, many unincorporated associations of persons, e.g., members' clubs. Such bodies derive their existence from contract, which regulates the rights of the members as between themselves and as regards any property acquired by these bodies. Here, there is no corporate identity, no legal personality in law, beyond that of the individual members. If goods are bought on behalf of the group, legal liability rests upon the individuals effecting the contract. Where an official of such an association engages a servant without authority, and the members of the association repudiate the engagement, he may be sued for breach of warranty of authority : *Collen* v. *Wright* (1857). Where the rules are sufficiently definite to constitute a contract between the members, the Courts may recognize it—allowing a member to be sued for the amount of his subscription, or permitting him to sue for wrongful expulsion.

Some form of statutory recognition has, however, been given to certain of these associations, e.g., Friendly Societies and Trade Unions. The former are now governed by the consolidating Friendly Societies Act, 1974.

Before *Taff Vale Railway Co.* v. *Amalgamated Society of Railway Servants* (1901), it was thought that since a trade union was neither a natural nor a legal person, it could not sue or be sued. In that case, however, it was held by the House of Lords, that a trade union *could be sued* for the wrongful acts of its servants. In *National Union of General and Municipal Workers* v. *Gillian* (1945), it was held that a trade union *could sue* for tort in its registered name, and that it could sue for defamation when the imputations made on it were imputations on it in its collective name and constituted a direct attack on its property.

The case of *Bonsor* v. *Musicians' Union* (1955) in the House of Lords established the following propositions : A trade union, though (in the state of the law obtaining at the date of the decision in that case) not an incorporated body, is capable of entering into contracts and of suing and being sued thereon as a legal entity distinct from its individual members. When a person's application to join a union is accepted, a contract comes into existence between him and the union, whereby he agrees to abide by its rules and it impliedly agrees that he will not be excluded otherwise than in accordance with those rules. If the union breaks this contract and expels him wrongfully he can sue the union as a legal entity. It may likewise, by reason of the rules, be under a contractual duty to him to render him legal assistance, e.g. in respect of an an accident claim for injuries sutained at work : *Buckley* v. *National Union of General and Municipal Workers* (1967).

By the Trades Disputes Act, 1906, section 4, trade unions were made immune from liability for the torts of their members or officials. However, this immunity was spelled out afresh in the Industrial Relations Act, 1971 (which aimed at securing better industrial relations and bargaining procedures) and restricted to trade unions (as well as employers' associations) duly registered under the Act. Such duly registered trade unions were automatically to receive corporate status on registration.

The Act of 1971 had but a short life, since (following a change of Government) it was repealed by the Trade Union and Labour Relations Act, 1974. For present purposes (other matters being dealt with elsewhere in the book—see e.g. *post* pp. 141 and 247) it is enough to say that the 1974 Act (amongst other things) redefined the legal status of a trade union, provided for the maintenance of a register of such unions and the rights of a member in respect of arbitrary or unreasonable exclusion or expulsion.

In particular, section 14 of the Act protects trade unions either in their own names or as against their members or officials from actions in tort in respect of acts done on their behalf in contemplation or furtherance of a trade dispute.

The Act of 1974 was in certain regards modified by the Trade Union and Labour Relations (Amendment) Act, 1976. One modification was to remove the statutory basis of the rights of a member in respect of exclusion or expulsion (see above) and thus, by inference, to relegate the rights to a voluntary system providing for appeal to a proposed non-statutory independent review body.

There is a form of unincorporated association which may be described briefly here, viz., Partnership.

## Partnership.

Partnership is the relation which subsists between persons carrying on a business in common with a view of profit. There are the following fundamental distinctions between a partnership and a registered corporation :—

(a) A firm has no legal personality apart from the personalities of its constituent members, whereas the essence of a registered company is that it is a legal personality in itself quite distinct from the personalities of its members.

(b) All partners, in the absence of contrary agreement, are entitled to share in the management ; not so the members of a company, who delegate the management of its affairs to directors.

(c) A partnership may consist of from two to twenty members, but there is no upper limit in respect of firms of solicitors, accountants or stockbrokers. A banking firm is restricted to ten members (twenty if the Department of Trade permits). In a public company there must be at least seven members, in a private company two, but there is no maximum, except in a private company, whose members are limited to fifty, not including employee-members.

(d) A partner is deemed to have authority to enter into contracts on behalf of the firm in the ordinary course of its business, but the members of a company, as such, have no such authority.

(e) A partner, other than a limited partner, is liable for the debts of the firm to the full extent of his private estate ; in the case of the ordinary limited company, a shareholder's liability is limited to the amount, if any, unpaid on his shares ; or to the amount of his guarantee, if the company is limited by guarantee.

(f) A partnership terminates on the death of a partner, while a company continues in existence despite changes in its membership.

CREATION. The relation of partnership arises from contract, express or implied, the terms of the contract usually being set out in a document termed the *Articles of Partnership*. On matters on which the Articles are silent, the Partnership Act, 1890, applies. A person, who is not a member of a firm, may become liable for debts contracted by the firm under the doctrine of " holding out ", a branch of the law of estoppel, applied expressly to partnerships by section 14 of the Act. A person who, by words or conduct has led another to alter his position to his detriment will not be permitted to recant, even to assert the truth. Thus, any person who by words or conduct either represents himself, or knowingly allows himself to be represented, as a partner to any person who has *on the faith of such representation* given credit to the firm, is liable as a partner in respect thereof, i.e., only to such person, and only in respect of such credit.

However, section 14 provides that, when a partner has died, the mere use of the old firm name, including the deceased's name, where the business is continued, shall not, of itself make his personal representatives, or his estate liable for any partnership debts contracted after his death.

TYPES OF PARTNER. A partner may be either (*a*) General—a partner in the fullest sense, or (*b*) Limited—a partner who takes no part in the actual management, and whose liability is limited to the amount of his capital invested in the business. Such a partner can exist only in a partnership registered as a limited partnership under the Limited Partnerships Act, 1907. A firm so registered must include at least one general partner fully liable for the partnership debts.

A general partner may be *active* or *dormant*. The former actually takes part in the management of the business, and is known to the world to be a partner ; the latter takes no such part, and is only liable to persons who know him to be a partner at the time of contracting with the firm. However, there must be borne in mind the Registration of Business Names Act, 1916 (as amended) which applies where the firm's name does not consist of the true surnames of all the partners who are individuals, and the corporate names of all partners who are corporate bodies, or where a partner has changed his name. Under this Act (which applies equally to individual traders) the true names of all the partners must be registered and also published on all the firm's letters, cards, circulars and publications. Thus, it is virtually impossible to conceal the names of the persons who are partners in a firm.

EVIDENCE OF PARTNERSHIP. The sharing of gross returns is never conclusive evidence of partnership, while the sharing of net profits is *prima facie* evidence of such a relation except in five cases. The ultimate test is : Was the business carried on by persons acting as the agents of the persons sought to be made liable and sharing profits with them?

AGENCY OF PARTNERS. Every partner is deemed to be an agent of the firm and of his other partners for the purpose of the business of the firm, and every act of a partner in the usual course of the firm's business will bind the other partners. Thus, a partner in a trading firm may bind the firm by drawing, accepting or indorsing bills of exchange.

The Articles may limit this implied or ostensible authority, but provided a partner has acted within this authority, it is immaterial that he has exceeded his actual authority : the firm will be liable to the third party, if he was unaware of the limitation of authority.

LIABILITY OF PARTNERS. Each partner, other than a limited partner is fully and personally liable for the debts of the firm. If he has to pay more than his proper share, he may seek contribution from his co-partners. But, his *contractual* liability is *joint only*. This means that there is only one cause of action, and if the aggrieved party has sued some only of the partners and obtained judgment against them, and the judgment is not satisfied, he cannot then sue the other partners, the original sole right of action being swallowed up in the judgment. But each partner is liable both *jointly* with his co-partners *and also severally* (i.e., *separately*) for torts committed by any of the partners within the scope of his authority or in the ordinary course of the business of the firm. Thus, if the injured party sues one partner and obtains judgment against him which is not satisfied, he may still sue any or all of the others until satisfied.

It should be noticed that the estate of a deceased partner is jointly and severally liable for debts contracted by the firm while the deceased was a partner.

A person is not liable for partnership debts contracted before he becomes a partner, unless he accepts such liability in a contract of " novation ", the consideration for which is, usually, the release from liability of a retiring partner. Similarly, an ex-partner is not liable for the debts contracted by the firm after his retirement provided he gives notice :—

(*a*) in the London Gazette—to bind future customers ;
(*b*) personally, to each existing, or " old " customer.

SECRET PROFITS. No partner may derive any benefit for himself from the use of the partnership property or name without the consent of the other partners. Moreover, if he carries on a *competing* business without such consent, he must account for and pay over to the firm all profits so made. During the partnership each partner must observe the utmost good faith, affording full information to his co-partners of all matters relevant to the business, and in all matters acting for the common advantage.

GENERAL RIGHTS OF PARTNERS. Subject to any special provision in the Articles, the Act prescribes certain rules as to the rights and duties of the partners amongst themselves. Examples are :—

(i) All partners are entitled to share capital and profits and to bear losses equally.

(ii) A partner is entitled to be indemnified for payments made or liabilities incurred in the ordinary course of the partnership business, or in preserving the firm's property.
(iii) A partner is entitled to interest on advances in excess of capital at the rate of five per cent. per annum.
(iv) Each partner has a right to take part in the management of the business and to inspect the books, which must be kept at the principal place of business.
(v) Ordinary business disputes are settled by a majority of the partners, but no fundamental change may take place in the partnership business without the consent of all the partners.
(vi) If the Articles do not so provide, a partner is not entitled to remuneration for acting as such.

DUTY OF GOOD FAITH. The relation of partnership is one which demands that the conduct of the partners must be of the utmost good faith. Each partner must afford full information to the others concerning all matters relevant to the business, and generally must act for the common advantage in everything affecting the partnership. A contract of partnership is, however, not strictly a contract *uberrimæ fidei*, for which the *preliminary negotiations* must be conducted with the utmost good faith.

TERMINATION OF PARTNERSHIP. A partnership is dissolved without any application to the Court :—

(i) By the expiration of the period (if any) fixed by the partnership agreement ;
(ii) By the completion of the undertaking for which the partnership was formed ;
(iii) By mere notice by one partner, if no term was fixed for the duration, or, if one was so fixed but the business has been carried on after the expiration thereof ;
(iv) By the death or bankruptcy of a partner ;
(v) Where the Court has granted a *charging order* against a partner's share, on the application of a private creditor. In this case, however, the other partners have the option of dissolution.

A charging order is a different matter from a partner's *voluntary assignment* of his share. This does not give the other partners the option of dissolution, and the assignee does not become a member of the firm or personally liable to the firm's creditors. He is, however, entitled (*a*) *before dissolution,* to receive the share of profits which would have come to the assignor, (*b*) *after dissolution,* to receive a share of the partnership assets.

On the application of a partner, the Court may decree a dissolution in any of the following cases :—

(i) When a partner is shown to the satisfaction of the Court to be incapable by reason of mental disorder of managing his own affairs ;
(ii) When a partner, other than the partner suing, becomes permanently incapable of performing his part of the partnership agreement ;
(iii) When a partner, other than the suing partner, has conducted himself in a manner prejudicial to the effective carrying on of the business of the firm, or has wilfully or persistently committed a breach of the partnership agreement, or has rendered co-operation by his co-partners impossible ;
(iv) When the partnership business can be carried on only at a loss ;
(v) When, in the opinion of the Court, it is just and equitable that the partnership be dissolved.

On dissolution, apart from any special provisions, each partner is entitled :—

(a) To require his colleagues to concur in all acts necessary to give public notice of the dissolution ;
(b) To have the property of the firm applied in payment of its debts and liabilities, and to have the surplus assets applied in payment of what may be due to the partners respectively.

Where a partner has paid a premium for admission to a partnership for a fixed term, and the partnership is dissolved before the expiration of that period, no refund can be granted by the Court if dissolution was due to the death of one of the partners, to the misconduct of the premium-paying partner, or to an agreement between the partners containing no provision for a return of any part of the premium. Otherwise, the Court will normally order a refund of a sum bearing the same proportion to the whole premium as the unexpired part of the partnership term bears to the whole period fixed. Thus, if the premium was £1,500 for a six-year term, which was terminated after three years, the Court will normally order a refund of £750, half of the premium.

If the cause of dissolution is the misrepresentation of a partner, an innocent partner has a lien on any surplus of the partnership assets after satisfaction of the partnership liabilities, and a right to an indemnity from the partner in fault against all the debts and liabilities of the firm.

DISTRIBUTION OF ASSETS. In the absence of contrary agreement, the following rules apply :—

(a) Losses, including deficiencies of capital, are paid first out of profits, next out of capital, and, lastly, if necessary, by the partners individually in the proportion in which they were entitled to share profits.
(b) The assets of the firm, including the sums, if any, contributed by the partners to make up losses or deficiencies of capital, are applied in paying :—
  (i) The debts and liabilities of the firm to persons who are not partners ;
  (ii) To each partner rateably what is due to him for advances as distinguished from capital ;
  (iii) To each partner rateably what is due to him in respect of capital.

The ultimate residue, if any, is to be paid to the partners in the proportion in which profits are divisible.

ACCRUAL OF INTEREST. Apart from any contrary agreement, the amount due to an outgoing partner or to the representatives of a deceased partner is a debt which accrues due at such outgoing or death. If the business is carried on by the continuing or surviving partners without a final settlement, the outgoing partner or the personal representatives of the deceased partner may claim either (1) the share of the profits attributable by the Court to the use of the former partner's capital, due allowance being made for the skill and services of the continuing partners, or (2) interest on the former partner's capital at the rate of five per cent. per annum.

Neither option, however, is available if the continuing partners have the option to purchase the former partner's share, and they exercise this right.

GOODWILL. " Goodwill is the whole advantage, whatever it may be, of the reputation and connection of the firm, which may have been built up by years of honest work or gained by a lavish expenditure of money " : Lord Macnaughten in *Trego v. Hunt* (1896).

The person who has acquired the goodwill of a business is alone entitled to represent himself as continuing or succeeding to the business of the vendor. Apart from any provision to the contrary, however, the latter may carry on a competing business and publicly advertise it but :—

(a) He may not solicit or circularize the customers of the old firm selectively and deliberately, although he may circularize a neighbourhood in which he knows some of them reside.

(b) He may not, by the use of the old name or otherwise, carry on business so as to give the impression that he is carrying on the old business. Where, however, a person is not himself a party to the disposition of his goodwill, he may solicit his old customers, as in the case of a bankrupt whose goodwill has been sold by the Trustee in bankruptcy.

It may be that on dissolution no arrangement was made for the disposal of the goodwill; in such an event each ex-partner who carries on business of a similar nature may use the old firm name, provided he does not thereby expose his former colleagues to risk of liability.

### Agency.

Something must now be said of that most common commercial association of persons, Principal and Agent. Agency is a relation existing between two parties, the function of one being to create a contractual bond between the other and third parties. The agent is thus an intermediary for a principal; and may be described as a projection of the legal personality of the principal.

In general, no particular form is required for the appointment of an agent, but there are the following exceptions :—

(i) An agent to contract under seal must be appointed by a deed called a " power of attorney " (complying with the provisions of the Powers of Attorney Act, 1971).
(ii) An agent to grant or surrender leases for more than three years must be appointed under seal.
(iii) An agent for a corporation must be appointed by deed except in the cases of trading corporations and the like.
(iv) To sign the prospectus of a company on behalf of a person named therein as a director, or to sign a director's consent to act, an agent must be appointed in writing.

TYPES OF AGENCY. Apart from *express* appointment, an agent may be appointed by *implication*, as when a master pays debts contracted on his behalf but without his authority : the doctrine of estoppel will prevent the master from denying liability in future similar transactions unless and until express notice of the withdrawal of his authority has been given. There is also agency *of necessity*, where, by reason of emergency, authority to act on behalf of another is conferred by law. Thus, a ship's captain, unable to communicate with the ship's owner, may, in cases of emergency, perform acts on the owner's behalf and bind the owner in his capacity as agent of necessity. Finally, there may be agency by *ratification*, where a contract made by a person without authority is subsequently adopted by the principal for whom he purported to contract.

The following conditions must exist before ratification can take place :—

- (a) The agent must contract expressly as such for a principal in contemplation and in existence at the time, who is named or adequately described.
- (b) The contract must be such as the principal could have lawfully made at the time of ratification.
- (c) The principal must have full knowledge of everything he seeks to adopt, or have dispensed with such knowledge.
- (d) Ratification must be of the whole contract.
- (e) Ratification must take place within a reasonable time, and before the time, if any, fixed for performance has expired.

A valid ratification acts retrospectively. That is to say, the parties are put in the position they would have occupied, if, in fact, the professed agent had, at the time when the contract was made, had the authority he purported to possess. But an unauthorized contract of fire insurance cannot be ratified after the subject-matter of the insurance has been destroyed by fire ; *Grover* v. *Matthews* (1910).

DUTIES OF AN AGENT. The following are the duties of an agent :—

- (1) An agent must perform his duties in person. There are certain obvious exceptions, as where delegation is authorized or necessitated by a sudden emergency.
- (2) In the case of a *gratuitous* agency, the agent must exercise the skill which he in fact possesses. He is liable only if he fails to do so, but he is not liable for non-feasance, a mere failure to act. A *paid* agent must exercise all the skill which, according to his profession, he ought to possess. He is liable for non-feasance as well as for misfeasance (doing a thing badly).
- (3) He must keep his principal informed of all matters relevant to the agency.
- (4) He must keep proper accounts and render them to the principal when required.
- (5) He must not use his position for his personal benefit to the prejudice of his principal.
- (6) He must not disclose to third parties information gained during the agency.
- (7) He must hand over all profits resulting directly or indirectly from the agency. Severe penalties are prescribed, civilly

and criminally, for agents who accept bribes and for third parties who offer them.

RIGHTS OF AN AGENT AGAINST HIS PRINCIPAL. An agent's rights may be summarized as follows :—

(1) An agent is entitled to be paid the agreed remuneration, commission and necessary expenses, or failing express agreement, to be paid such as is reasonable or can be implied from the custom or usage of the particular trade or profession, provided the agent has carried out the exact duties for which he was employed. *Turner* v. *Goldsmith* (1891) shows that in special cases (e.g., a fixed-term agency for a special business) the principal must not do or suffer anything to be done which will deprive the agent of the opportunity of earning commission.
(2) He has a right to be indemnified against all losses and liabilities incurred in the exercise of his duties, including the consequences of wrongful acts committed against third parties, if such were committed innocently and in good faith, and were committed within the scope of the agent's authority.
(3) In certain cases he may have a right of lien and the right of stoppage *in transitu* (in the course of transit) over the goods of the principal for agency charges.

RIGHTS OF THIRD PARTIES. Third parties enjoy important rights against principal and agent :—

(i) If the identity of the principal is disclosed at the time of the contract, and he is in existence, then the agent incurs no liability on the contract. This rule, however, is subject to the following exceptions :—

(a) Where an agent purchases goods on behalf of a foreign principal, there is a presumption that the agent incurs personal liability, but this may be rebutted.
(b) Where an agent signs a bill of exchange in his own name without clearly indicating that he signs merely as agent, then he, and not his principal, is liable on the bill.
(c) Where an agent contracts under seal on behalf of his principal, it is the former who must sue or be sued.
(d) The agent may be liable by custom. Thus, in the case of marine insurance, the broker is personally liable for the payment of the premium to the insurer.

Of course, it is always possible for the agent to undertake personal liability.

(ii) Where the agent contracts *as such*, but does not disclose his principal's *identity*, then, again, normally, the agent does not incur personal liability.
(iii) Where the agent conceals the *existence* of the principal, then, consistently with the doctrine of the undisclosed principal, the third party can *elect* whether he will hold the principal or agent liable, but he must make his election within a reasonable time and it must be unequivocal.
(iv) Where the agent purports to contract on behalf of a principal who is not yet in existence, such as a company not yet registered, the agent is personally liable, unless the contract is made subject to the condition precedent of the company's incorporation, and a special term is included exempting the agent from liability if the company is not incorporated within a specified time. This principle is, so far as companies are concerned, now incorporated in effect by the provision of section 9(2) of the European Communities Act, 1972.

BREACH OF IMPLIED WARRANTY OF AUTHORITY. A person who contracts as agent, professing to have an authority which does not exist, cannot be sued *on the contract*—there is no contract—but he may be sued for damages for breach of implied warranty of authority. This holds good even though he acted honestly, as where, unknown to him, his authority had been terminated by the death of his principal.

TORTIOUS LIABILITY OF THE PRINCIPAL. Although the actual wrongdoer is always liable, the principal may also be held liable if he actually authorized the agent's wrongful act, *or* if such was committed whilst the agent was acting within the scope of his ostensible authority.

TERMINATION OF AGENCY.—Agency may be terminated in the following ways :—
(1) By agreement between the parties.
(2) By expiration of the time fixed for the duration of the agency.
(3) By performance or completion of the object of the agency.
(4) By subsequent illegality, i.e., the occurrence of an event rendering continuance of the agency unlawful.
(5) By the death or supervening mental disorder of either party.
    Where the principal, however, has become insane, then, although the agency is terminated thereby, yet if the agent purports to enter into contracts with persons ignorant of

the principal's insanity, *to whom the principal when sane, has held out the agent as having his authority*, then he will be estopped from denying to those persons the continuance of the agency.

(6) By bankruptcy of the *principal*, not necessarily by bankruptcy of the agent.

With regard to the last two modes of termination certain qualifying remarks are necessary. An authority *coupled with an interest* is not terminated by the death, lunacy or bankruptcy of the principal, unless the agent consents. Such an authority is one given by deed or for valuable consideration for the purpose of effectuating any security or of protecting any interest of the agent, and is generally irrevocable during the subsistence of such security or interest. An example occurs where the principal is indebted to the agent, and forwards to him goods which the agent is to sell, recouping himself out of the proceeds of sale.

It should be pointed out that sections 4 and 5 of the Powers of Attorney Act, 1971 provide, in effect, that neither the death, incapacity or bankruptcy of the donor of a power of attorney (or of the donor in a body corporate by its winding up or dissolution) or anything done by him without the donee's agreement will revoke a power of attorney provided :—

(*a*) The power is expressed to be irrevocable ; and
(*b*) The power is given to secure a proprietary interest of the donee of the power, or the performance of an obligation owed to the donee, and these interests continue.

These two sections give protection both to an agent acting under a power of attorney (i.e., the donee) and a " purchaser " as defined in the Law of Property Act, 1925.

(7) Agency may be terminated by renunciation by the agent, but this may give rise to a right of action for breach of contract.

(8) Finally, subject to the terms of the contract, the principal may revoke the agency at any time. Here, again, there are the following qualifications :—

(*a*) If the agent has previously contracted with a third party on his principal's behalf, the latter must give such third party specific notice of revocation, otherwise the principal will still be liable on any future contract made by the agent with such third party, despite the fact of revocation.

(*b*) An agent's authority cannot be revoked by his principal if the agent, having partly executed his commission, would be exposed to loss or hardship by the revocation.

(c) An authority coupled with an interest cannot be revoked during the subsistence of such interest. Note also the provisions of the Powers of Attorney Act, 1971 set out above.

WIFE AS HUSBAND'S AGENT.—This matter has already been dealt with in Chapter III.

MASTER AND SERVANT.—The relationship of master and servant exists when a master or employer is so placed in regard to a person employed to do work for him—the servant or employee—that he has the right to tell the servant not only what to do but how to do it. This is the so-called " control test " of the existence of the relationship.

> The " control test " is not, however, exclusive today, for there are many contracts of service (especially of skilled professional men such as hospital doctors or civil engineers) where the " master " cannot really be said to control the manner in which the work is to be done. It was for that reason that Denning, L.J., in *Stevenson Jordon & Harrison Ltd.* v. *MacDonald & Evans* (1952), suggested the " integration " or " organization " test, by saying that : " One feature which seems to run through the instances is that, under a contract of service, a man is employed as part of the business [or organization]; whereas under a contract for services, his work, although done for the business [or organization] is not integrated into it but is only accessory to it." He put it in a similar way in *Bank voor Handel en Scheepvaart N.V.* v. *Slatford* (1952) ". . . the test of being a servant does not rest nowadays on submission to orders. It depends on whether the person is part and parcel of the organization . . ." Cp. *Beloff* v. *Pressdram Ltd. and another* (1973).
>
> Insurable employment within the meaning of the National Insurance Act, 1965, and the National Insurance (Industrial Injuries) Act, 1965 (see now the Social Security Act, 1975) depends on there being a " contract of service "—*Whittaker* v. *Minister of Pensions and National Insurance* (1966).

The relationship is usually created by a contract of service or employment and is thus basically contractual. Often a contract of service is entered into *ad hoc* and this will spell out the mutual obligations of the parties. The Contracts of Employment Act, 1972 (as read with the Employment Protection Act, 1975) requires an employer to deliver within a specified time to an employee employed to work for upwards of twenty-one hours weekly a written statement of the main terms of employment. In default of any special terms, the following may be said broadly to be the duties of the employer and employee respectively :—

(a) *On the part of the employer :*
  (i) To pay the appropriate remuneration ;
  (ii) To pay remuneration during the temporary absence of the employee owing to sickness ;

(iii) To reimburse the servant for expenditure reasonably and properly incurred by him in the lawful and authorized exercise of his tasks.

(b) *On the part of the employee :*

    (i) To obey the lawful orders of the employer ;
    (ii) To exercise care in executing his tasks and to do them efficiently ;
    (iii) To account to the employer for property and money coming into the hands of the employee on behalf of the employer ;
    (iv) To act with good faith and in the interests of the employer and not to make secret profits or divulge confidential information.

Among statutory provisions which have recently been enacted in the field of employment are the following :—

    (i) The Equal Pay Act, 1970 (in force from 29th December, 1975) providing for payment of equal remuneration as between the sexes, and to prevent discrimination as regards terms and conditions of employment between men and women.
    (ii) The Employment Agencies Act, 1973 (as amended by Schedule 13 to the Employment Protection Act, 1975) controls such agencies (as defined in the Act) by subjecting them to a system of licensing. Regulations may be made by the Secretary of State. Such Regulations may provide exceptions to the general rule laid down in the Act that an agency may not charge a fee to a person for finding or seeking to find him employment.
    (iii) The Sex Discrimination Act, 1975. Part II of the Act renders unlawful sex discrimination in the field of employment. It spells out situations in which it is unlawful for such discrimination to take place, namely terms of employment, opportunities for promotion and arrangements made for determining who shall be offered employment.
    (iv) The Employment Protection Act, 1975 (apart from putting on a statutory basis the Conciliation and Arbitration Service) contains provisions as to guarantee payments for work, payment to an employee suspended from normal work on medical grounds in consequence of health and similar regulations in a Schedule to the Act ; maternity pay and right to re-instatement in employment after childbirth ; right to reasonable time off to take part in specified trade union activities or to perform duties in connection with certain public offices or where the employee is dismissed because of redundancy, to look for new employment or arrange training for future employment.

**Termination may well be covered by special terms in the service agreement, but it must be borne in mind that under the**

1972 Act (as modified by the Employment Protection Act, 1975), employees working more than twenty-one hours a week (and have been in continuous employment for four weeks or more) are entitled to notice of the minimum length as follows :—

    (i) not less than one week's notice if his period of continuous employment is less than two years ;
    (ii) not less than one week's notice for each year of continuous employment of the employee if his period of continuous employment is two years or more but less than twelve years ; and
    (iii) not less than twelve weeks' notice if the period of continuous employment is twelve years or more.

The common law right to dismiss without notice in case of serious misconduct is specifically preserved by the Act.

The Redundancy Payments Act, 1965 (as amended), imposes an obligation on employers to make redundancy payments to employees (calculated on the basis of length of service of the individual employee—the minimum length being 26 weeks) dismissed by reason of redundancy, laid-off or kept on short-time.

An employer is not bound to give a testimonial to his servant or to answer questions from interested parties as to the servant's character and behaviour ; if he does, anything he writes to a stranger will be protected unless shown to have been written with malice sufficient to defeat the privilege otherwise accorded by the law of defamation to his communication.

An employee who has acquired confidential information or knowledge of secret processes during his employment may not sell, give away or otherwise misuse it after the employment has terminated, any more than he can whilst it is continuing. A breach of this duty would render him liable to damages and also subject to the operation of an injunction if the Court should see fit to grant one. Subject to that, the skill and knowledge an employee acquires is his to take with him to a new employment, into which he may freely enter unless prevented by any covenant in restraint which, if tested in the Courts, would be upheld as reasonable.

A wrongful dismissal by the employer amounts to a repudiation of contract (giving rise to an action for damages but not, in general, for injured feelings (see *Addis* v. *Gramophone Co.* (1909) but contrast *Cox* v. *Philips Industries* (1976)—where a virtual demotion was involved) and releases the employee from any covenants entered into by him : *General Billposting Co.* v. *Atkinson* (1909). The employee is under a duty to mitigate his damages by taking reasonable steps to secure other employment : see *Brace* v. *Calder* (1895) where it was held that the dissolution of a partnership operated as a wrongful dismissal of the firm's employees, but that the plaintiff (one of those employees) had failed to " mitigate " the damages, by not accepting re-employment by the continuing partners on terms as favourable as those of the terminated contract of employment.

An innovation of the Industrial Relations Act, 1971, was the concept of " unfair dismissal " as defined by the Act (and not to be confused with wrongful dismissal or redundancy referred to above). An employee (in any employment not excepted from the application of the material provisions of the Act) asserting unfair dismissal can lodge a complaint, which if he substantiates it, entitles him to compensation to be fixed as provided by the legislation or some other remedial measure such as reinstatement or conciliation. On the repeal of the 1971 Act by the Trade Union and Labour Relations Act, 1974 (see *ante* p. 127) these " unfair dismissal " provisions were, in substance repeated, but with some improvements.

Although the relationship of master and servant is basically contractual, the impact of legislation like the Factories Acts (in due course to be replaced by provisions in and Regulations issued under the Health and Safety at Work Act, 1974) and the development of the concept of the duty of care in connection with the tort of negligence (see Chapter VII) have produced duties incumbent upon an employer independent of contract. It has become recognized that an employer is under a duty, for the safety of his employees, to have reasonably safe premises, plant and machinery, to adopt a reasonably safe system of work and to employ reasonably competent staff. A breach of the statutory or common law duties causing damage or injury will give rise to an action for damages at the instance of the employee.

To round off the discussion, allusion must be made to the doctrine of vicarious liability under which a master may be liable in law for the acts of his servant. The doctrine will be discussed in detail in Chapter VII.

## CHAPTER VI

## LAW OF PROPERTY

**Conception of Property.**
 The term " property " is used in more senses than one. When the Sale of Goods Act, 1893, talks of the " property " in goods, it means the ownership of them. Usually, however, the word means the things capable of ownership and of possessing economic value. Things capable of ownership, however, need not exist in tangible form. Patents and copyright, for example, are property, but they are merely collections of rights to prevent others from gaining the benefit of certain inventions or works. The latter are, therefore, called *choses in action* or incorporeal chattels, that is, rights which can be enforced only by action and not by taking possession. Things having a tangible form, on the other hand, are called corporeal chattels or *choses in possession*, because the rights over those things are capable of physical assertion.

**Ownership and Possession.**
 Ownership and possession are quite distinct legal conceptions. In its essence, ownership is a right or an aggregate of rights. The owner of a thing is that person who has all the rights of enjoyment, destruction and disposition, subject to the rights of others. The owner of a field does not cease to be its owner because a neighbour has a right of way across it.
 Possession, on the other hand, is primarily a matter of fact. If the owner of a watch is robbed of it by a thief, the owner's rights remain intact, but his possession has gone. The thief on the other hand, may be in possession, but he acquires no right to the watch as against the owner.
 Possession of a thing involves a certain power of control over it, together with the intention to maintain that control. The degree of control and intention necessary for possession depends on the circumstances and the character of the thing possessed. Thus, the evidence of possession required in the case of a house would be different from that required in the case of a motor car.
 Possession is, however, evidence of ownership. Moreover, English law protects possession as against all persons but the owner. Thus, the finder of goods is, except as against the true owner, protected by the law against the whole world. Further,

even a wrongful possession, if continued for a certain length of time, will mature into what is indistinguishable from ownership. Thus, a wrongful possession of land by a " squatter " for twelve years destroys the former owner's title and gives the possessor a title which none can dispute. Even a thief can sue anyone (except the real owner or a person acting by his authority) who deprives him of the possession of the stolen property. This is the foundation of the maxim " Possession is nine points of the law ". A person cannot justify depriving a thief of the possession of the stolen property by pleading the theft.

Normally, possession is merely the external form in which a rightful claim asserts itself, and it is, therefore, usually to be found with ownership, the separation of the two being quite exceptional and resulting from accident, wrong or the special nature of the claim.

### Classification of Property.

Property is divisible into movables and immovables. This is the classification generally adopted in Continental legal systems. English law prefers to classify property as real and personal property, or, briefly, realty and personalty, the distinction between the two being historical in origin. Real property comprises all rights over land with certain additions and exceptions established by law, all other proprietary rights being included under personal property. Thus, leaseholds, although they are rights over land, are personal property, and trees which, while growing on land, are real property, become personal property the moment they are severed. Industrial crops, i.e., annual crops such as grain are, on the other hand, personal property.

At Common Law when the owner of real property was wrongfully dispossessed, he could bring an action, known as a " real " action, for recovery of possession. This remedy was not originally available to a dispossessed leaseholder, whose only remedy was an action for damages. Since his remedy was so restricted to a personal action (as opposed to a real action for recovery of possession) leaseholds were, as already stated, deemed personal property. This distinction was rendered obsolete by about the time of Henry VIII, when leaseholders were enabled to recover possession of their property by the same procedure as was available to dispossessed real property owners, but the legal principles applicable respectively to real and personal property have continued to develop along separate lines. Now, by the Law of Property Act, 1925, and the other statutes of that year, which completely remodelled the English law as to property in land, the law as to real and personal property has to a large extent been assimilated, and the chief distinction now is between property in land (immovables) and property in other subject-matter (movables).

The term, " chattels " (i.e., goods), and the expression " goods and chattels ", are used as synonymous with personalty, including debts, shares and patent rights. Chattels may be either *chattels real* or *chattels personal*. Chattels real indicate those forms of personalty associated at Common Law with the land law, e.g., leaseholds. Chattels personal, on the other hand, may be either corporeal chattels, i.e., tangible objects such as furniture or cattle, or incorporeal chattels, i.e., those not having an actual physical existence, such as stocks and shares, patents and copyright. This has given rise to the division, mentioned above, into *choses in possession* and *choses in action*.

Beneficial interests arising under trusts (see below) are known as equitable interests.

### Rights in Rem and Rights in Personam.

A right *in rem*, sometimes called a real right, corresponds to a duty imposed upon persons in general. A right *in personam*, or personal right, corresponds to a duty imposed upon definite individuals.

Property is an example of a right *in rem*, this phrase implying that such rights are enforceable against all persons. Other rights, called in Roman Law " obligations ", are rights *in personam*. A right *in personam* is enforceable only against certain persons. A right *in rem* is negative because it is nothing more than a right to be left alone. Most rights *in personam* are positive.

For example, if A trespasses on B's land, he is interfering with B's proprietary right, or property, in the land, which is a right *in rem* ; but the result of his trespass (which is a tort, or civil wrong) is to invest B with a right to sue A for at least nominal damages, and this right of B's is a right *in personam*.

The right to freedom of speech, and to one's good name, which are protected by various legal sanctions are also examples of rights *in rem*.

### Legal and Equitable Interests.

This is the classical division of property into legal interests, protected by the Common Law, and equitable interests, protected originally by the Chancellor. A large number of statutes have modified both Law and Equity, and since the Judicature Act, 1873, set up the present Supreme Court, Law and Equity have been administered side by side in the same Courts, the rules of Equity prevailing in case of conflict between the two systems. But the two systems still retain their separate existence as systems, and have, indeed, been remodelled so as to give the distinction a new significance by the property legislation of 1925. Equitable interests, as has been said, are of great importance as the only means by which future and concurrent interests in land can now be created.

## " Uses " and Trusts.

Something more must be said here about trusts, which have been mentioned in Chapter II. It was there pointed out how " uses " came into being in an attempt to circumvent the hardships which feudal laws imposed on feudal tenants, and how the beneficial, or equitable, interests of the beneficiaries were enforced by the Court of Chancery. These equitable interests came, in the course of time, to have almost the same standing as legal estates with one most important exception. This is that an equitable interest will not affect *a bona fide purchaser of the legal estate* out of which the equitable interest is carved, if such purchaser gives value and has no " notice " of the equitable interest. The doctrine of notice is referred to later in this Chapter.

The use became in course of time the foundation of the family settlement, which became the almost universal method of holding land during the Civil War, and seems to have increased in popularity during the succeeding two centuries. Unfortunately, settlements were so complicated and the beneficial interests under them were so split up, that the land became almost impossible to alienate. This led to the enactment of the various Settled Land Acts, the object of which is to render land subject to a settlement freely alienable. Settlements of land are treated in greater detail below. Trusts of personalty are quite as common as trusts of land.

Express trusts of land must be evidenced in writing, and are generally created by deed or will, but trusts of pure personalty (i.e., all personal property other than leaseholds) *may* be created orally.

In order to be effective a trust must be completely constituted, that is be perfectly created. It is not completely constituted unless all necessary steps have been taken to vest the legal estate in the trustees or there is a declaration of trust by the settlor. Where a trust is completely constituted it will, of course, be enforced even though the beneficiaries are " volunteers " (that is have provided no " consideration " in the legal sense). There is, however, no equity, to perfect an imperfect trust in favour of a volunteer. Where, however, valuable consideration is given or, in certain cases what is known as " marriage consideration " exists, an incompletely constituted trust will be treated as a contract to create a trust and will be enforced by Equity.

## LAW OF PROPERTY

The complete constitution of a trust is accomplished :—

(a) By the conveyance of the trust property to the Trustee. The mode of transfer appropriate to the particular property must be adopted. If this is not done, then the trust will fail unless the instrument of transfer contains a declaration of trust ; or
(b) By a declaration of trust by the settlor. If the trust relates to land it must be evidenced by writing. Otherwise the declaration may be oral, or be inferred from conduct.
(c) Where the trust is created by will, the death of the testator and probate of his will.

In addition to express trusts in the case of land, there are :—

(i) Resulting trusts ; e.g., where a testator leaves property on trust for a beneficiary and the beneficiary predeceases the testator, the trustee will hold the property for the benefit of the testator's representatives. Where a person purchases land or other property and the conveyance is taken in the name of another person, whom we may call the nominal purchaser, the nominal purchaser holds the property on trust for the real purchaser. This presumption of a resulting trust may be rebutted by what is known as the *presumption of advancement*. The last-mentioned presumption will generally be inferred from the relationship of the real to the nominal purchaser. Thus, if the real purchaser is the father or husband of the nominal purchaser, the presumption of advancement, i.e., that the real purchaser intended to benefit the nominal purchaser, will override the presumption of a resulting trust. In cases where there is no such close relationship, the presumption of a resulting trust will be overridden by actual evidence that the nominal purchaser was intended to benefit, although such intention will not be presumed.
(ii) Implied trusts ; e.g., where a person purchases property and has it transferred into the name of another person, there is the presumption of an implied trust for the purchaser.
(iii) Constructive trusts, as where a trustee obtains a renewal in his own name of a lease held by him as trustee.
(iv) Precatory trusts, which arise where a person gives property to another and expresses a wish, desire, or hope that the donee will deal with it in some particular way, e.g., for the benefit of a third person. The tendency of modern decisions is to hold that in these cases no trust is created because of the absence of one of the three " certainties " (see Chapter II).

Trusts may also be divided into *private* trusts, and *public*, or *charitable*, trusts. In the former case the intention is to benefit private individuals only, whilst in the latter case the intention is to benefit the public at large, or a defined section of it, hence the position that charitable trusts may, in the last resort, be enforced by the Attorney-General. Charitable trusts are usually divided into the following classes :—

(i) Trusts for the relief of poverty.
(ii) Trusts for the advancement of education.
(iii) Trusts for the advancement of religion.
(iv) Trusts for other purposes beneficial to the community, not falling under the first three heads.

A feature of a charitable trust distinguishing it from an express private trust is that, where a general charitable intention can be shown, a charitable trust does not fail for absence of certainty of objects as would be the case with a private trust. Moreover, where the objects of a charitable trust have become impossible of fulfilment, the application of the doctrine known as *cy-près* enables the court or the Charity Commissioners to direct a scheme whereby the charitable intention of the settlor or donor can be carried out *as nearly as can be* [the meaning of *cy-près*] to the declared intention.

The Charities Act, 1960, apart from consolidating and modernizing the law concerning charities and abolishing the law of mortmain, has extended the application of the doctrine to include cases where :—

(i) The original purposes have as far as is possible been fulfilled or cannot be carried out ; or

(ii) the original purposes provide a use for part only of the property ; or

(iii) the property given can be more effectively employed if used in conjunction with other property applicable for similar purposes ; or

(iv) the original purposes were laid down by reference to an area which then was, but has ceased to be, a unit for some other purpose, or by reference to a class of persons or an area which has ceased to be suitable having regard to the spirit of the gift and to its administration ; or

(v) the original purposes have been otherwise adequately provided for ; or ceased altogether ; or ceased to be an effective method of using the property.

Trustees may be either (1) individuals of full age and legal capacity ; (2) authorized corporations, known as " trust corporations " (e.g., the big Banks and some Insurance Companies) ; (3) the Public Trustee (as to whom see further *post* p. 149). Since corporate trustees are not affected by human mortality they are useful where continuity of function is of importance.

## Appointment of Trustees.

A trustee may be appointed by :—

(a) The creator of the trust, i.e., the *settlor*.

(b) The *beneficiaries*, if all are of full age and sound mind and entitled to the whole interest.

(c) *Any person having a power* under the trust instrument or under the Trustee Act, 1925, to appoint new trustees.

(d) The *Court*.

The Court will not appoint any person under disability or outside the Court's jurisdiction, unless the trust property or all the beneficiaries are abroad ; nor will it appoint any beneficiary or beneficiary's spouse or solicitor. A minor cannot be appointed trustee, although he can be a *constructive* trustee : *Re Vinogradoff* (1935).

Where a trustee :—

(*a*) Is dead ; *or*
(*b*) *Remains out* of the United Kingdom for more than twelve months ; *or*
[It was held in *Re Whitehead's Will Trusts* (1971) that (*b*) does not preclude the appointment (in exceptional circumstances) of a new trustee who is resident abroad.]
(*c*) Desires to be *discharged* ; *or*
(*d*) *Refuses* to act ; *or*
(*e*) Is *unfit* to act ; *or*
(*f*) Is *incapable of* acting ; *or*
(*g*) Is a *minor* ; *or*
(*h*) Being a corporation, is or has been *dissolved*.

Section 36 of the Trustee Act, 1925, provides that a new trustee may by writing be appointed in his place by :—

(*a*) The *person or persons nominated* by the trust instrument for the purpose of appointing new trustees ; *or*, if there is no such person or no such person able and willing to act,
(*b*) The *surviving or continuing trustee or trustees* for the time being ; *or*
(*c*) The *personal representatives of the last* surviving or continuing trustee.

If a testator shows an intention to create a trust but does not appoint a trustee, the personal representative is deemed a trustee. Similarly, on the death of a sole or last surviving trustee, his personal representatives, pending the appointment of new trustees, have all the powers of the deceased trustee. Where there are several co-trustees, upon the death of one, the survivors continue to officiate.

Under section 41 of the Act, whenever it is expedient to appoint a new trustee or new trustees, and it is found inexpedient, difficult or impracticable to appoint one in any other way, the Court may make the appointment, especially where the original trustee is convicted of a crime, is mentally disordered, a bankrupt, or a corporation which is in liquidation or has been dissolved.

## Disclaimer of Trustees.

A trustee may decline to accept office, but if he wishes to disclaim, he must do so promptly, so as to rebut the presumption, arising after a lapse of time, that he has accepted the office. It is desirable that a disclaimer should be by deed.

A trustee *cannot disclaim part* of a trust : he must disclaim all or nothing.

### Removal of Trustees.

A trustee can be removed :—

(a) *Under an express power* contained in the will or deed.
(b) *Under a statutory power.*
(c) *By the Court.* In this case, the paramount consideration of the Court is the welfare of the beneficiaries. The Court will not readily remove a trustee unless his conduct jeopardizes the trust property.

If a trustee becomes bankrupt, the Court can remove him under section 41 of the Trustee Act, 1925.

### Retirement of Trustees.

A trustee can retire :—

(1) *Under statutory authority.* Section 39 of the Trustee Act provides that a trustee may retire by deed, provided that :—
   (a) He leaves either a trust corporation or at least two individual trustees to carry on the trust ; *and*
   (b) The continuing trustees and such other person as is empowered to appoint new trustees consent to the retirement by deed. These conditions must be fulfilled if a trustee is to retire *without a new trustee being appointed in his place.*

(2) *By application to the Court by originating summons.* This method should be resorted to only when the trustee cannot be released from office in any other way, e.g., where there are beneficiaries who are minors or beneficiaries subject to some legal disability. It is entirely in the discretion of the Court whether a retirement will be sanctioned or not.

(3) *With the consent of all the beneficiaries,* provided they are *sui juris* and fully competent to give such consent.

### Trustee's Equitable Obligations.

A trustee's main duties are :—

1. *To carry out the directions in the settlement,* provided, of course, that these are legal. Further, he must be *diligent,* i.e., intelligent and careful in the performance of the directions. He may at any time, at the cost of the trust property, apply to the Court for authority to do any act or to undertake any transac-

tion regarded as expedient by the Court for solving problems in the administration of the trust.

2. *Prima facie, to preserve the trust property.* Thus, the trustees have no power of sale unless it is expressly provided for in the instrument. But they *must* sell in certain cases, e.g., where, on undertaking a trust, they find that some of the investments are in unauthorized securities, i.e., securities not authorized by the Trustee Investments Act, 1961, or the instrument creating the trust. This is because the trustee must reduce the property to its safest and simplest form.

The Act of 1961 repealed that part of the Trustee Act, 1925, which set out the list of authorized securities. In its place it enacted a virtual code, giving trustees extensive powers to invest not only in gilt-edged securities but also a certain portion of the trust funds in " equities ", while preserving the power to grant mortgages in respect of land under certain conditions.

3. *To pay over the trust income to the beneficiaries.*

4. *To exercise absolute impartiality between the different beneficiaries.* Thus, a trustee must realize investments of a wasting or hazardous nature, e.g., leaseholds, or shares in speculative companies, not only because of his duty (2) above, but also because of his duty to be impartial, for such investments, while probably bringing in more income (for the beneficiary entitled to the income for life), will not be so satisfactory from the point of view of those beneficiaries who are interested in the capital, e.g., children, perhaps unborn, who have some *future* interest in the capital.

5. *To render at all times full accounts to the beneficiaries.* If a trustee refuses to produce his accounts within a reasonable time, he must pay the costs of proceedings to compel him to do so.

6. *Not to make any profit, direct or indirect, out of his trust.* One example of this strict rule is the prohibition against a trustee buying any part of the trust property from the trust.

7. *Not to delegate his duties unless authorized.* He may, however, employ a solicitor, a banker or a stockbroker to carry out necessary transactions concerning the trust property.

Under the Public Trustee Act, 1906, a Public Trustee has been created. He can be appointed as a sole or as a new or additional trustee by the settlor, by the person having the power to appoint new trustees or by the Court. The advantages of such an appointment are continuity of office, avoidance of the difficulties which often arise in filling vacancies and a guarantee that the estate will be administered in a proper manner. The State is responsible for his breaches of trust.

## CHAPTER VI

### Liability of Trustees for Breach of Trust.

Breach of trust is some improper act, neglect or default by a trustee in respect of the trust. It renders a trustee liable to :—

(1) *Criminal prosecution* (in certain cases).
(2) *An action for damages, or for an order that he shall replace the loss.*

Beside these personal remedies against the trustee, beneficiaries injured by breach of trust have the following " real " or proprietary, remedies :—

(a) *The right to follow the trust property,* if it is identifiable, into the hands of anybody who has obtained it, except a *bona fide* purchaser of the legal estate or interest in it for value. A similar right exists to " follow " any property into which the trust fund has been converted.
(b) *The right to impound any beneficial interest which the trustee may himself have* under the trust.

On the other hand, the Court may relieve a trustee who has acted " honestly and reasonably ". And a claim against a trustee, except where the breach was fraudulent, or where the claim is to recover trust property or its proceeds still retained by the trustee or previously converted to his own use, will be unenforceable after six years, the time starting to run from the moment of the breach, in most cases whether the beneficiary knew of it or not. A trustee will also be relieved of liability if made bankrupt and discharged in bankruptcy, unless his breach of trust was fraudulent.

Further a beneficiary who acquiesces in the breach will have no right of action in respect of it, provided he knew all the facts and was of full age ; if another beneficiary who did not acquiesce sues the trustee in respect of the breach, the Court may in most cases order the trustee to be indemnified out of the interest of the beneficiary who instigated the breach.

### Variation of Trusts.

Where *all* the beneficiaries are *sui juris* (that is of full age and capacity) they can have the trust property dealt with by the trustees in any way the beneficiaries desire. In all other cases, since the trustees themselves or such of the beneficiaries as are *sui juris* cannot vary the trusts, the sanction of the Court must be obtained to any deviations from the terms of the trust. The Variation of Trusts Act, 1958, has facilitated applications for such sanction where it can be shown that the arrangements are in the interests of the beneficiaries.

## Incapacity of Minors.

Under the Law of Property Act, 1925 (as read with the Family Law Reform Act, 1969), a minor cannot hold a legal estate in land. He can, however, hold an equitable interest in land as a beneficiary under a trust. If land is left to a minor by will, the legal estate vests at first in the testator's personal representatives, who can retain the land until the minor attains the age of eighteen or appoint trustees to look after it for him. A minor can accept a gift of personal property, e.g., shares, but he can repudiate it when he comes of age.

As to alienation, generally speaking, a minor cannot make a binding disposition of his property to others. In regard to tangible movable property which he actually has in his hands, a minor has powers of alienation the limits of which have not been precisely determined. Thus, a sale of personal effects by a minor who has reached years of discretion will, in the absence of fraud or unfair dealing, be held to be binding. So also will a payment by him for goods bought, even though such payment could not have been enforced against him.

The assignment of an equitable interest in land requires writing, while for the transfer of stocks and shares, claims against debtors and interests held by others upon trust, a written document or a deed is necessary. In such cases, the minor's acts become binding on him only if, after attainment of full age, he fails to repudiate them within a reasonable time.

No minor can dispose of property by will, unless he is a soldier or airman on active service or a mariner at sea. In certain cases, however, a person of the age of sixteen can make what amounts in effect to a disposition by will. Thus, a member of a trade union or friendly society may, at that age, nominate in writing a person to receive moneys payable on his death by the union or society.

As to legacies to minors see *post*, p. 208.

As to a minor's transactions with a Building Society, see *ante*, p. 100.

## PERSONAL PROPERTY

### Transfer of Title to Chattels.

There is a legal maxim which runs : *Nemo dat quod non habet* (" No one gives what he has not "). In other words, if, for example, goods are sold by a person who has a defective title thereto and who does not sell them under the authority or with the consent of the owner, the buyer acquires no better title to the goods than the seller had. In the following cases, however, the buyer acquires a good title, notwithstanding the defect in the title of the seller or transferor :—

(a) In the case of the transfer of a negotiable instrument, e.g., a cheque, to a holder in due course. This follows the analogy of the transfer of current coin of the realm.
(b) Where, by the doctrine of estoppel, the owner is prevented by his conduct from denying the seller's authority to deal with the goods.
(c) Where a transaction falls within the provisions of the Factors Acts or similar enactments enabling the *apparent* owner of goods to deal with them as if he were the true owner.
(d) Where a sale is made under the order of a *Court* of competent jurisdiction.
(e) Where a vendor's title is not void but merely voidable, and has not been avoided at the time of the sale, the purchaser obtains a good title, provided he acts in good faith, with no notice of the defect in title.
(f) Where goods are sold in *market overt*. This is the description applied to a sale in recognized markets throughout the country or in any shop in the City of London (" the square mile ") of the goods usually sold in that shop. Market overt is held each day, except Sunday, in the City, but elsewhere only on the specific days set apart. To obtain the protection of the rule, the transaction must commence and finish in open market in full view of the public, between sunrise and sunset [see *Reid* v. *Metropolitan Police Commissioner* (1973)], and the buyer must act in good faith without notice of any defect in the seller's title. The following have been held *not* to be sales in market overt :—

(i) A sale in a room above or behind the shop or behind a curtain.
(ii) Where the goods were not of the kind usually traded in by the vendor.
(iii) Where the shopkeeper was the *buyer* of the goods. Even a purchaser in market overt will not obtain a good title where the goods belong to the Crown, or where the buyer knows the goods do not belong the the seller.

(g) Where a person sells goods but remains (with the buyer's consent) in possession of the goods or documents of title, and then transfers them to a third party, the first purchaser loses his right to the goods, unless the third party knew of the previous sale or otherwise acted in bad faith : section 25, Sale of Goods Act, 1893.
(h) Similarly, where a person, having bought or agreed to buy goods, obtains (with the seller's consent) possession of the

goods, or the documents of title thereto, then any disposition of such goods or documents of title by such person to a third person who acts in good faith, and with no notice of the prior rights of the original seller, will confer a valid title as if such sale were made by an authorized mercantile agent : section 25, Sale of Goods Act, 1893.

(*i*) In the case of a sale by a bankrupt of property acquired by him after being adjudicated bankrupt, before his Trustee has intervened to assert his title.

(*j*) In the case of a purchase of goods from a Sheriff selling under a writ of *fieri facias* (see Introduction) to enforce a judgment : *Curtis* v. *Maloney* (1950).

(*k*) In the case of certain motor vehicles as provided by Part III of the Hire-Purchase Act, 1964. (See *post*, p. 164.)

## Method of Transfer.

The ordinary everyday transfer of ownership of goods is accompanied by no special formalities : a mere physical handing over of the goods suffices, whether the transfer be by sale for value or by way of gift. Even the physical transfer of the goods is not always necessary. Thus, where there is an unconditional contract of sale of specific goods in a deliverable condition, ownership (and with it the risk of loss or damage) will pass by virtue of the contract itself, without any actual delivery of the goods. Similarly, the indorsement and delivery of a bill of lading, a document of title to goods on board ship, will transfer the ownership of the goods. In certain cases, however, some particular mode of transfer is required. Thus, to transfer ownership in a British ship, a special instrument known as a " bill of sale " (not to be confused with a similarly-named instrument to be described later) must be executed and registered in the shipping register. Also assignments of copyright must be *in* writing.

It will be appreciated that in many cases, from the very nature of things, some form of writing, often under seal, is required, accompanied by further formalities, e.g., the transfer of shares in companies, which must be completed by entry in the books of the company concerned.

In the case of a sale of goods, the intending buyer should, generally speaking, satisfy himself as to the quality of the goods or their fitness for any particular purpose, for the seller is under no duty to disclose defects in the goods. The maxim is *Caveat Emptor* (" Let the buyer beware "). Under the Sale of Goods Act, 1893 (as amended by the Supply of Goods (Implied Terms) Act, 1973), the following conditions are, however, implied :—

(1) That (except in the special circumstances now provided) the seller has, or will have, a right to sell ;
(2) Where goods are sold by description, that the goods shall correspond with the description ;
(3) Where the seller sells goods in the course of a business and the buyer expressly or impliedly discloses to the seller any particular purpose for which the goods are being bought there is an implied condition that the goods supplied under the contract are reasonably fit for that purpose, whether or not that is a purpose for which such goods are commonly supplied, except where the circumstances show that the buyer does not rely, or that it is unreasonable for him to rely, on the seller's skill or judgment.
(4) Where the seller sells goods in the course of a business, there is an implied condition that the goods supplied under the contract are of merchantable quality [an expression now defined in the amended Act] except that there is no such condition—
  (a) as regards defects specifically drawn to the buyer's attention before the contract is made ; or
  (b) if the buyer examines the goods before the contract is made, as regards defects which that examination ought to reveal.
(5) Where goods are sold by sample, that the bulk shall correspond in quality with the sample, that the buyer shall have a reasonable opportunity for comparing the bulk with the sample before acceptance, and that the goods are free from any defect rendering them unmerchantable, which is not apparent on reasonable examination of the sample.

N.B. It should be noted that the 1973 Act absolutely precludes the exclusion (by agreement) of the implied conditions in the case of a " consumer sale " (as defined in the 1973 Act) and in all other cases permits exclusion only where this would be fair and reasonable in the light of the guidelines given in the 1973 Act.

**Gifts.**

There are three types of gift :—

  (a) Gifts *inter vivos* ;
  (b) Gifts by will ; and
  (c) *Donationes mortis causa*.

These will be treated separately.

GIFTS *inter vivos*.

A gift *inter vivos* is a transfer of any property from one person to another without any consideration passing from the donee. The gift must be accepted by the donee to make it a valid gift. It may be made either by deed, or by transfer of possession with intent to pass ownership.

All forms of property, both real and personal, may be the subject of a gift *inter vivos*. Where a certain form of transfer is appropriate to a particular form of property, that form must be employed to make a valid gift.

Where the subject-matter of the gift admits of delivery, e.g., a book or other tangible article, mere delivery will suffice.

Gifts can be made subject to conditions precedent or subsequent. Thus, an engagement ring is a gift subject to an implied condition subsequent, i.e., that the parties shall marry. If the parties do not marry (except where the donor is at fault) the ring must be returned.

Where a trust is declared, it is binding on the declarer even if (as is usually the case) the beneficiary gives no consideration. But an imperfect gift (e.g., where the appropriate mode of transfer is not employed) will not be construed as a declaration of trust, and will thus not be enforceable against the donor.

## GIFTS BY WILL.

Both real and personal property can be given by will. A gift of personal property by will is known as a *bequest* or *legacy*, and the donee is known as a *legatee*. A gift of real property is known as a *devise* and the donee as a *devisee*.

There are three different classes of legacies, viz. :—

(a) *General legacies*, which are gifts of personal property not specifically distinguished from others of the same kind, e.g., " £100 " or " a horse ".

(b) *Specific legacies*, which are clearly distinct parts of the testator's personal estate, e.g., " my horse Dobbin ", or " the clock presented to me on my retirement ".

(c) *Demonstrative legacies*, which are money gifts payable out of a specific fund, e.g., " £100 payable out of my £1,000 War 3½ per cent. Stock ".

It is important to be able to determine the class to which a legacy belongs for two reasons :—

(a) In case *Abatement* is necessary.
(b) In case *Ademption* may have taken place.

Where the debts exhaust the estate to such an extent that the legacies cannot be paid in full, they will have to *abate*, i.e., to be reduced, proportionately.

Where, on the other hand, a specific article or fund is the subject of a legacy and the testator disposes of it in his lifetime, the specific legacy is said to be *adeemed*, i.e., to be revoked, and the legatee gets nothing.

The borderline between specific and demonstrative legacies is difficult to define, for demonstrative legacies are specific in that they do not abate until the fund demonstrated is exhausted, and general in that they are not subject to ademption.

Note that :—

(a) *As regards abatement*, general legacies abate before specific and demonstrative legacies ; *and*

(b) *As regards ademption*, only specific legacies can be revoked in this manner, except that where a general legacy is left to a child and subsequently to making the will the testator makes a gift (in the nature of an advancement) to the child, the general legacy is adeemed by or to the extent of the advancement. An advancement may be defined as the grant to a child of a portion of his share of capital before the time fixed for his attainment of an absolute interest in possession, frequently with the intention of setting the child up in life with the gift, e.g., a premium paid on articles.

If the fund out of which a demonstrative legacy is payable is non-existent at the time of the death, the legacy is not adeemed but becomes a general legacy payable out of the residuary estate.

Where the subject-matter of a specific legacy has not been completely disposed of by the testator, ademption *pro tanto* takes place, the legatee being entitled to the remaining portion. Ademption is also effected by the exercise, even after the testator's death, of an option to purchase the subject-matter of a specific legacy. A specific legacy is not affected, however, if its subject-matter has been changed in form only.

### Residue.

After the funeral expenses and debts of a deceased person and the death duties and costs of administration have been paid, and, where a will is left, all gifts have been distributed, a certain amount of property will probably remain ; this is called the residue. The will itself may state who is to receive this surplus, which is then called a residuary legacy if the property is personal property, or a residuary devise if the property is real property. If no such disposition is made by the will, a partial intestacy arises and the residue will devolve according to the laws of intestate succession (see page 210).

### Lapse.

If a person to whom a devise or legacy is left dies before the testator, the gift will usually lapse or fail, and an additional benefit will be acquired by the person who takes the residue of the estate. There is, however, an important exception to this rule, for, under section 33 of the Wills Act, 1837, if the devisee or legatee is a *descendant* of the testator and leaves issue which survive the testator, the gift will not lapse upon the death of the beneficiary. Instead, the gift will devolve as if the beneficiary had received it before his death, so that if the beneficiary dies intestate it will form part of his estate and be distributed according to the rules of intestate succession, and if he dies testate it will be disposed of according to the terms of his will. Thus, the devise or legacy does not necessarily benefit the issue of the deceased beneficiary, although the existence of such issue is essential in order to avoid the rule of lapse, as the devise or legacy falls to be dealt with as part of the residuary estate of the deceased beneficiary.

A lapsed share of a residuary legacy, however, is not given to the other residuary legatees, but will devolve as if the testator had died partially intestate, so that if the residue is left equally to $A$ and $B$, who are not issue of the testator, and $A$ dies before the testator, $B$ will still receive only half the residue, whilst the other half will devolve upon the testator's relatives according to the rules of intestate succession. The original testator's will may, of course, dispose of the lapsed share of residue in some other way, and may state that it is to be divided among the surviving residuary legatees, or there may be a " gift over " to the deceased residuary legatee's issue or estate.

If the lapsed legacy is given in satisfaction of an obligation of the testator to the legatee, there will be no lapse if the legatee predeceases the testator.

It will be noticed (page 211) that the predecease of an *intestate's* child automatically benefits the issue of that child. Thus, the intestate's grandchildren will necessarily receive between them their deceased parent's share. The predecease of a *testator's* child, however, does not necessarily mean that the child's issue will benefit. For the gift to the child under the will forms part of the child's residuary estate, and he may leave a will devising or bequeathing the residue to persons other than his issue.

### Donatio Mortis Causa.

This is a gift made in contemplation of death. The gift must be made on the condition that it is only to be complete and absolute on the donor's death, and that the subject-matter of the gift must be returned to the donor if he survives. The gift will also be revoked if the thing given is returned to the donor in his lifetime, or if the donee dies in the donor's lifetime. Such a gift can be claimed by the deceased donor's personal representative for payment of his debts if his other property is insufficient for the purpose.

A *donatio mortis causa* can only be made effectual by delivery. Such delivery need not of itself confer a legal title but it must be something more than a mere symbol. Delivery of a negotiable instrument is sufficient, but delivery of a cheque drawn by the donor is of no effect unless it is cashed or dealt with for value in the donor's lifetime. Delivery of the mortgage deed to the mortgagor has been held sufficient to extinguish the mortgage debt. Delivery may be made to the donee or his agent, but delivery by the donor to his agent, with instructions to deliver to the donee after the donor's death is not sufficient.

## Bailment

Bailment arises where the ownership and the possession of a chattel become vested in different persons. Thus where a chattel is pledged (given as security) the pledgor remains the owner of it and the pledgee acquires the possession of it, thus becoming its *bailee*.

A bailment is a delivery of goods on a condition, expressed or implied, that they shall be restored by the bailee to the bailor (the deliverer), or delivered according to his directions, as soon as the purpose for which they are bailed shall be fulfilled.

Bailments may be :—

(a) For the benefit of the bailor only, as in the case of a deposit without reward ;
(b) For the benefit of the bailee only, as in the case of a loan without interest ;
(c) For the benefit of both bailor and bailee, as in the hire of a thing for use.

The delivery to the bailee must be made for the purpose of giving the exclusive control of the goods, but it need not be made by the bailor. A, for example, may sell goods to B and with B's consent deliver them to a warehouseman to hold as bailee for B.

Generally, the identical goods, in the original or an altered form, have to be returned, but an auctioneer or a pledgee is none the less a bailee because he sells the goods. The bailee may return the goods to the bailor without an actual redelivery. Thus, he may, with the bailor's consent, deliver them to a third person to hold as bailee for the original bailor. This is bailment by *attornment*.

If the bailee does anything inconsistent with the terms of the bailment, the bailment comes to an end, and the right to possess reverts to the bailor as, for instance, where a carrier delivers the goods to the wrong person. If, however, a pledgee deals with the pledge otherwise than as allowed by law, the right to possession does not re-vest in the pledgor until he has paid or tendered what is due on the pledge.

The bailee will be liable for loss caused by the use of the goods for any purpose unauthorized by the bailor.

The case of *Coggs* v. *Bernard* (1703) furnishes a classic definition of bailments and states the liabilities of the bailee in different circumstances; however, modern cases (of which *Houghland* v. *R. R. Low (Luxury Coaches) Ltd.* (1962) is an example) have tended to discard the distinction formerly made between gross negligence and ordinary or slight negligence and to regard "the standard of care required in a case of bailment or any other type of case [to be] the standard demanded by the circumstances of that particular case" (per Ormerod, L.J.).

*Common carriers and innkeepers* are liable, however, by an older Common Law rule still surviving in their cases, for all loss " save by the act of God or the King's enemies " or the guest's own negligence. The Innkeepers Act, 1863, limited this strict liability in the case of innkeepers to the sum of £30, if the provisions of the statute were complied with. The Hotel Proprietors Act, 1956, however, repealed that Act and made hotel proprietors liable for loss of, or damage to, a guest's property, even though it was not due to their fault or that of their staff, but the liability :—

(a) Extends only to the property of guests who have engaged sleeping accommodation at the hotel;
(b) Is limited to £50 for any one article and a total of £100 in the case of any one guest, except in the case of property which has been deposited, or offered for deposit, for safe custody;
(c) Does not cover motor cars or other vehicles of any kind or any property left in them, or horses or other live animals.

Common Law protects the mere possessor of a chattel very efficiently. For example, the action of trespass is available to protect possession, whether of the owner or a mere bailee, and a mere bailee is able to recover the whole of the loss, though his interest may be trifling—for he may not, in the circumstances of the particular case, be liable to reimburse the owner for the loss. The bailee's right to possession is a right against all persons except the bailor.

Also a mere bailee will succeed in an action against any person who wrongfully takes the chattel from the bailee or wrongfully refuses to hand it over to him on demand; even if the bailee has no right to possess the chattel as against the owner. For the law will not allow such a wrongful taker or detainer to plead the *jus tertii*, or right of a third person. Thus, if B wrongfully takes a book in the possession of A, it is no defence to an action by A to prove that the book really belongs to C.

The bailee must always recognize the title of the bailor. He cannot, therefore, refuse to give back the subject of the bailment, even though he believes that the bailor is not legally entitled to it. Should he so refuse, he will be liable in an action for detinue or conversion.

If the bailment is for a specified period or purpose, the bailor cannot demand the return of the thing bailed until the period has expired or the purpose has been fulfilled, or until a sufficient time for the fulfilment of the purpose has elapsed.

The Disposal of Uncollected Goods Act, 1952, authorizes the disposal of goods accepted in the course of a business for repair or other treatment but not redelivered. The bailee must give the bailor written notice that the goods are ready for redelivery, and on the expiration of twelve months after such notice and not less than fourteen days before the sale of the goods, he must give the bailor written notice of his intention to sell the goods.

Where a dispute arises between bailor and bailee on the ground that the charges are excessive or that the repair or other treatment has not been properly carried out, the right to sell is suspended until the dispute is determined. Such a dispute is to be treated as having been determined if the bailee gives the bailor written notice to treat the dispute as determined and the bailor fails to object in one month.

> The Unsolicited Goods and Services Act, 1971 (as amended by the Unsolicited Goods and Services (Amendment) Act, 1975) contains provisions designed to restrict the sending of unsolicited and unordered goods by firms and individuals to persons who have not requested them for the purposes of a trade or business [a type of " involuntary bailment "].
>
> The main effect of the Act is to provide that, where unsolicited goods are sent to a person, that person may as between himself and the sender use and dispose of them as if such goods were an unconditional gift and the title of the sender of the goods shall be extinguished ; the loss of ownership of the goods themselves is, therefore, the " sanction ".
>
> There are various safeguards imposed by the Act to protect a sender who has, for instance, made a genuine mistake in despatching the goods and, generally speaking, an absolute title will not vest in the recipient until six months after the date of receipt by him. This period can be shortened by the recipient sending a notice to the sender requiring him to re-take possession of the goods within 30 days to expire at any time within six months of the date he received them.

### Hire-purchase and Credit-sale and like Transactions.

Many commodities are today acquired by way of hire-purchase and the following is an attempt to draw attention to the salient legal features of the system, the basic object of which has been stated by a writer to be " the deferred transfer of ownership " ; as the Crowther Report on Consumer Credit issued in 1971 (which led ultimately to the passing of the Consumer Credit Act, 1974) saw, however, the system was but one element in the economic-sociological phenomenon of consumer credit, the legal regulation of which stood in need of reform.

A " hire-purchase agreement " is defined in the 1974 Act as :

". . . an agreement, other than a conditional sale agreement. under which—
  (a) goods are bailed . . . in return for periodical payments by the person to whom they are bailed . . ., and
  (b) the property in the goods will pass to that person if the terms of the agreement are complied with and one or more of the following occurs—
    (i) the exercise of an option to purchase by that person,
    (ii) the doing of any other specified act by any party to the agreement,
    (iii) the happening of any other specified event."

A " credit-sale agreement " is defined in the same Act as :

" an agreement for the sale of goods under which the purchase price or part of it is payable by instalments which is not a conditional sale agreement "

The essential difference in law between the two is that under a hire-purchase agreement, there are two parties, namely, the " owner " and the " hirer ". During the currency of the agreement the parties retain these characters, the hirer being a bailee of the chattels hired, required to make certain payments over a given period. He is normally given an option to purchase on satisfying his obligations and making a certain additional payment. Until the exercise of the option the property remains with the owner. Under a credit-sale agreement, however, there is a relation of seller and buyer since the owner disposes of the chattel to the purchaser, who thereupon becomes the new owner, notwithstanding the fact that the full price is not paid on delivery, but is to be spread over an agreed period. The seller has, of course, a right of action in respect of any unpaid purchase money.

Important legal consequences flow from the difference outlined above and may be summarized as follows : Since the hirer under a hire-purchase agreement remains hirer, he is, until he exercises any option to purchase conferred upon him, not a person who has " bought or agreed to buy goods " within the meaning of section 25 of the Sale of Goods Act, 1893 (see *ante*, p. 154), and therefore he cannot pass a good title to a third person however innocent. Since, however, a credit-sale agreement constitutes a transaction which from its inception is a true sale under which the purchaser acquires ownership and not merely possession, section 25 will apply where the conditions laid down are satisfied and the third party will not normally be concerned with any prior or outstanding rights of the original seller of which he had no notice.

A " conditional sale agreement " is really a hybrid type of transaction. As defined in the 1974 Act, it is :

> " an agreement for the sale of goods ... under which the purchase price ... is payable by instalments and the property in the goods ... is to remain in the seller (notwithstanding that the buyer is to be in possession of the goods . . .) until such conditions as to payment of instalments or otherwise as may be specified in the agreement are fulfilled "

It is clearly also one involving consumer credit.

Statute has since 1938 closely regulated the matter of hire-purchase, credit-sale and conditional sale agreements. The relevant provisions so far as the rights of the parties are concerned are now contained in the 1974 Act which applies to any consumer credit agreement (this would include also a conditional bill of sale—see *post* p. 168 and a pawn—see *post* p. 170) between an individual (the " debtor ") and any other person (the " creditor ") by which the creditor provides the debtor with credit (credit being a cash loan or any other form of financial accommodation) not exceeding £5,000.

The Act (apart from controlling advertisements and establishing a system of licensing) very strictly regulates the formation of and the rights and liabilities under agreements within the monetary limits which agreements are treated for the purposes of the Act as " regulated agreements ". It requires agreements to take certain form and to contain certain minimum details as to cash price, instalment and other charges and terms ; the identity of the goods concerned and the right of the hirer to terminate the agreement ; it accords certain rights to cancel *ab initio* agreements and thus gives a cooling-off period and also treats the dealer as agent, for many purposes, of a Financing Institution. The Act causes certain conditions or warranties to be implied in relation to the character and quality of the goods [brought over (with changes in terminology only) from provisions in the Supply of Goods (Implied Terms) Act, 1973] ; restricts the remedies of the person to whom the instalments are payable and makes them exercisable under the control of the County Court ; and generally gives a thorough protection to the interests of the subordinate party.

Part III of the Hire-Purchase Act, 1964 (which Part is subjected to changes in terminology only in a Schedule to the 1974 Act) gives a measure of protection to third parties acquiring in good faith by private purchase motor vehicles the subject of unexpired hire purchase or conditional sale agreements of the existence of which agreements they have no notice. See also *ante* p. 155.

**Negotiable Instruments.**
A negotiable instrument is an example of a chose in action but it has special characteristics.

Negotiability is an attribute attaching to an instrument which evidences an obligation to pay money by virtue of which mere delivery of the instrument, or (if payable to order), indorsement and delivery thereof operates (and without the need to give formal notice of assignment) as a complete legal transfer of both the instrument and the rights created by it, and by virtue of which a transferee *in good faith and for value* is entitled to hold the instrument and enforce the obligation, notwithstanding any defect in, and free from any equity attaching to, or limitation of the title of the transferor. The transferee must take it *bona fide*, i.e., without notice of any fraud in its inception or negotiation. The negotiability of an instrument thus excludes the operation of the rule, *Nemo dat quod non habet*, and the instrument amounts virtually to current coin of the realm.

Examples are bills of exchange, cheques and promissory notes.

Negotiability must be distinguished from transferability. A transferable instrument is one that may be passed from hand to hand for value without the formalities of assignment so that the property in it is transferred from one person to another, but the right of the transferee is liable to be defeated by any defects of title or by any set-off or counter-claim that may be set up against the transferor. Thus, a British Postal Order is transferable but not negotiable. A negotiable instrument, on the other hand, e.g., a cheque, is not affected by any such defect, set-off or counter-claim. The special importance of a negotiable instrument is that a *bona fide holder of it for value* has a good title to it, even though afterwards it appears that he obtained it from a person who had no title to it.

A bill of exchange is an unconditional order in writing, addressed by one person (the drawer) to another (the drawee), signed by the person giving it, requiring the person to whom it is addressed to pay on demand, or at a fixed or determinable future time, a sum certain in money to or to the order of a specified person (the payee), or to bearer.

The essentials of a bill are, therefore, that :—

(1) It must be an order, i.e., its terms must be imperative, in writing.
(2) The order must be unconditional ; i.e., there must be no conditions attached to the making of the payment.

(3) It must be addressed by one person to another.
(4) It must require payment to be made to a specified person or his order, or to bearer.
(5) If the order is not to pay on demand, the time of payment must be fixed or determinable.
(6) It must order payment of a certain sum of money *only*.
(7) It must be signed by the drawer.

A cheque is a particular form of bill of exchange, namely one drawn on a banker, payable on demand.

A bill of exchange has three original parties, whereas a promissory note has but two. A promissory note is an unconditional promise in writing made by one person to another signed by the maker, engaging to pay, on demand or at a fixed or determinable future time, a sum certain in money, to, or to the order of, a specified person or to bearer. An IOU is not a negotiable instrument and amounts to no more than an admission of the existence of a debt.

A bill may be payable either to order or to bearer. Negotiation takes place when a bill is transferred from one person to another in such a manner as to constitute the transferee the holder of the bill. Under the Bills of Exchange Act, 1882, a "holder" is defined as "the payee or indorsee of a bill or note . . . in possession of it or the bearer thereof". Transfer of a bill payable to order is effected by the indorsement of the holder completed by delivery, but if the bill is payable to bearer, no indorsement is necessary, although it is always desirable in order to make the transferor liable as a party to the bill in case of dishonour by non-payment. If the transferor does not indorse it he simply warrants to his immediate transferee, being a holder for value, that the bill is what it purports to be, that he has a right to transfer it, and that at the time of transfer he is not aware of any fact which renders it valueless. Where the transferor indorses the bill, he becomes an indorser, and by his indorsement engages that on due presentment the bill will be accepted and paid according to its tenor, and that, if it be dishonoured, he will compensate the holder or a subsequent indorser who is compelled to pay it, provided that the requisite proceedings on dishonour are taken.

Only in regard to a holder in due course of a bill of exchange does the attribute of negotiability come into full play, affording such holder security of title and remedies against the other parties to the bill. Under the Act of 1882, in order to qualify for the description of "holder in due course" and attendant rights, a person must have taken the bill:—

(a) complete and regular on the face of it;

(*b*) before it was overdue ;
(*c*) in good faith ;
(*d*) for value ; and
(*e*) without notice of any defect in the title of the transferor.

Negotiation by a thief of a stolen bill or cheque payable to bearer will confer a good title on a holder in due course and that title will not be lost on the conviction of the thief for the theft.

Every party whose signature appears on a bill is *prima facie* deemed to have become a party to it for value received, and this consideration may consist of any *antecedent debt or liability*, thus constituting an exception to the rule that consideration must not be past.

A bill of exchange must not be confused with a bill of lading. When a person who wishes to send goods by sea makes an agreement with a shipowner to carry his goods without hiring any particular part of the ship, such an agreement is called a bill of lading. Although it is also a receipt for the goods to which it relates, it is not a bill of sale (see below), and although, where drawn to order or assigns, it is an assignable document of title to the goods, it is not a negotiable instrument, as it cannot generally confer a better title than the transferor possesses.

### Securities.

An owner of corporeal chattels (see *ante*, p. 141) may desire to raise money on the security thereof. The following methods are available to him :—

(*a*) *By bill of sale*. Here, the borrower retains possession only, while full legal ownership is given to the lender. In effect, this is a mortgage of personal chattels.
(*b*) *By pledge*. The legal ownership is retained by the borrower, the possession of the goods or documents of title being given to the lender.

In addition, a creditor may have a *lien*, i.e., a right to retain possession of his debtor's goods until his debt is paid. The creditor obtains no legal ownership. This will be dealt with presently.

Lastly, a person who has lent money to a company may have a debenture creating a charge on the company's assets.

### Bills of Sale.

Goods, as we have seen, may be transferred by merely handing them over, even when the transfer is for value. They may also be transferred by deed without delivery, and, where the transaction is for value, even by writing without seal. Such deeds or instruments generally require to be registered under the Bills of Sale Acts, which have been passed to prevent persons from obtaining credit by continuing to remain in possession of goods when they have secretly transferred their interest in them to others. A bill of sale is commonly used as a means of mortgaging goods, but it may also be used as an out-and-out conveyance.

A bill of sale is an instrument which purports to assign personal chattels—furniture, goods, stock-in-trade—which, however, remain in the apparent possession of the grantor (the person assigning the interest). There are two kinds of bill of sale :—

(a) An *absolute* bill. This is one which is given otherwise than as security for money and which vests the property absolutely in the grantee (the person in whose favour the bill is intended to operate), although the grantor retains possession. For the protection of creditors who might be induced to give credit on the strength of a fictitious appearance of " substance ", the Bills of Sale Act, 1878, sought to give publicity to such " secret " transactions by requiring registration.

(b) A *conditional* bill of sale, sometimes called a " security " or " mortgage " bill. This is one which gives a claim over the goods as security for the repayment of money lent by the grantee and which ceases to operate when the money is repaid. The Bills of Sale Act, 1882, sought to protect borrowers from oppressive or unconscionable conduct on the part of persons advancing loans.

The Court will always go behind the document used and ascertain the real nature of the transaction. If what purports to be a hire-purchase agreement is in fact a security for a loan, the agreement must be registered as a bill of sale. An ordinary receipt for purchase money is not a bill of sale, because it does not purport to pass the ownership in the goods.

The statutory requirements affecting bills of sale are :—

(1) In the case of an absolute bill :—
　(i) It must be duly attested by a solicitor, who must declare that he has explained the effect of the bill to the grantor.
　(ii) It must be registered within seven days of execution and re-registered every five years.
　(iii) It must truly state the consideration for which the bill is given.

(2) In the case of a conditional bill :—
　(i) It must be attested by one or more credible witnesses.

## LAW OF PROPERTY

    (ii) It must be registered within seven days of execution and re-registered every five years.
    (iii) It must truly state the consideration, *which must not be less than* £30.
    (iv) A schedule must be annexed containing an inventory of the goods comprised in the bill.
    (v) The bill must be given by the true owner of the goods.
    (vi) It must be in the statutory form.

The effect of non-compliance with the provisions of the Bills of Sale Acts is :—

(1) In the case of an absolute bill :—

    Non-compliance renders the bill void as against the Trustee in bankruptcy, or the trustee of an assignment for the benefit of creditors, or an execution creditor, of the grantor in respect of the goods comprised in the bill which are in the apparent possession of the grantor at the date of the bankruptcy, assignment or execution. As between the grantor and the grantee, however, the bill is perfectly valid.

(2) In the case of a conditional bill :—

    (i) If the consideration is less than £30, or if the bill is not in the statutory form, the bill is *totally void*. Even the covenant for repayment of money lent and interest, contained in the bill, is void, the only remedy being a Common Law action for recovery of the money lent, with interest at five per cent.
    (ii) If the bill is not duly attested or registered, or if the consideration is not truly stated, the bill is void as against all persons, as to the chattels comprised therein, but the covenant to repay remains valid and may be sued upon.
    (iii) If the inventory is defective, or if the grantor was not, at the time of the execution, the true owner of the goods described therein, then as regards chattels not specifically described or chattels of which the grantor was not the true owner, the bill is void except as against the grantor. If *no* inventory is attached, however, the bill is totally void, not being in the " statutory form ".

It remains to add that the grantee of a conditional bill may seize and sell the goods specified in the schedule :—

    (a) If the grantor makes default in the payment of the money due, or in the performance of any of the covenants in the

bill which are necessary for the maintenance of the security ; or
(b) If he becomes bankrupt ; or
(c) If he fraudulently removes his goods or allows them to be removed ; or
(d) If he fails, without reasonable excuse to produce, on the written demand of the grantee, the last receipts for rent, rates or taxes ; or
(e) If he allows execution to be levied against the goods under any judgment at law ; or
(f) If he allows the goods to be distrained for rent, rates or taxes.

The goods must not be removed for sale for five days from seizure, during which period the grantor may apply to the Court for relief on the ground of the irregularity of the seizure. The grantor has also a considerable measure of protection under the Consumer Credit Act, 1974.

**Pawn or Pledge.**
This is a delivery of goods, or of documents of title to goods, by one person, called the pawnor or pledgor, to another, called the pawnee or pledgee, as security for the payment of a debt or for the fulfilment of an engagement by the transferor. *The legal title to, or ownership of, such property still remains with the pawnor, while the possession or custody passes to the pawnee.* The effect of pawn is to transfer possession of the goods and consequent rights thereto, so that a *pawnee can sue for the return of the goods if they are taken from him.*

No memorandum or other formality is necessary to complete the security (except as provided in the Consumer Credit Act, 1974 mentioned below) and the Bills of Sale Acts do not apply : but before he can make an effective pledge, the *pledgor must have the property in the goods*, unless, as in the case of a factor, he is acting under special authority. By the act of pledging an article, the pledgor in general impliedly *warrants that it is his own property.*

The rights of the pawnee or pledgee are, briefly :—

(a) He can retain possession of the goods until the debt is paid ; and
(b) He can sell the pledged goods *if the debt is not paid* on the date fixed, or where no date is fixed, after reasonable notice demanding payment.

If the sale of the goods produces an amount larger than the debt, the pledgee must hand over the balance to the pledgor after deducting the amount of the debt with interest thereon and costs incurred. If, however, the sum produced does not amount to the sum lent, the pledgee can sue the pledgor for the balance.

The pawnee impliedly undertakes to return the goods pledged when the debt has been paid, unless his right of sale has already been exercised. He loses his rights if he parts with the possession of the goods to the pawnor or his agent, except in cases where he re-delivers them to the pawnor for a special purpose.

The liability of the pawnee or pledgee is as follows :—

(i) He must take reasonable care of the article pledged. If he acts as a prudent man, he will not be responsible for any loss which may be incurred.

(ii) He must not use the goods pledged, unless they are of a kind which will not deteriorate by wear ; even then, however, he uses them at his peril. But such use may be necessary or beneficial, as, for example, giving an animal which has been pledged a reasonable amount of exercise. In this case, the pledgee will be responsible only for damage arising through his negligence.

(iii) If the pledge is stolen property, he may be *sued for conversion* or *detinue* and be compelled to restore it to the rightful owner without any remedy other than his right of action against the pledgor.

The Consumer Credit Act, 1974 repealed the Pawnbrokers Acts, 1872–1960 which previously regulated the taking of chattels into pawn.

Under Part III of the Act of 1974 persons (with certain exceptions) carrying on (*inter alia*) the business of providing consumer credit (this would include a pawnbroker) require a licence. Under Part VIII of the Act there are special provisions concerning the taking into pawn of any article under a regulated agreement (this being defined generally in the Act as (amongst other things) a non-exempt consumer credit agreement). A consumer credit agreement is (as stated in Part II of the Act) an agreement between an individual (the " debtor ") and any other person (the " creditor ") by which the creditor provides the debtor with credit not exceeding £5,000. " Cerdit " includes a cash loan. The special provisions cover such matters as the giving of pawn-receipts and copies of agreements, redemption of pawn and re-delivery of the chattel pawned, as well as realisation of the pawn (after notice to the pawnor—except in the case of a sale by public auction) on failure by the pawnor to redeem. It is an offence for a pawnee to take any article into pawn from an individual known to him to be, or who appears to him to be, a minor. Other provisions in the Act (as generally applicable) empower the Court to reopen an extortionate credit agreement.

## Mortgages of Choses in Action.

Choses in action may be mortgaged, formally or informally. An example of the method in which shares in a company are formally mortgaged, may be helpful. The borrower in such a case assigns his shares to the lender by a formal transfer and hands over the share certificate to the lender, who will then obtain registration of himself as the new member of the company. Thenceforward he is entitled to receive all dividends out of which he may pay himself, or account therefor to the borrower according to the agreement made. This continues until repayment is made, when the borrower is entitled to have the shares retransferred to himself. As a rule the parties enter into an agreement setting out the terms of the transaction and recording that it is by way of mortgage and not an out-and-out sale.

Where shares which are not fully paid are offered as security, it may be inadvisable for the lender to take an absolute assignment thereof, as registration of the transfer will render him liable for all calls which may subsequently be made. In such cases and where there is a possibility of a call being made, a blank form of transfer is usually handed to the lender with the share certificate and a memorandum authorizing him to complete his title by registration, should the borrower fail to repay the loan by an agreed date. To ensure that the borrower does not transfer the shares to another party, the lender may have a "*notice in lieu of distringas*" served upon the company, which must then notify him if any transfer is lodged.

Where policies of assurance are assigned by way of mortgage, written notice of the assignment should be given to the assurance company at their principal place of business, for where the same policy is subject to more than one mortgage the mortgagees take priority according to the dates upon which notice is given: Policies of Assurance Act, 1867.

## Involuntary Transfer of Chattels.

There are several methods of involuntary transfer, i.e., cases where chattels are transferred from one person to another without any voluntary act on the part of their owner. These are :—

(1) *Accessio.* If A builds a house on C's land with B's bricks, the house belongs to C. B may sue A or C for conversion of the bricks. Similarly if A sews his coat with B's thread, the thread becomes part of the coat. The rule does not apply, however, if the chattel is altered in nature, e.g., if grain is made into malt.

(2) *Confusio.* Where A fraudulently mixes his goods with B's

so that reparation of their individual chattels becomes impossible, the whole mass belongs to B.
(3) *Limitation.* Under the Limitation Act, 1939, where A's goods have been wrongfully detained by B and A has omitted to bring an action for their recovery during the period of limitation (six years), A's title to the goods is extinguished, and they become B's.
(4) *Operation of Law.* An adjudication in bankruptcy vests the bankrupt's goods in the Trustee in bankruptcy. Again, a sale by the Court vests the property sold in the purchaser.

**Lien.**
There are three types of lien—*possessory, maritime* and *equitable,* of which the first is by far the best known. A *possessory lien* is the right of one man who is lawfully in possession of property belonging to another to retain it until certain demands of the possessor against the owner are satisfied. There are two types of possessory lien, viz., *general* and *particular.* A general lien arises usually only by express contract, by implication from previous transactions or by the custom of trade. A general lien allows the retention of goods until *any* debt due to the possessor from the owner has been paid, whether such debt is connected with the specific goods retained or not. Bankers and solicitors are amongst those who have general liens. A particular lien gives the possessor only the right to retain specific goods until the debt incurred in connection with *those* goods has been paid. Where any doubt exists the Court will construe a lien as particular, rather than as general.

It will be appreciated that the right of possessory lien is lost if the property subject to the lien is lost or surrendered—unless it is made clear that the lien is retained in the latter event. It is also lost, of course, if the possessor receives payment of the amount due, or agrees to give credit for it, or takes some other security for payment, such as a bill of exchange.

In general, the right is a purely passive one, a right of retention, and (save to the extent permitted by the Disposal of Uncollected Goods Act, 1952, previously mentioned) no power of sale is conferred.

A *maritime lien* is a right over a ship in connection with certain special classes of liability arising out of a maritime adventure. Examples are liens arising out of salvage claims, for seamen's wages or for damage by collision. It is enforceable by the arrest and sale of the ship through the medium of the Admiralty Court. Possession is not essential for the lien to attach or continue.

An *equitable lien* is a charge over property conferred by law on one who is not the owner of that property. It is so called because it was formerly enforceable only in a Court of Equity. Possession is not essential for such a lien to arise. Thus, even if a vendor executes an absolute conveyance of property to the purchaser, he still has an equitable lien on the property in respect of any part of the purchase-money that may remain unpaid. Similarly, a purchaser of land has an equitable lien on the property, before the actual conveyance to him, to the extent of any instalment of the purchase-money that he has paid.

**Patents.**

Certain intangible forms of property deserve some mention. They are patents, trade marks and copyright.

A *patent* is a grant by the Crown to an inventor, giving him for a limited period the monopoly of the right to make the articles, or to apply the processes which he has invented.

The subject of a valid grant must be a *manufacture* (not a mere idea), it must be *novel* (i.e., new within the United Kingdom), and it must be of some *utility* or advantage.

The law governing patents is contained in the Patents Acts, 1949–1957.

A register is kept at the Patent Office containing the names and addresses of grantees of patents, notifications of assignments and the like. The registration of a patent continues for sixteen years from the date of application, but an extension of five years may be obtained on petition to the High Court. In exceptional circumstances, an extension of ten years may be granted.

A patentee may assign his patent absolutely or conditionally, or limit the use of the same to any particular area of the United Kingdom or of the Isle of Man. Such an assignment is usually made under seal. The assignee applies to the Comptroller of Patents to register his title, and he then succeeds to the rights of the assignor. On the death of the patent-owner, the patent vests in his personal representative, and, on his bankruptcy, it vests in his Trustee.

**Trade Marks.**

A *Trade Mark* is a mark used, or proposed to be used, upon, or in connection with, goods for the purpose of indicating that they are the goods of the proprietor of such trade mark, by virtue of manufacture, selection, certification, dealing with or offering for sale. Registration of a trade mark is obtained on application to the Registrar in the prescribed manner, and the application may be for registration in Part A or B of the Register. Strict conditions must be observed for registration in Part A, but when it has been so registered, the proprietor is entitled to the exclusive use of the mark. During the first seven years its validity can always be attacked, but thereafter it can be attacked only on the ground of fraud, a tendency to deceive, or a contravention of law or morality. Any mark may be registered in Part B, if it is capable of distinguishing the proprietor's goods from other goods. Registration of this type affords the proprietor no protection against infringement if the Court holds that the infringement is not likely to deceive or cause confusion, or to indicate any trade connection between the goods and some person entitled, as proprietor, to use the mark. Registration in Part B is not improved at the expiration of seven years. Registration may be, and often is, effected in both Parts. The law on the subject is to be found in the Trade Marks Act, 1938.

Registration remains effective for seven years, but may be renewed from time to time. A registered trade mark may be assigned and transmitted either in connection with the goodwill of a business or not, and on assignment the assignee is entitled to be registered as proprietor.

On the death of the proprietor all rights in a registered trade mark vest in his personal representative under his will, or under the Administration of Estates Act, 1925, in the event of intestacy.

## Copyright.

The basic purpose of copyright is to afford a person a right to restrict reproduction without his consent of his original artistic, literary, dramatic or musical work, so that others may not unjustifiably profit from the toil of his brain.

Copyright is in substance governed by the Copyright Act, 1956.

Copyright protects the actual work as the form in which ideas are expressed; ideas themselves not expressed in concrete form are not the subject of copyright. Thus there is no copyright in news but only in the form in which it is conveyed.

Copyright attaches automatically without registration (except in cases of artistic work registrable under the Registered Designs Act, 1949). The symbol © followed by the year of publication to be seen in some printed books, is of significance only in respect of international copyright which is outside the scope of the present summary of English law.

Copyright subsists (broadly) for the life of the author and fifty years thereafter. Where material capable of copyright has not been published or performed during the lifetime of the author, copyright subsists for fifty years from the actual publication or performance. There are special rules as to photographs and as to the ownership of copyright where certain works are commissioned or are produced in the course of employment.

Infringement of copyright occurs where any person without licence or authority does anything the right to do which is, by the Act, conferred solely on the owner of the copyright. For practical purposes, the infringement would be unauthorized publication, reproduction or dissemination of the copyright matter.

The owner of a copyright has a choice of remedies open to him in the case of an infringement of his rights. He may proceed civilly and claim damages (which in gross cases may be punitive), an injunction, and the delivery up to him of all offending copies and plates; he may also claim an account and payment of profits received. He will not, however, be entitled to any pecuniary remedy other than costs if the defendant was not aware and had no reasonable grounds for suspecting that copyright subsisted in the work. Any action in respect of such infringement must it is thought be brought within six years of the infringement. Alternatively, he may proceed against the offender in a magistrates' court, which may impose a fine or imprisonment.

Under the Dramatic and Musical Performers Protection Act, 1958 (as amended by the Performers' Protection Act, 1963), it is an offence knowingly to make or sell records or films of or to broadcast the performance of a dramatic or musical work unless written consent has been given by the performers.

The owner of the copyright in any work may assign the right, either wholly or partially, and either generally or subject to limitation to any particular country, and either for the whole term of the copyright or for any part thereof, and may grant any interest in the right by licence.

No such assignment or grant will, however, be valid unless it is in writing, signed by the owner of the right in respect of which the assignment or grant is made, or by his duly authorized agent.

**Bankruptcy.**

The law provides means whereby a creditor may be recouped out of the property of his debtor. If judgment is obtained against the debtor, it may be enforced, or executed, against him in various ways, normally by seizure or sale of so much of the debtor's property as may be necessary to satisfy the debt. Imprisonment for debt no longer exists, execution is not against the debtor's person, but if after judgment a debtor has had the means of satisfying it and has deliberately abstained from so doing, the Court may imprison him for what is actually " contempt " of the Court's order.

It may be that the debtor's property is not sufficient to satisfy the claims of all his creditors. It would in such a case be unfair that one creditor should be paid in full and another sent empty away. Accordingly, centuries ago, bankruptcy proceedings were instituted, although, originally, these were applicable only in the case of insolvent traders. It came to be appreciated that a man's insolvency might well be due to his misfortune rather than to his reckless mismanagement of his affairs. Bankruptcy proceedings, therefore, enabled him, when he had done what was within his powers to satisfy his creditors, to make a fresh start, unencumbered by an initial load of debts.

Generally speaking, any debtor having the capacity to enter into a contract can be made bankrupt, provided that he is subject to the jurisdiction of the English Courts, that he owes £50 or more (a figure proposed to be raised to £300 under the Insolvency Bill before Parliament as this edition was being prepared) and that he has committed one of certain acts known as "acts of bankruptcy". An example of an act of bankruptcy is a fraudulent preference, i.e., a payment of money or a transfer of property to a creditor by an insolvent debtor with the dominant intention of giving the creditor a preference over the other creditors.

Since the passing of the Law Reform (Married Women and Tortfeasors) Act, 1935, a married woman has been subject to the law relating to bankruptcy in all respects as if she were a single woman.

The law of bankruptcy applies also to a minor in respect of enforceable debts.

The law of bankruptcy is now consolidated in the Bankruptcy Act, 1914 (as amended). Bankruptcy proceedings are commenced by petition, based upon some *act of bankruptcy* committed within the previous three months. There are several such acts, being various circumstances implying insolvency, such as a fraudulent preference mentioned above or the more frequent act of non-compliance with a bankruptcy notice, following a judgment obtained against him. A preliminary order, a *receiving order*, is made which does not divest the debtor of his property but places it under the control of the Official Receiver, an officer appointed by the Insolvency Division of the Department for Trade and Industry to act in bankruptcy matters, all actions against the debtor being stayed except by consent of the Court. Should no arrangement be arrived at between the debtor and his creditors, meeting with the approval of the Court, the debtor will eventually be adjudicated bankrupt, and will be divested of his property, which, with certain exceptions, will vest in the Trustee in bankruptcy and will become available for distribution amongst his creditors who have lodged proofs of their claims. This distribution is usually on a rateable basis, but certain debts, such as rates and taxes, wages of clerks and servants have preferential treatment. There are also provisions safeguarding the claims of secured creditors, i.e., creditors holding certain of the debtor's property to secure their loans.

There are two important aspects of bankruptcy law which should be mentioned here. The one is the doctrine of " Relation back " under which, although the Trustee's control does not commence until the making of the adjudication order, his *title* is ante-dated to the commencement of the bankruptcy, which is the act of bankruptcy on which the petition was founded, or any earlier act which the Trustee can prove committed within *three* months prior to the date of the petition. The other is the operation of the so-called " reputed ownership clause " by virtue of which there pass to the Trustee " all goods being, at the commencement of the bankruptcy, in the possession, order or disposition of the bankrupt, in his trade or business, by the consent and permission of the true owner under such circumstances that he (the bankrupt) is the reputed owner thereof. . . ."

The bankrupt may apply for his discharge from bankruptcy after adjudication : this will enable him to make a fresh start. Although he has been divested of his property, yet, if the Court grants the discharge, he will be freed from further anxiety as to claims provable in bankruptcy. In appropriate circumstances, the Court may refuse the application for discharge, or postpone it, or attach conditions to it.

The bankrupt is permitted to keep certain property, such as the tools of his trade, wearing apparel, etc., but if he remains undischarged, he is subject to certain disabilities. Thus, he must not obtain credit to the extent of £10 or upwards without disclosing that he is an undischarged bankrupt.

Reference should be made to Chapter IV with regard to rights of action which vest in the Trustee in bankruptcy.

Closely akin to bankruptcy is the procedure known as a Deed of Arrangement, whereby a person in financial difficulties can assign his property to a Trustee for the benefit of his creditors. The execution of such a deed does not render the debtor bankrupt, but the Deeds of Arrangement Act, 1914, provides that a certain proportion of the creditors must assent to the deed and the deed itself must be registered as provided by the Act. In fact, the execution of the deed is in itself an act of bankruptcy, but this cannot be taken advantage of by any creditor who has assented to the deed.

## REAL PROPERTY

**Property Acts of 1925.**

In 1925, some very important Acts were passed relating to land which came into operation on the 1st January, 1926. These are :—

The Settled Land Act.
The Trustee Act.
The Law of Property Act.
The Land Registration Act.
The Land Charges Act.
The Administration of Estates Act.

It has been said that the following were the main objects of the Property Legislation of 1925 :—

(a) The abolition of the artificial (as distinct from the real, or natural) distinctions between land and movable property.
(b) The assimilation of the law relating to real property and chattels real.
(c) The assimilation (as far as possible) of the law relating to real and movable property.
(d) To simplify and cheapen conveyancing.

With these objects in view, the following changes were made :—

(i) Where a person dies intestate, i.e., without leaving a will, or where his will does not effectually dispose of all his property, the property as to which there is no testamentary disposition descends now in the same way, whether it is realty or personalty.
(ii) Escheat (the right of the feudal lord to claim the land of his tenant in certain circumstances) was abolished.
(iii) Only two legal estates in land are allowed to exist : (a) the fee simple absolute in possession, and (b) the term of years absolute (see below). Certain legal interests are permitted (see *post*, p. 181).
(iv) Estates tail (see below) were abolished, and such interests can now exist only in Equity—they are known as " entailed interests ". Entailed interests can be created in any kind of property, whether realty or personalty.
(v) Future legal estates cannot now exist—future *interests* can exist only in Equity (see below).
(vi) Tenancy in common of a legal estate was abolished (see below).

## Tenure.

In theory all land is *held* of another, ultimately of the Crown. Tenure was formerly free or unfree, free tenure being the holding of land for *fixed* services. Of free tenure there were three types, *Knight Service* (where military services were rendered in return for the land), *Socage* (non-military, usually agricultural, services being rendered) and *Frankalmoin* (where lands were granted to the Church in return for spiritual services). After 1660, socage tenure was the only free tenure.

Unfree tenure was *villeinage tenure*, the unfree tenant or villein being merely a serf bound to perform any services required by his lord. Later, when certain privileged *villeins* had their rights recorded on the manorial records, of which they were given copies, a new tenure, *Copyhold*, came into being, but this was abolished by the Law of Property Act, 1922. At the present time there is for all practical purposes only one form of tenure, namely, socage, but frankalmoin still exists in theory.

## Legal Estates and Interests.

The holding of land may also be classified in respect of the estate or the duration of the tenant's interest in the land. With regard to the " quantum " of interest, there are two broad divisions :—

(i) *Freehold*.

The only freehold estate that is capable of existing now is the fee simple absolute in possession.

The fee simple is the largest estate in land known to the law, and is equivalent to absolute ownership, except that theoretically, as has been said, all land is still held by some person as tenant of the Crown. The term " absolute " seems to mean " without condition and not determinable upon the happening of any event ". For all practical purposes, the holder of a fee simple owns not only the surface but the space below and above it, " *usque ad centrum et usque ad coelum* " (" down to the centre and up to the sky "). All rights to coal are, of course, now vested in the State.

It should also be pointed out that the meaning of " land " in law is a very wide one, for it includes things which by themselves are not land, but once annexed to land become, as it were, merged into the land and are then treated as part of the land and so pass on any transfer of the land : they are " fixtures ". Difficult questions often arise in this field as between landlord and tenant, mortgagor and mortgagee or vendor and purchaser and other parties. In reaching a conclusion a Court will, in general, pay regard to the degree and the object of annexation. The following case is illustrative.

### Leigh v. Taylor (1902).

A tenant for life, the owner of a valuable tapestry, laid strips of wood over the drawing-room paper and fixed them to the walls with two-inch nails. Canvas was stretched over these strips and the tapestry was fastened by tacks to the strips. It was *held* that the tapestry had not become a fixture, because it was purely ornamental and was only lightly attached and so easily removable.

(ii) *Leasehold.*

The only other legal estate in land is the term of years absolute, which is the interest created by a lease. In this phrase the term "absolute" admits, under the Law of Property Act, 1925, terms which are determinable by notice, re-entry (as for breach of a condition of the lease) or various other events.

It is not necessary for a term of years to be "in possession" (i.e., it need not commence on or before the date of the lease), though it must not be limited to take effect more than twenty-one years from the date of the instrument creating it, or it will be void. Thus, in 1974, A can grant a lease of Blackacre to B for ninety-nine years commencing not later than 1995.

TENANCY FROM YEAR TO YEAR.

A tenancy from year to year continues from year to year indefinitely until terminated by a half year's notice given by either party. Although this tenancy is indefinite, it is covered by the phrase "term of years absolute", possibly because it can be terminated only at the end of the current year, the requisite period of notice having been given to expire on that date. Such a tenancy may be created expressly, e.g., a grant "to A for one year from the 1st January, 1975, and thereafter from year to year", or by implication, e.g., where a person is permitted to occupy land and pays rent calculated by reference to a year. Thus, if A is in possession of B's land and pays a rent of £52 per annum which is accepted by B, A is *prima facie* a yearly tenant. His position would be unaffected by the fact that the rent was payable weekly, *provided that it was calculated with reference to a year.* On the other hand, had the agreement been to pay so much a week, without reference to any yearly rent, then *prima facie* a weekly tenancy would be created.

TENANCIES OF SHORTER PERIODICITY.

(a) *Quarterly and Monthly tenancies.* In the case of *quarterly* and *monthly* tenancies, a notice *equal to the length of the tenancy* must be given *expiring at the end of a complete period of the tenancy.* Thus, e.g., a monthly tenancy requires a month's notice expiring at the end of a periodic month or on the preceding day.

(b) *Weekly tenancies.* If the premises are let as a *dwelling* (whether furnished or not) no notice to quit is valid (whether given by the landlord or the tenant) unless given not less than *four* weeks before the day on which it is to take effect: Rent Act, 1957. In the case of premises not let as a dwelling. e.g., a lock-up shop, the common law rules still apply, i.e., a week's notice to expire at the end of a complete period of the tenancy will suffice.

TENANCIES AT WILL.

A tenancy at will arises whenever a person is in possession of land *qua* tenant with the permission of the owner. A common example arises in practice in the case of purchases of land, where it is not unusual for the purchaser to be let into possession prior to completion. A tenancy at will is terminated by either party giving notice to the other party, or by either party doing some act incompatible with the continuance of the tenancy, e.g., where the lessor re-enters and resumes possession.

TENANCIES AT SUFFERANCE.

Such tenancies are created when a tenant under lawful contract of tenancy holds over, i.e., remains in possession, after the termination of his tenancy.

LICENCES.

Whereas a lease or tenancy postulates the granting to the tenant of exclusive possession of the property concerned, a licence confers merely personal rights on the person intended to be benefited and spares him from being sued as a trespasser so long as the licence is in force. A case of such a licence could arise where a houseowner permits his neighbour's guest to park the latter's car on vacant land of the houseowner for, say, a maximum of forty-eight hours.

FORMER LEGAL ESTATES.

Formerly, there were other legal estates known as life estates and estates tail. A life estate lasted only for the tenant's life. An estate tail, on the other hand, passed to the tenant's lineal descendants. An estate in tail-male descended only to males and only in the male line, while an estate in tail-female passed only to and through females, and an estate in special tail descended only to the issue of the tenant by a certain wife or husband. Under the Law of Property Act, 1925, these cease to be legal estates and become equitable interests of a kind called " entailed interests ".

DOCTRINE OF NOTICE.

A legal estate is a right *in rem*, enforceable against all persons. An equitable interest is a right *in personam*, enforceable only against a limited class of persons. Consequently, any person dealing with an equitable interest can only do so subject to the rights of the legal owner, but the purchaser of a legal estate is bound by equitable interests only if he has notice of them or ought to have had notice. This is the great Doctrine of Notice, which, however, has been greatly modified by the legislation of 1925. Thus, under the Law of Property Act, 1925, certain equitable interests may be over-reached, i.e., disregarded by a purchaser of the legal estate for value, even though he has actual notice of them. Other interests may be disregarded, if not registered under the Land Charges Act of the same year (or as subsequently replaced) whatever the state of knowledge of the purchaser (see below, p. 191).

The Law of Property Act, 1925, provides that the following legal *interests* in land may exist:

(a) Easements or similar rights held for an interest equivalent to a fee simple absolute in possession or a term of years absolute.
(b) A rentcharge in possession charged on land and being either perpetual or for a term of years absolute. Thus, if Blackacre is held by A subject to the payment thereout of a sum of £5 per annum to B for ever, or for a definite period of time, B has a legal interest in Blackacre.
(c) A charge by way of legal mortgage.
(d) Land tax and any similar charge on land not created by an instrument.

[Land tax was finally abolished by the Finance Act, 1963.]

(e) Rights of entry exercisable over or in respect of a legal term of years absolute or annexed for any purpose to a legal rentcharge. Thus, in the example quoted above where B is entitled to a rentcharge of £5 per annum charged on Blackacre, then if the rentcharge is twenty-one days in arrear, B has a right to enter on the land and to distrain (Law of Property Act, 1925, section 121). This right of entry is a legal interest.

Whereas, for the purposes of the Act, a legal *estate* is concerned with the legal rights of a person (the estate owner) over his own land, a legal *interest* is one concerned with legal rights of a person over the land of another.

Legal interests, as well as legal estates, are rights *in rem* and are binding on all persons acquiring any interest in the land concerned, irrespective of notice.

## Future Estates or Interests.

It was only with reluctance that the Common Law recognized future interests in land, i.e., interests which confer a right to the enjoyment of land at a future time, as, for instance, after the death of a living person. Before 1926 they were legal estates. They are now equitable interests. Future interests may be :—

(a) Reversions and Remainders. A reversion is the residue of an interest which remains in the grantor of a particular interest who has not disposed of his whole interest but merely deprived himself of present enjoyment and possession. Thus, where A, the owner in fee simple of Blackacre, grants a life interest in it to B, on B's death the land will revert to A, who retains the reversion. A remainder is an interest limited to take effect on the determination of a particular interest previously limited by the same instrument out of the same property. Thus, A, may grant a life interest to B, followed by a remainder in fee simple to C. Remainders are said to be either *vested* or *contingent*. Where the only event which need occur before a person becomes entitled to the enjoyment of his remainder is the determination of the prior estate, this is said to be a vested remainder. For example, in a limitation to A for life and after his death to B in fee simple, B has a vested remainder of which he will derive the benefit immediately A dies. But where some condition other than the mere determination of the prior estate must be satisfied before a remainder can take effect, this type of remainder is known as a contingent remainder. Thus, in a limitation to A for life and after his death to B if he attains the age of twenty-one years, B's remainder is a contingent remainder because A's death will not necessarily cause B's remainder to take effect. He might then be under twenty-one, in which case he must wait until he is twenty-one before he can benefit. It will be understood, however, that if B attains the age of twenty-one years before A dies, his remainder becomes vested.

(b) Springing and Shifting Uses. An example of a springing use is a grant of land to A and his heirs to the use of B and his heirs on the marriage of B. The use " springs " into being on the occurrence of a specified event.

An example of a shifting use would be a grant of land to A and his heirs to the use of B and his heirs until the marriage of C, and then to the use of C and his heirs. In this case the use would shift from B to C on the occurrence of C's marriage.

(c) Executory Devises. An executory devise is merely a future interest in land created by will, as where a testator by his will gives land to A when he attains the age of twenty-five years.

## Concurrent Interests.

Land may be granted to two or more persons concurrently in enjoyment and possession, as in the case of joint tenancies and tenancies in common. There is also coparcenary, confined, after 1925, to succession by female descendants to entailed interests. Only joint tenancy, however, can now exist as a legal estate, the other two being equitable interests.

In joint tenancy each tenant has a right to the whole estate jointly with the others. In the case of a tenancy in common, each tenant has a share but cannot point to a particular part of the property as representing his share. The shares are said to be " undivided " shares and are capable of transfer.

If one joint tenant dies the right to the estate *survives* to the other joint tenants, whereas, on the death of a tenant in common, his share passes to his personal representatives. Under the old law the purchaser of land held by a number of tenants in common was bound to investigate the title of each tenant. This often produced complications. Thus, where land was held by A, B and C as tenants in common, and A died, devising his interest to X and Y as tenants in common, and B died, devising his interest to L, M and N as tenants in common, an intending purchaser of the land would have to investigate the titles of no fewer than six persons. The new law aims at simplifying such conveyances. It achieves its object by vesting the *legal estate* in not more than four persons as joint tenants, and by establishing the principle that no tenancy in common can be created except as an equitable interest. Thus, a limitation which, before 1926, would have created a tenancy in common has now the following effect :—

(a) It invests with the *legal estate* certain persons who hold it as *joint tenants*. The property is notionally subject to a trust for sale, and the tenants in common are usually the trustees for sale.

(b) It invests with an *equitable interest* the tenants in common who enjoy the land (until sale) or the proceeds (after sale) as tenants in common.

Where, after 1925, property is held by joint tenants beneficially (i.e., they are entitled for their own benefit and not as trustees for others) the property is held on trust for sale, but the right of survivorship mentioned above is unaffected.

As an example, suppose that in 1927 land was conveyed to A and B as tenants in common. A and B hold the property on trust for sale and although, if B died, the legal estate (being vested in A and B as joint tenants) would now remain in A alone, the interest of B's estate in the proceeds of sale is unaffected. But if the property had been conveyed to A and B as joint tenants beneficially, then on the death of B, A becomes entitled solely to both the legal and equitable interest therein, i.e., he is the absolute owner, and the trust for sale is no longer operative.

**Easements and Profits à Prendre.**

In some cases, English land law confers no right to actual possession but entitles the holder of land to certain rights relating to land in the possession of another. Examples of such rights are easements and profits *à prendre*.

An easement is the right of the owner of land (1) to use the land of another for a certain purpose without the right to take anything from the land (subject to the exceptional easement of water), or (2) to prevent the owner of other land from using it in some particular manner.

Well-known examples are rights of way, rights of light, rights to take water or discharge water over the land of another. The basic rule with regard to easements is that there must be both a *dominant* and a *servient* tenement. Thus, if A gives B (who has no adjacent land) permission to cross his land, B has no easement but, at most, a licence. But if A, the owner of Whiteacre, grants a similar right to the owner of the adjacent Blackacre (who happens to be B), this is an easement. Whiteacre is the servient tenement, Blackacre the dominant tenement.

An easement must not be confused with a restrictive covenant. The latter is a contract between two neighbouring landowners (e.g., a vendor of land and a purchaser from him of part of the land) by which one of them acquires the right to prevent the other from putting his land to certain specified uses, e.g., from erecting shops on it. Thus, it imposes a negative burden. An easement, on the other hand, is generally positive in operation, the easement of light being an exception. Moreover, a restrictive covenant takes effect only in Equity, while an easement is a legal interest provided it is for a term of years absolute or in fee simple in possession. Finally, a restrictive covenant created after 1925 must be registered under the Land Charges Act, 1925 [now the consolidating Act of 1972—see *post*, p. 189], to be enforceable against subsequent purchasers of the land, whilst a legal easement does not require registration.

Profits *à prendre* are similar to easements in that they are rights existing over the land of another person, but they differ in that they allow the owner of the profit to *take* some substance from the servient tenement, e.g., a right to cut turf, dig for gravel or to pasture cattle on another's land. Another point of difference is that a profit may exist *in gross*, i.e., where the owner of the profit does not hold the right for the benefit of land owned by him, the right being merely personal, such as a right to take fish from a canal without limit.

There are various modes of acquisition of such rights. Easements may be acquired by statute, express or implied reservation or grant or by prescription. A " way of necessity " is an example of creation by implied reservation. Suppose A has land and sells off all of it save a plot entirely surrounded by the land sold off to others ; a reservation of a way is implied in favour of the land retained by A, for otherwise he would have no means of access to the land retained by him.

The Prescription Act, 1832, fixes the following periods for acquisition by prescription :—

(a) Easements other than Light :—

(i) Twenty years' uninterrupted user as of right creates a valid easement which an oral consent will defeat.
(ii) Forty years' similar user creates a valid easement which only a *written* agreement will defeat.
In each case the user must be open (i.e., not secret) and peaceable.

(b) Profits à prendre :—

Similar provisions apply but the periods are thirty years and sixty years respectively.

(c) Easement of Light :—

Here, there is only one period—twenty years' *uninterrupted* user (conferring what are popularly referred to as " ancient lights "). The only defence is that the enjoyment was by virtue of written agreement or deed. User need not be " as of right ". Thus money payment or oral consent will not defeat a claim.

[The Rights of Light Act, 1959, temporarily enlarged the period to meet certain cases but made permanent alterations to the law by providing for notional interruption of user by registration of a notice under the Land Charges Act.]

## Transfer of Real Property.

A transfer of the ownership of real property may take place in either of two ways. It may be a transfer by act of parties or it may be a purely involuntary transfer. This transfer by an owner or tenant of his interest in real or personal property to another is termed " alienation ".

## Transfer by Act of Parties.

The main methods by which a legal estate in land may be transferred are :—

(1) Conveyance of land by way of sale.
(2) Execution of a lease.
(3) Creation of a mortgage.
(4) Creation of a settlement.

## Conveyance by Way of Sale.

Successful negotiations for the sale of land lead to the conclusion of a contract. Such a contract is subject to the same rules as apply to contracts in general. Under section 40, Law of Property Act, 1925, a contract for the sale of land is unenforceable unless there is a memorandum of it in writing, signed by the party to be charged, or by some other person thereunto by him lawfully authorized. The memorandum must contain (*a*) an agreement for sale, (*b*) a description of the parties, (*c*) a description of the property and (*d*) a statement of the price. An oral contract may, however, be enforceable if the plaintiff can prove a sufficient act of part performance or if the defendant fraudulently prevented the creation of the written evidence. (See Chapter III.)

Under an *open contract* for sale (i.e., one which specifies merely the names of the parties, the description of the property and the price), the vendor must show title for fifteen years (the reduced period introduced by the Law of Property Act, 1969), commencing with a " good root of title ". A good root of title may be defined as one dealing with the whole of the legal and equitable estate in the property concerned, containing an adequate description of the property, and revealing no defect in title. He must also, at his own expense, abstract and, if under his control, produce the document which forms the root of his title, and all subsequent documents which affect the legal estate. Further, he must prove all facts which have affected the legal estate in the last fifteen years. This is called " deducing title " ; the purchaser on his side " investigates the title ". Upon a satisfactory investigation of title, the transaction proceeds to the conveyance of the property to the purchaser.

Under the Law of Property Act, 1925, when a legal estate is to be transferred, the conveyance of the land or of any interest therein must, with certain exceptions, be made by deed, the deed, on execution, being delivered to the grantee.

The deed must be carefully drawn to make clear who are the parties (transferor or transferee) the exact nature of the estate or interest transferred, the identity of the property and any exceptions or reservations to the grant and the scope of restrictive covenants imposed (if any).

### Registration of Title.

Investigation of title to land is sometimes very difficult and occasionally not inexpensive, and there has accordingly developed the system of registration of title.

The essence of this system is that the ownership of land is apparent from a Register maintained by officials at the Land Registry in London (whose chief is called " H.M. Chief Land Registrar ") or in Regional Offices. On registration of title, the old title deeds are, generally speaking, exchanged for a " Land Certificate " which is in effect an extract from the Register, and which is thereafter substantially the only proof of title necessary. The title shown by the Certificate is State guaranteed and investigation of title in the traditional manner is dispensed with. On a sale of registered land a very simple form of transfer is executed by the parties and lodged in the Registry, together with the vendor's Land Certificate. After registration of the transfer a new Land Certificate is issued in the name of the purchaser.

Under the Land Registration Act, 1925, registration of title became compulsory in the administrative County of London, the Counties of Kent, Middlesex and Surrey and the County Boroughs of Eastbourne, Hastings and Croydon. Registration has since (as a result of Orders issued under the Act) been made compulsory in very many other localities, mainly urban and it was expected that the extension would cover most of the built-up areas in the Country within a few years. However, for various reasons impetus was lost. The reorganization of local government areas taking effect from April 1974 has occasioned the issue of some Orders securing compatability of areas within the land registration scheme.

Any property, wherever situate *may*, however, be registered. The Land Registration Act, 1966, however restricted such voluntary registration except in the categories of cases announced by the Chief Land Registrar.

Only legal estates can be registered. The following leaseholds, however, *cannot* be registered :—

(a) Leaseholds with twenty-one years or less unexpired.
(b) Leaseholds held under a lease containing an absolute prohibition against assignment.
(c) Leaseholds held under a lease created for mortgage purposes, so long as there is a subsisting right of redemption.

## CHAPTER VI

The Register kept at the appropriate Land Registry consists of three parts :—

(1) The Property Register, containing a description of the land and estate, with such matters as easements, conditions and covenants *for the benefit* of the land.
(2) The Proprietorship Register, stating whether the title is absolute, good leasehold, qualified or possessory, and containing the name, address and description of the proprietor and any cautions, inhibitions and restrictions which may affect his right of disposing of the land.
(3) The Charges Register, containing charges and incumbrances affecting the land, all dealings with registered charges and incumbrances and notices relating to covenants, conditions and other rights *adversely* affecting the land.

" Overriding interests ", such as the rights of persons in actual occupation or rights of way, are not recorded in the Register or land certificate, but a purchaser from the registered proprietor takes subject to them.

Land may be registered with :—

(1) An absolute title. In the case of freehold land this confers on the person registered the fee simple in possession, subject to incumbrances and other entries appearing on the Register, to overriding interests unless the contrary is expressed in the Register and (where the first registered proprietor is not entitled for his own benefit) to any minor interests of which he has notice.
Registration of leaseholds with an absolute title vests in the first registered proprietor the possession of the leasehold interest, subject to the above qualifications and also to all express and implied covenants, obligations and liabilities incident to such leaseholds.
(2) A qualified title. In the case of freeholds, the registration has the same effect as registration with an absolute title, but it does not affect or prejudice the enforcement of any estate, right or interest appearing to be excepted. In the case of leaseholds, it has the same effect as registration with an absolute or good leasehold title, as the case may be, subject to the same qualifications.
(3) A possessory title. This has the same effect as registration with an absolute title, but the registration does not affect or prejudice any estate, right or interest adverse to the title of the first registered proprietor, subsisting or capable of arising at the time of his registration ; i.e., the State gives no guarantee regarding any matters adverse to the title

and capable of arising at the time of the first registration. A person may register with a possessory title if he is in possession or in receipt of the rents and profits, or has power to sell.

(4) A good leasehold title. This has the same effect as registration with an absolute title, except that it does not affect or prejudice the enforcement of any estate, right or interest in derogation of the title of the lessor to grant the lease. In other words, it vests in the registered proprietor the possession of the leasehold interest, subject to all express and implied covenants, obligations and liabilities, and to any right or interest in derogation of the lessor's title to grant the lease, in addition to the qualifications mentioned under an absolute title.

**Registration of Land Charges.**

Quite distinct from the registration of title to land itself is the system of registration of charges and incumbrances on land. It has been pointed out that the doctrine of "Notice" has been profoundly modified by the legislation of 1925. The nature of land is such that, although A may be the owner in fee simple, B may have a right of way thereover, C may have the right to discharge effluent thereover, and D may have an equitable mortgage thereon, and so on. Prior to 1926, whether or not a purchaser from A was bound by any such third party rights depended upon whether they were legal or equitable. In the former case the purchaser was bound irrespective of notice, but in the latter case he would take free of equitable interests provided he acquired the legal estate for value and without notice of such interests. After 1925, registration in the appropriate Register maintained under the Land Charges Act, 1925, has constituted *actual notice* to all persons and for all purposes, and a purchaser is bound by any registered interests irrespective of notice. Conversely an interest requiring registration and not in fact registered is not binding on a purchaser, even if he actually knows of such interest.

The Land Charges Act, 1972 consolidated all the relevant legislation concerning Land Charges (other than local land charges —as to which see below, p. 193) from the material sections of the Act of 1925 through those in the Matrimonial Homes Act, 1967, up to those in the Land Registration and Land Charges Act, 1971.

A further distinction between registration of title and registration of land charges is that the former is a *Register of property*, whereas the latter is a *Register of names* of the estate owners of the property affected. Thus, if it is desired to ascertain whether land has been registered under the Land Registration Acts,

1925–1971, it is necessary to complete a requisition for an official search, and to insert therein a description of the property, including, where necessary, a plan. If, however, it is desired to ascertain whether any charges or incumbrances have been registered under the Land Charges Act, it is necessary to complete the necessary requisition and to search against the names of the estate owners of the property concerned. A computer system is now in operation to facilitate such search. In practice, it is necessary to search only against the name of the vendor, as Certificates of Search, showing the results of searches against previous estate owners, are usually kept with the title deeds.

The following Registers are maintained in the Land Charges Department of the Land Registry :—

(1) Register of Pending actions, e.g., a bankruptcy petition.
(2) Register of Annuities, i.e., annual sums charged on land.
(3) Register of Writs and Orders affecting land, e.g., a Receiving Order in bankruptcy.
(4) Register of Deeds of Arrangement.
(5) Register of Land Charges, which fall into six classes :—

    (*a*) Class A Land Charges. These are statutory charges upon land made *pursuant to the application of some person*.

    (*b*) Class B Land Charges. These also are statutory charges, but they arise *otherwise than pursuant to the application of any person* ; i.e., they are imposed by the statute itself.

    (*c*) Class C Land Charges. These comprise :—

        (i) Puisne mortgages, i.e., legal mortgages not protected by a deposit of documents relating to the legal estate affected.

        (ii) Limited owner's charges. A limited owner's charge is an equitable charge on settled property which arises by statute in favour of the tenant for life of such property where he has discharged some liability out of income which should have been discharged out of capital, e.g., where he pays estate duty out of his own pocket.

        (iii) General equitable charges. A general equitable charge is an equitable charge which is not secured by a deposit of documents relating to the legal estate affected, and is not included in any other class of land charge, e.g., an *equitable* mortgage not protected by deposit of the title deeds, or the lien of a vendor who has parted with the deeds to the purchaser. Annuities *created after* 1925 are also registrable here.

(iv) Estate contracts, i.e., contracts by estate owners to convey or create a legal estate, including an option to purchase. Examples are contracts for the sale of land or to grant or assign a lease. The object of the registration is to protect the purchaser's rights under the contract against other purchasers who may acquire a legal estate from the vendor before completion of the purchase.

(d) Class D Land Charges. These comprise :—

(i) Charges for death duties.
(ii) Restrictive covenants affecting freehold interests, entered into after 1925. (See *ante*, p. 184). Such covenants entered into between *lessor* and *lessee* are *not* registrable.
(iii) Equitable easements created after 1925, e.g., an easement informally granted by writing not under seal.

(e) Class E Land Charges. Here must be registered annuities *created before* 1926.

(f) Class F Land Charges. Such as a charge affecting land by virtue of the Matrimonial Homes Act, 1967.

[Under the latter Act certain rights of occupancy are conferred on a spouse in the matrimonial home owned by the other spouse and these rights may be protected as against third parties by registration as a Land Charge.]

The effect of non-registration of a land charge varies with the class of land charge, and the position is :—

(a) Except in the case of estate contracts and land charges of Class D, any such charge unregistered is void against a purchaser for value of *any* interest in the land affected.
(b) In the case of estate contracts and land charges of Class D, any such charge unregistered is void against a purchaser of the *legal* estate for money or money's worth.
(c) Unregistered Petitions in Bankruptcy and Receiving Orders are void only against a *bona fide* purchaser of a legal estate for money or money's worth *without notice of an available act of bankruptcy.*

## Local Land Charges.

These are charges registered by Local Authorities, e.g., District Councils, the Council of any London Borough and the

Common Council of the City of London, under various statutes such as the Public Health Acts and the Private Street Works Act, 1892, and under various planning statutes, or by a landowner making use of the provisions of the Rights of Light Act, 1959, previously mentioned. They are different from land charges in that registration is (as under the Land Registration Act, 1925) against the property. They are now governed by the Local Land Charges Act, 1975, which provides for personal and official searches and for the payment of compensation to persons affected by non-registered charges or by defective official search certificates.

**Leases.**
Every lease to create a legal estate must be under seal, except a lease taking effect in possession for three years or less at the best rent reasonably obtainable without any capital payment. Such an excepted lease may be made verbally. An unsealed lease which the law requires to be under seal will be treated as an agreement for a lease, provided it is in writing, or (if it is verbal) provided there has been an available act of part performance. (*Walsh* v. *Lonsdale :* see Chapter II.)

A lease must be distinguished from a contract for a lease. A contract for a lease is an agreement to grant a lease, and under s. 40, Law of Property Act, 1925, it must be evidenced by a memorandum or note in writing, *no matter how short in duration* the term may be. Otherwise, it is unenforceable, unless there is a sufficient act of part performance (see Chapter III).

A leasehold is often called a term of years, though a tenancy for weeks or months is equally a leasehold.

During the subsistence of the lease, the lessor has the reversion, the most important incident of which is his right to the rent reserved by the lease, which (as will be seen below) can be enforced by action or distress, and in certain cases by forfeiture.

Where the lease does not contain express covenants and conditions, the following are implied :—

(a) *Obligations upon the lessee :—*
    (1) To pay rent.
    (2) To pay tenant's rates and taxes.
    (3) To keep in repair (but a weekly tenant is under no greater obligation than to take proper care of the premises : *Warren* v. *Keen* (1953)).
    (4) Where the landlord has covenanted to repair, to permit the landlord to enter and view the state of repair.

(b) *Covenant by the lessor for quiet enjoyment.*

A lease, however, normally contains express covenants, the most important of which are :—

(1) To pay rent.
(2) To pay rates and taxes.
(3) To repair.
(4) To permit the lessor to enter and inspect the state of repair.
(5) To insure.
(6) Not to carry on any trade or business.
(7) Not to assign or underlet without consent. By the Landlord and Tenant Act, 1927, this covenant is made subject to a proviso that such consent is not to be unreasonably withheld.

Liability of landlord or tenant to do repairs is, in the absence of special contractual terms a matter for the application of common law rules. It should be noted, however, that under the Housing Act, 1961, there is implied into a lease (including a tenancy) of a dwelling-house for a term of less than seven years a covenant by the landlord to keep the structure and exterior of the premises in repair and to maintain in proper working order the installations in the dwelling-house for the supply of water, gas and electricity and for space or water heating. The Act precludes a contracting out of the provisions without the leave of the County Court.

One important clause in a lease is the Proviso for Re-entry. This clause states that whenever any part of the rent shall have been in arrear for (generally) twenty-one days, whether the same shall have been legally demanded or not, or whenever the lessee shall commit a breach of any of his covenants, the lessor may re-enter upon the premises, and that thereupon the term granted shall come to an end. The lessee, however, may apply to the Court for relief against forfeiture.

Other remedies for breach of the covenant to pay rent are distress and an action for arrears. Distress is the landlord's right to seize the tenant's goods and sell them after five days. Some goods cannot be seized, e.g., the tenant's tools, clothes and bedding up to the value of £20. Under the Limitation Act, 1939, the landlord may by action recover six years' arrears of rent.

In regard to forfeiture for non-payment of rent, the lessee, under the Common Law Procedure Act, 1852, may *within six months* of ejectment, apply to the Court for relief against the forfeiture, and the Court may grant such relief if the tenant pays all arrears of rent and costs.

In regard to forfeiture for breach of other covenants, section 146, Law of Property Act, 1925, provides that, before proceeding to enforce the right of re-entry, the lessor must first serve on the lessee a notice specifying the breach complained of, requiring the lessee to remedy the breach if capable of remedy and requiring the lessee to make compensation in money for the breach.

The owner of a leasehold interest may dispose of it either by way of *assignment* or by way of *sub-lease*. In the former case he parts with his whole interest to the purchaser, who becomes in his place the tenant of the freeholder. Such a purchaser, or assignee, as he is called, is bound (so long as he owns the leasehold interest) to observe and perform all the covenants by which his vendor, the assignor, was bound. In the latter case, he himself grants an under-lease to the purchaser for the residue of the lease, less the last few days. Thus, if A, the fee simple owner, leases Blackacre to B for ninety-nine years, A is the freeholder and B is the lessee. If B sub-lets Blackacre to C for the residue of the original term, less the last ten days thereof, C becomes a sub-lessee, and B retains a reversion of ten days; i.e., when C's sub-lease expires, B has still ten days of the original lease unexpired. Generally speaking, a sub-lessee is not liable to the freeholder on the covenants in the lease, but he will usually be bound to the lessee by virtue of specific provisions in the sub-lease.

### Mortgages of Land.

A mortgage may be either legal or equitable.

A legal mortgage confers a legal estate or interest on the lender and enables him to take advantage of certain remedies afforded by law on default being made by the borrower.

At the present day, a legal mortgage of freeholds takes the form of either :—

(a) A lease of the mortgaged property to the mortgagee for a long term of years (usually three thousand) subject to cesser on redemption (i.e., the mortgagee's term comes to an end automatically on repayment) ; or

(b) A charge by way of legal mortgage, which confers on the mortgagee a legal interest, not a legal estate, but which entitles him to the same remedies as if the mortgage were by lease for a long term of years.

A legal mortgage of leaseholds takes the form of either :—

(a) A sub-lease to the mortgagee for the residue of the term less at least one day, subject to cesser on redemption ; or

(b) A charge by way of legal mortgage.

A first mortgagee will certainly insist on the title deeds being retained by him until the debt is repaid. If a second mortgage is created (i.e., a further charge on the property to secure a different loan) the title deeds, being held by the first mortgagee, cannot, of course, be handed to the second mortgagee, and to protect himself the latter must register his mortgage as a puisne mortgage (Land Charges, Class C (i) : see above).

## Equitable Mortgages.

Sometimes when the matter is urgent, or it is desired to avoid the trouble and expense incurred in drawing up a legal mortgage, an equitable mortgage will be created. The three usual methods of creation of such mortgages are :—

(a) A written agreement, signed as required by section 40, Law of Property Act, 1925, not accompanied by a deposit of the title deeds.
(b) A deposit of the deeds alone, not accompanied by a written agreement, if such amounts to a part performance of an agreement to give security.
(c) A written agreement, plus a deposit of the deeds.

Unless the mortgage is accompanied by a deposit of the title deeds, the mortgagee must register his mortgage as a general equitable charge [Class C (iii)]. A properly-framed deed will give the equitable mortgagee most of the remedies of a legal mortgagee (which result from the mortgage being a mortgage by deed under section 101, Law of Property Act, 1925), but he will not have the remedy of *taking possession*, this remedy arising from having a *legal* estate.

## Equity of Redemption.

This has been referred to in Chapter II.

It should in addition be noted that a purchase by the mortgagee of the equity of redemption, if subsequent to the mortgage, is not void. An option to purchase the equity of redemption, conferred by the mortgage deed, is, however, void as a clog, since it might enable the mortgagee to deprive the mortgagor of his right of redemption : *Samuel* v. *Jarrah Timber and Wood-Paving Corporation, Ltd.* (1904).

The equity of redemption exists until the mortgagee has exercised his power of sale or obtained an order for foreclosure, or until the right has become extinguished under the Limitation Act.

## Limitation Act, 1939.

Under section 12, Limitation Act, 1939, " when a mortgagee of land has been in possession of any of the mortgaged land for a period of twelve years, no action to redeem the land of which the mortgagee has been so in possession shall thereafter be brought by the mortgagor or any person claiming through him ". But "where a mortgagee is by virtue of the mortgage in possession of any mortgaged land and either receives any sum in respect of the principal or interest of the mortgage debt or acknowledges the title of the mortgagor or his equity of redemption, an action to redeem the land in his possession may be brought at any time before the expiration of twelve years from the date of the payment or acknowledgment ": section 23(3). At the expiration of twelve years, the mortgagor's title to the land is extinguished (section 16), and he, therefore, has no further claim to it.

Under section 18 of the same Act, no action can be brought to recover money secured by a mortgage or other charge on property, real or personal, after twelve years from the date when the right to receive the money accrued, and no action to recover arrears of interest in respect of any such money, or to recover damages in respect of such arrears, can be brought after six years from the date on which the interest became due.

### Rights of a Mortgagor.

The main rights of a mortgagor are :—

(1) To sue in his own name for rents and profits or for damage to the mortgaged property.
(2) When in possession, to grant leases on the same terms as a mortgagee, but the counterpart of any lease must be surrendered to the first mortgagee within one month. (This right may be and often is excluded by the terms of the mortgage.)
(3) To inspect and take copies or abstracts of the title deeds.
(4) To pay off the mortgage, on giving six months' notice to the mortgagee, unless the latter agrees to accept shorter notice, or unless the mortgagor pays an additional six months' interest in lieu of notice.
(5) To redeem so long as the "equity of redemption" subsists and to be given on payment off of the mortgage a discharge which will have the effect of bringing to an end any term of years under the mortgage. (As to "clogging the equity" see *ante* pp. 37 and 195.)

### Rights of Mortgagee.

The main rights of a mortgagee are as follows :—

(1) To sue on the personal covenant to pay. This is obvious and requires no comment.
(2) To take possession, if his mortgage is a legal mortgage. He can do this at any time after the deed is executed.
(3) To foreclose. This is a means of barring the equity of

redemption and leaving the mortgaged property outstanding in the mortgagee, subject nevertheless to any prior mortgages. The procedure is for the mortgagee to apply to the Court for an order *nisi* (which can be made at any time after the mortgage money is due) which requires the mortgagor to pay within a certain time (usually six months) the amount ascertained to be due to the mortgagee. In default of payment within this time the order is made absolute. Even after foreclosure absolute the mortgagee can still sue on the personal covenant, but the mortgagor is then given a further chance to redeem if he can then pay all that is due to the mortgagee.

(4) To sell. Where the mortgage is by *deed* and the mortgage money is due, the mortgagee can sell the mortgaged property and can convey the whole fee simple or term of years absolute (as the case may be) to a purchaser. Although the right to sell *arises* when the mortgage money is due, it is not *exercisable* until :—

  (a) Some interest is two months or more in arrear ; or
  (b) The mortgagor has failed to pay off the mortgage within three months after being requested in writing so to do ; or
  (c) There has been a breach of covenant contained in the mortgage or implied by the Law of Property Act, 1925, other than the covenant to pay principal and interest.

The purchase money received by the mortgagee shall be held in trust by him to be applied in the following order :—

  (i) In discharge of prior encumbrances ;
  (ii) In payment of the costs and expenses of sale ;
  (iii) In discharge of the mortgage debt and interest ;
  (iv) The residue to the person entitled to the mortgaged property, or the person authorized to give a receipt for the proceeds of sale.

(5) To appoint a Receiver. He can be appointed in the same circumstances as the power of sale can be exercised. Although he is appointed by the mortgagee, he is deemed to be the agent of the mortgagor, who is responsible for his acts and defaults. The Receiver is empowered to recover the income of the property and applies it (after payment of outgoings) in payment of the mortgage interest, and, if required in writing by the mortgagee, in payment of the capital of the mortgage.

(6) To insure, and keep insured the mortgaged property

against fire to the extent of two-thirds of the cost of replacement of the mortgaged property.

(7) To grant leases. Under section 99, Law of Property Act, 1925, a mortgagee who has taken possession can grant the following leases :—
   (a) Occupational or agricultural leases for a term not exceeding fifty years.
   (b) Building leases for a term not exceeding nine hundred and ninety-nine years.

(8) To cut and sell timber, if he has taken possession.

It should be noted that the above remedies are cumulative, not alternative, and can be exercised concurrently. Thus, a mortgagee can take possession, and while in possession he can grant a lease, and can sell or appoint a Receiver if the statutory conditions are complied with.

## Settlements of Land.

A strict settlement of land, so called to distinguish it from a settlement by way of trust for sale (see below), is created with the object of keeping the land intact in the family. It is usually executed when the settlor is about to marry, and it secures that :—

(a) The settlor has a life interest in the property ;
(b) His wife is provided for (should she survive him) by means of a rentcharge for her life, i.e., a certain sum of money per annum to be raised out of the land and paid to her ;
(c) Capital sums, known as " portions ", are raised and paid to the *younger* children of the marriage ; and
(d) Successive entailed interests are conferred on the male issue of the marriage and, failing male issue, the daughters of the marriage are entitled as tenants in common.

By this means, the land becomes " tied " until the eldest son attains majority, when, usually, family sentiment and personal interest induce an agreement between father and son to bar the entail (i.e., to obtain a fee simple in remainder, which will take effect on the father's death), and then to resettle the property on similar terms. The son cuts down his entailed interest in remainder in return for an immediate annuity charged on his father's life interest. Successive remainders in tail are conferred on the *son's* children. If this system, known as " disentailing and resettlement " is followed each time an eldest son attains his majority, the land can be tied up " in the family " for generations.

The fundamental evil of the system, however, was that the tenant for life, the actual tenant in possession, had no power of disposition of the lands, and situations would often arise when it was necessary, if the property was to be maintained in good order, to expend considerable sums of money for this object. Human nature being what it is, very often the limited owner, the tenant in possession, was reluctant to expend his private fortune largely for the benefit of posterity. Thus, estates, in some instances, fell into ruin.

The main object of the Settled Land Acts (dating from the nineteenth century) has been to make land and buildings freely alienable, and thus to prevent their deterioration in the hands of impecunious tenants for life. To achieve this object, they have given the tenant for life under the settlement wide powers of dealing with the land by sale, exchange, leasing or mortgaging, free from the trusts of the settlement and without the necessity of making any application to the Court, and they have protected the rights of the beneficiaries, in the case of a sale, by shifting the settlement from the land to the purchase money which has to be paid into the hands of the trustees. The Settled Land Act, 1925, continued this policy by vesting the fee simple of settled land in an " estate owner " of full age, generally the tenant for life, and by providing that the beneficial interests of the persons entitled under the settlement shall be equitable merely and capable of being overreached by the sale of the fee simple. It extended the scope of the powers of the tenant for life, and facilitated the separation of the equitable interests from the legal fee simple by providing that all settlements *inter vivos* must be effected by two different deeds, the Vesting Deed and the Trust Instrument. The Vesting Deed gives a description of the land and vests the legal fee simple in, i.e., passes it to, the tenant for life or statutory owner, while the Trust Instrument sets out the trusts on which that fee simple must be held. An intending purchaser of the land need look only at the Vesting Deed; he is not concerned with the trusts. He must, however, pay the purchase money to the trustees named therein, who thus have more than nominal duties and must employ the funds in the manner authorised by law.

A settlement may be created by will, in which case the will becomes the trust instrument. After the personal representatives have completed their administration duties, they will execute a document, called a Vesting Assent, vesting the settled land in the tenant for life.

## Trust for Sale.

The " strict " settlement must be distinguished from a settlement by way of trust for sale. In the latter case the object is to sell the land, and the land is conveyed to trustees on trust for sale, but, usually there is no obligation to sell immediately. The deed directs that the proceeds of sale are to be held on the trusts declared in a trust instrument, executed on the same day and between the same parties as the conveyance to the trustees. Until sale, the trustees have all the powers of a tenant for life under the Settled Land Act.

Other occasions (and they are statutory) where a trust for sale arises are (a) in connection with concurrent ownership (see *ante*, p. 185) and (b) on an intestacy (see *post*, p. 210).

### Rule against Perpetuities.

The law discourages the " tying-up " of property (of any type) indefinitely. The Rule against Perpetuities (as crystallized in 1833 in the case of *Cadell* v. *Palmer*) therefore provides that the vesting of real or personal property may not be postponed for a period longer than a life or lives in being at the date when the instrument creating the limitations takes effect, and for 21 years after the cesser of such life or lives, with the addition, if necessary, of a period of gestation.

An instrument takes effect in the case of a deed on its execution and in the case of a will on the death of the testator.

The Perpetuities and Accumulations Act, 1964, made important changes in the law, but for present purposes it is only necessary to state (a) that section 1 of the Act made it possible for an alternative perpetuity period to be specified in respect of a disposition under an instrument taking effect after 16th July, 1964 (the date of coming into force of the Act) namely a period not exceeding 80 years, and (b) that whereas in considering the application of the pre-1964 Rule, possible events, and not actual or likely events, have to be considered (so that where a gift might have failed under the pre-1964 Law because there was a *possibility* that it would vest outside the perpetuity period) section 3 of the 1964 Act introduces a useful " wait and see " rule in relation to instruments within the 1964 Act. This has the effect that such a disposition is to be treated as if it were not affected by the Rule against Perpetuities until such time as it is established that the disposition will *in fact* vest outside the perpetuity period.

The effect of a limitation which offends the Rule is that the instrument takes effect as if the void limitation were struck out. This, as section 6 of the 1964 Act appears to contemplate, may have the effect of accelerating the vesting of an interest (itself not void under the Rule) subsequent to the void limitation. Prior interests are not affected.

### Accumulations of Income.

Distinct rules apply as to the accumulation, or tying up, of income. A settlor who wishes to accumulate income (i.e., who directs that the capital of his estate is to be invested, and the income from the investments added to the capital) may do so for not longer than one of the following periods :—

(a) The life of the settlor ;
(b) Twenty-one years from the making of the disposition (if by deed) or after the death of the settlor (where the disposition is by will) ;
(c) The minority of any persons living or *en ventre sa mère* at the making of the disposition or the death of the settlor (as the case may be) ;
(d) The minority of any persons who would, if of full age, have been entitled to the accumulated income under the terms of the settlement.

Where an accumulation is directed which exceeds the period allowed, then if the period also exceeds that allowed by the Perpetuity Rule, *no* income may be accumulated. If, however, the Perpetuity Rule is not offended, income may be accumulated for the longest period allowed, the direction only being void as to the excess. Consequently, a trust for accumulation for the life of any person other than the settlor is valid for twenty-one years after the settlor's death. But a simple trust for accumulation for one hundred years, without reference to " lives " offends the Perpetuity Rule and is totally void.

## INVOLUNTARY TRANSFERS

### Requisites of a Valid Will.

English law from an early date recognized the power of a man to provide for the disposition of his personal property after his death. The recognition of a similar power of disposition with regard to his real property was a much later development. A person is said to die testate when he dies leaving a will disposing of all his real and personal property. He dies intestate when he leaves no will, and partially intestate when part of his property is not disposed of by his will. A will is said to be ambulatory until the testator's death, which means that he can revoke it at any time before death. It is also said to " speak from death ". That is to say, it is construed, with reference to the property disposed of, to take effect as if it had been executed immediately before the testator's death. Thus, it may affect property other than that which was in existence at the date when the will was made.

By the Wills Act, 1837, the formalities to be observed in the disposition of both realty and personalty were made uniform.

These were :—
(1) The will must be in writing.
(2) It must be signed "at the foot or end thereof" by the testator or by some person in his presence and by his express direction.
(3) The signature must be made or acknowledged by the testator in the presence of at least two witnesses, *both being present at the same time.*
(4) The witnesses must attest and subscribe the will in the presence of the testator but not necessarily in the presence of each other.

The testator must be of full age and sound mind. The qualification as to age has, however, no application to soldiers and airmen in actual military service or mariners "at sea". Moreover, the formalities set out above do not apply to the wills of such persons, who are allowed to make nuncupative wills, i.e., mere oral declarations before witnesses.

> Part III of the Administration of Justice Act, 1969, for the first time enables the Court to authorize the making of a will or codicil on behalf of a mentally disordered person otherwise incapable of making a will.

If any benefit is purported to be given by a will to a witness thereto, or to the spouse of such witness, the gift is void, although the validity of the rest of the will is not affected.

> The effect of this provision (in section 15 of the Act of 1837) has to to a certain extent been mitigated by the Wills Act, 1968, which prevents forfeiture where the will is otherwise duly attested by two independent witnesses.

All alterations in a will are presumed to have been made *after* execution. They must, therefore, be separately signed and attested, initials, instead of full signatures, being sufficient for this purpose.

The essential validity of a will may, in appropriate circumstances, be challenged in a "Probate Action" brought in the Chancery Division of the High Court (see Chapter IX).

## Freedom of Testamentary Disposition.

Unlike systems of law founded on Roman Law (e.g., Scots, French and German law) there was in this country until comparatively recently, complete freedom of testamentary disposition, and, accordingly, a man might with impunity "cut off with a shilling" his widow or other member of his family morally entitled to a fair "expectation" on his death.

> However, under the Inheritance (Family Provision) Act, 1938, as amended by the Intestates' Estates Act, 1952, the Family Provision Act, 1966, and the Family Law Reform Act, 1969,

where a testator or testatrix left a widow (or widower), an unmarried daughter, a son who was a minor or who, although no longer a minor, had not attained the age of 21, or a son or daughter incapacitated by mental or physical disability and failed to make reasonable provision for them, the Court might, on application by any of the above mentioned dependants within six months from the grant of representation (a period which in the unfettered discretion of the Court might be extended), order that reasonable provision shall be made for the maintenance of such dependants. The periodical payments made under the Court's order to such dependants ceased on the death or remarriage of the widow (or widower), the death, attainment of the age of 21 or cesser of disability of a son or the death, marriage or cesser of disability of a daughter.

It is to be noted that in the case of a person dying after the coming into force on 1st January, 1970, of the Family Law Reform Act, 1969, his illegitimate son or daughter was (under that Act) to be treated as his dependant in any case in which a legitimate son or daughter of his would be so treated. Adopted children (adopted under an order made in the United Kingdom) have always been within this Family Provision legislation.

The Court had power to make interim orders and payments by way of lump sum. The Court took into consideration the nature of the testator's property, the reasons given for his dispositions, the financial position of the dependants and their conduct towards the testator.

The provisions of the legislation applied to cases where persons died intestate, for the Act of 1952 provides that " the court . . . shall not be bound to assume that the law relating to intestacy makes reasonable provision in all cases ".

By the Inheritance (Provision for Family and Dependants) Act, 1975, new provisions were enacted to replace those outlined above and to apply to the death on or after 1st April, 1976 of a person domiciled in England and Wales.

The new Act extends the categories of eligible claimants surviving the deceased to include not only the surviving spouse, an unmarried or incapacitated daughter or a son so incapacitated, but also a child (as such and although having reached the age of majority) of the deceased ; any person (not being a child of the deceased) who in the case of any marriage to which the deceased was at any time a party, was treated as a child of the family in relation to that marriage ; a former spouse of the deceased who has not remarried ; any person (not included in the foregoing cases) who immediately before the death of the deceased was being maintained either wholly or partly by the deceased making a substantial contribution in money or money's worth towards the reasonable needs of that person. The latter category would include a mistress or other person with whom the deceased was cohabiting.

The Act repeats the need for any application to be made within six months from the date on which representation with respect to the estate of the deceased is first taken out (unless the Court extends the time) ; any such application is to be made " on the ground that the disposition of the deceased's estate effected by his will or the law relating to intestacy, or the combination of his will and that law, is not such as to make reasonable financial provision for the applicant."

" Reasonable financial provision " is expressed to mean in the case of a surviving spouse (other than one under a continuing separation following a decree of judicial separation) such financial provision as it would be reasonable in all the circumstances of the case for a husband or wife to receive, whether or not that provision is required for his or her maintenance ; in other cases it is such financial provision as it would be reasonable in all the circumstances of the case for the applicant to receive for his or her maintenance.

The Act extends the orders which the Court can make. For example, the Court may deal with the case where no financial relief was granted in divorce or like proceedings. The property to be treated as part of the " net estate " within the meaning of the Act is more closely defined and the property available for financial provision now includes (*inter alia*) property or money nominated by the deceased or comprised in a *donatis mortis causa* ; there are wide powers to upset dispositions intended to defeat applications under the Act.

**Revocation of a Will.**

An essential feature of a will is that it is revocable till death. This is what is meant by saying that a will is ambulatory until the death of the testator : there is always the possibility of a change of mind. A will may be revoked in various ways :—

(i) By the execution of a new will expressly revoking the former will, or inconsistent with it in whole or in part. A Codicil—an instrument executed as a will—is often attached not so much to revoke the will but rather to supplement it. It may make an isolated alteration of some provision.

(ii) By the testator or someone in his presence and by his direction destroying the will, provided that the act of destruction, e.g., burning or tearing, is done with the intention to revoke the will. There must be both the destruction and the intent. An accidental destruction does not affect the validity of the will, the contents of which may be proved otherwise—even , in exceptional circumstances, by the recollection of a person well acquainted with the circumstances. If a will known to have been made cannot be found on the death of the testator, he is presumed, in the absence of evidence to the contrary, to have revoked it by destruction. The best evidence of non-revocation is proof of the will's existence after the testator's death. Loss or destruction after that date will not prevent the obtaining of a grant of probate, although of course evidence must be given as to its contents.

(iii) By the complete and intentional obliteration of a provision. It must be impossible to determine the original provision. A mere purported alteration which leaves the original provision apparent is of no effect unless signed by the testator and attested by two witnesses as in the case of a will.

(iv) By the subsequent marriage of the testator. This does not apply when the will is expressly made in contemplation of a specified marriage, which takes place in due course.

## Personal Representatives.

Both on an intestacy and under a will, all property vests in the personal representatives. Personal representatives may be appointed by a will or by the Court. Representatives appointed by the will are "Executors", and as such are entitled to probate. If no executor is named in the will, or the person named in the will cannot or will not apply for probate, or dies before obtaining probate, some person interested in the estate will have to apply to the Court for "letters of administration". This is called administration *cum testamento annexo* (with the will annexed). The person thus appointed is an "Administrator", but the distribution of the estate follows the terms of the will. A person appointed where there is no will, i.e., in the case of intestacy, is also an administrator, but the estate is administered in accordance with the provisions of the Administration of Estates Act, 1925, as amended by the Intestates' Estates Act, 1952, and subsequent legislation.

Where a sole or last surviving executor dies after obtaining probate but before completing the administration and without appointing an executor of his own, or where a sole or last surviving administrator dies after obtaining letters of administration but before completing the administration (whether or not he appoints an executor of his own), a grant of administration *de bonis non administratis* ("in respect of property not administered") is made to some person interested in the estate.

There may be an executor *de son tort*. This is a person, not named as an executor by the will, who intermeddles with the estate before any grant of representation has been made by doing some act which should ordinarily be done only by a personal representative. He incurs the obligations of an executor.

*Special* executors may be appointed by the testator for some special purpose, as, for example, to administer his property abroad, or in respect of settled land which does not cease to be settled on his death. In the latter case, in the absence of such an express appointment, the Trustees of the settlement are *deemed* to have been appointed special executors and will take out a grant limited to the settled land. Thus, suppose that land is settled on A for life, remainder to B for life, remainder to C in fee simple, and X and Y are trustees of the settlement. On A's death the land continues to be settled land, as B is then entitled to a life interest. Consequently, A will be deemed to have appointed X and Y as special personal representatives and they will take out a grant limited to the settled land. They will then vest the settled land in B by means of a vesting assent.

The duties of personal representatives are, very briefly :—

(a) To collect all the assets of the estate. Thus, for example, they may have to sue for a debt due to the estate.

(b) To pay the funeral and testamentary expenses and all the deceased's debts and, if necessary, to sell part of the estate for this purpose. If the estate is insolvent, the personal representative must follow the order of administration provided by section 34 and Part I of the First Schedule to the Administration of Estates Act, 1925 (which, subject to qualifications, is that obtaining in bankruptcy).

(c) To give effect to any legacies bequeathed and to distribute the residue of the estate among the persons entitled thereto under the will or intestacy of the deceased.

In order to give effect to an actual or notional disposition of *land* by the deceased, the personal representatives will execute in favour of the beneficiary a document called an " assent ". Stocks and shares would be transferred by the usual form of transfer and other types of property would be made over to the beneficiary by the method appropriate to the type of property—thus a chattel the subject of a specific bequest would pass by mere delivery, since it is a chose in possession.

The payment of a pecuniary legacy to a minor creates a problem since (in the absence of an express provision in the will) a minor cannot give a receipt to the personal representatives which will effectually discharge them. The problem can normally be overcome by the representatives availing themselves of the statutory power to appropriate the legacy to specially appointed trustees. Those trustees will then be able to resort to the legacy fund for the maintenance and advancement of the beneficiary until majority is reached under the powers conferred by the Trustee Act, 1925.

There is a peculiar doctrine in connection with executors known as " the chain of representation ". Where a sole executor dies, after taking out a grant of probate, *and has appointed an executor of his own will*, the latter executor, on proving his testator's will, automatically becomes executor of the original testator also. In any other circumstances the chain of representation is broken, and a grant of letters of administration, with the will annexed, must be taken out by some person to complete the administration of the testator's estate.

**Lapsed Gifts.**

Where a person to whom a legacy (a gift of personal property) or a devise (a gift of real property) is given predeceases the testator, the gift made to him lapses, i.e., fails. No lapse, however, occurs :—

(a) On the gift of an entailed interest, where the donee leaves issue who survive the testator and who are capable of inheriting under the entail. The gift takes effect as if the donee had died immediately after the testator. Thus, if land is left by will in trust for X in tail male, and X predeceases the testator, leaving male issue alive at the testator's death, the entail descends to the eldest son of X.

(b) Where the testator has made a gift to his *issue*, the gift will not lapse, provided the donee leaves issue alive at the testator's death, but will take effect as if the child had died immediately after the testator. The effect in this case is not to give the property which is the subject of the gift to the issue of the donee, but to make it form part of the donee's estate, and to devolve accordingly. Thus, if the donee had made a will, the property would pass thereunder ; otherwise, it would devolve as on intestacy. Where there *is* a lapse of a specific gift, the lapsed property will fall into the residue of the testator's estate. Where, however, there is no residuary gift, or the lapsed property itself forms part of the residue, the lapsed property will devolve as on intestacy. Thus, if by his will A leaves £1,000 to B (a friend) and B predeceases A, the £1,000 is not payable and the residue of the estate, i.e., the amount left after all specific gifts and the estate debts have been paid, is increased by £1,000. This sum is, therefore, said to " fall into residue ". Where there is no residuary gift, the £1,000, together with the other property not specifically disposed of, will pass as if the deceased had died intestate. If the initial gift is a part of the residue and there is a lapse of that gift, that part of the residue is also distributed as on intestacy.

## Modern Rules of Succession.

Until the 1st January, 1926, on the death of a person intestate, the distribution of his property was made in accordance with rules that were different from those observed today. The intestate's real estate was distributed according to one set of rules and his personal estate according to another. As from that date, however (and except that the old rules still regulate the descent of an entailed interest), the Administration of Estates Act, 1925, as amended by the Intestates' Estates Act, 1952, the Family Provision Act, 1966 (and as read with the Family Law Reform Act, 1969, and the Family Provision (Intestate Succession) Order, 1972, has (apart from directing that the estate of an intestate is to be held on trust for sale) provided a uniform set of rules for all kinds of property. These rules are :—

(1) If the intestate leaves a husband or wife and—

    (a) No issue and no parent or brother or sister (or issue thereof) of the whole blood.

        The whole estate goes to the surviving husband or wife.

    (b) Issue.

        The surviving husband or wife takes :—
        (i) Personal chattels (i.e., furniture, motor-cars and articles of personal use or ornament, but not chattels used for business purposes) ;
        (ii) £15,000 free of duty and costs with interest (payable out of income) at 4 per cent. per annum from the date of death ; and
        (iii) A life interest in one half of the balance.
        [This involves the investment of capital from which the surviving spouse will derive income for life.]
        The residue goes on the statutory trusts (explained below) to the issue subject to the life interest of the surviving husband or wife.

    (c) No issue but a parent or a brother or sister (or issue thereof) of the whole blood.

        The surviving husband or wife takes :—
        (i) Personal chattels ;
        (ii) £40,000 free of duty and costs

with interest (payable out of income) at 4 per cent. per annum from the date of death; and
(iii) Half the residue absolutely.
The other half of the residue :—
(iv) Where the intestate leaves one or both parents, goes to such parent or parents absolutely.
(v) Where the intestate leaves no parent, goes on the statutory trusts to the brothers and sisters (or issue thereof) of the whole blood—

(2) If the intestate leaves no husband or wife but leaves—

(a) Issue. The residue is held on the statutory trusts for the issue.

(b) No issue but one or both parents. The residue passes to the parent or parents absolutely.

(c) No issue or parents but other relatives. The residue goes in the following order to :—
 (i) Brothers and sisters (or issue thereof) of the whole blood on the statutory trusts.
 (ii) Brothers and sisters (or issue thereof) of the half-blood on the statutory trusts.
 (iii) Grandparents absolutely.
 (iv) Uncles and aunts (or issue thereof) of the whole blood on the statutory trusts.
 (v) Uncles and aunts (or issue thereof) of the half-blood on the statutory trusts.

(d) No relatives. The residue goes to the Crown as ownerless property (*bona vacantia*).

The statutory trusts are to divide the property equally among the beneficiaries within the class, each share vesting at the age of eighteen or prior marriage. Where a beneficiary has predeceased the intestate, his share goes to his issue in the same way.

" Issue " has been extended by the Family Law Reform Act, 1969, to include illegitimate offspring.

A surviving spouse is given the right, in normal circumstances, to require the personal representatives to appropriate to the surviving spouse the matrimonial home, the market-value of which would on such appropriation be deducted from the other benefits accruing under the intestacy.

Although no direct reference is made in the tables to nephews, nieces or cousins, yet they may take interests under an intestacy, for nephews and nieces may be entitled under the statutory trusts in favour of brothers and sisters, and likewise cousins under the statutory trusts in favour of uncles and aunts. Thus, if A is survived only by a brother B, and two nephews X and Y, children of a deceased sister C, the estate is divisible into two parts, of which B takes one part and X and Y the other part equally. The same would apply if B was an uncle, and X and Y cousins, the children of a deceased aunt.

There may be, as has been said, a *partial intestacy*, e.g., where the deceased's will contains no residuary gift or where there is a lapse of part of the residue. In these cases the part of the estate undisposed-of is distributed in accordance with the above rules. Consequently, if A dies without issue and leaves his estate to be divided between his wife B and his brother C, and C predeceases A, there is a lapse of one-half of the residue and a corresponding partial intestacy.

It sometimes happens that a person who is entitled to a share in the estate has already benefited either under the will, in the case of a partial intestacy, or from a gift by the intestate before his death, in the event of a total intestacy. If this has happened, there are three cases (apart from express provisions in wills) when the benefit already received must be brought into account before calculating the beneficiary's share in the intestate's estate. This is known as bringing the benefit into " hotchpot ".

Firstly, it is provided that where an intestate's property is held upon the statutory trusts for the issue, or any money property which has been paid to or settled upon any *child* of the testate, must be taken as paid or settled in total or partial satisfaction of the share which such child can claim upon the death of the parent intestate, unless the circumstances show a contrary intention.

Moreover, where grandchildren obtain a share of an intestate's estate owing to the death of their parent before the intestate, any advance made to the deceased parent must be brought into hotchpot by the grandchildren. Thus if A dies intestate leaving property valued at £5,000 to be divided between his two sons X and Y and it happens that X has received an advancement of £1,000 during A's lifetime, this must be brought into hotchpot, so that X would receive £2,000 and Y £3,000. Should X have predeceased A leaving children surviving, those children will receive only £2,000 between them, as the advance made to X must be brought into hotchpot.

It must be noted, however, that this provision relates only to advances made to a *child* of the intestate, advances to grandchildren and remoter issue being excluded. Gifts made to brothers or sisters, or indeed to any person other than a child of the deceased, are not deemed to be advances and so need not be brought into account.

Secondly, where assets are held on the statutory trusts for issue on a partial intestacy, any gift by *will* to *issue* of the deceased must be brought into hotchpot. Thus a son benefiting under the partial intestacy must account for any gifts to his children, as well as those to himself, under the will.

No benefit can be derived from the hotchpot in the two cases mentioned by any person who is not a descendant of the intestate, for the purpose of the rule is to equalize the shares of the issue and so the share of a widow or widower is deducted before bringing the advances into account.

The third provision is that any beneficial interest received by a surviving spouse under a will must be set off, in the case of a partial intestacy, against the lump sum (known as the statutory legacy) of £15,000 or £40,000, as the case may be, but *not* against any other benefit due to the spouse under the intestacy.

## Involuntary Transfer of Real Property to Creditors.

The land of a debtor is liable to be seized at the instance of a creditor in satisfaction of unpaid debts. This may happen in three ways :—

(a) When a mortgagee obtains a foreclosure decree absolute.
(b) When a debtor is adjudicated bankrupt, his land is transferred to his Trustee in bankruptcy, who will dispose of it for the benefit of the creditor.
(c) On the death of a debtor, his property devolves on his personal representatives, in whose hands it becomes assets for the payment of his debts.

## Social Control of Land.

Severe restrictions are imposed by modern legislation on the freedom of a landowner to do what he likes with his land. Most of the restrictions come by way of the Town and Country Planning Acts (now consolidated in the Act of 1971 and subsequently amended), which subject the use of land to the condition that any " development " must be sanctioned by the appropriate planning authority charged with the formulation and carrying out of planning schemes. " Development " means not only the construction of buildings, or the alteration of existing buildings (e.g., the conversion of a house into flats) or the execution of engineering works, but also anything whereby an existing use of land or buildings is materially changed. Permission for the development must be obtained and supporting plans lodged. A Statutory Order lists a number of cases where " development " may be made without planning permission, but they are comparatively minor and innocuous matters. The last word does not however, lie with the planning authority, since there is a right of appeal to the Secretary of the Environment. The scheme of the Acts also envisages the compulsory acquisition of private land for planning purposes.

Much modern statute law interferes with freedom of contract in the matter of leaseholds. Thus the Rent Acts (for the most part consolidated in the Rent Act, 1968) present a maze of legislation too complicated to summarize, but the purpose of which may be said to afford security of tenure in respect of, and to control the level of rents payable under, tenancies of dwelling-houses privately let and under certain prescribed limits of rateable value. The Rent Act, 1974 extends full rent protection to residential furnished tenants and affords in most cases, a measure of security of tenure in respect of such tenancies.

The legislation makes it a criminal offence for a landlord to dispossess his tenant without a Court order or to harass the tenant.

The Landlord and Tenant Acts, 1927-1954, afford tenants of business and professional premises rights to compensation for improvements and (except in recognized cases) to renewal of their tenancies.

The Agriculture Act, 1947, gives effect to the policy of controlling the efficiency of farming operations, by laying down standards of good estate management for the owner and good husbandry for the occupier. The Agricultural Holdings Act, 1948 (as amended), protects a tenant of an agricultural holding against eviction without good cause and against excessive rents.

The Housing Act, 1961 (referred to on page 193) imposes certain obligations as to repairs on certain landlords.

The Leasehold Reform Act, 1967 (which has been estimated to affect upwards of 1,000,000 residential tenants in this Country) makes provision for the acquisition against agreed or officially ascertained compensation to the freeholder of the freehold by a residential tenant holding under a long lease at a low rent. The tenant is given alternative rights to a renewal of his lease for fifty years if he opts against this " leasehold enfranchisement ".

Legislation exists (and is likely to be extended) providing for the compulsory purchase or acquisition by governmental agencies or local authorities of land ripe for development for housing and other needs. A recent example is the Community Land Act, 1975.

All these things reflect the tendency in the present century to subject land to various forms of social control. The matters already mentioned may be grouped under four rubrics :—

(i) Planning control.
(ii) Agricultural control.
(iii) Protection of tenants.
(iv) Making land available for development.

# CHAPTER VII

## ELEMENTS OF TORT

**Liability for Tort.**
*A tort is a wrong independent of contract, giving rise to an action for damages.*

There are three factors : (*a*) an act or omission not being a breach of a purely contractual undertaking ; (*b*) an act or omission unauthorized by law ; (*c*) injury inflicted of a kind that is special, private and peculiar to an individual, as distinguished from injury to the public at large.

In every tort there are usually two elements : (i) *damnum*, i.e., damage—substantial loss of money, comfort, health, and (ii) *injuria*, i.e., unauthorized interference with some right conferred by law.

There are certain fundamental propositions which must be borne in mind :—

(*a*) *Damnum absque injuria* ("loss without legal wrong") is not actionable. An example would be harm resulting from ordinary and lawful trade competition.

(*b*) *Injuria sine damno* ("legal wrong without loss") is not actionable in most cases ; i.e., if there is the violation of a legal right but no loss occasioned, then, in general, no action will lie. But certain torts are actionable *per se*, i.e., without proof of special damage, e.g., trespass to land and libel. In many cases, however, damage is the gist of the action, e.g., fraud, malicious prosecution, nuisance and negligence.

There may be a tort arising from the infringement of a *public* right, one enjoyed by all men in common, e.g., obstruction of the highway. This is a *public* nuisance, and for an individual to have a right of action in such a case he must prove special, peculiar and substantial damage to himself over and above that incurred by the public at large, e.g., that he fell into an unauthorized trench, dug across the highway, and broke his leg.

(*c*) *Ubi jus, ibi remedium* ("Where there is a right there is a remedy"). Thus, there are as many actions in tort as there are infringements of non-contractual rights.

*There is a mental element in tort.* There must be *volition* : a hiker knocked by a motor car from the highway on to adjoining land is not a trespasser against that land ; but failure to appreciate the probable consequences of one's act or omission is of no avail as a defence. Ignorance of the tortious character of the act usually affords no excuse.

Malice in the sense of spite or ill-will is usually irrelevant, but there are exceptions, e.g., in the tort of malicious prosecution and as regards the defence of qualified privilege in defamation. An evil motive does not render wrongful an act that would not otherwise be so. Thus, in *Bradford Corporation* v. *Pickles* (1895), it was held not to be actionable to dig wells on one's lands, thereby interfering with water flowing in *undefined* channels, which the plaintiff was relying upon to augment the town supply, although the object was to force the purchase of the land at an unduly high price. On the other hand, a good motive will not render lawful an otherwise unlawful act.

An act or omission *prima facie* tortious is not actionable if there is lawful excuse for it. Among lawful excuses may be mentioned:—

(1) *Act of State*. This requires the following essentials:—

   (a) It must be an act done to a foreign State or to a subject of a foreign State, and, if such subject is an alien friend, the act must be done outside the realm.
   (b) The act must be one of sovereign power, e.g., the annexation of territory by an arbitrary act.
   (c) The act must be that of the State itself acting through authorized agents, but authorization may arise through subsequent ratification.

**Buron v. Denman (1848).**

A British naval officer destroyed a Spaniard's barracoons for slaves on the African coast. His act was formally approved by the Secretary of State.

*Held* that this was an act of State, and that no action lay in respect of it.

There cannot be an act of State between *Crown and Subject*; that is to say, it is no defence to an action by a British subject to plead the exercise of sovereign power by the Executive, i.e., the persons and bodies by whom governmental policy is carried out. Thus, the State cannot compulsorily acquire land without paying compensation to its owner, except, of course, under statutory authority. Cp. *Nissan* v. *Attorney-General* (1967).

(2) *Judicial Immunity*. A Judge is immune from any proceedings in respect of his *judicial* acts, even though he may have acted unlawfully, provided those acts were done within his jurisdiction. Thus, a Judge cannot be sued in respect of anything said or done by him within his jurisdiction.

(3) *Statutory Authority*. There is a general implication that the authorization does not cover negligent execution of the authorized

act. A distinction is drawn between a statute which merely authorizes an act if it *can* be done *without* causing injury to others, and a statute which authorizes an act to be done which must *necessarily* cause injury to someone. In the latter case, the statute will be construed as authorizing the doing of the act in any event.

(4) *Volenti non fit injuria* (" No injury can be done to a willing person "). A person who consents to an act being done or who takes upon himself the risk of suffering damage cannot bring an action in respect of that act or damage. But a man's mere *knowledge* of the danger does not amount to consent to incur the risk. The maxim must be applied with caution when the relation of master and servant exists. Thus, it cannot be applied when the action in question arises out of the servant's ordinary duty, unless the particular occupation is an inherently dangerous one, such as working in an explosives factory. " A man, however, whose occupation is not one of a nature inherently dangerous but who is asked, or required, to undertake a risky occupation, is in a difficult position . . . It is not enough to show that, whether under protest or not, he obeyed an order or complied with a request, which he might have declined as one which he was not bound to obey or comply with. It must be shown that he agreed that what risk there was, should be on him " : Lord Goddard, C.J., in *Bowater* v. *Rowley Regis Corporation* (1944). The maxim is excluded where the servant's action is based on the master's breach of statutory duty.

Nor does the maxim apply when a man has been compelled " to make a choice of evils " in an emergency created by another's default.

The maxim does not apply inevitably where a man is injured in his voluntary efforts to save another person from injury. Here, the test is : Did he intervene to rescue another, put in peril in consequence of the negligence of another ? Was his act such as could be expected from a man of ordinary courage and ability, situated in similar circumstances ? If no person is put in peril, the volunteer acts at his own risk.

An illustrative case is :—

### Haynes v. Harwood (1935).

The defendant's servant negligently left a two-horse van unattended in a street in Rotherhithe. A mischievous boy threw a stone at the horses and thus caused them to bolt. The plaintiff, a police constable, on coming out of the police station whence he had seen what was happening, saw that a woman and some children were in danger of being injured if nothing were done to stop the unnerved horses. Accordingly he seized one of them and succeeded in pulling them both up before any mischief occurred. However, one of the horses fell on and injured him. The Court of Appeal *held* that the maxim *volenti non fit injuria* did not apply and the plaintiff was entitled to recover, for as a policeman he was under a moral duty to prevent injury to people lawfully using the highway. The injury was a direct consequence of the defendant's negligent act (through their servant) of leaving horses unattended.

The principle of *Haynes* v. *Harwood* was followed in *Baker* v. *T. E. Hopkins & Sons, Ltd.* (1959), where a brave doctor lost his life in attempting to rescue workmen who had become overcome by fumes in a well being cleared of water by a petrol pump placed some feet down the well in circumstances disclosing negligent indifference by the men's employers to the safety of the workmen.

The consent to undergo the risk may be implied, as in participation in games or in the case of spectators at sports and exhibitions, but failure to take reasonable precautions may negative the defence in these circumstances.

The test to be applied in relation to *volenti non fit injuria* is an objective one : *Burnett* v. *British Waterways Board* (1972).

> It should be noted that under section 6 (5) of the Animals Act, 1971, where a person employed as a servant by a keeper of an animal incurs a risk incidental to his employment he is not to be treated as accepting the risk voluntarily.

## Who May Sue or be Sued.

In general, any injured person except an alien enemy may sue. The term "alien enemy" for this purpose includes a British subject voluntarily residing or carrying on business in an enemy country or an enemy-controlled country.

There are, however, certain qualifications. Thus before the Law Reform (Husband and Wife) Act, 1962, a husband could not sue his wife in tort and a wife could not sue her husband in tort except for the protection and security of her own property. However, the Act provides that " each of the parties to a marriage shall have the like right of action in tort against the other as if they were not married ". Nevertheless, the Court is empowered, where an action in tort is brought by one spouse against the other during the subsistence of the marriage, to stay the action where it appears (*a*) that no substantial benefit would accrue to either party from the continuation of the proceedings ; or, (*b*) that the question in issue could more conveniently be disposed of under that section of the Married Women's Property Act, 1882, which provides for the determination of questions between husband and wife as to the title to or possession of property (see *ante*, p. 108).

The general rule of liability is that all persons are liable in tort, minority and mental disability notwithstanding. A minor, however, is liable only for his " naked " torts ; i.e., he cannot be sued for a tort if the action would be an indirect mode of enforcing a contract against him ; even so he is answerable for tortious conduct which also happens to be a breach of an important contractual term. Cp. *Burnard* v. *Haggis* (1863). Further, the fact of minority must be considered if the tort is one requiring the presence of a mental element. Accordingly in dealing with an allegation of contributory negligence of a minor the Court would adopt standards of care referable to the actual age of the minor rather than those of the adult " reasonable man " : *Gough* v. *Thorne* (1966). A parent is not liable *as a parent* for the torts of his child, though he may be liable himself if he is personally negligent, e.g., in allowing his child to possess and use without supervision a dangerous object, like an air-gun, and injury is caused to a playmate or stranger, as happened in *Newton* v. *Edgerley* (1959).

There are also certain qualifications upon the general rule. Thus, it used to be said that the " Queen can do no wrong ". The full operation of this maxim has, however, been curtailed by the Crown Proceedings Act, 1947, which makes the Crown generally liable for the torts committed by its servants or agents in the course of their duty, but provides that no proceedings can be taken against the Queen in her private capacity. See *ante* p. 111.

The immunity from legal proceedings is also extended to foreign sovereigns and potentates and to foreign ambassadors and their accredited staffs, but in these instances the immunity may be waived, the privilege being one of immunity from legal proceedings and not immunity from liability.

A corporation can act only through its agents or servants and its liability for the torts of those agents or servants is the same as that of any other principal or employer. In other words, a corporation is not liable for the wrongful acts of its agents or servants if such acts were outside the scope of their general authority or duty.

As to trade unions see *ante* pp. 127 and 141 and *post* p. 247.

## Vicarious Liability.

In certain circumstances a man is liable not only for his own acts but for the acts of others. This arises in particular when the relation of master and servant exists. Thus, a master is always liable for the wrongful acts done by his servants under his specific orders, but he is also liable for the wrongful acts of his servants committed *in the course of their employment* or *within the scope of their authority*. If, at the time of the commission of the wrongful act, the servant was " out on a frolic of his own ", as in the case of a chauffeur who, without his master's knowledge, uses his master's car for his own private purposes, then the master will not be liable. Similarly, a master is not liable for injury sustained by an unauthorized passenger carried in a vehicle owned by him and driven by his servant : *Conway* v. *George Wimpey & Co.* (1950).

A master is not responsible for the consequences of his servant's act during the period of his employment, unless the act was one which the servant was employed to perform. Thus, in *Crook* v. *Derbyshire Stone, Ltd.* (1956), where a lorry driver, having left his lorry to visit a café, was involved, whilst crossing the road, in a collision with a motor cyclist, the latter failed in his action against the driver's employers.

Moreover, a servant has, in general, no implied authority to delegate his authority, and, thus, the master is not liable for the wrongful acts of a delegate, unless the very act of delegation amounts to negligence in the mode of carrying out the duty entrusted to him, as in the case of an omnibus driver allowing the conductor to drive " for a change ". When the act done is one of a class which the servant was employed to do, there are three " areas " of liability :—

(a) Negligence of the servant in the course of his employment.
(b) Excess or mistake of the servant in the execution of his duty—not gratuitous assault, or mere capricious acts.
(c) Wilful wrong committed by the servant in the course of employment, although forbidden expressly by the master, even though constituting a crime, and committed solely for the benefit of the servant himself.

Even if the relation of master and servant or principal and agent does not exist, a person may be liable for the tortious acts of another whom he has urged to embark on concerted action with him.

**Brooke v. Bool (1928).**
The defendant enlisted the aid of X, a passer-by, to trace the source of a leakage of gas. X caused an explosion by trying to discover the source with a naked light. The plaintiff's goods were in consequence destroyed.
*Held* that the defendant was liable for the negligence as joint tortfeasor.

An employer is not liable, however, for the negligence of an *independent contractor*. An independent contractor is a person who is to achieve a specified end by his own means, whereas a servant is directed to attain a specified end by specified means. A servant is under his master's control not only as to *what* he is to do, but as to *how* he is to do it, whereas an independent contractor is under the employer's control only as to *what* he is to do, having full discretion as to the manner of doing it. A servant is employed under a contract of *service*; an independent contractor engages to render acts in the nature of *services*. In certain cases, however, an employer is liable for the negligence of an independent contractor, e.g., where the employer personally interferes in the work or creates special hazards to third persons, or where the work directed is in itself wrongful.

## SUBSTANTIVE TORTS

**Trespass.**

There are three types of trespass :—

(a) *Trespass to the Person.*
   (i) Assault. This is an attempt or offer to apply unlawful force to the person of another, there being an *apparent* present ability to execute such threat. The essence of the wrong is that a person is put in present fear of violence. Thus, if A points an unloaded gun at B, there is an assault if B believes the weapon to be loaded. There must be some type of action. Thus, words alone cannot make an assault, but they may *unmake* one, as where a man says, " If that policeman were not watching me, I would strike you with my stick ".
   (ii) Battery. This is the execution of the threat involved in an assault, the touching of a person hostilely or against his will. The slightest contact will suffice, e.g., kissing a girl against her will. The injury may be wrongful in that it is force applied intentionally, or, as the result of negligence. Mere jostling in ordinary social intercourse is not a battery.
   (iii) False Imprisonment : the totally restraining, by force or show of authority of the liberty of another, without lawful justification. There must be a *total* deprivation of liberty of action. It is not false imprisonment to prevent a person from walking along *one* side of the street. It is not essential that the plaintiff should be aware of the fact of imprisonment ; thus, a man who is asleep, may yet suffer false imprisonment. Yet there is no false imprisonment when the defendant merely abstains from doing an act which he is under no obligation to do, e.g., where an employer refuses to provide facilities to enable his employee to leave his place of employment before the time stipulated in the contract of employment.

There are the following defences to an action for trespass to the person :—

(1) *Self-defence.* This includes defence, not merely of oneself, but of those whom one has a legal or moral obligation to protect. It also applies to protection of property. But in all cases no more force must be used than is commensurate with the necessity.
(2) *Parental or similar authority.* Thus, moderate chastisement inflicted by a parent on his child, or by a schoolmaster on his pupil by way of delegation of the parents' authority, is not actionable.
(3) *Judicial authority.* This includes the right to arrest.

(*b*) *Trespass to Land.* An example of this is an entry on land in the possession of another without lawful authority. As in other cases of trespass, it is not necessary to prove actual damage. Nor is ignorance a defence. Apart from the ordinary forms of trespass, there are many other varieties, e.g., driving nails into a wall, or the defendant's horse kicking the plaintiff's horse through a fence. It is trespass even to use the highway for some purpose other than the lawful right of passing and repassing.

It should be observed that under the Civil Aviation Act, 1949, it is provided that " no action shall lie in respect of trespass or in respect of nuisance by reason only of the flight of an aircraft over any property at a height above the ground, which, having regard to wind, weather and all the circumstances of the case, is reasonable . . ."

Trespass is essentially a wrong against possession not against ownership. The plaintiff must have been in possession, actually or constructively. Thus, a landlord may sue in trespass only if some permanent injury has been inflicted, e.g., the destruction of his property, or a serious impairment of the value thereof. The fact that a third person was lawfully entitled to the possession of the land and that the plaintiff's possession as against such person was unlawful is no defence to an action of trespass against some other person. This is what is meant by saying that a wrongdoer cannot set up the *jus tertii* (right of a third person).

There is a curious doctrine whereby a person whose original entry was lawful may yet become a trespasser by his *subsequent* conduct. This is known as *trespass ab initio.* Thus, where the defendant has authority conferred upon him *by law*, as distinct from authority conferred by the plaintiff, to enter upon land for a particular purpose, he is not a trespasser on entry. But should he use his authority for any other purpose than that authorized, he becomes a trespasser, and, moreover, the abuse relates back *to his original* entry, provided that the abuse is a misfeasance (an improper act) and not a mere nonfeasance (an omission to act). This latter point is illustrated by the *Six Carpenters Case* (1610).

Carpenters entered a public inn and ordered wine for which they paid. They ordered more for which they refused to pay. They were not trespassers *ab initio* (from the beginning) because although they had authority by law to enter, they were guilty of nonfeasance, not of misfeasance.

> In *Chic Fashions (West Wales) Ltd.* v. *Jones* (1968) (alleged irregular seizure by police (under a search warrant and following a lawful entry) of goods believed to have been stolen), Diplock, L.J., considered that the question of " what application, if any, the rule applied in the *Six Carpenters' Case* has in the modern law of tort may some day call for re-examination. . . .". Lord Denning, M.R., went further and said ". . . I know that at one time a man could be made a trespasser *ab initio* by the doctrine of relation back ; but that is no longer true. The *Six Carpenters' Case* was a by-product of the old forms of action. Now that they are buried, it can be interred with their bones."

A person enjoying a revocable licence over land (see *ante* p. 182) becomes a trespasser once the licence has been revoked and he has had reasonable time in which to withdraw but has failed to withdraw.

Apart from the remedy by action, there is an extra-judicial remedy, " self-help ", whereby the person in possession of land may, having first requested the trespasser to depart peaceably, eject him, using such force as is reasonably necessary.

> In the case of trespass by animals, the occupier had at Common Law the right of Distress Damage Feasant, which was the right to seize the animals and detain them until their owner made compensation, but he could not sell them.
> 
> The remedy has been abolished in respect of animals by the Animals Act, 1971, section 7(1) of which provides that " the right to seize and detain any animal by way of distress damage feasant is hereby abolished." The remaining subsections of section 7 afford new remedies (including an ultimate right of sale).

(c) *Trespass to Goods.* This may occur by wrongfully taking goods out of the plaintiff's possession, or by forcibly interfering with them whilst in his possession. It involves direct physical interference as where a misguided person removes the wheels of a motor-car parked in a quiet country lane.

The essence of the wrong is the interference with possession, and thus it differs from two other torts, *Detinue* and *Conversion*, of which the trespass is often the first stage. Detinue is wrongfully detaining the goods of another to the immediate possession of which that other is entitled. An action for detinue is brought where restoration has been demanded and refused and where the plaintiff seeks both damages and the return of the specific goods.

Conversion is the usurpation of the powers of the true owner, as by taking away, destroying, delivering to a third person or otherwise depriving the plaintiff of goods, to the possession of which the plaintiff is entitled. The moral innocence of the defendant is immaterial. Thus, if A steals B's watch and sells it to C, who is ignorant of the theft, then unless the case falls within one of the exceptions mentioned in Chapter VI, C is liable to A for conversion. If C sells to D, D to E, and so on, each person acquiring the watch is similarly liable to A.

The leading case on conversion is :—

### Hollins v. Fowler (1875).

The defendant, a cotton broker, honestly purchased from a third party, who had obtained possession by fraud, a quantity of cotton belonging to the plaintiff, and sold it to a manufacturer. Although the defendant acted in good faith, the sale and delivery by him of the cotton was held to be a conversion, since the defendant's acts were inconsistent with the plaintiff's title.

Purely "ministerial dealings", e.g., carrying or warehousing goods, do not amount to conversion, for such acts are done without reference to the question of property in the goods.

## Nuisance.

There are two types of nuisance, Public and Private.

*A Public Nuisance* is some unlawful act or omission endangering or interfering with the lives, comfort, property, or common rights of the public, e.g., the obstruction of a highway or keeping dangerous premises near a highway. A public nuisance is a crime, and the normal remedy lies in criminal proceedings, but it is actionable at the suit of a private individual if he has suffered peculiar damage over and above that suffered by the public as a whole, or if the public nuisance is also an interference with his private rights or property. Thus, to dig a ditch across the highway without authority creates a public nuisance. But if A, in the dark, falls into the ditch, or if the ditch as such interferes with his right of access from his premises to the highway, he may sue in tort for a private nuisance.

*A Private Nuisance* is an unlawful interference with a man's user of his property, or with his health, comfort or convenience according to the standard existing in his neighbourhood. It is a wrongful act causing material injury to property or sensible personal discomfort. There are three chief classes of private nuisance :—

(a) Nuisances affecting ownership. Here there is a similarity to trespass, but, whereas in the latter the cause of action is the interference with another's right, in the former it is the damage resulting from such interference which is the cause of action.

Examples are permitting gutters or roots or branches of trees to project over or encroach upon neighbouring land.
(b) Nuisances affecting the rights which people may have over the property of others, e.g., an interference with a right of way or of light, provided that it is an appreciable interference with user of such right. Within the same class come nuisances arising from interference with natural servitudes, the law concerning which, in a nutshell, is as follows : So far as land unburdened with buildings and unweakened by excavations is concerned, that land has, in law, a natural servitude (easement) of support from the adjoining land. There is, however, no natural servitude of support to buildings either from the adjoining land or from other buildings. Nevertheless a right of support for a building can be acquired by express or implied grant or by open enjoyment for twenty years. An interference with that right of support would amount to a private nuisance.
(c) Continued interferences with another's health or comfort or enjoyment of his property.

In considering whether an act or omission is a nuisance within class (c) the following points are relevant :—

(1) There need be no direct injury to health ; it suffices that a person has been prevented to an appreciable extent from enjoying the ordinary comforts of life.
(2) The standard of the ordinary comforts of life obviously varies with the neighbourhood in which they are enjoyed—there is no uniformity of standard between Park Lane and Whitechapel. (This does not apply to light : to sew requires the same amount of light wherever one may be.)
(3) An operation may become a nuisance by reason of its cumulative effect in conjunction with previously existing operations. Moreover, in general, it is no defence to allege that the complainant " came to the nuisance ". Yet a person cannot take advantage of his peculiar sensitivity to noise and smells. There must be some " give and take " ; a man cannot expect the same amenities in a crowded industrial town as he has enjoyed in the country.
(4) The character of the alleged nuisance has no bearing on the question of nuisance or no nuisance. Limekilns, tanneries, pigstyes and breweries are doubtless material to the well-being of the community ; nevertheless, if they are erected or carried on so as to constitute an infringement of a man's right to the ordinary comforts of life, they are nuisances.
(5) Nuisances affecting property must affect such property to a *material* extent. If an alleged nuisance does not affect the enjoyment of a house used in its ordinary capacity, it does not become a nuisance because it prejudices a non-ordinary use of the land for some particular purpose.
(6) The modes of annoyance are infinitely various, e.g., bell-ringing, circus-performing, excessive use of the wireless, causing queues to assemble so as to prevent access to a house or place of business.
(7) A nuisance may result from the cumulative acts of several wrongdoers, where the acts of each taken separately would not have constituted an interference with the rights of others. Any one of the participants may be proceeded against for nuisance, and he cannot plead that the nuisance was a cumulative one.

(8) In certain circumstances malice or evil motive may become the gist of the offence. Thus, in *Hollywood Silver Fox Farm, Ltd.* v. *Emmett* (1936), the defendant was held liable in nuisance in that he deliberately fired guns on his own land for the purpose of disturbing the silver foxes on his neighbour's land, and so injuring his business of *breeding* silver foxes. This evil motive was evidence that he was not using his property in a legitimate manner. This decision in no wise affects the decision in *Bradford Corporation* v. *Pickles* (see page 214), because the presence of malice was proof of the defendant's *unreasonable user* of his land, thus rendering his act a nuisance.

(9) It is possible to acquire a right to create a private nuisance by prescription—twenty years' continuous operation since the act complained of *first constituted a nuisance.*

### Sturges v. Bridgman (1879).

For more than 20 years the defendant, a confectioner, had used a pestle and mortar in his kitchen in Wigmore Street. Then, the plaintiff, a physician in Wimpole Street, built a consulting room in his garden, abutting on the confectioner's kitchen. The noise made by the confectioner detrimentally affected the use of the consulting room.

*Held* that the defendant had not acquired a prescriptive right to create the nuisance, as the nuisance only arose when the consulting room was built.

A right to commit a public nuisance cannot be acquired by prescription.

PARTIES TO SUE AND BE SUED. The actual occupant of the property affected by a nuisance is the person to sue, but the landlord may sue in the event of permanent injury. The general rule is that the person who creates the nuisance is the person liable. *Sedleigh-Denfield* v. *O'Callaghan* (1940) shows, however, that an occupier may be liable even though he did not himself actually create the nuisance. In that case a trespasser laid a pipe and grating in the defendant's ditch. The grating having become choked, water overflowed on to the plaintiff's premises. The House of Lords held that it was the occupier's duty in such a case to abate a nuisance of the existence of which he knew or ought to have known. A landlord may be liable, e.g., if he created the nuisance and then leased the property, or where the nuisance is due to the landlord's breach of covenant, or where he authorized the tenant, expressly or impliedly, to create or continue the nuisance.

REMEDIES. The party injured by a private nuisance may :—

(i) Abate the nuisance himself, provided he causes no unnecessary damage, provided he does no wrong to an innocent third party, and provided where entry on defendant's land is necessary [*Lemmon* v. *Webb* (1894)] notice requesting removal of the nuisance is first given. The abator who lops branches overhanging his land is not entitled to retain them or their fruit—if he does he commits conversion: *Mills* v. *Brooker* (1919) ;

(ii) Sue for damages

(iii) Seek an injunction if he can prove that damages will not be an adequate remedy and that the injury will continue and be irreparable unless the injunction is granted.

## Negligence.

Negligence is now an independent tort and has become so as a result of rapid legal development running parallel with the growth of a machine age.

Briefly, negligence is the breach of a duty to take care. The plaintiff must prove :

(a) The existence of a duty to take care owed by the defendant to him, the plaintiff ;
(b) A breach of such duty by the defendant ;
(c) Resulting damage to him, the plaintiff.

As regards the first essential it has been said, " Negligence is not a ground of liability unless the person whose conduct it impeached is under a duty of taking care " : *Butler* v. *Fife Coal Co. Ltd.* (1912) (per Lord Shaw of Dunfermline). Again, " A man is entitled to be as negligent as he pleases towards the whole world if he owes no duty to them " : *Le Lievre* v. *Gould* (1893) (per Lord Esher).

The question of the existence of a duty to take care is one of law ; the nature of the relation giving rise to such a duty eludes precise definition, but it was stated in *Donoghue* v. *Stevenson* (1932) to exist between the doer and his " neighbours ", i.e., " persons who are so closely and directly affected by (the) act that (the doer) ought reasonably to have them in contemplation as being so affected when directing (his) mind to the acts or omissions which are called in question " (per Lord Atkin). This relationship is one of proximity in the legal (not necessarily also geographical or physical) sense.

### Donoghue v. Stevenson (1932).

A man bought from a retailer a bottle of ginger-beer, manufactured by the defendants. He gave the bottle to his lady friend who was made very ill because the bottle contained the decomposed remains of a snail ; since the bottle was made of opaque glass and had a closed top, it was impossible to detect the snail until most of the liquid had been consumed. The consumer sued the manufacturer in negligence and recovered damages.

The case is of considerable importance for, as Jenks says, it established the " existence of a general liability for harm resulting from carelessness " and " as a general rule a person is bound to use reasonable foresight whenever he ought to realize that he is likely to cause damage to others ".

Situations in which a duty to take care arises are manifold. The obvious one is use of the highway.

In the House of Lords case of *Hedley Byrne and Co.* v. *Heller and Partners* (1963) (overruling the majority decision and preferring the dissenting view of Denning, L.J. in the Court of Appeal case of *Candler* v. *Crane, Christmas and Co.* (1951)) it was held that liability for financial loss caused by negligent misstatements could arise not only by virtue of a contractual or fiduciary relationship, but also (in tort) on the voluntary assumption of responsibility (as by a banker giving a reference in unconditional terms) creating a situation occasioning a duty to take care.

In *Home Office* v. *Dorset Yacht Co. Ltd.* (1970) (H.L.) it was held that prison authorities keeping an open borstal institution owed a duty of care to those in the neighbourhood and that duty was capable of giving rise to liability in damages for damage to property shown to have resulted from negligent supervision of the system which permitted the escape of inmates of the prison.

As regards the second essential—the breach of such duty, negligence, " is the omission to do something which a reasonable man, guided by those considerations which ordinarily regulate the conduct of human affairs, would do, or doing something which a prudent and reasonable man would not do ".

Thus, the standard of care required is not that of a particularly conscientious man, but that of an average prudent man in the eyes of the jury. Only when a man has undertaken a duty which requires extraordinary skill will he be expected to use extraordinary care.

> The standard of care was discussed by the House of Lords in *Barnes* v. *Hampshire County Council* (1969) in relation to school authorities and it was held that it was negligent to release children five minutes before scheduled school-closing time from a school adjoining a main road when all the parents might not reasonably be expected to have arrived to escort their children home. On the other hand it is not necessarily negligent to leave children unsupervised in the playground during the few minutes before school starts for the day : *Ward* v. *Hertfordshire County Council* (1970) (C.A.).

The third element—resulting damage—will be discussed in connection with the topic of remoteness of damage (*post* p. 245).

FUNCTIONS OF JUDGE AND JURY. It is for the Judge to decide whether the alleged facts are sufficient to support the plea of a failure of duty, it is for the jury (if any) or for the Judge when sitting alone to decide whether they do in fact make out such plea. Normally the onus of proving negligence rests upon the plaintiff, but if a thing is solely under the management of the defendant or that of his servants, and the accident is such as, in the ordinary course of events, does not happen if those having the management of such things use proper care, there is *prima facie* evidence of negligence. This principle is known as "*Res ipsa loquitur*" ("The thing speaks for itself"). Thus in *Byrne* v. *Boadle* (1863) where a person was walking along a public street, and a barrel of flour fell upon him from a window of the defendant's house, it was held sufficient *prima facie* evidence of negligence to cast upon the defendant the onus of proving that his want of care was not the cause of the accident. Barrels do not usually fall out of windows unless there has been want of care. The principle does not, however, do more than shift the burden of proof to the defendant, who must satisfy the Court that he was not, in fact, negligent. He need not, therefore, prove exactly how and why the accident happened : *Turner* v. *National Coal Board* (1949). In *Moore* v. *Fox* (1956), it was further explained that it was not sufficient for the defendant merely to show that the accident could have happened without negligence on his part, but that he must show either that he had not been negligent or that the accident was due to a specific cause not connoting such negligence.

CONTRIBUTORY NEGLIGENCE. A person is guilty of contributory negligence if he has by his own want of care so far contributed to the damage caused by the negligence of the other party that, if it had not been for his own want of care, the damage would not have occurred.

It was pointed out in *O'Connell* v. *Jackson* (1971) (C.A.) that a plaintiff who has suffered damage in consequence of an accident for which the defendant is wholly responsible may be guilty of contributory negligence, although his conduct in no way contributed to the accident itself, if his act or omission contributed to the nature or extent of the injuries he has sustained as a result of the accident. Accordingly a motor cyclist who fails to wear a crash helmet in circumstances where a prudent road-user would do so and who is injured in an accident may be held in part responsible for the injuries which he would not have received if he had been wearing a helmet, even though he was in no way to blame for the occurrence of the accident. The Court gave approval to the dictum of Denning, L.J., in *Jones* v. *Livox Quarries Ltd*. (1952) that "just as actionable negligence requires the foreseeability of harm to others, so contributory negligence requires the foreseeability of harm to oneself". The principle in the dictum of Denning, L.J., in *Jones* v. *Lirox Quarries* was applied by the Court of Appeal in *Froom* v. *Butcher* (1975) in holding that the driver or front-seat passenger sustaining injury in a collision between two motor vehicles is guilty of contributory negligence if he was not wearing a seat-belt at the time of the collision occasioning him personal injury.

Formerly, a plaintiff guilty of contributory negligence could not recover any damages, unless the defendant could, with reasonable care, have avoided the consequences of the plaintiff's want of care. However, the law as to contributory negligence has been amended by the Law Reform (Contributory Negligence)

Act, 1945, which makes liability, in such circumstances, apportionable between the plaintiff and the defendant, as for long has been the rule with regard to collisions at sea. Thus, the claim will not be defeated by reason of the fault of the plaintiff, but the damages recoverable will be reduced having regard to the plaintiff's share in the responsibility.

When a person is suddenly put in a position of imminent personal danger by the negligence of another, any imprudent act that he does in " the agony of the moment " is not treated as contributory negligence, provided he shows as much judgment and self-control in attempting to avoid the danger as can reasonably be expected in the circumstances. Thus, a passenger jumping off a runaway bus, reasonably believing that it will crash at the bottom of a hill, and breaking his leg in doing so will not be prejudiced by the mere fact that the driver regains control and the anticipated crash is averted. This is sometimes called the doctrine of alternative danger.

### Liability of Occupiers of Premises to Persons Suffering Injuries Thereon.

The law on this subject has been affected by the Occupiers Liability Act, 1957, the following being a summarized statement of the present law :—

The liability of the occupier of premises to persons who, whilst on such premises, suffer injuries from defects thereon, depends on the character in which such persons come upon his premises.

Before the Occupiers Liability Act, 1957, such persons would be regarded in law as entering either (a) in pursuance of a contract with the occupier, or (b) not in pursuance of contract but as (i) invitees, (ii) licensees or (iii) trespassers and the duty towards them was measured according to the particular character they answered, it being governed by the express or implied terms of the contract under (a) and being of descending scope in the case of (b) (i), (ii) and (iii).

The Occupiers Liability Act, 1957, while not rendering otiose the above characterization creates in effect, although not explicitly, the dichotomy of (a) lawful visitors, (b) unlawful visitors.

To all his lawful visitors the occupier owes the same duty, the " *common duty of care* " except in so far as he is free to and does extend, restrict or exclude that duty to any visitor or visitors by agreement or otherwise. The " common duty of care " is expressed in the Act to be " a duty to take such care as in all the circumstances of the case is reasonable to see that the visitor will be reasonably safe in using the premises for the purpose for which he is invited or permitted by the occupier to be there ".

Since the Act does not (to quote its language) " alter the rules of the common law as to the persons on whom a duty is so imposed or to whom it is owed ", trespassers must, as at Common Law, be treated as "unlawful visitors" within the virtual dichotomy of the Act. The duty to them remains after the Act what it was before ; it was re-examined and re-stated in the case in the House of Lords of *British Railways Board* v. *Herrington* (1972) (as interpreted in the subsequent case in the Privy Council of *Southern Portland Cement Co.* v. *Cooper* (1974)) as involving an occupier in a duty towards potential trespassers, to do what a humane man with the occupier's financial and other limitations would do to prevent injury. The position of the trespasser as uninvited entrant was considered by the Law Commission in Law. Com. 75 published in 1976 to which was appended a draft Bill intended to clarify the law.

To revert to the common duty of care owed to the lawful visitor, the following additional things may be said : (i) The circumstances relevant include the degree of care and of want of care which would ordinarily be looked for in the visitor, so that an occupier must be prepared for children to be less careful than adults and may expect that a person, in the exercise of his calling, will appreciate and guard against any special risk ordinarily incident to it, so far as the occupier leaves him free to do so ; (ii) warning of danger will be judged from the standpoint of whether in all circumstances it was enough to enable the visitor to be reasonably safe ; (iii) the occupier is not liable for the faulty work of his independent contractor where he had taken reasonable steps to satisfy himself that the contractor was competent and had properly done the work.

The Act provides (section 5) that where the visitor enters under contract with the occupier the duty, in so far as it depends on a term to be implied in the contract by reason of its conferring the right to enter, is to be the common duty of care.

Section 4 of the Act (in the amended version contained in the Defective Premises Act, 1972) deals with the duty of care imposed on a landlord in virtue of an obligation or right to repair premises let under a tenancy or premises in respect of which a right of occupation has been given by contract or any enactment.

Subsection (1) of the section reads as follows :—

" Where premises are let under a tenancy which puts on the landlord an obligation to the tenant for the maintenance or repair of the premises, the landlord owes to all persons who might reasonably be expected to be affected by defects in the state of the premises a duty to take such care as is reasonable in all the circumstances to see that they are reasonably safe from personal injury or from damage to their property caused by a relevant defect."

## CHAPTER VII

**Liability for Dangerous Chattels.**

" Anyone who :—
  (i) leaves a dangerous instrument, as a gun, in such a way as to cause danger, or
  (ii) without due warning supplies to others for use an instrument or thing which, to his knowledge from its construction or otherwise, is in such a condition as to cause danger, not necessarily incident to the use of such an instrument or thing, is liable for injury caused to others by reason of his negligent act " : *Heaven* v. *Pender* (1883).

There are the following possibilities :—

(*a*) The possessor of chattels allows or " invites " another to use goods dangerous in themselves, e.g., loaded firearms, explosives, inflammable gases. Here, the duty of the circulator is to take precautions to secure the persons or property of others from injury and damage.

A frequent immediate cause of such damage is the intermeddling of the injured party himself, or some third party. " A loaded gun will not go off unless someone pulls the trigger, and a poison is innocuous until someone takes it." Nevertheless, such interference is no defence, if it is what the circulator might well have expected on the part of a person unaware of the danger, or incapable of appreciating it. To leave a loaded gun with young children is " asking for trouble ". But the position is obviously different if such interference is the deliberate act of the intermeddler, e.g., if a potential murderer avails himself of the opportunity provided by the loaded gun. There is, however, no duty to secure safety if the recipient is well aware of the dangerous character of the article, and the duty is discharged if adequate warning is given.

(*b*) The goods may not be dangerous *per se*, i.e., in themselves, but dangerous in the peculiar circumstances. Of course, if a contractual relation exists between the parties, the extent of liability will depend, primarily, upon the terms, express or implied, of the contract. But, apart from contractual liability, a duty is cast upon a vendor to give due warning where he knows or ought to have known of the dangerous character of the particular goods supplied, and, knows that the person supplied is not aware of it : *Clarke* v. *Army & Navy Co-operative Society* (1903).

(*c*) The Rule in *Donoghue* v. *Stevenson* (1932).

A manufacturer of articles or products which he sends forth in such a form as to show that he intends them to reach the ultimate user or consumer in the form in which they left him with no reasonable possibility, or no reasonable expectation, of intermediate examination, and with the knowledge that the absence of reasonable care in the preparation or putting up of the articles or products will result in injury to the user's or consumer's person or property, owes a duty to the user or consumer to take such reasonable care.

The facts of the case are set out *ante* p. 227.

It will be observed that there was no contractual relation between the parties, the duty to take reasonable care being owed to "all the potential users of his commodities". The duty results from the direct relation created by the manufacturer between himself and the ultimate consumer, the retailer being the mere instrument of transmission of the products to the consumer, these being by their nature precluded from inspection or interference in any way; at least, there was no reasonable expectation that such would take place. It was thought, formerly, that there must be *no* opportunity of intermediate examination, but it is now held that the Rule applies even although such examination was possible, if such could not reasonably have been anticipated.

### Herschtal v. Stewart and Ardern, Ltd. (1940).

The plaintiff bought on hire-purchase terms a car, which had been reconditioned. The day after delivery, whilst the plaintiff was driving, a wheel came off owing to the insufficient tightening of the nuts and the stripping of the threads. The defendants pleaded that the plaintiff had had an opportunity for examination.

*Held* that the defendants would not reasonably have anticipated such examination, and, being guilty of negligence, they were liable.

The Rule is not confined to articles of food and drink. Thus in *Grant* v. *Australian Knitting Mills, Ltd.* (1936), it was applied to a pair of woollen pants in which, owing to the negligence of the manufacturers, irritant acid had been left, causing the plaintiff to contract a skin disease. A learned author, referring to this decision, said : "the Judicial Committee of the Privy Council relegated poisonous pants to the company of dead snails interred in ginger-beer bottles, mischievous hairwashes, motor car wheels made of sawdust, nails in mincepies, and other intrusive elements in manufactured articles".

Of course, the Rule does not apply if the defect is known to the user, or, where the manufacturer has taken reasonable care, as by the provision of a foolproof device for filling bottles.

The term "manufacturers", in connection with the Rule, is used in a general sense, including suppliers and repairers of goods ; hence the decision in *Herschtal* (*supra*).

Retailers may be under liability in contract to buyers from them by virtue of provisions of the Sale of Goods Act, 1893. (See *ante*, p. 155.)

## Liability for Damage Done by Animals.

### (1) Outside the Animals Act, 1971.

A person having the custody or control of an animal may be liable for injury or damage to person or property caused by that animal under one or other of the following heads :

(i) *Nuisance :* Keeping pigs too near a neighbouring house ; *Aldred's Case* (1610) ; *Pitcher* v. *Martin* (1937)—dog on highway held on an excessively long lead became entangled with an old lady's legs causing her to fall (Defendant alternatively liable in negligence).

(ii) *Intentional act :* deliberately setting a dog on a harmless citizen (trespass to the person through assault and battery) ; onlooker on the highway setting his dog to steal a golf ball on adjacent golf course (trespass to goods, per Atkin, L.J., in *Manton* v. *Brocklebank* (1923)) ; slander through an indoctrinated parrot (first and third illustrations given in " Winfield and Jolowicz on Tort " second deduced from " Street on Torts ").

(iii) *Negligence :* This arises from " the ordinary duty of a person to take care that his animal or chattel is not put to such use as is likely to injure his neighbour " (per Lord Atkins in *Fardon* v. *Harcourt-Rivington* (1932). Examples are failing to keep under proper control a dog brought on to the highway : *Pitcher* v. *Martin* (supra) ; *Gomberg* v. *Smith* (1962) ; failing properly to control Alsatian dogs escaping through inadequate dividing hedge and injuring neighbour's young son : *Draper & Another* v. *Hodder* (1972) (C.A.). Cp. *Bativala* v. *West* (1970).

Contrast *Gayler & Pope Ltd.* v. *Davies & Son Ltd.* (1924)—pony attached to a milk van left unattended bolting into shop (owner liable) with *Tillet* v. *Ward* (1882) —ox lawfully on the highway enters shop and causes damage without negligence on the part of the drover (farmer not liable).

### (2) Under the Animals Act, 1971.

The Animals Act, 1971, re-stated and amended the law on civil liability for dangerous animals, cattle trespass and injury to livestock by dogs and created a new liability in negligence in respect of animals straying on to the highway from unfenced land.

For liability for dangerous animals of a kind previously classified as *ferae naturae* (but in section 6(2) of the Act defined as of " a dangerous species " being a species not commonly domesticated in the British Isles and whose fully grown animals normally have such characteristics that they are liable, unless restrained, to cause severe damage . . .) strict liability (that is, regardless of negligence) is continued as heretofore [section 2(1)] but it now attaches to the " keeper " as defined in section 6(3). This definition shows that a person is a keeper of an animal if (*a*) he owns the animal or has it in his possession or (*b*) he is the head of a household of which a member under the age of sixteen owns the animal or has it in his possession.

Liability in respect of animals not of a dangerous species [previously classified as *mansuetae naturae*] continues to be based on *scienter*, but the expression is not used in the Act and the conditions are carefully spelled out in this regard in section 2(2).

These conditions, in essence, postulate knowledge or presumed knowledge of vicious or mischievous propensities. As in the case of animals belonging to a dangerous species, strict liability attaches to the " keeper " as defined in section 6(3).

As the dogs, the law contained in the Dogs Acts, 1906–1928 (now repealed) is re-stated. Section 3 states shortly : " where a dog causes damage by killing or injuring livestock (this includes poultry—see section 11) any person who is a keeper of the dog is liable for the damage, except as otherwise provided by this Act."

The killing of or injury to dogs worrying livestock is dealt with in section 9 which affords in civil proceedings a defence under carefully regulated conditions where such action is necessary for the protection of livestock.

Strict liability for livestock straying on to the land of another and causing damage to that other's land or property is covered by section 4 which makes their owner the person responsible to pay damages or expenses caused. " Livestock " is defined in section 11 as cattle, horses, asses, mules, hinnies, sheep, pigs, goats and poultry and also deer not in the wild state. " Owner " is for the purpose of the section the person in whose possession it is. Damage for this purpose does not appear to include personal injury, so the decision to the opposite effect in *Wormald* v. *Cole* (1954) under the pre-1972 law is no longer valid.

Section 5 contains provisions as to exemptions from the strict liability under sections 2–4 so far discussed. They include the situation where the damage suffered was due wholly to the fault of the person suffering it ; voluntary assumption of risk (except where section 6(5) applies—see *ante*, p. 216) ; special provisions as to trespassing persons.

Section 8 abolished the Rule in *Searle* v. *Wallbank* (1947) so that, as respects damage caused by animals straying on to the highway, it is no longer open to a defendant sued in negligence to plead that he was under no duty to fence or otherwise prevent his animals straying. Exceptions are afforded in the case of straying from common land or town or village greens.

The Act contains detailed provisions for the detention and sale of trespassing livestock (replacing (amongst other things) the old " distress damage feasant " regime). See *ante*, p. 221.

### The Rule in Fletcher v. Rylands.

This case is better known as *Rylands* v. *Fletcher* (1868), because the decision was affirmed in the House of Lords under that name.

The Rule may be stated thus : A person who, for his own purpose, brings and keeps on land in his occupation anything likely to do mischief if it escapes, must keep it in at his peril, and if he fails to do so, he is liable for all damage naturally arising from the escape. This applies whether the things brought on the land are " beasts, water, filth or stenches ".

Thus, the duty is one of strict liability independent of negligence, provided the use to which the land is put is a non-natural one. In the case which gave rise to the Rule, the defendant had constructed a reservoir on his land, employing *competent* workmen. Water escaped from the reservoir, percolated through certain old mine shafts, which had been filled in with marl and earth and eventually flooded the plaintiff's mine. The defendant was held liable in that he had collected water on the land, not naturally there, and it had escaped and done damage.

In *Read* v. *J. Lyons & Co., Ltd.* (1946), where the plaintiff was injured by an explosion in an ordnance factory in respect of which no negligence was averred or proved, the House of Lords held that the strict liability existing in *Rylands* v. *Fletcher* was conditioned by two elements, (1) the condition of " escape " from the land of something likely to do mischief if it escaped, and (2) the condition of " non-natural use " of the land. " Escape ", for the purpose of the Rule, meant escape from a place in the occupation or under the control of the defendant to a place outside his occupation or control. There having been no such " escape " from the defendants' factory, the first condition at any rate was absent, and the defendants were, therefore, not liable.

Their Lordships were not called upon to determine whether the Rule applies to injury to the person as well as to injury to property, but their inclination appeared to be against the view that there can be *Rylands* v. *Fletcher* liability for personal injury, Lord Macmillan being definitely of the opinion that proof of negligence is essential to a claim in respect of personal injuries.

The Rule has been applied in a very wide range of circumstances, e.g. :—

(a) To yew trees, planted by the defendant, which projected over his fence, causing the death of the plaintiff's horse, which ate of the branches ;
(b) To electricity, which escaped and disturbed the regularity of a telegraph company's current ;
(c) To an accumulation of sewage ;
(d) To damage caused in a market garden by creosote fumes escaping during road operations on the highway.
(e) To vibrations from pile-driving causing damage to adjacent buildings.

But there is no liability under the Rule (although there may be in Nuisance) for damage caused by the escape from land of things which are naturally there, e.g., the spread of thistledown from the land of an idle farmer upon his neighbour's land. A person, however, may be liable if he has artificially accumulated such things as rabbits or rats, and they escape and do damage.

Moreover, a man will be liable for directing a natural accumulation of flood water, from his own land to that of his neighbour, thereby causing damage to the latter. But this does not prevent a man from *anticipating* a danger, as by taking active steps to prevent a *threatened* flooding—even if damage is inevitably caused to his neighbour's land by the diversion of the flood water when it accrues.

There are certain possible defences to proceedings under the Rule, viz. :—

(i) That the plaintiff himself caused the escape by his own default.
(ii) That the escape was due to an Act of God. This can rarely be pleaded because of the modern stringent definition of an Act of God for *this* purpose—" Circumstances which no human foresight can provide against, and of which human prudence is not bound to recognise the possibility."
(iii) That the escape was due to the independent wrongful act of a stranger, over whom the defendant had no control, e.g., damage caused by a malicious stranger plugging up the waste-pipe of a lavatory basin and turning on the taps.
(iv) That the source of the damage was an artificial work created for the common benefit of the plaintiff and the defendant, e.g., a water cistern installed at the top of a house for the common benefit of landlord and tenant, from which water escapes, damaging the tenant's furniture.
(v) Statutory authority.

Under the Atomic Energy Act, 1954, and the Radioactive Substances Act, 1960, the Atomic Energy Authority is under an absolute liability in respect of damage from ionizing radiation to persons or property. This liability exists in respect of damage caused by the Authority either on the premises or elsewhere.

## Defamation.

A defamatory statement is one concerning any person which exposes him to hatred, ridicule or contempt, or which causes him to be shunned or avoided, or which has a tendency to injure him in his office, profession or trade. Where such is in a permanent form, it is *libel*. It need not be in writing or print, it may be an effigy, a statue, a caricature or a film picture. The Defamation Act, 1952, provides that the broadcasting of words is libel. Cp. section 4, Theatres Act, 1968, under which publication by performance of a play is (with the exceptions set out in section 7) to be treated as publication in permanent form for the purpose of the law of libel and slander.

Where the statement is in a mere transitory form, e.g., spoken words or gestures, it is *slander*.

It is presumed that a libel entails damage, but special damage must be proved in slander, with certain limited exceptions. Whereas, libel may be both a crime and a civil wrong, slander is only a civil wrong.

Words are not defamatory unless directed at a particular individual. A class of persons cannot be defamed under the civil law. The plaintiff must prove that he was the person marked out by the words, but he need not be the individual to whom the defendant intended to refer. The plaintiff need only prove that reasonably-minded people who knew him connected the defamatory statement with him.

### Hulton v. Jones (1910).

A newspaper article contained words defamatory of " Artemus Jones ", intended by the writer to be a fictitious character in a fancy sketch of life abroad, but there was, unknown to the writer, an actual individual of that name. The Judge directed the jury that, if reasonably-minded persons thought that the words related to the genuine individual, they might find a verdict for the plaintiff. Witnesses testified that they thought the words referred to the plaintiff and the jury found for the plaintiff. The House of Lords held that he was entitled to judgment.

The principle in *Hulton* v. *Jones* was extended to circumstances where the statement related in truth to a real (as opposed to a fictitious) person, A, and was mistakenly, but reasonably, thought to refer to another real person, B.

### Newstead v. London Express Newspaper, Ltd. (1940).

The defendants in one of their newspapers made reference to the fact that " Harold Newstead, thirty-year-old Camberwell man ", had been convicted of bigamy. This was true of a Camberwell barman of that name, but it was untrue of this plaintiff, Harold Newstead, aged about thirty, who assisted his father in a hairdressing business in Camberwell. The defendants were *held* liable to Harold the hairdresser.

Cp. *Morgan* v. *Odhams Press Ltd.* (1971) (H.L.) (where incidentally it was held that (*inter alia*) the fact that a reader does not believe the defamatory allegations against the plaintiff is no defence.

It is not necessary to make express reference to the plaintiff by name. Where one of a class is defamed, but it is not certain which of them, no action will lie. Further, no civil action will lie for defamation of a deceased person. The personal reputation of the plaintiff must be impugned. It is not sufficient that his title to property is disparaged, or that his goods are disparaged.

It is for the Judge to consider whether the words *can* convey a defamatory meaning. If he so decides it is the task of the jury to determine whether they *did* bear such meaning.

If a plaintiff pleads *innuendo*, viz., that words not ordinarily defamatory were defamatory in the peculiar circumstances of his case, he must aver in his statement of claim the peculiar defamatory meaning of the words and show how they came to possess such meaning. Moreover, he must satisfy the jury that facts were known to the person to whom the alleged defamatory statement was communicated, from which a defamatory meaning could reasonably be construed from that statement. An example of innuendo is afforded by the case of *Cassidy* v. *Daily Mirror Newspapers* (1929), where the paper published a photograph of a man and woman and underneath it the caption " Mr. A and Miss B, whose engagement has been announced ". The plaintiff was the lawful wife of Mr. A, and she alleged the innuendo that she was immorally cohabiting with Mr. A. On proof that several of her friends thought that this was in fact the case, the plaintiff was awarded £500 damages, although the defendants acted quite innocently.

> The *innuendo* must be explicitly set forth in the pleadings and sufficiently proved by the plaintiff : *Tolley* v. *Fry* (1931) ; *Allsop* v. *Church of England Newspaper Ltd.* (1972) ; *S and K Holdings Ltd.* v. *Throgmorton Publications Ltd.* (1972).

PUBLICATION. No action for libel or slander will lie unless the alleged defamatory words are published, i.e., communicated to some person other than the person defamed. There need not be direct publication : it suffices that the writer of a libel knows that it is likely to be opened by some person other than the person to whom it is addressed, e.g., his clerk. It is presumed that third parties will read postcards, but not that they will extract letters from an envelope, even although unsealed. If the writer of a letter reveals its contents to some persons other than the addressee, e.g., to the writer's clerks, typists, etc., there is publication, but such may be privileged. Communication of a statement which defames a third person by a husband to his wife is not publication ; but, communication of a statement defaming one spouse made to the other is publication. The jury decide upon the existence or otherwise of the facts relied upon to support a claim of publication, the Judge decides whether such facts do constitute publication.

SPECIAL DAMAGE. The plaintiff in an action for libel need prove only the defamatory nature of the statement and its publication. The plaintiff in an action for slander must go further: he must prove special damage, i.e., that he has suffered some actual temporal loss.

In the following cases, however, slander is actionable *per se*, i.e., without proof of special damage :—

(a) Where the words impute guilt of a criminal offence punishable by imprisonment without the option of a fine. This is not an imputation of *conviction*.

(b) Where the words impute the presence of a contagious disease rendering the person so infected liable to be excluded from society. The imputation must be of a present, not a past, infection.

(c) Where the plaintiff is a woman or girl, and the words impute adultery or unchastity to her (Slander of Women Act, 1891).

(d) Where the words impute unfitness, incompetence or misconduct in an *office of profit*, profession or trade. Under the Defamation Act, 1952, where words are calculated to disparage the plaintiff in any office, profession, calling, trade or business held or carried on by him at the time of publication, it is not necessary to allege or prove special damage, whether or not the words are spoken of the plaintiff in respect of his conduct in that office, profession, calling, trade or business. An imputation of insolvency against a trader would be actionable *per se*.

(e) Where the words impute misconduct in an honorary office such as would justify removal from that office. To say of a city councillor that he was drunk at a council meeting is not actionable *per se*, but to say that he has used his public office to further his private business affairs is so actionable. It is suggested that the words must impute corrupt conduct in office.

REPETITION OF A DEFAMATORY STATEMENT. It is no defence for a man to plead that he did not originate the statement, but merely repeated it. It makes no difference if he believed the statement to be true, unless he repeated it on a privileged occasion. This liability for repetition may have a curious result in the case of a slander not actionable *per se* when first uttered. If the special damage necessary to support an action flows from the repetition and not from the original publication, then the repeater is liable, but not so the originator, i.e., unless the originator authorized the repetition, or unless he uttered the statement in the presence of a person whom he knew to be under a duty to repeat it.

If the person who circulates a defamatory statement takes a merely subordinate part, he will not be held liable, e.g., the porter who delivers libellous handbills, unaware of the contents thereof.

The retailer of a newspaper containing a libel can discharge his *prima facie* liability by proving that he did not know of the libel, that his ignorance was not due to negligence, and that there was no ground for him to suspect the paper as being likely to contain a libel. A circulating library is in a similar position.

The repetition may consist of a failure to act. Thus, if an unauthorized person posts a placard defamatory of A upon B's garage door, B, if he appreciates or should reasonably have appreciated its defamatory character, must remove the placard or be liable as a repeater of the defamatory statement. If the removal of matter constituting a libel will involve great expense, e.g., if it is so engraved on property as to require actual destruction of the property in order to eliminate the offending statement, he would probably escape liability.

DEFENCES TO AN ACTION FOR DEFAMATION.

1. Justification. If the defendant proves the truth of the alleged defamatory statement, he has an absolute defence in tort. He must prove that the alleged defamatory statement is substantially true. But in an action for libel or slander in respect of words containing two or more distinct charges against the plaintiff, the defence of justification is not to fail merely because the truth of every charge is not proved, provided the words not proved to be true do not materially injure the plaintiff's reputation, having regard to the truth of the remaining charges : Defamation Act, 1952. If a defamatory statement is true, the plaintiff cannot have suffered damage to his reputation, or he has been enjoying a reputation which he did not deserve to enjoy. But a man may be " lucky after the event ", i.e., he may discover that his statement was in fact true, although he was unaware of it at the time of utterance. Justification is, however, a somewhat dangerous defence, as failure to establish the defence will almost certainly increase the damages awarded.

It may be mentioned that pursuant to the Rehabilitation of Offenders Act, 1974, the defence of justification is not available to a defendant in respect of the " publication " by him, made with malice, of a " spent conviction " of the plaintiff within the meaning of that Act.

2. Fair Comment on a Matter of Public Interest. The Judge decides whether a matter is of public interest. If he so decides, and considers that there is evidence that the comment was not fair, the jury must *decide* the question of fairness.

It is not fair comment to attack the character of an author under the cloak of a criticism of his book. The term " fair " means honest, relevant and free from malice. The defendant must confine his criticism to actual facts : he cannot plead fair comment when he has invented a foundation on which to build his remarks. Irrelevant comment is not protected ; nor is comment which is really invective : *Harris* v. *Lubbock* (1971).

As to matters of public interest, the field of criticism is confined to :—

 (*a*) Matters of interest to the general community—the conduct of the Government and of persons in public offices and affairs generally.
 (*b*) Matters laid open to the public by the voluntary act of the person concerned, e.g., books, pictures, plays, etc. But the private life of an author or dramatist is not a matter of public interest.

3. **Privilege.** There are two types of privilege, absolute and qualified. In the former case malice is immaterial, in the latter, the presence of malice destroys the immunity conferred by the privilege. Malice means an unjustifiable intention to inflict injury upon the person defamed. Such may be deduced from evidence as to the existence of persistent ill-feeling or the manner of publication.

Examples of absolute privilege are :—

 (*a*) Statements made in Parliament. Cp. *Church of Scientology* v *Johnson-Smith* (1972).
 (*b*) Reports ordered to be published by either House of Parliament.
 (*c*) Judicial proceedings.
 (*d*) Official communications by one officer of State to another.

Examples of qualified privilege are :—

 (*a*) Fair, impartial and contemporary reports of Parliamentary and judicial proceedings and of the proceedings of any public meeting and of the meetings of public bodies and persons specified by section 4, Law of Libel Amendment Act, 1888.
 (*b*) Defamatory statements made in pursuance of a legal, moral or social duty, e.g., to a father or guardian concerning his child or ward, by an assistant master to his headmaster. The duty may be one owed to a man himself in self-defence. Where A has made an attack upon B, he cannot complain if the latter makes a public defence containing statements defamatory of A, provided the defence does not go beyond the necessities of the situation so as to lead a jury to infer malice, which will destroy the privilege. References given to ex-employees are also privileged if given without malice ; likewise illustrations of statements made in performance of a duty are the following : auctioneers cheated by a rogue warning other auctioneers in the district [*Boston* v. *W. S. Bagshaw & Sons* (1966).] ; M.P. referring to Law Society and to Lord Chancellor complaints from one of his constituents about the management of his affairs by his solicitors [*Beach and another* v. *Freeson* (1971)] ; discussions at a meeting of a local authority : [*Horrocks* v. *Lowe* (1972) (C.A.)]
 (*c*) Defamatory statements which the maker and the recipient have a mutual interest in publishing and receiving. Such a community of interest may arise in connection with family affairs, money matters, a particular calling or profession. Statements of this kind must not be more general than is warranted by the community of interest. Professional communications between solicitor and client are an example.

4. **Apology.** This is a statutory defence, restricted to publications in newspapers and similar periodical publications. There must be absence of malice and culpable negligence. The defendant must insert a full apology in the offending newspaper or publication before or at the earliest opportunity after the commencement of the action. There must be payment of a sum of money into Court along with this special plea, and no other defence may be coupled with it. This special plea is different from the tendering of an apology with a view to the mitigation of damages, which is available in all cases of defamation.

Moreover, a person who has published defamatory words may, if he claims that they were published innocently, make an offer of amends, i.e., an offer to publish a suitable correction and a sufficient apology. If the offer is accepted by the aggrieved party and is duly performed, proceedings for libel or slander between the parties are to be barred. If the offer is not accepted by the aggrieved party, it shall be a defence in proceedings by him for libel or slander to prove that the words complained of were published innocently and that the offer was made as soon as practicable and has not been withdrawn : Defamation Act, 1952, section 4. This section is intended to mitigate the hardship resulting from cases containing elements of coincidence like the *Jones* and *Newstead* cases set out above.

Statements are under section 4 (5) of the Act deemed to be " innocent ", if (*a*) the publisher did not intend to publish them of and concerning the plaintiff and did not know of circumstances by which they might be understood to refer to him ; or if (*b*) the words were not defamatory on the face of them, and the publisher did not know of circumstances by virtue of which they might be understood to be defamatory of the plaintiff ; and in either case the publisher exercised all reasonable care in relation to the publication.

INJUNCTIONS AND DEFAMATION. Apart from a claim for damages, an allegedly defamed person may seek an injunction restraining further publication. Such may be an *ordinary* injunction granted at the trial of the action, or an interim injunction pending the trial of the action. The Court is reluctant to grant an interim injunction, because this involves a decision as to libel or no libel before the jury decides whether there is one or not. " It (the jurisdiction) ought only to be exercised . . . where any jury would say that the matter complained of is libellous and, where if the jury did not so find, the Court would set aside the verdict as unreasonable. The Court must also be satisfied that in all probability the alleged libel was untrue, and, if written on a privileged (i.e., qualified) occasion, that there was malice on the part of the defendant. It follows from these rules that the Court can only on the rarest occasions exercise the jurisdiction ": Lord Esher in *Coulson* v. *Coulson* (1887). The applicant for an injunction must act promptly, prove an intended continuance of the offending publication and that such intended continued publication will entail immediate and irreparable injury.

**Fraud.**

So far as concerns its effect upon contracts, fraud has been discussed in Chapter IV. The present Section is concerned with the tort of fraud, or deceit, as it is sometimes called.

Fraud (or deceit) is a false representation of fact, made with a knowledge of its falsity or without belief in its truth, or in reckless disregard whether it be true or false, with the intention that it should be acted upon by another. To be actionable at the suit of that other, the following conditions must be satisfied :—

(a) The statement must be an untrue statement of *fact*. Thus, a statement of mere opinion cannot be fraud unless it can be proved that the opinion was not held. A suppression of the truth may amount to a suggestion of falsehood, e.g., if the owner of a house conceals a defect in one of the walls in order to effect a sale. However, if there is no duty to disclose, mere non-disclosure is not fraud.

(b) The maker of the representation must know it to be untrue, or be without belief in its truth or be recklessly indifferent whether it be true or not.

If the maker of the statement believed it to be true, then, even if he had no reasonable ground for such belief, he would not be liable, for negligence does not amount to fraud. (Persons who issue company prospectuses are under a special liability : they are liable for mere carelessness in making statements if such results in damage to subscribers.) Although this is the doctrine the Court's knowledge of human nature serves to modify its operation. The Court will not support a plea of ignorance where there were grounds which should have made the most stupid man aware of the falsity of his statement. A man culpably ignorant of the untruth of his statement is just as liable as if he knew that it was untrue.

(c) The statement must be made with the intent that the plaintiff should act upon it. It need not be made directly to the plaintiff, provided that it is intended that he shall act upon it. In *Langridge* v. *Levy* (1837), a gunmaker sold a gun to X for the use of X and his sons, and fraudulently represented it to be sound. The gun burst while Y, one of X's sons, was using it and he was thereby injured. The

Court held that Y could bring an action of fraud against the gunmaker because the statement as to the soundness of the gun, though made to X, was intended to be communicated to, and to be acted upon by, Y. The fact that the untrue statement was made without any corrupt motive of gain to the maker or injury to the plaintiff is immaterial, provided that it was made with a knowledge of its falsity, and that the plaintiff has suffered damage. But the defendant is not liable to *all* persons who act upon his statement. He is only liable to such persons as were intended to act upon his statement or who can be reasonably construed to have been in his mind at the time of making such statement. Thus, in the case of *Peek* v. *Gurney* (1873), directors were held liable to original allottees of shares, taking their shares from the company, for false statements contained in a prospectus, but not liable to purchasers of shares on the open market.

(*d*) The plaintiff must have been deceived. Deceit which does not deceive is not fraud. If the plaintiff ignored the misrepresentation, relying upon his own judgment, he cannot succeed in an action based on fraud. But it does not matter that he need not have been deceived if he had made full use of his opportunities of independent investigation.

(*e*) The plaintiff must have suffered damage by his reliance upon the misrepresentation, and such damage must be the natural and probable consequence of acting upon the defendant's statement.

If the misrepresentation is as to the conduct or credit of another and made with intent to procure for him credit, money or goods, it must be in writing, and signed personally by the maker thereof, before an action will lie : Lord Tenterden's Act [Statute of Frauds (Amendment) Act, 1828].

## Malicious Prosecution.

In an action for malicious prosecution the plaintiff must prove :—

(1) That the defendant *instituted* criminal (or bankruptcy) proceedings against him ;
(2) That such proceedings terminated in his, the plaintiff's favour ;
(3) That the proceedings were instituted without reasonable and probable cause ;
(4) Malice, i.e., that the defendant's motive in instituting proceedings was an improper motive and not the furtherance of justice ;

(5) That the plaintiff suffered damage by reason of those proceedings.

In *Abrath* v. *N.E. Railway Co.* (1886), Bowen, L.J., said : " The plaintiff has to prove, first, that he was innocent, and that his innocence was pronounced by the tribunal before which the accusation was made ; secondly, that there was a want of reasonable and probable cause for the prosecution or, as it may otherwise be stated, that the circumstances of the case were such as to be in the eyes of the Judge, inconsistent with the existence of reasonable and probable cause, and lastly, that the proceedings of which he complains, were initiated in a malicious spirit, that is, from an incorrect and improper motive and not in furtherance of justice." It is no defence for the defendant to show that he instituted proceedings under an order of Court if the Court was moved by his evidence—not necessarily at his request—to give the order, and if the proceedings in the prosecution involved the repetition of the same falsehood.

An action will lie against a corporation, if the wrongful proceedings were instituted by a servant of the corporation acting in the course of his employment and in what he supposed to be the interests of the corporation.

The bringing of an ordinary civil action, however malicious and destitute of reasonable and probable cause, will not support an action for malicious prosecution.

DISTINCTION BETWEEN MALICIOUS PROSECUTION AND FALSE IMPRISONMENT.

In brief, the test may be said to be : Did the defendant set a ministerial or a judicial officer in motion? In the latter case, the defendant exposes himself to an action for malicious prosecution, in the former case to an action for false imprisonment.

" Imprisonment is *prima facie* a tort, prosecution is not so in itself." Thus arises the striking distinction that, whereas in the former case the onus of proving reasonable and probable cause is upon the defendant, in the latter case the burden of proof is, in the first place, upon the plaintiff to show that the defendant had no reasonable and probable cause for his conduct.

### Interference with Contractual Relations.

1. It is a tort knowingly, *and without lawful justification*, to induce a person to commit a breach of contract with the result that the other party to the contract suffers damage.

Originally, the tort was confined to unjustifiable inducements to procure a menial servant to break his contract of service with his employer, but the tort has been extended to cover all contracts. Thus, where a famous singer contracted to sing in an opera under one manager, it was held to be a tort when a rival manager induced her to break her contract in consideration of a promise of higher remuneration : *Lumley* v. *Gye* (1853). Yet, it is possible to plead " justification " as a defence to an action of this type. Circumstances amounting to justification have not as yet, however, been clearly defined. It is suggested with confidence that a father might set up this defence, if he induced his daughter to break her promise of marriage, always assuming that he acted in what he supposed to be the interests of his daughter.

Again, a doctor may well be absolved from liability if he has advised his patient to break his contract of employment on the ground that continuance therein would be fraught with grave consequences to the health of his patient.

2. It is not a tort for *one* person to induce another not to enter into a contract with another, or to terminate an existing contract in a lawful manner, provided that no unlawful form of persuasion, e.g., threats of violence, is employed.

3. Neither is it *prima facie* actionable for a combination of persons to induce another not to enter into a contract or to terminate his contract in a lawful manner, provided no unlawful means of persuasion are employed.

The combination will, however, be liable in tort if its *predominant* motive is " malice ", i.e., spite, an intent to injure its rivals. If, however, its predominant motive is not such, if it is merely to further its legitimate interest—not necessarily trade interests—there is no tort, even though others may suffer incalculable damage in consequence.

Apparently, the basis of liability, malice in this sense having been established, is the fact of combination ; there is a conspiracy. Many may do harm where one cannot. Accordingly, it would appear that an *individual* who, without resorting to unlawful means, induces another not to enter into a contract, or induces him to terminate a contract in a lawful manner, is immune from liability, however " malicious " he may be.

Under section 13 (1) of the Trade Union and Labour Relations Act, 1974 (as amended by the Trade Union and Labour Relations (Amendment) Act, 1976) an act done by a person in contemplation or furtherance of a trade dispute is not actionable in tort on the ground only that it (*a*) induces another person to break a contract or induces any other person to interfere with its performance or (*b*) consists in his threatening that a contract (whether one to which he is a party or not) will be broken or its performance interfered with, or that he will induce another person to break a contract or to interfere with its performance or (under section 13 (2)) that it interferes with another's trade, business or employment or with another's right to dispose of his capital or labour as he wishes. An agreement or combination between two or more persons to do any act in contemplation or furtherance of a trade dispute is not actionable in tort if the act is one which if done without such agreement would not be actionable.

### Slander of Title.

This is the making of a false statement injurious to the material interests of another, such as the unwarranted disparagement of the quality of the goods manufactured by him. It is to be distinguished from defamation, in that in the latter tort, the personal reputation of the plaintiff is at stake, whereas, in the former, his material interests are injured by the making of false or unwarranted statements to third persons.

### Remoteness of Damage.

Formerly, only such damages were recoverable as were considered to have been the " natural and probable consequences " of the wrongful act. The question was : Would an ordinary reasonable man, situated in similar circumstances, have expected that to happen which did happen? If not, the damage was too " remote ".

However, in the case of negligence (and the rule has been extended to other torts) once negligence has been established, then the defendant is liable for all the *direct* consequences thereof, even though they could not have been foreseen by an ordinary reasonable man situated in similar circumstances.

#### Re Polemis and Furness Withy & Co. (1921).

Stevedores were unloading the hold of a vessel which contained cases of petrol. By leakage the hold was filled with highly inflammable vapour. One stevedore negligently knocked a plank into the hold, where in its fall it struck a spark, setting the vapour alight. This caused a fire which destroyed the ship.

*Held* that negligence having been established, the employers of the workman were liable for the destruction of the ship, this being the direct consequence of the negligent act, although that consequence could not have been reasonably foreseen or anticipated.

Pending a definitive ruling by the House of Lords, the continuing validity of the Rule in *Re Polemis* is doubtful, particularly in the light of the repudiation of the Rule by the Judicial Committee of the Privy Council in *Overseas Tankship (U.K.) Ltd.* v. *Morts Dock and Engineering Co. Ltd.* (1961). In that case (generally referred to by commentators as *The Wagon Mound*) the defendants' servants negligently allowed furnace oil to flow on to the waters of a bay in which the plaintiffs had their wharf. The oil caught fire and the structure was badly damaged. It was held that because the defendants did not know and could not reasonably be expected to have known that the furnace oil was capable of being set alight when spread on water, they were not liable for the damage occasioned. A defendant should be liable only for damage which a reasonable man would foresee might follow from the negligent act. It must be remembered, however, that a decision of the Judicial Committee has but persuasive authority (see *ante* p. 11 and *post* p. 287 and indeed it has in fact been followed in a number of subsequent cases at various judicial levels, such as *Hughes* v. *Lord Advocate* (1963) (a Scottish appeal to the House of Lords) and treated as establishing the principle that the damage sustained must be of the same kind as the foreseeable damage. Thus in :—

**Bradford v. Robinson Rentals (1967).**
Plaintiff recovered damages for breach of the duty to adopt a safe system of work in the following circumstances. He was a television engineer of some fifty-seven years (normally working indoors) who was sent by the defendants his employers on a five-hundred-mile journey in an unheated van which had a defect necessitating frequent halts for " topping up " the radiator. The weather was bitterly cold and he suffered frostbite causing him permanent physical injury. Rees, J., found that the defendants had failed to take steps to protect the plaintiff their employee against the reasonably foreseeable hazards (of which frostbite was one of the kinds just as much as pneumonia) of weather conditions and were, therefore, liable for negligence.

In the meantime it has been held that the rule in personal injury cases that a defendant must take his victim (the plaintiff) as he finds him still holds good ; thus he cannot escape liability because of circumstances peculiar to the person injured, e.g., that he is a haemophilic subject or has an unusually thin skull.

Difficulty arises when the act of a stranger intervenes between the wrongful act and the damage suffered by the plaintiff—*novus actus interveniens* (" a new act intervening "). What degree of interference will constitute such a break in the chain of consequences as to exempt the damage suffered from being the direct consequence of the original wrongful act? The test is : Was the intervention such as was likely to happen in the circumstances? If so, the defendant will still be liable. Thus, A throws a lighted squib into a market, and it falls upon B's stall. B hastily throws it away, it falls upon C's stall, and C throws it away. Ultimately it explodes, putting out D's eye. Here there is no vital break in the chain of circumstances, and A is liable to D : *The Squib Case, Scott* v. *Shepherd* (1773).

If, however, the intervention is such as could not reasonably have been anticipated, the original wrongdoer will not be liable for the ultimate consequences.

### Weld-Blundell v. Stephens (1920).

The plaintiff wrote a letter to a chartered accountant containing statements defamatory to two officials of a company. The accountant's partner negligently left it at the company's office, where the manager read it. Having taken a copy of it, the manager showed it to the two officials, who successfully sued the writer for damages for libel.

*Held* that the damages and costs, which the writer was compelled to pay, were too remote to be recovered by him from the chartered accountant.

NERVOUS SHOCK. At one time it was held that illness resulting from nervous shock was not a ground of liability, but this view has been exploded. A definite illness produced by nervous shock as the result of another's wrongful act is as truly damage as a broken leg. Moreover, provided a definite illness results from the nervous shock, it is immaterial that the fear induced by another's conduct was fear of injury to *others* and not to *oneself*.

### Hambrook v. Stokes Brothers (1925).

A mother saw her children go round a bend in a narrow, steep road. Then she saw a lorry rushing round the bend towards her. Fearing for her children's safety, she was taken ill and died from shock.

*Held* that, if the shock was due to what she had seen herself, then her representatives had good ground for an action. If, however, the shock was induced by what she had been told by bystanders, then there was no right of action.

Thus, a person, Y, on the footpath, who sees a fatal accident in the street arise from the negligence of X, and who suffers shock and consequent illness, will have a right of action against X, even though the victim of the accident is unknown to Y, provided that Y *saw*, and was not " told of ", the accident.

## Effect of Death.

The maxim formerly was, *Actio personalis moritur cum persona* (" A personal action dies with the person "). That is to say, if an injury was done either to the person or the property of another for which damages were the only remedy, the action died with the person to whom, or by whom, the wrong was done.

This principle was modified considerably by the Law Reform (Miscellaneous Provisions) Act, 1934, whereby in most cases the right to sue and the liability to be sued for torts does not cease on the death of either party. But this does not apply to a cause of action for defamation.

But even though a cause of action has survived against the estate of a deceased person, no proceedings are maintainable unless either :—

(a) Proceedings were pending against him in respect of such cause of action at the date of his death ; or
(b) Proceedings are taken in respect thereof not later than six months after his personal representative took out representation.

Quite apart from the 1934 Act (which was concerned with the survival of rights of action vested in a deceased or maintainable against his estate) it has been possible since the passing of " Lord Campbell's Act "—the Fatal Accidents Act, 1846—for an action to be brought for the benefit of certain dependent relatives of a person killed by the tortious act of another where the dependants can show they suffer economic loss by reason of the death. The Act of 1846 has been amended and since the passing of the Fatal Accidents Act, 1959, the class of persons for whose benefit an action may be brought has become enlarged to include not only the wife, husband, parent, grandparent, child (whether adopted or illegitimate) of the deceased but also a stepchild, grandchild, nephew or niece. The relatives themselves may sue if there is no personal representative or if no action is brought by him within six months of the death. Although the Fatal Accidents Acts give rise to a new cause of action, that cause rests upon the condition that the person killed would, had he survived, have had a cause of action against the wrongdoer, e.g., for negligence. The damages recoverable are such as may compensate the relatives for the pecuniary loss to them resulting from the death of the deceased as " bread-winner ". The amount awarded is apportioned by the Court among the relatives shown to be " dependants ".

[N.B. The dependancy of a widow is no longer to be affected in the assessment of damages by her remarriage or prospects of remarriage : Law Reform (Miscellaneous Provisions) Act, 1971, section 4 (i). Her remarriage prospects will still affect awards to her children : *Thompson* v. *Price* (1973).]

Whereas damages recovered against a tortfeasor under the 1934 Act will be held by the personal representatives of the person who, but for his death, could have sued, as part of the deceased's estate to be administered like the rest of the deceased's property and so to be applied in the payment of his debts and then distributed amongst those beneficially entitled under his will or intestacy, damages recovered under the Fatal Accident Acts are *ex hypothesi* to be held not for the benefit of the estate but for the dependants shown to be entitled. Where claims are made both under the 1934 Act and under the Fatal Accidents Acts the Court may have to make adjustments to preclude a dependant from taking a double benefit.

The governing legislation is now the Fatal Accidents Act, 1976 (a consolidating Act).

### Effect of Bankruptcy.

Where the person injured by a tort subsequently becomes bankrupt, the cause of action is not affected. The plaintiff's Trustee in bankruptcy cannot, however, claim the damages recovered by the bankrupt, unless he can show that the wrong caused some loss to the bankrupt's estate. Thus, damages for personal injury or for defamation may be retained by the bankrupt.

If a person who is guilty of a tort is adjudicated bankrupt, the right of action is not affected, but the liability for damages does not pass as against the Trustee in bankruptcy of the wrongdoer. It follows that a discharge from bankruptcy will not affect the liability, which remains enforceable against the wrongdoer.

### Limitations of Actions.

Generally speaking, actions on torts must be brought within six years of the cause of action arising. If, at the time when the cause of action arises, the plaintiff is a minor or of unsound mind, time does not commence to run against the plaintiff until his disability ceases. When the time has once begun to run, however, subsequent disabilities do not affect the operation of the statute. In one or two cases special periods of limitation have been prescribed. Thus, an action under the Fatal Accidents Act, 1976, must be brought within three years of the death of the injured party, and, in the case of an action for damages for negligence or nuisance where personal injuries are involved, the period of limitation is three years : Law Reform (Limitation of Actions, Etc.) Act, 1954. The period may in exceptional cases be extended by leave of the Court pursuant to the Limitation Act, 1975, e.g., where the Court is satisfied as to certain specified matters, such as that the material facts relating to the cause of action were outside the knowledge of the claimant plaintiff at a time when he could otherwise have brought his action and he has taken or sought to take proceedings within one year of acquiring such knowledge. See *ante* p. 93.

### Remedies.

Remedies in tort are :—

    A. *Judicial.* The judicial remedies are :—

        (1) Damages. The general principle is that a successful plaintiff is to be awarded fair and adequate compensation for the injury suffered by him to his person or property.

            Damages are *nominal* where a right of the plaintiff has been infringed but he can prove no actual loss (*injuria sine damno*) ; they may be *contemptuous* when the Court considers the claim proved but unmeritorious and so awards only a trifling sum ; they are *substantial* (and so compensatory) where there is both *injuria* and *damnum* and they may be inflated or "aggravated" by reason of the motives or conduct of the defendant ; they are *exemplary* (or punitive) when awarded to show the disapproval of the Court of the defendant's conduct or to operate as a deterrent to others against committing a similar tort—when they are additional to *compensatory* damages.

In *Rookes* v. *Barnard* (1964) the House of Lords considered that exemplary damages would be appropriate in three cases :—

(a) In cases of oppressive, arbitrary, or unconstitutional acts by government servants ;
(b) In cases where the defendant's conduct has been calculated by him to make a profit for himself which might well exceed the compensatory damages paid to the plaintiff ;
(c) In cases expressly authorised by statute.

The principles and categories enunciated by Lord Devlin in *Rookes* v. *Barnard* (*supra*) were re-affirmed and slightly extended by a majority in the House of Lords in the libel case [case (b) above—published work] of *Broome* v. *Cassell & Co. sub. nom. Cassell & Co.* v. *Broome* (1972).

(2) Injunction. See *ante*, pp. 4, 36 and 243.

In *Warder* v. *Cooper* (1970) Stamp, J., granted an injunction to a licensee (i.e., a person permitted to occupy premises—see *ante*, p. 182—deemed to be a tenant for the purpose of section 32 of the Rent Act, 1965) asserting harassment under that section and so claiming in tort for a breach of statutory duty lying on the landlord. If an injunction was refused leaving the licensee to a remedy in damages for the tort, the Court would be allowing just the mischief which the section was designed to prevent.

B. *Extra-judicial*. Developed law favours judicial remedies and so recourse to the Courts, but allows in the nature of things, a certain measure of "self-help" of which the following are instances :—
(1) Use of force in self-defence where necessary and proportionate to the dilemma ;
(2) Forcible re-taking of chattels if the force used is reasonable ;
(3) Abatement of nuisance (see *ante*, p, 226).

# CHAPTER VIII

## ELEMENTS OF CRIME

**Nature of Crime.**

It is not possible to give a logical and scientific definition of crime so as to distinguish a crime from other wrongs. As regards a breach of contract the distinction is clear : a breach of contract is a breach of an obligation incurred voluntarily, whereas a crime is an act forbidden, or an omission to perform an act commanded, by the general law. But this does not distinguish a crime from a tort. A man does not agree not to trespass on his neighbour's lands or defame his character ; yet if he does so trespass, if he does so defame, the injured party has his remedy in damages. It is sometimes said that a crime is an injury to the community as a whole. But every illegal act has this consequence nor can any absolute distinction be based on the gravity of the consequences to the community. A breach of trust, the mismanagement of the affairs of a company, neither of which need involve the commission of a crime, may be fraught with incomparably more serious harm to the community than the stealing of a packet of cigarettes.

Moreover, the same act may be at once a crime, a breach of contract and a tort. Thus, if A lends a book to B, and the latter decides to retain it permanently, he commits the crime of theft, a breach of contract and the tort of conversion. Apart from committing a theft, he is also guilty of a breach of the term implied in all contracts of bailment that the property bailed shall be returned to the bailor as soon as the purposes for which it is bailed have been fulfilled. In addition, by depriving A of his property in the book, B can be sued for conversion.

However, a line of distinction may be drawn from a consideration of the respective legal consequences of various wrongs. Criminal law is that part of the law which deals with acts that may be the subject of criminal proceedings ; whether a wrong is a crime or a civil injury is determined by the remedy available, for a crime is *punished*, whereas *compensation* is the remedy appropriate for a tort or civil injury. Accordingly, Courts of criminal or civil jurisdiction become seized of the matter according to the remedy sought ; there being, thus, either a *prosecution* in a criminal court or a *civil action* in a court of civil jurisdiction, as the case may be. Thus, although no true definition is attempted, one may say that a crime is a wrongful act, viewed not from the standpoint of the individual sufferer, but from that of the whole community, for which the wrongdoer is *punished* by the State. In *Board of Trade* v. *Owen* (1957) the House of Lords adopted as a correct definition of a crime, that appearing in Halsbury's Laws of England, namely, " A crime is an unlawful act or default which is an offence against the public and renders the person guilty of the act liable to legal punishment." On the other hand, a civil injury involves primarily a violation of the civil rights of the individual, for which the wrongdoer has to provide *compensation* in damages or otherwise.

There is one clear line of demarcation. A person injured by the tort of another may, if he so chooses, condone such wrongful act, but in the case of a crime only the Crown can remit the punishment, and even the Crown may not pardon a public nuisance whilst it remains unabated, or the offence of sending a person to prison outside the realm to avoid the operation of the Habeas Corpus Acts. Bearing these matters in mind, Professor Kenny concluded that, " Crimes are wrongs whose sanction is punitive, and is remissible by the Crown, *if at all* ".

In the past the main pre-occupation of the Criminal Law was the protection of persons and property, but with the development of a complicated society in a machine or industrial age, attention has had to be given to wider fields and this has, of course, been done through the statute-book. Thus the increased use of the motor vehicle has led to legislation of a penal nature concerning the use of such vehicles on the highway and scientific development of such things as drugs has led to legislation (previously consolidated in the Dangerous Drugs Act, 1965, and now more carefully worded in the Misuse of Drugs Act, 1971) regulating the manufacture of these substances and more importantly the unauthorized possession or misuse thereof in a social background of permissiveness. Protection of consumers is to some extent secured by the Trade Descriptions Act, 1968 (as amended). On the other hand suicide has ceased to be a crime and abortion may now be carried out under what some regard as an inadequate system of control; these and other changes in the law reflect current *mores*.

The Children and Young Persons Act, 1969, set out to give effect to currently held theories about the liability and treatment of these young people.

The Criminal Justice Act, 1972, strengthened the powers of the Court to impose compensation orders on convicted persons ; to make criminal bankruptcy orders in certain cases as well as to make community service orders on persons who had attained the age of seventeen and had been convicted of offences punishable with imprisonment ; and made numerous miscellaneous provisions connected with the administration of criminal justice. The bulk of the Act has (along with numerous other statutory provisions) now been consolidated in the Powers of Criminal Courts Act, 1973.

In practice, a Court of criminal jurisdiction makes a compensation order only in the simplest of cases, e.g., in an uncomplicated case under the Theft Act, 1968 (see below), or following a conviction for an offence under the Trade Descriptions Acts, 1968–1972. The power of the Court to order compensation does not militate against the analysis of the essential difference between a tort and a crime attempted at the beginning of this Chapter. Nor does the existence of the Criminal Injuries Board set up in 1964 to operate a Scheme allowing for the award of compensation to victims of crimes of violence.

## Classification

According to the mode of trial, crimes are (*a*) indictable—all crimes are such unless by statute they are made triable summarily, (*b*) non-indictable, i.e., offences triable summarily. But this classification is not rigid. Many indictable offences may, in certain circumstances, be tried summarily, certain summary offences may, if the accused wishes, be tried upon indictment, and some offences may be tried either on indictment or summarily.

The historical classification of crimes was under the heads of (*a*) *Treasons*, (*b*) *Felonies* and (*c*) *Misdemeanours*. Treasons were in fact felonies, but, being the rarest and most heinous, they were classified separately. A felony, in the original sense, was a crime conviction of which, prior to the Forfeiture Act, 1870, entailed automatic forfeiture of goods and lands, but since the abolition of this penalty, certain crimes were declared felonies by statute. Misdemeanours were all crimes which were not treasons or felonies. Although originally there was a clear distinction between a felony and a misdemeanour based on their relative heinousness, this ceased necessarily to be so in later development. Indeed, certain misdemeanours were punishable more severely than certain felonies. Thus, the maximum penalty for simple larceny, a felony, was five years' imprisonment, whereas, perjury, a misdemeanour, was punishable by seven years' imprisonment.

Various consequences flowed from the distinctions between a felony and a misdemeanour. The *bare concealment* of a treason or felony was the misdemeanour of misprision ; there was no corresponding offence in connection with a misdemeanour. Other differences lay with the power to arrest without warrant, degrees of complicity (as principals or accessories whether before or after the fact) and procedural rules.

The Criminal Law Act, 1967, adopted the major recommendations of the Criminal Law Revision Committee—see *ante*, p. 25.

Under the Act " all distinctions between felony and misdemeanour are hereby abolished " and " on all matters on which a distinction has previously been made between felony and misdemeanour, including mode of trial, the law and practice in relation to all offences cognisable under the law of England and Wales . . . shall be the law and practice applicable at the commencement of this Act in relation to misdemeanours ".

The Act regulates the powers of arrest without warrant in respect of an " arrestable offence " (defined in the Act as one for which the sentence is fixed by law or for which a person is liable by statute to imprisonment for at least five years and to attempts to commit any such offence).

Other provisions of the Act are dealt with in their due places in this Chapter.

## Constituent Elements of a Criminal Offence.

As a general rule, the commission of a crime necessarily involves two elements—the performance of a *guilty* act and the existence of a *guilty mind*. Thus the cardinal maxim is *Actus non facit reum nisi mens sit rea*, i.e., an act does not make a person guilty unless the mind is guilty. The mental attitude which, at Common Law, is an essential constituent element of every criminal offence is often summarized by the expression *mens rea*, but this phrase does not denote any single mental condition, for the mental element may assume various forms varying from a specific intention to commit an illegal act to mere negligence in the case of certain crimes. The requirement of the presence of some degree of *mens rea* applies almost universally. But there are certain statutory exceptions, e.g., selling adulterated food without knowing it to be such, selling intoxicating liquor to a drunken person without knowledge of his condition. But in all such exceptions there is the justification that in the peculiar circumstances there would be extreme difficulty in proving any specific state of mind.

There is another maxim to which there is no exception : **A bare intent, however criminal, is not punishable unless followed by a criminal act.** The law cannot take cognizance of a mere intent, unless and until it is translated into action. Thus, an act is necessary even in the case of the treason of compassing or imagining the death of the Queen because the guilty mind must be *manifested* by an overt act, i.e., an act capable of being observed by someone else. The crime of conspiracy may appear to be an exception in that the crime is complete, even although no act is done in pursuance of the conspiracy. But there can be no conspiracy without an agreement, and such connotes communication, which obviously involves an act.

Although the accused must intend to do the act which is part of the crime, it does not matter that he did not intend to commit the particular crime which in fact resulted from his conduct. He is presumed to intend the natural and probable consequences thereof.

In cases where a particular attitude of mind alone constitutes the *mens rea*, the onus is on the prosecution to prove that the accused had that particular attitude of mind. Thus, killing is murder only if done with the particular mental attitude known as " malice aforethought ", and, therefore, the onus is on the prosecution to prove, not merely that the deceased was killed by the accused, but intention on the part of the accused to kill or to do grievous bodily harm. In other words the prosecution must prove (1) causation of death, and (2) malice aforethought.

## Qualifications as to Liability.

(*a*) COERCION.

By this term is meant compulsion by the threats of other people. Where actual physical force is used in the sense that A presses B's finger on the trigger of a gun, which is thereby fired, the act is, obviously, that of A, not B. Coercion may be :—

(i) *Public*.—This is a defence only to acts committed under the physical compulsion of rebels, under threat of immediate death or grievous bodily harm. The coerced person must avail himself of the first opportunity of escape, otherwise he will lose the benefit of this defence.
(ii) *Private*.—This is rarely a good defence even when it takes the form of threats of the immediate infliction of death or grievous bodily harm. In *R*. v. *Singh* (1973) Lawton, L.J., rejected the view that a man who commits a crime at the request of a blackmailer whom he fears can plead duress, and said : " Duress arises from threats of violence, not exposure." Conjugal subjection has always been a good defence to a wife committing offences, other than treason or murder, in the presence of her husband. Indeed the Common Law presumed coercion in such circumstances, but the Criminal Justice Act, 1925, abolished the presumption, whilst preserving the defence ; i.e., if the wife can prove actual compulsion by her husband she will be free from liability.

(*b*) MISTAKE.

A mistake *as to the law* is never an excuse for a wrongful act.

A mistake of *fact* will be a defence if :—(i) It is reasonable ; (ii) It is as to the existence of facts which, if true, would make the act guiltless.

In addition, the statutory definition of a crime may provide that it is a valid defence to prove that the accused acted under a mistaken claim of right made in good faith, e.g., the definition of larceny in the Larceny Act, 1916.

Mistake as to the *consequences* of an unlawful act provides no defence.

(c) AGE.

For the purpose of determining criminal liability youngsters are divided into two classes :—
  (i) There is an irrebuttable presumption of law that a youngster under the age of ten is incapable of crime.
  (ii) Between the ages of ten and fourteen a youngster is presumed to be incapable of guilty intent, but this presumption may be rebutted by proving " precocity ", i.e., that a particular youngster was " old beyond his years ". Young people of fourteen years and upwards are fully liable, but there are several peculiarities as to procedure and punishment. Thus, a young person, under the age of eighteen, at the time of the commission of the offence cannot be sentenced to death for murder.

[When the Children and Young Persons Act, 1969, is in full force—it is to be brought into force by stages—no criminal proceedings other than for homicide will be competent against persons under 14 years and special provisions will apply to young persons over that age.

The powers of the Courts in respect of young offenders are regulated by statute, including (apart from the 1969 Act just mentioned) the Criminal Justice Act, 1948, the Homicide Act, 1957, the Criminal Justice Act, 1961, the Children and Young Persons Act, 1963, the Criminal Justice Act, 1967, and the Criminal Justice Act, 1972. As to the latter Act, see Powers of Criminal Courts Act, 1973 (see above p. 256).]

(d) INSANITY AND DIMINISHED RESPONSIBILITY.

The extent to which insanity will provide a defence is still governed by the principles laid down in *M'Naghten's Case* (1843). Thus :—
  (i) Everybody is presumed sane until the contrary is proved. This means that the burden of proof of insanity rests upon the accused.
  (ii) For the defence of insanity to succeed the accused must be proved to have been suffering at the time of the commission of the crime charged, under such a defect of reason from disease of the mind that he did not know the nature or quality of his act, or, if he did know it, that he did not know that it was wrong to do it. " Wrong " means " contrary to law " : *R.* v. *Windle* (1952).

In *R.* v. *Clarke* (1972) the Court of Appeal stressed that the M'Naghten rules do not apply to those who retain the power of reasoning, but who in moments of confusion or absentmindedness fail to use their powers to the full (shoplifting).

Formerly, if the defence was successful, the verdict was the illogical one of " Guilty but insane ". This amounted to an acquittal and the accused could not appeal against such verdict. However, by virtue of the Criminal Procedure (Insanity) Act, 1964, the special verdict in cases of insanity is now to be " Not guilty by reason of insanity "—an acquittal in form as well as in substance. From this there may be an appeal.

> The powers of the Courts in relation to persons suffering from mental disorder who are concerned in criminal proceedings are regulated by Part V of the Mental Health Act, 1959 (as amplified by the Criminal Procedure (Insanity) Act, 1964).

DIMINISHED RESPONSIBILITY. The Homicide Act, 1957, introduced the new defence of *diminished responsibility* which applies where a person kills or is a party to the killing of another, yet was suffering from such abnormality of mind at the time as to substantially impair his mental responsibility in doing or being a party to the killing. As to this defence the following points should be noted :—

(i) If pleaded successfully the defence of *diminished responsibility* results in the accused being convicted of manslaughter and not of murder, thereby giving the judge a very wide choice of punishment (including detention or submission to treatment under the Mental Health Act, 1959). In contrast, if the defence of insanity is pleaded successfully the court orders the accused to be detained in a hospital until ordered by the Home Secretary to be discharged.

(ii) The defence of *diminished responsibility* applies only to the crime of murder, and, unlike insanity, it is not a general defence.

(iii) The abnormality of mind required to bring the defence of *diminished responsibility* into operation must (in the words of the Act) arise from " some arrested or retarded development of mind or any inherent causes " or have been " induced by disease or injury ". This requirement excludes from the ambit of the defence persons who commit murder as a result of sudden outbursts of passion or rage, but who are not otherwise mentally abnormal. It is for the jury to say whether upon the evidence they are satisfied or not that the case comes within this sub-section.

(iv) As with the defence of insanity, the burden of proving *diminished responsibility* rests upon the accused and need only be established on a balance of reasonable probabilities and not beyond all reasonable doubt : *R.* v. *Dunbar* (1957).

(*e*) INTOXICATION.

Intoxication is not of itself a defence to a criminal charge, but where a specific intent is an essential element of the offence charged, evidence of drunkenness may be admitted to rebut the presumption that the accused intended the natural consequences of his acts. In other words, the drunkenness may be indicative of the state of the accused's mind, and *may* support the inference that he could not have formed the specific intent which is an essential element of the offence charged. If the drunkenness be involuntary, *e.g.*, contrived by the prisoner's enemies, or carried so far that the prisoner is completely incapable of distinguishing right from wrong, it will be a good defence : *Director of Public Prosecutions* v. *Beard* (1920). Self-induced intoxication is no defence to a charge of assault : *D.P.P.* v. *Majewski* (1976) (H.L.).

(*f*) NECESSITY.

An act or omission which amounts to a criminal offence cannot be justified by mere personal necessity. It is murder for a person, in order to save his own life, to take away the life of another who is guiltless of any illegality to anyone : *R.* v. *Dudley and Stephens* (1884). But a criminal act or omission may be excused if the motive was to prevent the execution of an illegal purpose and the act or omission was necessary to prevent it, e.g., the motive of self-defence against a forcible crime.

(*g*) ACCIDENT.

No one can be criminally responsible for an accident due to some external agency over which he had no control, or for the unintended consequences of a lawful voluntary act done without negligence, e.g., where a boxer is killed in a lawful boxing contest.

(*h*) AUTOMATION.

If a person's actions are purely automatic and his mind has no control over the movement of his limbs, he will be in the same position as a person in an epileptic fit, and no responsibility will rest on him : *R.* v. *Charlson* (1955).

In addition to the above qualifications there are certain exemptions from liability, e.g. :—

(*a*) *The Sovereign.*
(*b*) *Foreign sovereigns and potentates.*
(*c*) *Foreign ambassadors.*
   These may be liable for acts affecting the existence or safety of the State, and for an attempt against the life of the sovereign, but even so they are not amenable to ordinary criminal law. In such case they may be arrested and will normally be returned to their own country.
(*d*) *Corporations.* The Criminal Justice Act, 1925, enables corporations to be indicted. Answers to such questions as must be put to a prisoner, and the plea of " Guilty " or " Not guilty " or any special plea are made by a representative of the corporation. Yet, it follows from the very nature of a corporation that it cannot be guilty of such crimes as

treason, murder, bigamy and the like. Nor is it capable of a crime which can be punished only by some form of corporal punishment. Yet, through the medium of its servants a corporation has been held guilty of an intent to deceive [*Director of Public Prosecutions* v. *Kent and Sussex Contractors* (1944)], of common law conspiracy to defraud [*R.* v. *I.C.R. Haulage, Ltd.* (1944)], and of infringements of purchase tax regulations [*Moore* v. *Bresler* (1944)]. It should be noted that there is a growing tendency for statute to provide in relation to an offence committed by a corporation that a director or other officer of the body corporate who has consented to or connived at the offence shall be likewise guilty of the offence and be punished accordingly. Instances are to be found in the Theft Act, 1969, the Trade Descriptions Act, 1968, the Employment Agencies Act, 1973, and the Employment Protection Act, 1975.

### Degrees of Complicity.

Before the Criminal Law Act, 1967 came into operation, a person might be involved in a felony as a principal in the first or second degree or as an accessory before or after the fact and this categorisation of complicity produced over-refined rules (which do not call for treatment in an elementary book such as the present one beyond the statement that broadly the categorisation depended on the degree of participation whether as actual doer of the criminal act, or assisting its perpetration, or shielding the doer from being brought to justice) as well as different consequences in the matter of punishment. The categorisation applied only to felonies, for in treason all persons implicated were treated as principals and the same was true of misdemeanours (including persons aiding and abetting) the participants being, in theory, liable to the same punishment as principals.

There were also the independent offences of misprision of felony and of compounding a felony.

As we saw earlier (see *ante* p. 256) the Act of 1967 abolished the distinctions between felony and misdemeanour and provided that the law and practice relating to misdemeanour were to prevail.

At the same time the Act (in order to deal with the consequential abolition of the category of accessory after the fact) provided that :

" Where a person has committed an arrestable offence, any other person who, knowing or believing him to be guilty of the offence or of some other arrestable offence, does without lawful authority or reasonable excuse any act with intent to impede his apprehension or prosecution shall be guilty of an offence ". [No proceedings are however, to be instituted in respect of such an alleged offence without the consent of the Director of Public Prosecutions.]

Similarly, (in order to deal with matters formerly within the domain of misprision or compounding) the Act provides:

"Where a person has committed an arrestable offence, any other person who, knowing or believing that the offence or some other arrestable offence has been committed, and that he has information which might be of material assistance in securing the prosecution or conviction of an offender for it, accepts or agrees to accept for not disclosing that information any consideration other than the making good of loss or injury caused by the offence, or making of reasonable compensation for that loss or injury, shall be liable on conviction on indictment to imprisonment for not more than two years". [There is a similar limitation on taking proceedings without the consent of the Director of Public Prosecutions.]

The provision was considered by the Court of Appeal (Criminal Division) in *R.* v. *Brindley*; *R.* v. *Long* (1971) and it was held that it is not necessary to prove that the accused, charged with an offence under the section knew the identity of the person who had committed the principal offence. What has to be proved is: first, that a person has committed an arrestable offence; second, that another person knew or believed that the first person committed it; third, that the second person did an act with intent to impede the apprehension or prosecution of the first person; fourth, that the act was done without lawful authority or reasonable excuse.

Incitement to commit a crime is an independent misdemeanour at Common Law.

## SUBSTANTIVE CRIMES

### A. AGAINST THE PERSON

**Homicide.**

Homicide involves the death of one human being as the result of the conduct of another. In criminal law there can be no "human being" until there has been complete extrusion from the womb, and a child must be born alive before it can be killed. Death may be caused by an omission, e.g., when a parent deliberately refuses to supply food or medical aid to his child.

Homicide may be lawful or unlawful. Examples of the former are killing in defence of persons against some forcible and atrocious crime, if the force used was commensurate with the emergency, and the execution of a criminal sentenced by a competent Court, carried out in a lawful manner by the lawfully appointed official. There are the following types of unlawful homicide:—

(a) Murder.

This is committed *when a person of sound mind and discretion unlawfully kills any human creature in being and under the Queen's peace with malice aforethought, death resulting within a year and a day of the unlawful act or omission.*

Apart from the administration of poison, it was thought at one time that the death must result from the application of force in some form. But it is now probable that on proof of malice aforethought, death from nervous shock will be recognized as murder, as where caused by the despatch of an alarming telegram to a woman known to have a weak heart brings about her death from shock, because medical evidence may prove a direct unbroken chain of causation between the telegram, shock and death.

But a default in the performance of a mere moral duty will not create liability for murder, nor will the procuring of another's death by perjury.

It is not sufficient for the prosecution to prove that A killed B ; the prosecution must prove that A acted with malice aforethought. It is not for the accused to establish his innocence, but for the prosecution to prove his guilt : *Woolmington v. Director of Public Prosecutions* (1935).

Malice aforethought is peculiar to the crime of murder and distinguishes if from other forms of homicide.

Since the Homicide Act, 1957, it would appear that the expression malice aforethought includes only an intention :—

(a) to kill ; or
(b) to inflict grievous bodily harm.

The Homicide Act, 1957, introduced categories of capital and non-capital murders, the defence of diminished responsibility (discussed *ante* p. 259) and altered the law in other respects.

However, the Murder (Abolition of Death Penalty) Act, 1965, abolished the death penalty for murder and substituted life imprisonment, the sentencing Court being empowered at the time of sentence, to recommend a minimum period of confinement. The Lord Chief Justice, and if possible the trial judge, is to be consulted before the Secretary of State releases on licence a person convicted of murder.

The Act was to continue in force until 31st July, 1970, when it was to expire unless Parliament by affirmative resolutions of both Houses otherwise determined. It was thus experimental. However by a majority resolution of both Houses of Parliament at the end of 1969 the abolition of the death penalty for murder was made permanent.

Formerly, it was necessary to produce the body of the alleged victim, but where the fact of death is definitely established by other means, this is no longer essential : *R.* v. *Onufrejczyk* (1955).

(*b*) **Manslaughter.**

In general terms, manslaughter is unlawful homicide unaccompanied by malice aforethought. It may be voluntary or involuntary.

Originally the expression " voluntary manslaughter " was used in relation to those homicides which were reduced from murder to manslaughter owing to provocation. However, since the Homicide Act, 1957, the expression has also embraced :—

(*a*) a killing by a person in pursuance of a suicide pact with the person killed (see below) ; and,
(*b*) a killing by a person suffering from " diminished responsibility " (see above).

In order that provocation may reduce a *prima facie* charge of murder to manslaughter :—

(*a*) It must be such as to deprive an ordinary reasonable man—and the accused may not be such—of self-control.
(*b*) It must have caused the accused *himself* to lose self-control.
(*c*) The killing must follow closely upon the provocation, so that " cooling time " has not elapsed, whereby the accused should have recovered his self-control.
(*d*) There must be some proportion between the nature of the provocation and the mode of retort : *Mancini* v. *D.P.P.* (1942).

Often the provocation is a physical blow, but there may be other circumstances in which provocation arises. Thus if a man suddenly discovers his wife in the act of adultery, and he kills either her or her paramour immediately, he will be guilty of manslaughter.

The *reasonable man* test has now received statutory recognition. Section 3 of the Homicide Act, 1957, provides that in determining the question of provocation " the jury shall take into account everything both said and done according to the effect which, in their opinion, it would have on *a reasonable man.*"

The reference in section 3 to things " both *said* and done " indicates a retreat from the position reached by the House of Lords in *Holmes* v. *D.P.P.* (1946) in which it is stated that words alone can only constitute provocation " on the rarest of occasions ", and, in particular, that a sudden confession of adultery could never suffice. It may be that, as a result of section 3, the judges will decide that such confessions may be taken into account by the jury.

It is for the jury to decide as a matter of fact whether there was sufficient provocation or not, although the judge will have to decide, in the first place, if there is enough evidence of provocation to be left to the jury.

The defence of provocation is available only on a charge of murder to reduce the offence to manslaughter; it is not available on any other charge such as malicious wounding: *R. v. Cunningham* (1958).

Involuntary manslaughter is unlawful conduct consisting of :—
  (i) An unlawful act which, although not dangerous to life, is dangerous to human safety;
  (ii) An act of culpable negligence;
  (iii) An omission to do an act when there is a legal duty to take care, e.g., failure to provide medical aid, in cases of necessity, if such failure caused or accelerated death.

(c) Suicide.

This is self-killing by a person *of sound mind* and years of discretion.

The Suicide Act, 1961, abrogated the rule of law that suicide is a crime. Consequently, attempted suicide is also no longer a crime.

The Act makes it an indictable offence to aid, abet, counsel or procure the suicide of another or an attempt by another to commit suicide. Such complicity is a misdemeanour and a person charged with murder or manslaughter may be charged with it.

Prior to the Homicide Act, 1957, the survivor of a suicide pact was guilty of murder. However, section 4(1) of the 1957 Act provided that it should be " manslaughter and not murder for a person acting in pursuance of a suicide pact between him and another to kill the other or be a party to the other killing himself or being killed by a third person. A suicide pact was expressed to mean " a common agreement between two or more persons having for its object the death of all of them, whether or not each is to take his own life " but it was declared that the accused must have had " the settled intention of dying in pursuance of the pact ".

The Suicide Act, 1961, amended section 4(1) of the 1957 Act by repealing the words " killing himself or " therein, so that a survivor of the deleted category would now be guilty of the new offence of counselling suicide and not of manslaughter.

(d) Road Deaths.

Section 1 of the consolidating Road Traffic Act, 1972 (repeating a provision in the earlier Act of 1960), makes it an independent offence, punishable with five years' imprisonment as a maximum, to cause the death of another by reckless or dangerous driving as defined in the section. It remains possible to charge the accused with manslaughter or culpable homicide in appropriate circumstances, but recent statistics show that the statutory offence is now more commonly relied upon.

(e) *Infanticide.*

Under the Infanticide Act, 1938, where a woman by any wilful act or omission causes the death of her child, being a child under the age of twelve months, but at the time of such act or omission the balance of her mind was disturbed by reason of her not having fully recovered from the effect of child-birth or by the reason of the effect of lactation consequent upon the birth, she shall be guilty of the offence of infanticide, punishable as manslaughter. On these grounds a charge of murder may be reduced to that of infanticide.

INFANT LIFE PRESERVATION ACT, 1929 ; ABORTION.

Although, as has been said, it is not murder to kill a child not yet born, yet under this Act any person who, with intent to destroy the life of a child capable of being born alive, by any wilful act causes a child to die before it has an independent existence, is guilty of child destruction, punishable by imprisonment for life. The prosecution must prove that the act which caused the death of the child was not done in good faith for the purpose only of preserving the life of the mother. Cp. *R.* v. *Bourne* (1939).

The Abortion Act, 1967 (which creates no new offence), attempts to amend and clarify the law relating to termination of pregnancy by registered medical practitioners.

In effect the Act does little more than give statutory force to the summing-up to the jury in the leading case of *R.* v. *Bourne* (*supra*) but spells out specifically the conditions which must exist before an abortion may lawfully be carried out ; provides for a system of notification to be followed by the practitioner who authorizes or performs an abortion ; excuses from participation in a medical termination of pregnancy persons who have a conscientious objection to such participation. All treatment for termination of pregnancy must be carried out in a National Health Service hospital or other place approved by the Minister of Health.

## B. AGAINST PROPERTY

**Theft and Related Offences.**

Before considering the nature of this crime it is necessary to have some idea of the meaning of the terms *property, possession* and *custody*. *Property* is the right of ownership. *Possession* means physical control exercised over a corporeal thing with the intention and for the purpose of excluding all other persons from its use and enjoyment. Actual physical control is not essential. There is still possession although the subject has been entrusted to a servant ; he has custody, but possession remains with the master. Where A the owner of a car, hires it to B, who lends it to his friend C, who instructs his chauffeur, D, to drive the car to his garage, A has the ownership, B has the right *to* possess, C has the *immediate* right of possession and D has mere custody.

Under section (1)(1) of the Theft Act, 1968 a person is guilty of theft " if he dishonestly appropriates property belonging to another with the intention of permanently depriving the other of it. . . ."

The Act of 1968 completely reformed the law relating to theft and kindred offences and repealed the Larceny Act, 1916, under which the definition of larceny had involved a fraudulent taking and carrying away without the consent of the owner and without a claim of right made in good faith of anything capable of being stolen with intent, at the time of such taking, permanently to deprive the owner thereof.

The quoted definition in the 1968 Act (coupled with the definitions of " dishonestly " ; " appropriates " ; " property " ; " belonging to another " ; and " with the intention of permanently depriving the other of it " given in sections 2–6 of the Act) is wide enough to cover what, under the previous law, had been the separate categories of simple larceny, larceny by a bailee, by a trick, intimidation or finding as well as embezzlement and fraudulent conversion. It also covers the situation where a person gets property of another through the mistake of that other.

Although (subject to the special provisions of sections 6 and 12 of the Act) the mere borrowing of goods is not, in ordinary circumstances, an offence, section 12 of the Act (repeating and extending previous statutory provisions) does make it an offence for any person to take for his own or another's use without the consent of the owner or other lawful authority any motor vehicle or other conveyance. It remains a defence that the accused believed that he had lawful authority or would have the owner's consent if the owner knew of the taking and the attendant circumstances. A sub-section makes it a summary offence for a person to take for his own or another's use a pedal cycle without the consent of the owner or other lawful authority.

Under section 30 of the Act husband and wife are for the first time made fully amenable to the law of theft in relation to each other's property. A prosecution requires the consent of the Director of Public Prosecutions.

## Handling Stolen Goods.

Replacing the earlier law on the subject of " receiving stolen property ", the Theft Act, 1968, creates the offence of handling stolen goods. Under section 22 this offence is committed by a person who knowing or believing goods to be stolen dishonestly receives them or dishonestly undertakes or assists in their retention, removal, disposal or realization by or for the benefit of another person, or if he arranges to do so.

## Obtaining Property or Pecuniary Advantage by Deception.

The Theft Act introduced new provisions to cover the offences formerly known as obtaining property by false pretences or obtaining credit by fraud.

Under section 15 of the Act it is an offence for any person by any deception dishonestly to obtain property belonging to another with the intention of permanently depriving the other of it. " Deception " means any deception (whether deliberate or reckless) by words or conduct as to fact or as to law, including [and this is an advance on the previous law] " a deception as to the present intentions of the person using the deception or any other person." " Property " is given a wide definition in section 4 of the Act and includes a thing in action such as a cheque : *R.* v. *Dunn* (1973).

Under section 16 it is an offence for a person by any deception dishonestly to obtain for himself or another any pecuniary advantage. Cp. *R.* v. *Watkins* (1976) (Bank overdraft).

## Robbery.

Under section 8 of the Theft Act, 1968, a person is guilty of robbery if he steals, and immediately before or at the time of doing so, and in order to do so, he uses force on any person or puts or seeks to put any person in fear of being then and there subjected to force.

## Blackmail.

Under section 21 of the Theft Act, 1968, a person is guilty of this offence if, with a view to gain for himself or another or with intent to cause loss to another, he makes any unwarranted demand with menaces. Such a demand is unwarranted unless the person making it does so in the belief (*a*) that he has reasonable grounds for making the demand ; and (*b*) that the use of the menaces is a proper means of reinforcing the demand.

## Burglary.

*Burglary* (as re-defined in section 9 of the Theft Act, 1968) is committed by a person if (*a*) he enters any building as a trespasser and with intent to commit stealing anything therein, of inflicting on any person therein any grievous bodily harm or raping any woman therein or of doing unlawful damage to the building or anything therein ; or (*b*) having entered any building as a trespasser he steals or attempts to steal anything therein or inflicts or attempts to inflict on any person therein any grievous bodily harm. *Aggravated burglary* (attracting a more severe penalty) arises where firearms or weapons of offence are used.

This is an improvement on the previous law as it obviates the technicalities of " breaking and entering ", makes no distinction between offences committed during day or night-time and embraces the former disparate offences of burglary, housebreaking, larceny in a dwelling-house and sacrilege. Underlying the offence is entry as a trespasser.

### Criminal Damage.

The Criminal Damage Act, 1971, implemented the recommendations of the Law Commission in Law Com. No. 29. It thus modernized and simplified the law and repealed most of the provisions of the complicated and unsatisfactory Malicious Damage Act, 1861.

In essence, the Act created (*a*) one basic offence to cover the whole field of damage to another's property without lawful excuse, with a maximum penalty of ten years, except where it is committed by the use of fire [to be charged as arson as before], when the penalty is life imprisonment ; (*b*) one aggravated offence, with a maximum penalty of life imprisonment ; the aggravating element being the endangering of life.

The *mens rea* required is intention or recklessness and the word " maliciously " used in the 1861 Act is not employed in the 1971 Act.

### Forgery.

Under the Forgery Act, 1913, forgery is the making of a false document in order that it may be used as genuine.

The offence may be analysed as follows :—

(*a*) *The Instrument* or *Document* : No comprehensive definition is possible, but a document may be defined as any writing the words of which purport in themselves to carry legal consequences.

The varieties of " documents " are infinite—a theatre ticket, the credentials of a clerk in Holy Orders, a used postage stamp from which the cancellation has been eliminated in order that it may be used again. An illustration that " the varieties of documents are infinite " is afforded by the case of *R*. v. *Potter* (1958). There A, a qualified driver, took a driving test representing that he was B and, having successfully concluded the test, signed in B's name the certificate of competence which was subsequently used by B to obtain a licence from the council. A was convicted of forgery, the trial judge holding that the certificate was a document within the meaning of the Forgery Act, 1913, and that there had been an intent to defraud.

(b) *The Falsity* : It is not sufficient that a document tells lies, it " must tell a lie about itself ".

Thus, if A writes a letter containing statements which, to his knowledge, are untrue, he does not commit forgery ; but if A writes a letter in which he says nothing that is untrue but, without authority, signs the letter in X's name, A has committed forgery, if he acted with intent to defraud.

The signing of a fictitious name or the name of a dead man will be forgery if the effect of such signature is to make a document appear to be that which it is not. It is even a forgery to sign one's own name under such conditions as to lead a third party to believe that such is the signature of another. But, no forgery is committed by a person who signs a document in an assumed name, but puts it forward to another as emanating strictly from himself. Such other person gives credit not on the signature, but to the actual maker of it.

(c) *The Making* : A document may be forged by affixing a stamp to it. There may be forgery by omission, e.g., where a person, with the necessary intent, omits a provision from a will which he is drafting at the testator's dictation. A document may be produced in Court as having been forged by the accused, although that is the first occasion on which he has seen it, as, for example, where the document is a telegram made out by the receiving telegraphist.

(d) *The Mens Rea* : For the purpose of *public* documents, e.g., marriage licences, an intent to *deceive* will suffice ; but, usually, there must be an intent to defraud. To *deceive* is, by falsehood, to induce a state of mind, to *defraud* is, by deceit, to induce a course of action. For instance, a receipt for moneys paid being a private document, the forging thereof will not be a criminal offence unless there is an intent to defraud. So if a clerk, having already issued a receipt signed by his employer for moneys actually paid, issues a duplicate and signs it himself without authority, these facts do not constitute forgery, as there is no intent to defraud. But if the money had not, in fact, been paid, the issue of the receipt with intent to defraud the employer amounts to forgery.

## C. AGAINST PUBLIC RIGHTS

Under this head are considered crimes which affect a man in his capacity as a member of the State and concern rights common to all subjects of the realm.

## Treason.

This involves a breach of allegiance owed to the Queen. An alien may be convicted of treason if owing local allegiance by reason of residence within the realm. Where he has once so resided, his duty of allegiance does not cease on quitting the realm if he continues to use a British passport : *Joyce* v. *Director of Public Prosecutions* (1946). In all types of treason there must be an *overt act*, i.e., an act manifesting the criminal intent and tending towards the accomplishment of the criminal object.

Of the treasons specified in the Treason Act, 1351, only two require especial mention :—

 (a) *Levying War*. This comprises any forcible insurrection of a widespread nature, involving a general defiance of the government. A war-like array is necessary, although actual disturbance need not occur. In this respect it differs from a riot, which occurs when an unlawful assembly begins to carry out its unlawful purpose with a show of violence. But the basic distinction lies in the object which the participants have in mind : if such is of a public and general nature, the offence is treason ; if of a private and local nature, then a riot is committed.

 (b) *Adhering to the Queen's enemies*. This means giving assistance or succour to the subjects of a foreign State at war with Her Majesty. Thus, adherence to rebel subjects of the Queen is not within this species of treason, although it may amount to " levying war ". The assistance may be given either within or without the realm. Thus, in *R.* v. *Casement* (1917), a British subject was held guilty of treason in that he had incited British prisoners of war to join the enemy forces, and participated in an expedition in a submarine having for its object the landing of arms in Ireland.

## Sedition.

This embraces malicious words, deeds or writings, not amounting to treason, which cause or are intended to cause or excite discontent or dissatisfaction, ill-will between different classes, public disturbance or civil war, or hatred against the Sovereign or the government.

## Unlawful Meetings.

Unlawful assemblies, routs and riots, both Common **Law and** statutory, have been dealt with in Chapter V.

## Perjury.

By the Perjury Act, 1911, this offence is committed when

"any person, lawfully sworn as a witness or interpreter in a judicial proceeding, wilfully makes a statement, material in that proceeding, which he knows to be false or does not believe to be true".

A person is "lawfully sworn" if he gives his evidence on affirmation or solemn declaration, and it is the Judge's duty to ascertain the "proper" form of oath, i.e., the form of oath which a witness considers to be binding upon him.

A "judicial proceeding" includes a proceeding before any Court, tribunal or person having by law power to hear, receive and examine evidence on oath. The person authorized to hear evidence on oath must be present when the false statement is made. Thus, when a registrar in bankruptcy, who was presiding over the examination of a debtor, left the room, but instructed the solicitor to continue questioning the debtor, false answers given in his absence were held not to constitute perjury : *R. v. Lloyd* (1887).

There are three elements essential to a statement on oath to constitute perjury. Such a statement must be :—

(a) Wilful ;
(b) False or believed by the accused, when he made it, to be false ;
(c) Material.

All three elements must exist, for even if a statement is false, and wilfully false, there is no perjury if such a statement is not material.

The question of materiality is one to be determined by the Judge.

A person may commit perjury even although his statement is true, if he did not believe it to be so.

A person may not be convicted of perjury on the uncorroborated evidence of one witness. The required corroboration may consist of the following :—

(1) The evidence of two witnesses directly contradicting him ;
(2) The evidence of one witness directly contradicting him, where such evidence is corroborated by a second witness ;
(3) The evidence of one witness directly contradicting him, and proof that he has himself made a contradictory statement on another occasion ;
(4) Evidence that he has on other occasions made contradictory statements and proof of facts tending to show that those statements were true ;
(5) The evidence of two witnesses that he has on two occasions made statements contradicting his evidence.

Under section 11(1) of the European Communities Act, 1972, "a person who, in sworn evidence before the European Court [in Luxembourg] makes any statement which he knows to be false or does not believe to be true shall, whether he is a British subject or not, be guilty of an offence and may be proceeded against and punished :—

(a) in England or Wales as for an offence against section 1(1) of the Perjury Act, 1911 ..."

## Bigamy.

The offence of bigamy is committed by any person who, being married, marries any other person during the life of the former spouse, whether the second marriage takes place in England or Ireland or elsewhere : Offences Against the Person Act, 1861, section 57.

The original marriage must have been valid, substantially and ceremonially, and must be still subsisting at the date of the second " marriage ". The essence of the offence is the profanation of the marriage ceremony, so that, if the due formalities have been observed on the celebration of the second " marriage ", it is immaterial that a valid marriage was not in any case possible owing to some personal incapacity apart from the existence of the prior marriage.

The following possible defences exist :—

(a) Seven years' absence of the spouse of the accused. It must be established that (i) the accused's wife or husband has been continuously absent for seven years, and (ii) that he or she has never been heard of by the accused at any time during such period. Proof of the first requisite raises a presumption as to the existence of the second, but this may be rebutted by the prosecution. This defence is available no matter how many so-called " marriages " the defendant contracts. Thus, where A was lawfully married to B in 1925, and, not having heard of her for twenty years, " married " C in 1946 and D in 1948 (B being, in fact, still alive) it was held that he could not be convicted of bigamy in respect of the " marriages " with C or D ; *R.* v. *Taylor* (1950).

(b) If the accused had a *bona fide* and *reasonable* belief in the death of his or her spouse, even if seven years have not elapsed, a second marriage will not be an offence.

### R. v. Tolson (1889).

Mrs. T honestly believed her husband to be dead, having learned on reliable authority that he had travelled by a ship which had gone down with all hands. Although seven years had not elapsed since she had seen her husband, she remarried, and then discovered that he was still alive.

*It was held* that she was not guilty of bigamy.

(c) A second marriage after a divorce or nullity decree by a Court of competent jurisdiction. An honest belief (although mistakenly held) that the marriage has thus been dissolved

will exonerate a spouse who remarries : *R.* v. *Gould* (1968).
(d) If the second marriage was not contracted in England, Wales or Northern Ireland, the accused not being a British subject.

It was held in *R.* v. *Dolman* (1950), that, where A had reasonable cause to believe that his first marriage with B was invalid on the ground that B was already married, he could not be convicted of bigamy by reason of his having gone through a form of marriage with C, although his marriage with B was, in fact, valid.

Where the accused successfully pleads the defence of reasonable belief in the death of the other spouse, the second " husband " or " wife " cannot be guilty of aiding and abetting even though he or she had knowledge that such spouse was alive. But if, with such knowledge, the second ceremony resulted from the persuasion of the second " husband " or " wife ", the latter is guilty of incitement.

The spouse of the accused is a competent, but not a compellable, witness for the prosecution. This means that although the spouse cannot be compelled to give evidence against his or her will, if he or she elects to give evidence for the prosecution, such evidence is admissible.

## Criminal Libel.

Libel is both a civil wrong and a criminal offence. As a civil wrong it has already received notice in Chapter VII. The essence of the criminal offence is its tendency to cause a breach of the peace. It is not necessary, therefore, as it is in the case of civil libel, to prove *publication to a third person*. Publication to the prosecutor alone is enough. There are other respects in which the criminal offence differs from the civil wrong. Thus, criminal, though not civil, proceedings are possible in respect of :—

(a) Libels on deceased persons tending to provoke their families.
(b) Libels tending to defame persons in high positions abroad.
(c) Libels against a class.
(d) Libels that are true, unless their publication is for the public benefit.

The defences to a charge of criminal libel are :—
(1) Privilege.
(2) Fair comment.
(3) That the publication was accidental or without the defendant's authority or knowledge.
(4) That, though the libel is true, its publication is for the public benefit.

Privilege and fair comment have been sufficiently discussed in Chapter VII.

## Public Mischief.

Some crimes are crimes at Common Law. Conduct causing, or tending to cause, public mischief constitutes, it has been said, a misdemeanour at Common Law. " All offences of a public nature, that is, all such acts or attempts as tend to the prejudice of the community are indictable " : *R.* v. *Manley* (1933).

> In that case the accused made a false statement to the police to the effect that she had been robbed of some money. Police officers wasted their time in investigating these false allegations, and innocent persons were exposed to suspicion and arrest. There being no statutory crime with which she could be charged, she was indicted for having effected a public mischief. The definition of a public mischief as an act or attempt that tends to the prejudice of the community is exceedingly wide and suggests the possibility of a dangerous extension of the crime in times of stress. Since the decision in *R.* v. *Newland* (1953), it seemed that public mischief cases would in future be treated, where appropriate, as lying within the realm of the law of conspiracy, and that an unconcerted action of an individual would be indictable only if it was itself a Common Law or statutory offence. The Court of Criminal Appeal said that in its opinion the safe course was no longer to follow *R.* v. *Manley*. Following the reasoning in *R.* v. *Newland* (*supra*) the House of Lords (by a majority) in *Shaw* v. *Director of Public Prosecutions* (1961) held that a conspiracy to corrupt public morals is a crime at Common Law as injurious to the public interest. Cp. *D.P.P.* v. *Bhagwan* (1970) (H.L.) ; *Knuller* (*Publishing, Printing and Promotions*) *Ltd.* v. *D.P.P.* (1972) (H.L.). These latter cases were upheld in *D.P.P.* v. *Withers* (1974) (H.L.) but it was held that a conspiracy to effect a public mischief was not an offence known to law and that conspiracies must remain within the previously recognized categories of perverting the course of justice, to corrupt public morals or to defraud.

It is perhaps to be welcomed that conduct of the type which figured in the controversial case of *R.* v. *Manley* (*supra*) has now become the subject of statutory provision in the Criminal Law Act, 1967 in the following terms :—

> "Where a person causes any wasteful employment of the police by knowingly making to any person a false report tending to show that an offence has been committed, or to give rise to apprehension for the safety of any persons or property, or tending to show that he has information material to any police inquiry, he shall be liable on summary conviction to imprisonment for not more than six months or to a fine of not more than two hundred pounds or to both ".

## D. INCHOATE CRIMES

As we have seen, the commission of a crime involves both a guilty mind and a guilty act. There are, however, three classes of incipient or inchoate crimes where there is no, or no complete, guilty act.

## I. Conspiracy.

A conspiracy is the agreement of two or more to do an unlawful act, or to do a lawful act by unlawful means with a view to injuring another.

It is obvious that a man cannot conspire with himself and, thus, if only two are indicted and one is acquitted, the other must be acquitted, even though he may have pleaded guilty. At Common Law it was considered that for all legal purposes husband and wife were one, and although this principle has been largely negatived by statute it is still the rule that husband and wife cannot be convicted of conspiracy.

The crime is complete as soon as the agreement is made, even though nothing is done in pursuance thereof. The object may be a crime; a tort involving fraud or intending to injure another; or conduct offensive to public morals. Cp. *Shaw* v. *Director of Public Prosecutions* (*supra*) and the other cases cited with it; also *D.P.P.* v. *Withers* (*supra*). The Law Commission has recently issued a Report on the topic of conspiracy (Law Com. No. 76).

In order to constitute the crime :—

(a) Each conspirator must know and approve the intention of the others.
(b) There must be an act showing intention, but, as stated above, the agreement itself is a sufficiently guilty act.
(c) There must be an intention to carry out the conspiracy.

Where the existence of the conspiracy has been established the acts or statements of any one of the conspirators are admissible in evidence against the other or others, even though not done or said in their presence. This is contrary to the general rules of evidence.

## II. Incitement.

To incite or solicit another to commit an offence is itself a misdemeanour at Common Law, but statutory provision has been made for the special punishment of certain forms of incitement, e.g., incitement to commit murder or perjury.

The offence is complete even though the incitement is ineffectual, and even though the incitement does not come to the knowledge of the person to be incited, as, for example, where a letter of incitement is lost in the post.

If the incited crime *is* committed, those responsible for the incitement are (in the light of the Criminal Law Act, 1967) liable as principals.

## III. Attempt to Commit Crime.

To constitute an attempt to commit a crime, the act done must be more than mere preparation for the intended offence. It must be a step actually taken towards its completion and directly connected with it.

### R. v. Robinson (1915).

A jeweller, having insured his stock against burglary, falsely represented to the police that burglary had been committed at the shop, in the hope that the police would make a report by which the insurers might be induced to pay. Before he himself could make a claim to the insurers, the fraud was discovered and he was charged with an attempt to obtain money by false pretences.

*It was held* that he could not be convicted of the attempt, his act being merely one of preparation.

An attempt has been defined as " an act done with intent to commit a crime, and forming part of a series of acts which would constitute its actual commission if it were not interrupted ".

It was at one time thought that it was no defence that it was physically impossible to complete the offence. Thus, for a person to put his hand into another's pocket with intent to steal was held to be an attempted larceny even though the pocket was empty: *R.* v. *Ring* (1892). However, the analysis of attempt made by their Lordships in *Haughton* v. *Smith* (1973) (H.L.) showed that *R.* v. *Ring* (*supra*) was wrongly decided, as were the cases which followed it, in that they were based on the theory that guilty intention (without more) should be punished " so that a man who stabs a corpse may be as deserving of punishment as a man who attempts to murder a living person " (*per* Lord Reid). Thus *R.* v. *Osborn* (1919) was rightly decided in holding that if a man enters the room of his enemy and, believing the latter to be in bed, strikes the pillow with a hatchet, when the intended victim is, perhaps, miles away, however guilty a mind the assailant may have, he is not guilty of an attempt. In *Haughton* v. *Smith* (*supra*) an appeal against conviction of an attempt to handle stolen goods (see *ante* p. 269) was allowed when it appeared that at the time of the handling the goods (contrary to the belief of the accused) were no longer " stolen goods."

## CHAPTER IX

## ENGLISH LEGAL SYSTEM

Having finished our general survey of the " content " of English law, we may find it instructive to take a glance at the Courts in which it is administered and at the rules of evidence by which they are guided in their administration of justice.

Before doing so a brief mention must be made of the Constitutional independence of the judiciary. Since the Act of Settlement, 1701, High Court Judges have been freed from royal control, hold office during good behaviour and can only be removed for misconduct on an address presented by both Houses of Parliament. Moreover, their independence is further secured by the fact that their salaries are paid out of the Consolidated Fund and are thus free from annual criticism by Parliament; and by the immunity referred to *ante* p. 216.

## COURTS OF CIVIL JURISDICTION

### House of Lords.

At the head of the judicial system is the High Court of Parliament, the House of Lords, the ultimate Court of appeal in civil cases for England, Scotland and N. Ireland.

It has also jurisdiction to try peerage claims.

In practice the constitution of the House for *judicial* (as opposed to legislative) business comprises the Lord Chancellor, ex-Lord Chancellors and the Lords of Appeal in Ordinary. A quorum of three is essential.

### Supreme Court of Judicature.

In the time of Henry II, the *Curia Regis* (" King's Council ") was the Court that tried all crimes and many civil actions as well. It was from this Court that the Common Law Courts originated. The Court of Exchequer was the first to emerge as a separate Court, deciding questions between the Crown and the taxpayer and, later, disputes between one subject and another. Next came the Court of Common Pleas, which was the principal Court for deciding disputes between subject and subject. The King's Bench was the last Court to separate from the *Curia Regis*, and exercised both civil and criminal jurisdiction. Later there came into existence a Court of Appeal known as the Court of Exchequer Chamber. There were also Courts of Assize held in various towns.

Apart from these Courts, there came into existence later Courts exercising more specialized jurisdictions, such as the High Court of Admiralty, the Court of Probate and the Court for Matrimonial Causes.

The Judicature Act, 1873, amalgamated all these Courts into the Supreme Court of Judicature, comprising the Court of Appeal and the High Court of Justice. The High Court originally consisted of five Divisions, namely, the Chancery Division, the Probate, Divorce and Admiralty Division, the Common Pleas Division, the Exchequer Division and the Queen's Bench Division. In 1880, the last three were merged in the Queen's Bench Division, so that there are now only three Divisions of the High Court of Justice. The results of the reorganization of the work of those three Divisions effected by the Administration of Justice Act, 1970, are set out below when discussing the High Court.

Under the Act the High Court may sit at any place in England or Wales and at any time.

The Courts Act, 1971, added the newly established Crown Court as a limb of the Supreme Court.

### The Court of Appeal (Civil Division).

The members of the Court are (a) *ex-officio* Judges, viz., the Lord Chancellor, the Lord Chief Justice, the Master of the Rolls, the President of the Family Division, the Lords of Appeal in Ordinary and ex-Lords Chancellors, but of these only the Master of the Rolls sits habitually, and he is virtually the head of the Court; (b) a certain number of permanent Judges known as Lords Justices of Appeal. The Court generally sits in separate Divisions of three Judges.

The Court has jurisdiction to hear and determine appeals from judgments or orders of a Divisional Court, final judgments or orders of the High Court in civil proceedings, interlocutory orders of Judges in Chambers (i.e., orders made during the progress of an action) in matters of practice and procedure, decisions of County Court Judges, and the Mayor's and City of London Court (which latter has, under the Courts Act, 1971) the status of a County Court.

In civil matters appeal from the Court lies to the House of Lords by leave from the Court of Appeal itself or the Appeal Committee of the House of Lords.

Under Part II of the Administration of Justice Act, 1969, provision is made in limited circumstances for an appeal to go direct from a judge of the High Court or a Divisional Court to the House of Lords (bypassing the Court of Appeal, Civil Division).

## High Court of Justice.

This comprises the Queen's Bench Division, the Chancery Division and the Family Division. Theoretically, all the Divisions are of equal competence, but for convenience certain matters are allocated to each of the Divisions. Thus :—

(a) The Queen's Bench Division has a criminal jurisdiction and is the Court of trial for many civil actions of a common law kind such as breach of contract or negligence causing injury to property or person. Admiralty jurisdiction is now exercised by this Division and a Commercial Court is attached to the Division.

(b) The Chancery Division has assigned to it various " equitable " matters, e.g., the dissolution of partnerships, the foreclosure of mortgages, the execution of trusts, the construction of wills and the administration of estates. Also, it exercises the jurisdiction of the High Court under the Companies and Bankruptcy Acts and in revenue matters. It has now jurisdiction in contentious probate matters.

(c) The Family Division to which are assigned the matrimonial jurisdiction previously exercised by the Probate, Divorce and Admiralty Division ; non-contentious probate and the wardship of minors.

Each Division has power to form a Divisional Court consisting of two or more Judges sitting together. Amongst other matters the Divisional Court in the Queen's Bench Division makes orders of *Mandamus, Prohibition* and *Certiorari*, issues the writ of *Habeas Corpus*, and determines questions of law on cases stated by the Crown Court or Magistrates' Courts. *Mandamus, Prohibition, Certiorari* and *Habeas Corpus* have been referred to in Chapter V.

The Judges of the High Court consist of the Lord Chancellor, who is President of the Chancery Division, the Lord Chief Justice who is President of the Queen's Bench Division, the President of the Family Division, and certain *puisne* (or junior) Judges, styled Justices of the High Court, a certain number of whom are assigned to each Division by the Lord Chancellor in his capacity as head of the judicial system. Judges of the superior Courts are addressed as " my Lord ".

## County Courts.

The bulk of civil litigation in England is determined in the various County Courts first established in 1846 and now governed by the consolidating County Courts Act, 1959 (as amended). Upwards of a million and a half cases are dealt with in these Courts annually, of which, however, only some thirty thousand are determined after a hearing in Court, the balance consisting of undisputed claims settled before trial or cases where plaintiff obtains judgment on defendant's default. In the High Court, the average number of proceedings per annum for the three Divisions is but one hundred and seventy thousand.

The whole country is divided into districts, and the Courts in each district are presided over by a Judge, a barrister of at least seven years' standing, appointed and removable on the recommendation of the Lord Chancellor and addressed as "your Honour". Under a provision in the Courts Act, 1971, every Circuit judge shall, by virtue of his office, be capable of sitting as a judge for any County Court district. Each Court has its registrar, a solicitor of at least seven years' standing, similarly appointed and removable. He acts as clerk of the Court and has power (extended by the Administration of Justice Act, 1970) to try certain small cases as Deputy for the Judge.

JURISDICTION :—There are limitations as to place, and as to the nature and amount of the claim. The general rule is that the plaintiff must bring his action in the Court of the district where the defendant or one of several defendants, dwells or carries on business. Where land is concerned the action must be brought in the Court of the district wherein it is situate.

As regards the nature and amount of the claim, the jurisdiction may be summarized as follows :—

(a) Common Law jurisdiction :—
   (i) Contract claims not exceeding £1,000.
   (ii) Tort claims not exceeding £1,000—but not defamation.
   (iii) Actions of replevin (i.e., actions to recover possession of goods unlawfully distrained on for rent) to any amount, subject to qualifications.
   (iv) Actions by a landlord to recover possession, where the net annual value of the land for rating does not exceed a defined amount.
   (v) Any Common Law action where the parties agree in writing that it shall be tried by the County Court.

(b) Equitable Jurisdiction :—In such matters as execution of trusts, foreclosure or redemption of mortgages, dissolution of partnerships—provided that the property or sum involved does not exceed £5,000.

(c) Miscellaneous Jurisdiction :—
- (i) Probate jurisdiction where the value of the deceased's estate is less than a defined amount.
- (ii) Admiralty jurisdiction in certain cases.
- (iii) Company liquidations where the paid-up capital does not exceed a defined amount.
- (iv) Jurisdiction under the Bankruptcy Act, 1914, the Landlord and Tenant Acts, 1927–1954, the Rent Acts, and numerous other statutes (including the Race Relations Acts, 1965–1968, the Consumer Credit Act, 1974, the Children Act, 1975, and the Inheritance (Provision for Family and Dependants) Act, 1975).
- (v) Jurisdiction in undefended matrimonial causes as provided by the Matrimonial Causes Act, 1967.

Appeal lies from a decision of the County Court Judge to the Court of Appeal : always on a point of law and in certain cases where fact alone, or mixed questions of law and fact are involved. Appeals from decisions of the Court of Appeal have already been mentioned.

Under a provision in the County Courts Act, 1959, there is power to transfer from the High Court an action into the County Court.

**Restrictive Practices Court.**

This Court set up under the Restrictive Trade Practices Act, 1956, pronounces upon the validity of agreements covered by the Act. It was given further functions by the Resale Prices Act, 1964. Its jurisdiction has now been covered by the consolidating Restrictive Practices Court Act, 1976, and the substantive provisions as to agreements are now to be found in the Restrictive Trade Practices Act, 1976.

## COURTS OF CRIMINAL JURISDICTION

**House of Lords.**

The House in its judicial capacity hears appeals in criminal matters by prosecutor or defendant (on points of law of general public importance requiring consideration by the House and by leave from the Criminal Division of the Court of Appeal as provided by the Criminal Appeal Act, 1968, or a Divisional Court of the Queen's Bench Division as provided by the Administration of Justice Act, 1960.

### Court of Appeal (Criminal Division).

Under the Criminal Appeal Act, 1966 this Court succeeded to the jurisdiction of the Court of Criminal Appeal set up in 1907.

Any person *convicted* on indictment, criminal information or coroner's inquisition may appeal :—

(a) Without leave, on a question of law ;
(b) With leave of the Court or on the certificate of the Judge of the Court of trial, on a question of fact, or mixed fact and law, or on any other ground which appears to the Court to be a sufficient ground of appeal ;
(c) With the leave of the Court of Appeal (Criminal Division) only, against sentence, unless such is fixed by law.

The Court has power to dismiss an appeal, to quash a conviction or to vary a sentence (but not to make that sentence more severe). If satisfied that no substantial miscarriage of justice has occurred, the Court may dismiss an appeal although properly made. Under the Criminal Appeal Act, 1968 (replacing provisions first introduced by the Criminal Appeal Act, 1964), the Court may, where it allows an appeal against conviction by reason of additional evidence adduced before it, if the interests of justice so require, order the appellant to be retried. Except for the limited power conferred by the 1968 Act just referred to, the Court has no power to order a new trial. But if it considers the former proceedings were abortive, and so did not constitute a trial at all, it may send the appellant to stand his trial. This procedure is a survival of the ancient power of the Court of King's Bench to issue a writ of *venire de novo*. An example is *R.* v. *Hancock* (1931) (where the prisoner, after being put in charge of the jury, confessed his guilt and was sentenced without the jury's verdict being taken).

The Court is empowered, when dismissing an appeal or application for leave to appeal, to order the appellant or applicant to pay the whole or any part of the costs, of the appeal or application.

> The Court has no jurisdiction to entertain an interlocutory appeal or any appeal not covered by the statutory jurisdiction conferred on it : *R.* v. *Collins* (1969).

### Queen's Bench Division.

It has original and appellate jurisdiction. In exercise of the former jurisdiction it can try indictments from the judicial areas of Middlesex and London, misdemeanours committed by public officials outside the realm, offences against the Official Secrets Acts and indictments moved from other Courts, but this jurisdiction is rarely exercised. It may direct that a trial be removed to the Central Criminal Court, instead of to the Queen's Bench Division itself, where it is impossible to obtain a fair trial elsewhere, or a difficult question of law is likely to arise.

The appellate jurisdiction is exercised by a Divisional Court, usually of three Judges, sitting without a jury. It hears appeals from decisions of Justices of the Peace, and other inferior Courts, in respect of some point of law.

## Crown Court (Replacing Courts of Assize).

The country was, until 1971, divided into six Circuits, and assizes were held in each county three times, in some instances four times, in each year. The Courts had jurisdiction over all indictable offences. The Judges, who always included two Judges of the Queen's Bench Division, were known as Commissioners inasmuch as they sat by virtue of four commissions. These were (a) the Commission of *Oyer and Terminer*, i.e., to hear and determine all treasons and offences committed within the Circuit; (b) the Commission of *General Gaol Delivery*, i.e., to try and deliver every person in gaol, or released on bail, at the time of their arrival, whatever the charge; (c) the *Commission of the Peace*; (d) the *Commission of Assize*.

The Criminal Justice Administration Act, 1956 (in an experiment affecting large conurbations) set up the Crown Court at Liverpool and the Crown Court at Manchester as new Courts of Assize exercising jurisdiction by virtue of the Commissions of *Oyer and Terminer* and *General Gaol Delivery*, the Judges being the Judges of the High Court and the Recorders of Liverpool and Manchester. The new Courts sat also as Courts of Quarter Sessions for Liverpool and Manchester respectively.

The recommendations of the Beeching Committee on Assizes and Quarter Sessions were much more comprehensive and thoroughgoing in the case of courts exercising criminal jurisdication than they were in the field of civil jurisdiction.

Accordingly, the ensuing Courts Act, 1971, made substantial changes in the organization of the criminal courts. Assizes (see above) the Crown Courts of Liverpool and Manchester (see above) and Quarter Sessions (see below) were abolished. In their place a single Crown Court, centrally administered, was established in England and Wales as a superior court of record and empowered to sit at any place in England or Wales and at any time.

The jurisdiction and powers of the Crown Court are to be exercised by:

- (a) any judge of the High Court, or
- (b) any Circuit judge or Recorder, or
- (c) a judge of the High Court, Circuit judge or Recorder sitting with justices of the peace (where required by the Act).

All proceedings on indictment are to be brought before the Crown Court (section 6).

The distribution of business (on a basis of relative weight or seriousness of the crime in question) is fixed by Practice Direction issued by the Lord Chief Justice.

### Central Criminal Court.

In effect this was the " Assize Court " for Greater London. See section 1(1) Administration of Justice Act, 1964 (occasioned in part by the London Government Act, 1963). In general, the Court is constituted of (*a*) one or more Judges of the Queen's Bench Division—hearing the most serious cases ; (*b*) the Recorder of the City of London ; (*c*) the Common Serjeant ; and (*d*) the Judge of the City of London Court. Each sits separately with a jury.

Under section 4(7) of the Courts Act, 1971, the Crown Court sitting in the City of London may continue to be known as the Central Criminal Court.

### Crown Court (Replacing Courts of Quarter Sessions).

Until the Courts Act, 1971, there were County Quarter Sessions and, in some instances, Borough Quarter Sessions. In counties, the Court was composed of the county magistrates of whom there had to be at least two present. In boroughs which had been granted a separate Court of Quarter Sessions, the Recorder—a barrister of at least five years' standing, appointed by the Crown on the advice of the Home Secretary—was the sole Judge.

A court of Quarter Sessions had appellate jurisdiction from Petty Sessions and might in certain cases deal with persons convicted by a magistrates' court, following the hearing of a case summarily, where the magistrates had committed the accused to Quarter Sessions for sentence. In counties the appeal was heard by the Appeals Committee without a jury. It had original jurisdiction over all indictable offences except treason, other capital offences and any offence punishable by imprisonment for life and certain " difficult " crimes, e.g., bigamy and perjury.

Appeals from a Court of Quarter Sessions were heard by the Criminal Division of the Court of Appeal. Quarter Sessions might state a case on a point of law for the decision of the Divisional Court of the Queen's Bench Division, if the matter arose out of an appeal from Petty Sessions.

By virtue of section 3 of the Courts Act, 1971, courts of quarter sessions were abolished and their jurisdiction (original and appellate) was transferred to the Crown Courts.

## Courts of Petty Sessions.

The great majority of justices of the peace are unpaid (except that under the Justices of the Peace Act, 1968, they are entitled to financial loss allowances for earnings lost because of their magisterial duties) and thus, like the jury, constitute an important lay element in the administration of justice. Appointments are made by the Lord Chancellor after taking advice from the appropriate advisory bodies. Stipendiary magistrates, who are solicitors or barristers of seven years' standing, may be appointed for certain specially defined areas.

Within the Inner London area there are metropolitan police magistrates, who are barristers and who are paid. The latter sit alone and have all the powers of two justices of the peace in a petty sessional Court. Stipendiary magistrates have similar powers, but lay justices may sit with them. By the Justices of the Peace Act, 1949, it is provided that no person may be appointed a justice of the peace for a particular area unless he resides within fifteen miles thereof. No Justice of the Peace can be a member of a juvenile Court if he is over 65 and, in general, must retire on reaching 70 years of age.

Justices exercise two main functions. *As a Court of trial*, any two of them, in Petty Sessions, try persons accused of minor offences and, in the case of certain indictable offences, normally triable by a jury, the justices may try the issue if the accused consents. In the case of children, i.e., those under fourteen years of age, and young persons, i.e., those aged fourteen but under seventeen years of age, the offence not being homicide, proceedings are conducted in special Courts, known as Juvenile Courts, and are, as far as possible, shielded from publicity. *As a Court of preliminary investigation*, which may be conducted by one justice in any place and at any time, and from which the public may be excluded, the justices determine whether there is a *prima facie* case to go for trial before a jury. In addition, the justices have a certain civil jurisdiction, e.g., in minor disputes between masters and servants, and a considerable quasi-civil jurisdiction, e.g., in affiliation and matrimonial proceedings.

A person convicted at Petty Sessions may appeal to the Crown Court against conviction or sentence, unless he pleaded guilty, when he may appeal only against sentence. Either party, or any person aggrieved, may appeal by way of case stated, to the Queen's Bench Division, on a point of law or a plea that the justices have exceeded their jurisdiction.

If the justices cannot conclude their examination at one sitting, they may grant bail; i.e., the accused may be granted his liberty pending trial subject to certain persons undertaking to be responsible for his appearance at the trial; if they commit the accused for trial they may also grant the accused bail—but not on a charge of treason, and, *in practice*, not in cases of murder. If they refuse bail on a charge of misdemeanour, the accused must be informed of his right to appeal to the Queen's Bench Division. The discretion as to the granting of bail will be affected (*a*) by the gravity of the charge ; (*b*) by the means of the person charged ; (*c*) by the possibility of the accused interfering with the witnesses for the prosecution.

There are complicated provisions as to bail in the Criminal Justice Act, 1967.

The procedure of the Magistrates Courts is governed by the Magistrates Courts Act, 1952 (as amended) and Rules made thereunder.

## OTHER COURTS.

**Coroner's Court.**

This is a Court of enquiry, not of trial. It is the duty of the coroner to hold an inquest into the cause of death, where there is reason to believe that the deceased died a violent or unnatural death, or that he died a sudden death the cause of which is unknown, or has died in prison. He must summon a jury of not fewer than seven nor more than eleven persons : (*a*) where he has reason to suspect that the deceased came by his death by murder, manslaughter or infanticide, or where the death occurred in prison ; (*b*) where the death was caused by an accident arising out of the use of a vehicle in a street or public highway ; (*c*) where the death occurred in circumstances the continuance or possible recurrence of which is prejudicial to the health or safety of the public ; (*d*) where there is reason to suspect that the death was caused by an accident, poisoning or disease of which notice must be given to a Government Department.

If during his enquiry the coroner is informed that a person has been charged before examining justices with the murder, manslaughter or infanticide of the deceased, he must adjourn the inquest to await the outcome of the criminal proceedings. The inquest may then be resumed, but the coroner's jury may not return a verdict in conflict with that given in such proceedings.

A coroner's verdict as to death is reviewable by the High Court. In a recent such review it was held that a coroner should not presume a death by suicide in the absence of affirmative evidence, but in such a case should return an " open verdict."

A coroner has also jurisdiction to hold an inquest as to treasure trove, that is any money, coin, gold, silver, plate or bullion found hidden in the earth or other private place. It belongs to the Crown, unless the owner appears to claim it. Any person concealing treasure trove from the Crown was at Common Law liable to a fine or imprisonment. That offence of concealment of treasure trove was (along with certain other common law offences) abolished by section 32(1)(a) of the Theft Act, 1968. Nevertheless, a dishonest appropriation of such treasure trove would now amount to theft within that Act. The modern practice is for the objects found to be sent to the British Museum, which makes a payment to the finder.

## Judicial Committee of the Privy Council.

This Committee is regulated principally by the Judicial Committee Act of 1833 " for the better administration of justice in His Majesty's Privy Council ". However, there are still traces of the theory that the Judicial Committee is an executive Council and not a Court of law. Its decisions do not take the form of judgments but of reports tendering advice to Her Majesty. It does not consider itself bound by its previous decisions, but normally it will follow such. The English Courts are not bound by the decisions of the Committee, but attach great importance to them. The Committee is composed of :—

(a) Privy Councillors who hold, or have held, high judicial office in the United Kingdom ;
(b) Certain Judges and ex-Judges of the superior Courts of the Dominions ;

The Committee hears appeals from :—

(a) The Ecclesiastical Courts (in certain cases) ;
(b) The Prize Court ;
(c) The Superior Courts of the Channel Islands and the Isle of Man, of overseas territories and those of the former Dominions which have not abrogated this appeal to the Committee under the powers conferred on them by the Statute of Westminster, 1931.
(d) Certain Courts established by the Foreign Jurisdicton Act, 1890.

Appeals are not allowed in criminal matters, unless there has been a flagrant violation of justice, and leave to appeal therein must first be petitioned for. Questions concerning Commonwealth affairs may also be referred to it by the Crown, as in the Labrador Boundary dispute of 1927 ; likewise questions arising under the House of Commons Disqualification Act, 1975, or in connection with parliamentary privilege.

## Barristers and Solicitors.

The barrister speaks in Court for his lay client, presenting the case, and looking after the lay client's interests in Court generally. Another of his functions is to advise a lay client, when approached through a solicitor ; the lay client accordingly obtains " counsel's opinion ".

Ancillary to his conduct of a case in Court, the barrister drafts the pleadings, and other documents connected with the litigation, except where these are unimportant.

The solicitor is the person first approached by the lay client. He advises the lay client, and, in the event of litigation, or of the possibility of litigation, prepares the lay client's case, except for the matters mentioned above that are undertaken by the barrister ; instructs the barrister to carry out these matters and *briefs* him to appear and represent the lay client in Court. Only in certain inferior Courts (such as the County Courts and the Magistrates' Courts or where otherwise permitted under the relaxation introduced by the Courts Act, 1971) has a solicitor the right of audience, and even in these Courts it is customary to brief a barrister except in very unimportant cases.

*Other* important points of difference between the duties and liabilities of barristers and solicitors are the following :—

(1) Barristers cannot make binding contracts with clients in respect of their fees ; solicitors can.
(2) Barristers cannot bind their clients by anything they say ; solicitors can, as they are agents for their clients.
(3) Barristers are not liable for negligence in the conduct of a case in Court (as advocates that is) ; it is not finally settled whether solicitors are, but it is clear that they are liable in damages for negligently handling their client's affairs : *Rondel* v. *Worsley* (1967).
(4) Barristers may not, as a matter of strict professional usage or etiquette, deal with their lay clients, broadly speaking, except through the instrumentality of solicitors ; solicitors may deal with their clients directly.
(5) Barristers are not officers of the Court and the Court has no special control over them, although it has an inherent power to suspend from practising any barrister guilty of professional misconduct. On the other hand, solicitors are, in fact, officers of the Court and are subject to the Court's disciplinary jurisdiction over its officers.
(6) The qualifications for call to the Bar, etiquette, etc., are entirely dependent on tradition and custom, as expounded by the Inns of Court on their own authority ; in the case of

solicitors, such matters, except to a minor extent, are fixed by statute.

(7) Barristers need to a greater degree an intellectual grasp of the law, and dialectical skill ; solicitors are to a far greater degree business men, and are in much closer touch with their clients.

Points of similarity between the two branches of the profession are :—

(1) Both have a complete legal immunity in the lawful conduct of their clients' lawsuits ; e.g., they are immune from liability for libel or slander in respect of defamatory statements made in the course of carrying on their clients' lawsuits.
(2) Both are bound not to divulge any facts which may have come to their knowledge affecting their clients' interests in the course of, or preparatory to, litigation.
(3) Both are liable to censure and penalties, at the hands of professional bodies, for conduct contrary to the rules of their profession.

In recent years there have been suggestions for the fusion of the two branches of the legal profession under one governing body and a common training. There are arguments both ways in this matter. On the one hand, those who support fusion contend that the advantages to be derived would be the lower cost of legal assistance because fewer legal personnel would be involved and normally one adviser-advocate would handle a matter from inception to end. On the other, those against fusion would seem to point to the countervailing disadvantages that the Bench of judges would no longer be recruited from a highly skilled and successful group of experienced advocates and that specialization in various departments of the practice of the law would no longer be the rule. The benefits to be derived from a common training are self-evident.

## Queen's Counsel.

These are leading barristers who have been appointed counsel to the Queen on the recommendation of the Lord Chancellor. They wear silk gowns and are, therefore, known as " silks ".

The chief rule relating to these senior barristers is that no Queen's Counsel may appear in Court unless another barrister is briefed with him as his " junior ".

## Other Judicial Officers.

(a) LORD CHANCELLOR.

Although the Lord Chancellor is the head of the Judiciary, his is, in fact, a ministerial office, and he is a member of the Government. He is appointed by the Crown on the advice of the Prime Minister. In his judicial capacity he is President of the Court of Appeal and of the Chancery Division of the High Court. He is also *ex-officio* Speaker of the House of Lords (when sitting in its legislative capacity) and presides at judicial proceedings on appeal thereto. He is also an *ex-officio* Judge of the Court of Appeal. The Lord Chancellor is responsible for the appointment of Justices of the Peace.

(b) VICE-CHANCELLOR.

The Administration of Justice Act, 1970, empowers the Lord Chancellor to nominate one of the puisne judges for the time being attached to the Chancery Division to be Vice-Chancellor, to be responsible for the organization and management of the business of that Division.

(c) MASTER OF THE ROLLS.

The Master of the Rolls is one of the permanent members of the Court of Appeal and exercises important functions as to the admission of solicitors to the Roll of Solicitors.

(d) ATTORNEY-GENERAL and SOLICITOR-GENERAL.

These are known collectively as the Law Officers of the Crown. Both offices are political appointments. The Attorney-General is the head of the English Bar. His duties are to represent the Crown in legal proceedings, to conduct Crown prosecutions and to act as legal adviser to the various Government Departments. He is also a necessary party to any assertion of public rights, e.g., for the abatement of a public nuisance. The duties of the Solicitor-General are similar, but he is subordinate to the Attorney-General. When the office of the latter is vacant, the Solicitor-General carries out the necessary functions.

(e) COMMON SERJEANT.

The Common Serjeant is a barrister exercising special judicial functions in the Mayor's and City of London Court and in the Central Criminal Court. He acts as adviser to the City of London Corporation.

(f) TAXING MASTERS.

These are officials of the Supreme Court concerned with the taxation of costs, i.e., the fixing by the Court of the amount which one party to an action is directed to pay to another party. They are solicitors of at least ten years' standing and are appointed by the Lord Chancellor with the concurrence of the Treasury.

### (g) Official Referee.

He was a barrister who tried cases involving examination of accounts, documents and other matters of lengthy detail. Since the Courts Act, 1971, the functions of this officer (the office as such being abolished) are to be performed by a designated Circuit Judge. An appeal lies from his decision to the Court of Appeal on a point of law only.

### (h) Director of Public Prosecutions.

This official is a barrister or solicitor of at least ten years' standing, who acts under the general direction of the Attorney-General. His main duties are:

(1) To give advice to Government Departments and to the police as to criminal prosecutions;
(2) To receive reports from the police of certain specified offences;
(3) To prosecute all offences punishable by death, cases referred to him by Government Departments, or cases which appear to be of special difficulty or importance.

### (i) Queen's Proctor.

This officer is responsible for making inquiries as to whether a divorce case has been improperly prosecuted, e.g. (as the law stood before the Divorce Reform Act, 1969, a petitioner had failed to disclose his own adultery). He may intervene in any divorce suit.

### (j) Official Solicitor to the Supreme Court of Judicature.

This officer acts for mental patients who are involved in litigation; in High Court proceedings for the adoption of children and also watches the interests of persons committed to prison for contempt of court. He came into prominence in June 1972 in the case of three unofficial dock strikers threatened with contempt proceedings by the National Industrial Relations Court set up under the Industrial Relations Act, 1971 (now abolished and repealed respectively).

## General Principles of English Justice.

(1) All trials are held in open Court, to which the public has free access, and both sides must be heard, the parties having the right to be represented professionally.
(2) The burden of proof is (in almost every case) on the accuser, i.e., the prosecution in criminal cases, and the plaintiff in civil cases. In criminal cases the prosecution must discharge their burden of proof *beyond all reasonable doubt*, that is satisfy the jury of the guilt of the accused: *Woolmington* v. *Director of Public Prosecutions* (1935).

(3) The only facts that may be taken into account in arriving at a decision are those that have been adduced in evidence.

(4) In all serious criminal cases (i.e., all except those which can be tried summarily by magistrates) the accused must be tried not by a Judge alone but before a jury, which is the *sole judge of fact*, that is, of what really happened and whether the facts fit in with the legal definition given by the Judge in his summing-up.

Under provisions in Part II of the Criminal Justice Act, 1972, brought into force in the spring of 1974 a person aged between 18 and 65 who is on the register for Parliamentary and local government elections and has been resident in the United Kingdom for at least five years is liable to jury service (the property qualification dating from 1825 having been abolished). Persons connected with the administration of justice such as judges and lawyers are ineligible (as are likewise the clergy) and certain other persons may claim to be excused as of right such as Members of Parliament, full members of the Forces and those in the medical and similar professions. Certain convicted persons are disqualified from service on a jury. The Court may exclude from jury service anyone whose physical disability or insufficient understanding of the English language makes doubtful his ability to act effectively as a juror. These provisions have now been worked into the consolidating Juries Act, 1974.

Under the relevant statutory provisions jurors are entitled to travelling and subsistence allowances as well as to compensation for loss of earnings and for additional expenses incurred.

Unlike the situation in a criminal trial (where an accused being tried on indictment is always entitled to be tried by jury) the use of the jury in *civil cases* has become very restricted. Nowadays a jury is used in *civil cases* only where the case is one of defamation, false imprisonment, or where there is an allegation of fraud or where, in other cases, the Court in its unfettered discretion orders trial by jury. A jury is sometimes found in contested divorce or probate cases. Section 39 of the Courts Act, 1971, makes provision for the acceptance in given circumstances of a majority verdict of a civil jury.

The retention of the jury for the trial of serious criminal cases would appear to be justified by the following considerations which may perhaps be described as psychological. The jury are judges of fact and under direction by the judge as to the applicable law are really the final arbiters between prosecution and defence. An accused may normally be expected to feel that the verdict of twelve reasonable men and women will result from a careful weighing of the evidence and on his being given the " benefit of the doubt " in a case not patently forlorn.

The Criminal Justice Act, 1967 introduced (subject to safeguards) the possibility of accepting a verdict by majority in a criminal case in contradistinction to the age-long rule that the verdict of a jury must be unanimous.

(5) The judgment of the Court is delivered in public, and, where a professional Judge is presiding, reasons are given for it.

(6) There is, in substantially all proceedings, a right of appeal.

(7) There is control over possible **Contempt of Court.**

Contempt of Court may be either civil or criminal. Civil contempt arises where there has been disobedience to an order of the Court made in a civil case. The punishment is by fine or imprisonment. The offender (or " contemnor " as he is technically called) may secure his release from imprisonment by making a full and sincere apology and so " purge his contempt ".

Criminal contempt, on the other hand is a common law misdemeanour occasioned by various acts interfering with the course of justice, such as outrageous conduct in the face of the Court, interference with jurors or witnesses, or the publishing of statements prejudicial to the fair trial of a pending case. It is generally punishable by fine or imprisonment, but superior courts may punish by attachment or committal. An inferior court of record has no jurisdiction over contempt unless it is committed in the face of the court ; however, the Queen's Bench Division has power to protect such a court.

By virtue of s. 13 of the Administration of Justice Act, 1960, appeal lies from the decision of a court punishing for contempt to the Divisional Court, Court of Appeal or House of Lords, as the case may be. The Act also introduced alterations of the rigorous common law rules affecting publishers and distributors of information concerning judicial proceedings.

The *raison d'être* of the power to punish contempt of court is obviously the preservation of the integrity and effectiveness of the administration of justice and not merely the security of the judges themselves. It should be added that genuine criticism made in good faith of the conduct or result of a judicial proceeding or of any aspect of the law or of a judicial organ or institution is not proscribed. Were it otherwise, law reform would be tardier than it is and the legal periodicals would be hard pushed for contributions from writers and publicists.

## Evidence.

It is not within the scope of this small book to give even an outline of this topic, but it is proposed to mention some of the main principles.

CLASSIFICATION OF EVIDENCE.

Evidence may be classified as :—

(i) *Primary and Secondary Evidence.*

Primary Evidence is the best evidence, e.g., the production of an original document. It is a general principle that " the best evidence must be given of which the nature of the case permits " : *Macdonnel* v. *Evans* (1852). The so-called best evidence rule is now virtually confined to documents.

Secondary Evidence is substitutionary evidence, indicating the existence of a more original source of information, e.g., a copy of a document the original of which has been lost.

(ii) *Direct and Circumstantial Evidence.*
Direct Evidence consists of the testimony of a witness who was present when the fact happened, or of the production of the document which constitutes the fact.
Circumstantial Evidence is evidence as to other facts which go to show that the fact to be proved did or did not exist.

(iii) *Original and Hearsay Evidence.*
Original Evidence is evidence of a witness who speaks of the facts from his own knowledge. [This could, it is thought, come by way of a tape-recording of alleged slanderous words or other matters. Cf. *R.* v. *Robson*; *R.* v. *Harris* (1972).]
Hearsay Evidence is evidence of a witness whose information has been derived entirely from one or more other persons. Hence the saying " What the soldier said is not evidence ".

CIRCUMSTANTIAL EVIDENCE.

There is considerable, and not entirely justified, prejudice against the admissibility of such evidence. Even the value of direct testimony may be affected by the risks of mistake, forgetfulness and falsehood. It is argued that the value of circumstantial evidence is further subject to the risk of error in the deduction which the jury must make from the chain of facts constituting such evidence. On the other hand, " Witnesses can lie ; circumstances cannot ". " Circumstantial evidence ", said Thoreau, " may be very strong, as when you find a trout in the milk ". Also much so-called direct evidence is actually circumstantial. You can see A stab B, but you cannot see A shoot B, unless tracer bullets are used. Moreover, in many cases the only evidence available is circumstantial. Persons do not usually commit adultery, or murder, before an audience. Where several independent facts are attested by witnesses which, taken together, form a complete chain of evidence leading to but one conclusion, this evidence is likely to be at least as reliable as direct evidence which may be tinged by prejudice, mistake in observation and untruthfulness. But the case is very different when the circumstantial evidence consists of one isolated fact.

For a modern example of admissible circumstantial evidence, see *Hampson* v. *Powell* (1970)—identity of lorry (and of its driver) not stopping after colliding with private car, established from various sources.

In *McGreevy* v. *D.P.P.* (1973) (H.L.) it was held that while in a criminal trial it is the duty of the judge to make clear to the jury in terms which are adequate to cover the particular features of the case that they must not convict unless they are satisfied beyond reasonable doubt of the guilt of the accused, there is no rule that, where the prosecution case is based on circumstantial evidence, the judge must as a matter of law, give a further direction that the jury must not convict unless they are satisfied that the facts proved are not only consistent with the guilt of the accused, but also such as to be inconsistent with any other reasonable conclusion.

RULES OF EVIDENCE GENERALLY.

(i) If a person brings a charge, the burden of proof is, in the first place, on him to make out a *prima facie* case.

(ii) An advocate may not put leading questions to his own witness. (A leading question is one which, although it is capable of being answered in various ways, yet suggests that a particular answer is required.)

(iii) The evidence of a witness is his recollection of the matters in question, not his judgment of the deduction to be drawn from them—unless he is an expert witness.

(iv) Evidence must be relevant.

(v) Where the contents of a document are sought to be given in evidence, the document itself must be produced or its absence explained.

(vi) Hearsay evidence is not normally admissible. That is to say, a witness is not allowed to quote a statement in the nature of a narrative of facts which he has received from some other person for the purpose of establishing the truth of the facts; but where such statement is part of the *res gestae*, that is a part of the transaction in issue or **relevant to the issue, or accompanies and explains a fact which is in issue or which is relevant to the issue**, evidence may be given that it was in fact made. It is on this basis that proof can often be given of the publication of a defamatory statement (see *ante*, p. 237). Cp. *Ratten v. Reginam* (1971) in the House of Lords (evidence of telephonist at local exchange as to call received).

There are the following numerous exceptions to the rule :—

(*a*) Admissions by an interested party, by conduct or otherwise, when made against him, but not when in his favour ; (*b*) confessions (voluntarily made) ; (*c*) certain statements made by persons since deceased ; (*d*) statements contained in public documents ; (*e*) statements made in previous proceedings in certain circumstances, e.g., if the witness is dead ; (*f*) matter admissible under the Criminal Evidence Act, 1965, (that is certain records compiled in the course of a trade or business); (*g*) matter admissible in civil proceedings under the Civil Evidence Acts, 1968 and 1972.

(vii) The extreme youth or mental disorder of a witness does not of itself incapacitate him from giving evidence. The question is : " Are such persons capable of comprehending the facts about which they are to testify ? "

(viii) There are certain questions which may be put to a witness in proceedings other than criminal proceedings, but which he cannot be compelled to answer, e.g., a question the answer to which may tend to incriminate him, that is to expose him to criminal proceedings or to proceedings for a penalty.

(ix) Documents put in evidence must be accompanied by proof of their genuineness.

(x) A court [this includes a jury : *R.* v. *Jones (Reginald William)* (1969)] is entitled to take " judicial notice " of certain classes of facts to the extent of not requiring actual proof of the facts. Examples are Acts of Parliament (which are said " to prove themselves ") or the facts of nature, like " night " and " day " and the normal period of gestation, which are notorious facts. Judicial notice has been taken of the domestic reception of television : *Bridlington Relay* v. *Yorkshire Electricity Board* (1965).

In *R.* v. *Jones* (*supra*) the Court of Appeal held that judicial notice could be taken of the fact that a much used breathalyser for tests under section 1(1) of the Road Safety Act, 1967, had been approved by the Home Secretary and thus formal proof of approval was no longer necessary. In *British Railways Board* v. *Herrington* (1972) (H.L.) Lord Diplock said that " a Court may take judicial notice that railway lines are regularly patrolled by linesmen and gangers " and in *Mount* v. *Oldham Corporation* (1973) Lord Denning, M.R., said that the Court will take judicial notice of the usage that a parent wishing to withdraw his boy from a fee-paying school, may do so at any time, but he must either give a term's notice or pay a term's fee in lieu of notice.

Under section 3(2) of the European Communities Act, 1972, judicial notice is to be taken of the Treaties referred to in the Act (including " the Treaty of Rome ") of the Official Journal of the European Communities and of any decision of or expression of opinion by, the European Court. Under section 3(1) of the Act questions of Community law, are to be treated as questions of law and not of fact.

COMPARISON OF EVIDENCE IN CIVIL AND CRIMINAL CASES.

(1) In civil cases issues are normally to be proved by a " preponderance of evidence " or " balance of probabilities ";

ENGLISH LEGAL SYSTEM 299

in criminal cases the jury must be satisfied beyond all reasonable doubt. The " standard of proof " is, therefore, not the same in the two branches.

(2) In civil cases a complaint made by the plaintiff in the absence of the defendant is not admissible in evidence; complaints in criminal cases may in certain circumstances and for certain purposes be admitted.

(3) Admissions are always receivable in evidence in civil cases and (subject to safeguards) may now be admissible under the Criminal Justice Act, 1967 in criminal proceedings other than committal proceedings; confessions (criminal cases) must be voluntary

(4) In civil cases both parties and their spouses are compellable witnesses; in criminal cases the accused is never a compellable witness, nor is the spouse usually compellable, nor even, in certain cases, competent.

(5) In civil cases the rules of evidence may be waived by consent.

(6) Dying declarations are admissible only in criminal cases, i.e., on charges of murder or manslaughter.

(7) In civil proceedings the defendant's character is not generally relevant; in criminal proceedings the character of the accused may be brought into issue in circumstances defined by the Criminal Evidence Act, 1898 (e.g., when he attacks the character of witnesses for the prosecution).

(8) In criminal cases children too young to understand the nature of an oath may give unsworn evidence, if they understand the duty of speaking the truth. But such evidence must be corroborated.

(9) In criminal trials the accused may make unsworn statements in lieu of, or in addition to, his sworn testimony.

(10) While in civil proceedings first-hand hearsay may now be admitted under and subject to the safeguards provided by the Civil Evidence Act, 1968 (as read with the Civil Evidence Act, 1972), in criminal proceedings the rule against hearsay still basically and generally applies.

FUNCTIONS OF JUDGE AND JURY.

The general rule is that the Judge decides questions of law, and the jury decide questions of fact; but the Judge decides whether there is any or sufficient evidence to go to the jury. To this general rule, however, there are certain exceptions.

**Subpoenas.**

A subpoena is a writ issued in a civil action requiring the person to whom it is directed, under a penalty (*sub poena*), to be present at a specified time and place for a specified purpose. The varieties most in use are:—

(1) The *subpoena ad testificandum* to compel a witness to attend and give evidence.
(2) The *subpoena duces tecum* to compel a witness to attend and bring with him certain documents in his possession which are specified in the subpoena.

In criminal proceedings such attendance or production is secured by a witness order or witness summons issued under the Criminal Procedure (Attendance of Witnesses) Act, 1965. In both civil and criminal proceedings disobedience amounts to contempt of court.

**Legal Aid.**

As a person's legal rights are of little avail if he cannot afford the cost of legal proceedings to vindicate them, it is perhaps fitting that this small book should provide a short account of the system of legal aid introduced by the Legal Aid and Advice Act, 1949, and now regulated by the consolidating Legal Aid Act, 1974, and Regulations made thereunder.

Under this legislation a scheme of legal aid is administered by the Law Society, the body responsible for the maintenance of discipline in, and the regulation of the affairs of the solicitors' profession. Panels of solicitors and barristers willing to operate the Act are maintained, from which a person granted legal aid (known as an "assisted person") may make a selection.

Legal aid in civil matters is available for the taking or defending of proceedings (including matrimonial causes) in the High Court or the Court of Appeal and proceedings in the County Court; to appeals to the House of Lords and to domestic proceedings and those in relation to the care and protection of children in Magistrates' Courts as well as proceedings before the Lands Tribunal and in proceedings under Part III of the Fair Trading Act, 1973, in the Restrictive Practices Court. Legal aid has now been made available in proceedings in the Employment Appeal Tribunal established under the Employment Protection Act, 1975. Whether or not a person is eligible for legal aid depends upon his "disposable capital" and "disposable income". A person's disposable income is his gross annual income less certain specified deductions, and where the disposable income does not exceed the amount for the time being statutorily fixed the person in question can be granted legal aid. His contribution towards the cost of the proceedings in respect of which the Certificate is granted is assessed by the Supplementary Benefits Commission. This contribution, of course, depends on the resources of the assisted person and his actual contribution towards the costs of the proceedings will only rarely exceed his assessed contribution.

Applications for legal aid are made on prescribed forms and are submitted to local committees of solicitors who must satisfy themselves that the applicant has reasonable grounds either for taking or (as the case may be) defending the proceedings in question. After a certificate for legal aid is granted, the assisted person will select a solicitor from the panel, who will conduct the proceedings in the ordinary way. Professional fees are payable to solicitors and barristers out of the Legal Aid Fund, and there is paid into this Fund all costs recovered from the opposing party.

No legal aid is available in actions for defamation.

The legislation gives a discretion to the Court to order payment out of the Legal Aid Fund of costs incurred on a party and party basis by an unassisted litigant against whom proceedings have unsuccessfully been brought by a litigant granted legal aid. Before making the order the Court must be satisfied that it is just and equitable to make it in the light of the fact (*inter alia*) that undue financial hardship would otherwise be imposed on the unassisted litigant.

Legal advice, i.e., oral advice in legal questions by a solicitor participating in the Law Society's scheme, has now become available to any person who cannot afford to obtain it in the ordinary way. He may be required to pay a low prescribed fee for each interview. In certain situations a solicitor may without special authority give advice and assistance within a certain limit (at present £25); assistance beyond that limit requires authority from the legal aid authorities.

Legal aid in criminal proceedings is governed by Part II of the 1974 consolidating Act and Regulations. A person granted such legal aid may in certain circumstances be called upon to make a contribution towards the costs of his defence.

**Arbitration.**

Instead of bringing an action in a Court of Law to settle a dispute, e.g., as to whether there has been a breach of contract, a party may decide to submit the dispute to arbitration. Arbitration is the reference of a matter in dispute to the decision of one or more persons called arbitrators. This extra-judicial method of settling disputes is often resorted to (particularly in commercial matters) because of its privacy, simplicity and alleged speed and economy. Generally, arbitrations are proceedings out of Court, but a Court has power to refer questions to arbitrators (e.g., under section 4 of the Administration of Justice Act, 1970, or in respect of County Court proceedings under the County Courts Act, 1959, as amended by the Administration of Justice Act, 1973).

Any matter which may be made the subject of a valid contract or which affects purely private rights may be submitted to arbitration, but criminal matters and divorce suits cannot be so submitted.

The parties who desire to adopt this method of settling a dispute make what is known as a submission, i.e., an agreement to appoint some person or persons to decide the dispute and to regard his or their decision as binding. A submission may be oral, but it is better that it should be in writing, for a written agreement enjoys many advantages under the Arbitration Act, 1950, which is the governing statute.

Where the reference is to two arbitrators, they are required by the Act to appoint an umpire immediately. The parties and their witnesses are examined on oath or affirmation, and the award, i.e., the decision, is made with due dispatch. If the arbitrators fail to agree, the umpire hears the whole matter through and gives a decision covering the whole dispute.

An arbitrator or umpire must act in a judicial manner and regulate the proceedings as far as possible on the model of Court proceedings. He must follow the ordinary rules of evidence and must take the evidence personally in the presence of both parties. He may be removed by the Court for misconduct, e.g., for showing bias.

No appeal can be made from an award, but the Court, on the application of a party, may in certain circumstances and in exercise of its supervisory powers of control set it aside entirely, e.g., if the arbitrator makes use of evidence other than that adduced by the parties or if new evidence is discovered.

An award on a written arbitration agreement may, by leave of the High Court, be enforced in the same manner as a judgment.

## Administrative Tribunals.

The idea of having special " Courts " for special purposes outside the ordinary system of Common Law Courts is not new. The Mercantile Courts, the Ecclesiastical Courts and the Royal Forest Courts were special Courts set up for special purposes. The tendency, however, was for these special Courts to be absorbed by the Common Law Courts. In the 19th century, however, the first Tribunals were set up to deal with special branches of the law, e.g., the Railway and Canal Commission. In the present century a large number of such Tribunals has been set up. They are a phenomenon resulting from a rapid and marked extension of governmental action and are not generally staffed by lawyers.

The reasons for the establishment of special Tribunals include :—

(i) The ordinary Courts are already over-burdened with work.
(ii) The costs of proceedings in ordinary Courts would be heavy.
(iii) Matters which involve a public service are best administered by specialists in that service.
(iv) Where policy decisions must be made, these are best settled by administrative authority.

The advantages of Administrative Tribunals are :—

(i) Expert knowledge is required in many non-legal fields, e.g., the operation of a health service, or the granting of a pension. Most of such Tribunals are staffed by experts.
(ii) Lawyers are trained in sifting facts and deciding on the basis of them and not in administering social and economic policies.
(iii) Lawyers, trained in the freedom of the Common Law, are likely to be most unsympathetic to policies which restrict the traditional freedom of person and property.
(iv) Administrative tribunals are quick and cheap and can dispose of many cases in a short time. Usually no fees are payable.
(v) They suit the litigant in person, to whom the complicated procedure of a Court is often terrifying and confusing.
(vi) They have wide discretionary powers and so avoid the rigidity that the doctrine of precedent sometimes imposes on the law.

The disadvantages of such Tribunals, on the other hand, have, in some quarters, been felt to be the following :—

(i) Their discretion is often so wide as to make their decisions completely unpredictable.
(ii) The public is excluded from many such hearings, and the lack of publicity arouses suspicion as to what takes place behind closed doors.
(iii) In many cases parties are not allowed to be represented by solicitor or counsel, which increases public mistrust.
(iv) It is not always the practice to publish reasons for the Tribunal's decision, but merely to inform the applicant of it. This makes it impossible to advise him and strengthens the impression of arbitrary bureaucracy.
(v) The technical knowledge that fits an administrator to formulate a policy does not equip him to find the facts on which his policy is to be based ; he needs the corrective of the chairmanship of a legally-trained assessor.

(vi) Tribunals have not always been sufficiently independent of the Minister or Department with whom or with which they work. Many Tribunals have been staffed with officials of the Ministry involved, with no independent members, thus giving the impression that they were under departmental influence and were regarded as machinery of administration rather than of adjudication.

(vii) The absence or restriction of rights of appeal.

The general rule of English law is that all Tribunals are subject to the control of the High Court, unless there is a provision to the contrary in the Statute which sets up the Tribunal. Where the power of control is not so excluded, the Queen's Bench Division has power, by means of the Orders of *Certiorari, Prohibition* and *Mandamus* (see Chapter V) to keep Tribunals within their jurisdiction and to ensure that they observe the rules of natural justice when acting in a *judicial* or *quasi-judicial* capacity.

> The rules of natural justice may be stated as (a) a tribunal must not be biased ; (b) the party interested must be told of the case against him and be given an opportunity of being heard : *audi alteram partem*.

Whereas administrative tribunals are concerned with questions of policy and the weighing of private against public interest, the traditional or orthodox courts are concerned in the main with questions of liability conceived on the plane of criminal or civil law and in the latter with reciprocity of rights and duties. The judges enjoy independence ; they are specialists as a result of long experience at the Bar. The law of evidence and of procedure, the distinction between questions of law and of fact and the right to have issues tried by a jury and in open court ; the enunciation of reasons why the Court takes the action it does in the case before it, and the use of the doctrine of binding precedent ; a system of appeals, are elements which allow it to be asserted that " openness, fairness and impartiality " characterize the scheme and labours of the orthodox courts.

The Franks Committee (which in 1956 considered the constitution and working of administrative tribunals) wished the quoted qualities to be characteristic of administrative tribunals likewise and made recommendations accordingly.

The operation of the Tribunals and Inquiries Act, 1958 (which was enacted soon after the Franks Committee reported in 1957 and has, with other cognate legislation, been consolidated in the Tribunals and Inquiries Act, 1971) may be expected to rationalize the system and to secure the possession by the tribunals generally of the essential qualities referred to. The Council on Tribunals set up will review the constitution and working of tribunals ; the Lord Chancellor will have a voice in the appointment of certain members of the tribunals ; the Council will give guidance in the matter of procedural rules ; certain rights of appeal are conferred and generally speaking reasoned decisions must be given by the tribunals to which the Act applies.

The labours of the Franks Committee have borne fruit not only in the 1958 Act just referred to, but in various other ways : the provisions of the Town and Country Planning Act, 1962 (now to be found in the consolidating Town and Country Planning Act, 1971) enabling aggrieved persons to challenge the validity of certain orders or Ministerial action under the basic legislation, by an application to the High Court, afford an example ; so do the amended Rules made under the Registered Designs Act, 1949, which now require the Registrar to hear any disputes relating to a registered design as a rule in public. Moreover, a noticeable tendency is to place newly-created tribunals under the supervision of the Council on Tribunals. A recent example is that concerning the value added tax tribunals established under the Finance Act, 1972. A full list of tribunals under the general supervision of the Council is given in a schedule to the Tribunals and Inquiries Act, 1971 ; that schedule must now be added to by reason of the fact that the Director General of Fair Trading created by the Fair Trading Act, 1973 has, under a provision in the Consumer Credit Act, 1974, been brought under the supervision of the Council in respect of his adjudicating functions.

# INDEX

## A

| | PAGE |
|---|---|
| Abatement | 157 |
| Abridgments | 12 |
| Acceptance, *see* Contract | |
| Accumulations of Income— | |
| Rules as to | 202 |
| Act of Parliament, *see* Statute | |
| Act of State | 216 |
| Ademption | 157 |
| Administrative Tribunals | 302 |
| Adoption— | |
| Legal effect of | 103 |
| Sanction of Court to | 104 |
| Agency— | |
| Breach of implied warranty of authority | 137 |
| Definition of | 134 |
| Gratuitous | 136 |
| Of wife | 67, 139 |
| Ratification of | 135 |
| Rights of third parties | 136 |
| Termination of | 138 |
| Tortious liability of principal | 138 |
| Types of | 135 |
| Agents— | |
| Appointment of | 134 |
| Duties of | 135 |
| Necessity of | 135 |
| Paid | 136 |
| Rights against principal | 136 |
| Agreement, Nature of | 47 |
| Alienation | 188 |
| Aliens— | |
| Capacity to contract | 70 |
| Status of | 109 |
| Allegiance | 114 |
| Animals | 233 *et seq.* |
| Animals, Liability for Damage by | 233 |
| Annulment of Marriage | 106 |
| Appeals— | |
| Civil cases, in | 280 |
| Criminal cases, in | 283 |
| House of Lords, to | 279 |
| Privy Council, to | 289 |
| Queen's Bench Division, to | 284 |
| Appropriation of Payments | 88 |
| Arbitration | 301 |
| Arson | 270 |
| Artificial Persons | 121 *et seq.* |
| Assault | 221 |
| Assignment— | |
| By operation of law | 85 |
| Choses in action, of | 40, 83 |
| Contractual rights, of | 83 *et seq.* |
| Equitable | 41 |
| Attachment of Earnings | 5 |

## B

| | PAGE |
|---|---|
| Bailee | 160 |
| Liability of | 160 |
| Bailment | 160 |
| By attornment | 160 |
| Bankruptcy— | |
| Relation back | 178 |
| Reputed ownership | 178 |
| Barristers | 289 |
| Battery | 221 |
| Beneficial Interest | 39 |
| Bigamy | 274 |
| Bill of Exchange | 165 |
| Bill of Lading | 167 |
| Bills of Sale | 167 *et seq.* |
| Absolute | 168 |
| Conditional | 168 |
| Remedies of grantee | 169 |
| Statutory requirements of | 168 |
| Blackmail | 269 |
| Burglary | 269 |

## C

| | PAGE |
|---|---|
| Canon Law— | |
| Application of | 14 |
| Declining influence of | 42 |
| Capacity to Contract— | |
| Aliens | 70 |
| Corporations | 68 |
| Intoxicated persons | 67 |
| Married Women | 67 |
| Mentally disordered persons | 67 |
| Minors | 64 *et seq.* |
| Case Law | 9 |
| Cases— | |
| Principle of decision in | 12 |
| Reports of | 11 |
| *Caveat Emptor* | 155 |
| *Certiorari*, Order of | 117, 281 |
| Chain of representation | 208 |
| Chancellor— | |
| Jurisdiction of | 28 |
| Petitions to | 29 |
| Chancery Division | 280, 281 |
| Chattels— | |
| Corporeal | 143, 145 |
| Incorporeal | 143, 145 |
| Involuntary transfer of | 172 |
| Method of transfer of | 155 |
| Personal | 145 |
| Real | 145 |
| Transfer of title to | 153 |
| Cheque | 166 |
| Children— | |
| Adoption of | 103 |
| Illegitimate | 101 |

# INDEX

**Children** (*continued*)—
Legitimated . . . . . . 102
Choses in action . . . . 143, 145
Choses in possession . . . 143, 145
Circuit System . . . . . . 8
Codification . . . . . . 2
Common Law . . . . . . 8
  Derivation . . . . . . 8
  Inflexibility of . . . . . 28
  Riot . . . . . . . . 120
  Statute law and . . . . 17
Companies . . . . . 123 *et seq.*
  Capital of . . . . . . 125
  Kinds of . . . . . . . 124
  Meetings of . . . . . . 125
  Powers of . . . . . . 124
Condition . . . . . . . 78
Conditions, implied in sale of goods . . . . . . . 155
Conflict of Laws . . . . . 111
*Consensus ad Idem* . . . . 47
Consideration—
  Executed . . . . . . 53
  Executory . . . . . . 53
  Forbearance to sue as . . . 56
  Past . . . . . . . . 55
  Rules relating to . . . . 54
  Valuable . . . . . . . 54
Conspiracy . . . . . . . 276
Contempt of Court . . . . 294
Contract—
  Assignment of rights . . 83 *et seq.*
  Breach of . . . . . 88 *et seq.*
  Classification of . . . . 44
  Contrary to public policy . . 71
  Determinable . . . . . 51
  Discharge of . . . . 85 *et seq.*
  Duress, effect of . . . . 82
  Essentials of . . . . . 51
  Executed . . . . . . 47
  Executory . . . . . . 47
  Express . . . . . . . 46
  For a lease . . . . . . 194
  Form of . . . . . . . 48
  Frustrated . . . . . 90 *et seq.*
  Fundamental term . . . 57, 78
  Gaming . . . . . . . 72
  Illegal . . . . . . . 72
  Implied . . . . . . . 46
  Impossibility . . . . . 74
  Interpretation . . . . . 99
  In writing . . . . . . 48
  Limitation of actions . . . 92
  Misrepresentation in . . 78 *et seq.*
  Mistake in . . . . 74 *et seq.*
  Offer and acceptance in . 56 *et seq.*
  Performance . . . . . . 86
  Reality of consent in . . . 74
  Record, of . . . . . . 44
  Rectification of . . . . . 78

**Contract** (*continued*)—
  Remedies for breach of . 93 *et seq.*
  Restraint of trade, in . . . 71
  Seal, under . . . . . . 44
  Simple . . . . . 44 *et seq.*
  Specialty . . . . . 44 *et seq.*
  Substantial performance . . 96
  *Uberrimae Fidei* . . . . 81
  Undue influence, effect of . . 82
  Unenforceable . . . . . 52
  Use of post, in . . . . . 61
  Use of telephone, in . . . 62
  Void . . . . . . . . 51
  Voidable . . . . . . . 51
  Wagering . . . . . . . 72
  Waiver . . . . . . . 85
  Written evidence, requiring . 49
Contractual Relations, Interference with . . . . . 246
Conversion . . . . . . . 224
Conveyance by Way of Sale . . 188
Copyhold . . . . . . . 180
Copyright . . . . . . . 175
  Assignment of . . . . . 176
Coroner . . . . . . . . 288
Corporations—
  Capacity to contract of . . 68
  Characteristics of . . . . 122
  Classification of . . . . 123
  Crimes of . . . . . . 261
  Torts of . . . . . . . 219
  *Ultra vires* doctrine . . . . 69
Court—
  Appeal, of . . . . 280, 283
  Central Criminal . . . . 286
  Chancery . . . . . . . 28
  Commercial . . . . . . 281
  Common Law . . . . . 28
  Coroner's . . . . . . . 288
  County . . . . . . . 281
    Jurisdiction of . . . . 282
  Criminal Appeal, of . . . 283
  Crown . . . . 280, 286 *et seq.*
  Family . . . . . 3, 43, 281
  High . . . . . . . . 281
  Judicial Officers . . . . 291
  Maritime . . . . . . . 15
  Merchant . . . . . . 15
  Petty Sessions, of . . . . 286
  Pie-Powder, of . . . . . 15
  Record, of . . . . . . 3
  Restrictive Practices . . . 283
  Staple, of the . . . . . 15
  Supreme . . . . . . . 279
Credit-sale Transactions . . . 162
Crimes—
  Against property . . 267 *et seq.*
  Against public rights . . 271 *et seq.*
  Against the person . . 263 *et seq.*
  Attempt to commit . . . 277

# INDEX

Crimes (*continued*)—
   Classification of . . . 256
   Constituent elements of . . 257
   Degrees of complicity in . . 262
   Inchoate . . . . 276 *et seq.*
   Liability for, qualifications on 258 *et seq.*
   Nature of . . . . . 254
   Substantive . . . . 263 *et seq.*
Criminal Damage . . . . . 270
Crown—
   Action against . . . 113, 216
   Institution of proceedings against . . . . . 113
   Servants of . . . . . 114
*Curia Regis* . . . . . . 279
Custom . . . . . . . 9
   Distinguished from usage . . 9
   Judicial recognition of . . 9
   Laws derived from . . . 9

## D

Damages . . . 4, 35, 94 *et seq.*
   Contemptuous . . . . 252
   Distinguished from penalty . 95
   Exemplary . . . . 94, 252
   Liquidated . . . . . 95
   Nominal . . . . . 94, 252
   Special . . . . . . 94
   Unliquidated . . . . 94
Dangerous Chattels, Liability for . . . . . 231 *et seq.*
Deceit, *see* Fraud
Declaratory Judgment . . . 118
Declaratory Order. . . . . 36
Deed of Arrangement. . . . 178
Defamation, *see* Libel and Slander
Delegated Legislation—
   Checks upon abuse of . . 22
   Reasons for increase of . . 22
   Types of . . . . . . 22
Desertion . . . . . . 106
Detinue . . . . . . . 223
Diminished Responsibility . . 259
Director of Public Prosecutions . 292
Divorce . . . . . . 106
Doctrine of Alternative Danger . 230
Doctrine of Substantial Performance . . . . . . 96
Documents—
   Rectification of . . . . 36
   Cancellation of . . . . 36
Domicile . . . . . . 111
*Donatio Mortis Causa.* . . 156, 159
Duress . . . . . . . 82

## E

Easements . . . . . . 186
Ecclesiastical Courts . . . 14
*Ejusdem Generis* Rule. . . . 21

English Justice, Principles of . 293
English Law, Sources of . . . 8
English Legal System. . 279 *et seq.*
Entailed Interest . . . . . 182
Equitable Interests . 145, 183, 185
Equity—
   Contributions of . . . 35 *et seq.*
   Fusion of law and . . . . 31
   History of . . . . 28 *et seq.*
   Main fields of . . . . . 42
   Maxims of . . . . 32 *et seq.*
   Nature of . . . . . . 27
   Remedies of . . . . 35 *et seq.*
Equity of Redemption . . 36, 197
   "Clog" upon . . . . 37, 197
*Escrow* . . . . . . . 44
Estate—
   Contract . . . . . . 193
   Freehold . . . . . . 180
   Future . . . . . . 183
   Leasehold . . . . . 181
   Legal . . . . . . 180
   Life . . . . . . . 182
   Tail . . . . . . . 182
Estoppel . . . 45, 53, 93, 129, 135
European Economic Community 26
Evidence . . . . 295 *et seq.*
   Circumstantial . . . . 296
   Classification of . . . . 295
   Functions of Judge and jury . 299
   Rules of . . . . . . 296
Executor . . . . . . 206
   *De son tort* . . . . . 207
   Special . . . . . . 207

## F

False Imprisonment . . . . 221
   Distinguished from malicious prosecution . . . . 246
Family Division . . . 3, 43, 281
Fee Simple Absolute . . . . 180
Felonies . . . . . . 256
Fixtures . . . . . . 180
*Fletcher* v. *Rylands*, Rule in . . 235
Forgery . . . . . . . 270
Fraud . . . . . . 80, 243
Frustration (of Contract). . 90 *et seq.*

## G

Gaming and Wagering Contracts 72
Gifts . . . . . . . 156
   By will . . . . . . 157
   *Inter vivos* . . . . . 156
   Lapsed . . . . . 158, 208
Goods—
   Transfer of Title . . . . 153
Grant *cum testamento annexo*. . 206
Grant *de bonis non administratis* 207
Guarantee . . . . . . 49
Guardians, Duties of . . . . 101

# INDEX

## H
| | PAGE |
|---|---|
| *Habeas Corpus*, Writ of | 117, 119, 281 |
| Health Service, National | 116 |
| Hire-purchase | 162 |
| Homicide | 263 et seq. |
| Hotchpot | 211 |
| Hotel Proprietors | 161 |

## I
| | |
|---|---|
| Illegitimacy | 101 |
| Incitement | 277 |
| Indemnity | 49 |
| Independent Contractor | 220 |
| Infanticide | 267 |
| Infants, *see* Minors | |
| Injunction | 4, 27, 33, 35, 96 |
| Defamation | 243 |
| Interlocutory | 36 |
| Mandatory | 36 |
| Perpetual | 36 |
| Prohibitory | 36 |
| Tort | 253 |
| Innkeepers | 161 |
| Insurance (National)— | |
| Benefits | 115 |
| Health Service | 116 |
| Industrial injuries | 116 |
| Interests— | |
| Concurrent | 185 |
| Equitable | 145, 185 |
| Future | 183 |
| Legal | 180, 185 |
| Intestacy | 179, 209 et seq. |
| Partial | 211 |
| Intoxicated Persons— | |
| Capacity to contract | 67 |
| I.O.U. | 166 |

## J
| | |
|---|---|
| Judicial Committee of the Privy Council | 289 |
| Judicial Immunity | 216, 279 |
| Judicial Independence | 279 |
| Judicial Notice | 298 |
| Judicial Precedent, Doctrine of | 9 |
| Binding force of | 10 |
| Justices of the Peace | 286 |

## L
| | |
|---|---|
| Land— | |
| Charges, registration of | 191 et seq. |
| Conveyance of | 188 |
| Interests in | 180 et seq. |
| Legal estate in | 180 |
| Legal interests in | 145, 180 |
| Local charges | 193 |
| Meaning of | 180 |
| Mortgages of, *see* Mortgage | |
| Registration | 189 |
| Settlements of, *see* Settlements | |
| Social control of | 212 et seq. |

| | PAGE |
|---|---|
| Lapse of legacies | 158, 208 |
| Lapse of time | 92 |
| Law— | |
| Administrative | 21 |
| Canon, *see* Canon Law | |
| Common, *see* Common Law | |
| Divisions | 6 |
| European Economic Community | 26 |
| Judge-made | 13 |
| Merchant | 15 |
| Equity and | 16 |
| Nature of | 6 |
| Private | 7 |
| Public | 6 |
| Reform | 25 |
| Reports | 11 |
| Roman, *see* Roman Law | |
| Rule of | 116 |
| Sources of | 8 |
| Leases | 194 et seq. |
| Legacies | 157 |
| Legal Aid | 300 |
| Legal Profession, Division of | 289 |
| Legal Treatises | 24 |
| Legitimation | 102 |
| Libel | 237 |
| Criminal | 275 |
| Defences to action for | 240 |
| Newspaper, in | 242 |
| Publication of | 239 |
| Licence (Land) | 182, 186 |
| Lien | 173 |
| Equitable | 173 |
| Maritime | 173 |
| Possessory | 173 |
| *Litera Legis* | 19 |
| Lords, House of | 283 |

## M
| | |
|---|---|
| Malicious Prosecution | 245 |
| Distinguished from false imprisonment | 246 |
| *Mandamus*, Order of | 117, 281 |
| Manslaughter | 264 |
| Market Overt | 154 |
| Marriage— | |
| Banns | 105 |
| Decree of nullity | 106 |
| Judicial separation | 107 |
| Licences | 105 |
| Solemnisation of | 105 |
| Void | 106 |
| Voidable | 106 |
| Married Women— | |
| Capacity to contract | 67 |
| Liability for tort | 215 |
| Master and Servant | 139, 219 |
| Material Alteration (Contract) | 93 |
| Memorandum in Writing | 49 |
| Contents of | 49 |

# INDEX

| | PAGE |
|---|---|
| **Memorandum in Writing** (*contd*)— | |
| Effect of non-compliance | 50 |
| Nature of | 49 |
| *Mens Rea* | 257, 271 |
| Mental Disorder | 67, 108 |
| Merger | 45, 93 |
| Minors | 100 |
| Action in Courts | 101 |
| Capacity to contract, of | 63 *et seq.* |
| Criminal responsibility | 259 |
| Legacy to | 208 |
| Liability for tort, of | 219 |
| Money paid by | 66 |
| Testamentary capacity of | 100 |
| Misdemeanours | 256 |
| Misrepresentation (Contract)— | |
| Fraudulent | 78 *et seq.* |
| Innocent | 78 |
| Negligent | 80 |
| Mistake (Contract) | 74 *et seq.* |
| Mortgage— | |
| Choses in action of | 172 |
| Effect of lapse of time on | 197 |
| Equitable | 197 |
| Land, of | 196 |
| Legal | 196 |
| Mortgagee Rights of | 198 |
| Mortgagor Rights of | 198 |
| Murder | 263 |

### N

| | |
|---|---|
| Nationality | 109 |
| Naturalisation | 110 |
| Natural Persons | 100 *et seq.* |
| Negligence | 227 *et seq.* |
| Contributory | 229 |
| Negotiability | 165 |
| Negotiable Instruments | 165 |
| *Nemo dat quod non habet* | 153 |
| *Non est factum* | 74 |
| Notice, Doctrine of | 145, 182, 191 |
| Notice *in Lieu of Distringas* | 172 |
| Notice to Quit | 181 |
| Novation | 84, 130 |
| Nuisance | 224 *et seq.* |
| Private | 224 |
| Public | 215, 224 |

### O

| | |
|---|---|
| *Obiter Dictum* | 13 |
| Occupiers of Premises, Liability of | 230 *et seq.* |
| Offer, *see* Contract | |
| Official Receiver | 177 |
| Official Referee | 292 |
| Ownership | 143 |

### P

| | |
|---|---|
| Parents, Duties of | 101 |

| | PAGE |
|---|---|
| **Partners**— | |
| Active | 129 |
| Agency of | 130 |
| Dormant | 129 |
| General | 129 |
| General rights of | 131 |
| Liability of | 130 |
| Limited | 129 |
| Types of | 129 |
| Partnership— | |
| Charging order | 132 |
| Creation of | 129 |
| Dissolution of, by Court | 132 |
| Distinguished from company | 128 |
| Distribution of assets | 133 |
| Evidence of | 130 |
| Goodwill of | 134 |
| "Holding out" in | 129 |
| Premium, return of | 133 |
| Secret profits | 131 |
| Termination of | 131 |
| Part Performance, Doctrine of | 50 |
| Patents | 174 |
| Assignment of | 174 |
| Pawn | 170 |
| Liability of pawnee | 171 |
| Rights of pawnee | 170 |
| Performance (of Contract) | 86 *et seq.* |
| By payment | 86 |
| By tender | 86 |
| Impossibility of | 74 |
| Perjury | 272 |
| Perpetuities, Rule against | 202 |
| Personal Representatives | 206 |
| Personalty | 144 |
| Persons— | |
| Artificial | 121 *et seq.* |
| Natural | 100 *et seq.* |
| Pledge, *see* Pawn | |
| Possession | 143 |
| Power of Attorney | 134 |
| Precedent— | |
| Declaratory | 10 |
| Judicial, Doctrine of | 9 |
| Original | 10 |
| Persuasive | 11 |
| Prerogative— | |
| Orders | 117 |
| Writs | 117 |
| Privilege | 241 |
| Privy Council, Judicial Committee of | 289 |
| Probate, Divorce and Admiralty Division | 281 |
| *Prohibition*, Order of | 117, 281 |
| Promissory Note | 166 |
| Property | 143 *et seq.* |
| Classification of | 144 |
| Conception of | 143 |
| Equitable interests | 145, 183, 185 |

# INDEX

| | PAGE |
|---|---|
| Property (*continued*)— | |
|   Immovables | 144 |
|   Incapacity of minors | 153 |
|   Involuntary transfers | 203 *et seq.* |
|   Legal interests | 145, 182 |
|   Legislation of 1925 | 178 |
|     Objects of | 179 |
|   Movables | 144 |
|   Obtaining by Deception | 269 |
|   Ownership and possession | 143 |
|   Personal | 144, 153 *et seq.* |
|   Real | 144, 178 *et seq.* |
|   Transfer | 187 *et seq.* |
| Proprietary Rights | 144 |
| Proviso for re-entry | 195 |
| Public Mischief | 276 |
| Public Trustee | 148, 151 |

## Q

| | |
|---|---|
| *Quantum Meruit* | 95 |
| Quasi-Contracts | 97 |
| Queen's Bench Division | 280, 281, 284 |
| Queen's Counsel | 291 |
| Queen's Proctor | 293 |
| *Quia timet* action | 36 |

## R

| | |
|---|---|
| *Ratio Decidendi* | 13, 19 |
| Realty | 144 |
| Receiver, Appointment of | 36, 177, 199 |
| Reports | 11 |
| Residue | 158 |
| *Res gestae* | 297 |
| *Res Ipsa Loquitur* | 229 |
| Restraint of Trade | 71 |
| Restrictive Covenants | 186, 193 |
| Rights— | |
|   *In personam* | 145 |
|   *In rem* | 145 |
| Riot | 120, 272 |
| Road Deaths | 266 |
| Robbery | 269 |
| Roman Law, Influence of | 41 |
| Rout | 120 |

## S

| | |
|---|---|
| Sealing of Contracts | 44 |
| Securities | 167 |
| Sedition | 272 |
| Settlements | 200 |
|   On trust for sale | 185, 201 |
|   Strict | 200 |
| "Silks" | 291 |
| Slander | 237 |
|   Defences to action for | 240 |
|   Of title | 247 |
|   Publication | 239 |
|   Special damage | 239 |
| Solicitors | 289 |
| Specific Performance | 4, 27, 33, 35, 96 |

| | PAGE |
|---|---|
| Statute | 17 |
|   Citation and numbering | 18 |
|   Codifying | 2 |
|   Consolidating | 2 |
|   Full title | 18 |
|   Interpretation, rules of | 19 |
|   Law | 6 |
|     Common Law and | 8 |
|   Obsolete | 19 |
|   Official reference | 18 |
|   Short title | 18 |
| Statutory Authority | 216 |
| Statutory Instruments | 19, 22 |
| Statutory Trusts | 210 |
| Stipendiary Magistrate | 287 |
| Subject— | |
|   Duties of | 115 |
|   Equality before law | 117 |
|   Liberty of discussion | 119 |
|   Personal freedom of | 118 |
|   Right of public meeting | 119 |
| Subpoenas | 299 |
| Succession, Modern Rules of | 209 |
| Suicide | 266 |

## T

| | |
|---|---|
| Tenancies | 181 |
| Tenant— | |
|   In common | 185 |
|   Joint | 185 |
| Tenure | 180 |
| Term of Years | 181 |
| Testamentary Disposition, Freedom of | 204 |
| Theft | 267 *et seq.* |
| Title, Registration of, *see* Land Registration | |
| Tort | 215 *et seq.* |
|   Definition of | 215 |
|   Effect of bankruptcy on | 251 |
|   Effect of death on | 250 |
|   Elements of | 215 |
|   Husband and wife | 218 |
|   Limitation of actions | 251 |
|   Remedies | 252 |
|   Remoteness of damage in | 247 |
|   Right to sue in | 218 |
|   Vicarious liability | 219 |
|   When not actionable | 216 |
| Trade Marks | 174 |
|   Registration of | 175 |
| Trade Union | 127 |
| Transferability | 165 |
| Treason | 256, 271 |
| Treasure Trove | 288 |
| Trespass— | |
|   To goods | 223 |
|   To land | 222 |
|   To the person | 221 |
| Trust | 38 *et seq.*, 146 |

|                              | PAGE     |                              | PAGE     |
|------------------------------|----------|------------------------------|----------|
| Trust (*continued*)—         |          | Unlawful Assemblies          | 120      |
|   Administration   | 38       | "Uses"                       | 38, 146  |
|   Breach of        | 152      |                              |          |
|   Certainties, the three | 39 | **V**                        |          |
|   Charitable       | 147      | Vicarious Liability          | 219      |
|   Corporation      | 148      | *Volenti Non Fit Injuria*    | 217      |
|   For sale         | 185, 201 |                              |          |
|   Types of         | 147      | **W**                        |          |
|   Variation        | 152      |                              |          |
| Trustees                     | 148      | Waiver (of Contract)         | 85       |
|   Appointment      | 148      | Warranty                     | 78       |
|   Breach of trust  | 152      | Way of Necessity             | 187      |
|   Disclaimer       | 149      | Will                         | 203      |
|   Equitable obligations of | 150 |   Codicil      | 206      |
|   Removal          | 150      |   Freedom of disposition by | 204 |
|   Retirement       | 150      |   Lost             | 206      |
|                              |          |   Requisites of valid | 203   |
| **U**                        |          |   Revocation of    | 205      |
| *Ultra vires* doctrine       | 69       | Writ System                  | 28       |
| Unborn Persons               | 267      |                              |          |
| Undue Influence              | 82       | **Y**                        |          |
| Unincorporated Associations  | 126      | Year Books                   | 11       |

# Expert POSTAL Tuition

### *for professional examinations:*

**Accountancy, Company Secretaryship, Law, Marketing, Management**

**for B.Sc.(Econ.), LL.B. and other external Degrees of London University**

**for G.C.E. 'O' and 'A' Levels.**

At these examinations Metropolitan College students have gained more than 375,000 SUCCESSES and hundreds of honours and prizes. This excellent record of achievement and the testimonies of countless satisfied students provide an assurance that Metropolitan College postal coaching is both thoroughly practical and reliable, and the best way to obtain a professional qualification that will command success, a high income and security.

The College also provides many intensely interesting non-exam. courses in business subjects; particularly useful to the executive wanting to add to his management skills.

### *Guarantee of Coaching until Successful*

For details of the college tutorial service, write, stating interest, or subjects required, to the Secretary, Dept. G.33.

Founded 1910

## Metropolitan College
## Aldermaston Court
## Reading RG7 4PW

or call in at our London Advisory Office,
4 Fore Street Avenue, London EC27 5EJ

*Accredited by the Council for the Accreditation of Correspondence Colleges.*

*Member Association of British Correspondence Colleges.*